Review of Adult Learning and Literacy

VOLUME 7

Connecting Research, Policy, and Practice

Review of Adult Learning and Literacy

VOLUME 7

Connecting Research, Policy, and Practice

Edited by

John P. Comings
Barbara Garner
Cristine Smith

Routledge
Taylor & Francis Group
New York   London

First published by Lawrence Erlbaum Associates, Inc., Publishers
10 Industrial Avenue
Mahwah, New Jersey 07430

Transferred to digital printing 2010 by Routledge

Routledge

270 Madison Avenue
New York, NY 10016

2 Park Square, Milton Park
Abingdon, Oxon OX14 4RN, UK

Cover design by Kathryn Houghtaling

Library of Congress Cataloging-in-Publication Data

Review of Adult Learning and Literacy, Volume 7:
Connecting Research, Policy, and Practice

ISBN 978-0-8058-6164-8 - ISBN 0-8058-6164-5 (cloth)
ISBN 978-0-8058-6165-5 - ISBN 0-8058-6165-3 (pbk)
ISBN 978-1-4106-1523-7 - ISBN 1-4106-1523-5 (e book)

Copyright information for this volume can be obtained
by contacting the Library of Congress.

Table of Contents

Foreword *Patricia Bennett*	vii
Preface	xi
List of Tables and Figures	xv
1 The Years 2004 and 2005 in Review *Noreen Lopez*	1

2 Persistence: Helping Adult Education
   Students Reach Their Goals
   John P. Comings
	23

3 Achieving Adult Education Program Quality:
   A Review of Systematic Approaches
   to Program Improvement
   Mary Ziegler and Mary Beth Bingman
	47

4 Assistive Technology and Adult Literacy:
   Access and Benefits
   Heidi Silver-Pacuilla
	93

5 Individualized Group Instruction:
   A Reality of Adult Basic Education
   Perrine Robinson-Geller
	137

6 Health Literacy: An Update of Medical
   and Public Health Literature
   *Rima E. Rudd, with Jennie Epstein Anderson,
   Sarah Oppenheimer, and Charlotte Nath*
	175

7   Research on Professional Development
    and Teacher Change: Implications
    for Adult Basic Education   205
    Cristine Smith and Marilyn Gillespie

8   Opportunities, Transitions, and Risks:
    Perspectives on Adult Literacy
    and Numeracy Development in Australia   245
    *Rosie Wickert, Jean Searle, Beth Marr
    and Betty Johnston*

9   Adult Basic Education and Training in South Africa   285
    Veronica McKay

10 Annotated Bibliography on Workplace Education   311
    Connie Nelson

About the Editors   331

About the Contributors   333

Author Index   341

Subject Index   355

Foreword

Impact of Research on an Adult Education Practitioner

I am aware as I write this that the ability of the adult education field to access research on adult basic education is facing a serious challenge. Indeed, this could be the last edition of this publication. The Bush administration's unfortunate decision to end funding for a national research and development center for adult learning and literacy will have a deleterious effect on the ability of state and local programs to meet mandates for education reform and the expectations of students. It is ironic that, at a time when adult education has been challenged to meet the "gold standard" of research, the national funding supporting an adult education research center is being eliminated.

Growing numbers of individuals are in need of adult education and literacy services. The recent publication of the National Assessment of Adult Literacy (NAAL) reveals that 93 million residents in the United States would benefit from adult education and literacy instruction. Our country's ability to compete on the global stage, described in *The World Is Flat* (Friedman, 2005), depends on the knowledge and skills of all of our available workers. We need families strengthened by improved literacy and parenting skills to interrupt the intergenerational cycle of illiteracy and to create new role models for achievement.

Like other states across the country that are part of the national adult education and literacy network, Maryland is faced with enormous challenges. Maryland invested in a State Assessment of Adult Literacy (SAAL) as part of the National Assessment of Adult Literacy. Maryland's SAAL identified 1.5 million adults at the basic and below-basic skill levels—approximately 20% of Maryland's adult population. With a state unemployment level below 4%, our economy is in desperate need of knowledgeable and skilled workers now. We do not have the luxury of waiting for the students currently working their way through the K–12 school system to enter the workforce. Maryland is one of the top 10 destinations in the country for new immigrants and the need for services for English-language learners is expanding. Our students require, and are demanding, services targeted to their needs and goals. They also require services that align with their work schedules and family responsibilities.

Federal and state governments, as well as the public, demand that public funds be used effectively and deliver results in a timely way. Indeed, one argument posed by the Bush administration for decreasing the funding for adult education in the 2006 budget proposal was a flawed report by the Office of Management and Budget, which erroneously concluded that adult education was not effective. A system with tremendous needs, inadequate resources, and students who cannot afford to invest years in their education does not have the luxury of stumbling blindly through the labyrinth to find a path that works. To achieve results, we need an effective compass and a road map. Research provides these tools.

The research presented in this and previous volumes of the *Review of Adult Learning and Literacy* has been extremely helpful to me, as a state director of adult education, in informing many of the routine and strategic decisions facing our state. Our most recent experience using research has been one of the most valuable and potentially far-reaching. Maryland's state investment in adult education has seriously lagged behind what was needed to make a significant impact on the target population. Historically, we enrolled less than 4% of the eligible target population annually and, in Fiscal Year 2003, were investing only $77 per student; students were receiving an average of 40 contact hours of instruction annually.

In 2005, Maryland established a Superintendent's Panel on Excellence in Adult Education to develop recommendations to ensure that adult education programs and students achieve results. The Panel, with leadership from the business community and representation from business, labor, local school systems, local government, community-based organizations, higher education, finance, and adult education, used a standards-based finance approach to education to develop recommendations. The Panel established the cost of delivering services that result in student achievement. Their report, *Stepping Up to the Future: Adult Literacy Challenges at Work, at Home, and in the Maryland Community,* made recommendations to ensure that Maryland's adult students have sufficient resources to meet national and state student achievement standards.

The Panel began its study with a survey of current national research and evidence-based practice that has been demonstrated to produce results, as defined by the National Reporting System. The research provided a guide to the components that should be included in a quality adult education and literacy program. These components included well-qualified instructional staff, appropriate class size, instructional support services, and other resources necessary to achieve results. Research also answered the critical question of how much instruction is necessary for the students with the characteristics of Maryland's adult learners. Having used research to develop the model for the program, it was an easy step to develop a cost structure.

Research was also essential in developing stakeholder support for the financial resources necessary to implement the Panel recommendations and the prototype model. Research by a labor economist using the Maryland wage database and 4 years of actual adult education student data identified the financial return on investment from wage gains. Research also answered the critical question of how long it takes to see a return on investment. The data for Maryland indicates a $3.15 return for every $1 invested by the state, which accrues within 18 months of student exit.

Since the Panel issued its report in December 2005, the state budget for adult education has increased by 43% for Fiscal Year 2006. Maryland's governor proposed an additional 60% increase in funding for Fiscal Year 2007. In January 2006, the Maryland General Assembly introduced two bills to establish Maryland's first-ever state funding formula for adult education. If the bills are passed, the formula will increase adult education funding to $23 million in 5 years. The research foundation of the Panel's work provided a basis to communicate the rationale for the needed investment, the components that would be added to the program, and the results that can be anticipated.

Research at both the national and state level provided Maryland with the information needed to create a road map to the future. Regardless of funding outcomes, the Panel established a prototype program model that can be implemented as resources become available. It provides a foundation for the professional development and other program reforms necessary to ensure students achieve at the level and in the time frame required by our economy, our students, and our community.

Here in Maryland and across the nation, adult educators have more challenges ahead. In addition to the inadequacy of national funding for research, there is also a lack of high-quality research that is specific to the characteristics of adult learners. Assuming that what works with children will be effective with adult learners is no longer sufficient. As a practitioner,

I need access to research in adult learning and the opportunity to apply the findings in partnership with the research community. Venues such as the National Adult Education Practitioner-Researcher Symposium (December 2004 in Sacramento, California) are needed to provide an opportunity for dialogue on the implications of, and continuing questions posed by, current research.

Significant challenges in building a learning community within state and local delivery systems remain. These challenges are complicated by an overwhelmingly part-time workforce, a diverse delivery system, and expanding learner needs. Research that can enhance services keyed to diverse student needs is especially valuable. I need more research to inform our efforts to incorporate the best and most applicable practices into the classroom and to build an effective state delivery system that serves all adult students. Most critically, I need more research that demonstrates the value added from adult education and literacy gains for learners, families, the economy, and the community.

Although I regret the gap in applicable research facing the adult education community in the future, I feel honored to introduce this volume to you and recommend it to all of my colleagues. We can embrace its riches and use it to help us find the path to the future.

—*Patricia Bennett*

Preface

The National Center for the Study of Adult Learning and Literacy (NCSALL) and Lawrence Erlbaum Associates are pleased to publish the *Review of Adult Learning and Literacy, Volume 7: Connecting Research, Policy, and Practice* (formerly *The Annual Review of Adult Learning and Literacy*). The *Review* aspires to serve as the source of record for the field of adult learning and literacy, reaching those policymakers, scholars, and practitioners who are dedicated to improving the quality of practice in adult basic education (ABE), adult English for speakers of other languages (ESOL), and adult secondary education (ASE) programs.

Each review begins with an overview of significant developments in the field of adult education and literacy during the year. In this case, we cover both 2004 and 2005, as so much national advocacy and policy work happened during this time period. Each review concludes with an essay and bibliography on a topic of current interest to the field; in this volume, workplace education is the focus. The chapters included in the core of the volume are both theoretical and practical, covering a wide range of topics critical to the success of adult education and literacy services in the United States.

In the foreword, Patricia Bennett, adult education state director in Maryland, discusses the way research has been useful in her state, as she has sought funding and policy changes to better support adult learners.

In chapter 1, "The Years 2004 and 2005 in Review," Noreen Lopez documents the major policy, funding, and research initiatives across these 2 years, including the national effort to restore full funding for adult education that was cut from President Bush's Fiscal Year 2006 budget. The grassroots activism and advocacy effort of practitioners and adult students across the country succeeded in restoring level funding for adult education services. Lopez also covers the efforts to reauthorize the Workforce Investment Act and welfare-related legislation, both of which were stalled in the Congress.

In chapter 2, John P. Comings, NCSALL Director, based at the Harvard Graduate School of Education, reviews the literature and recent research on adult student persistence, including his own studies, to understand what factors affect and support student persistence in adult education. Comings argues that, in addition to providing supports to students that help them persist in coming to classes, we need to restructure program participation "in ways that make it easier for adults to pursue episodes of program participation and self-study to achieve their learning goals."

In chapter 3, Mary Ziegler and Mary Beth Bingman at The University of Tennessee provide an overview of systematic approaches to improving adult education program quality. After a review of national and state-level quality improvement efforts in government and private industry, the authors discuss recent efforts in the field of adult education. In case studies of the Analyze, Identify, Develop, Document, and Evaluate (AIDDE) model in Oregon, the Baldrige Criteria in Tennessee, and the Equipped for the Future model in Vermont, the article concludes with a call for a national accountability system that not only provides proof of programs' performance, but also provides elements that can help improve the quality of services adult learners receive.

In chapter 4, Heidi Silver-Pacuilla of American Institutes for Research discusses the role of assistive technology and how it might be used to help adult students improve their reading and writing skills. She describes the categories of assistive technology and reviews the research about the use of technology, including computer software, in helping learning-disabled K–12 students improve their basic skills. She provides examples of how such technologies as text enhancement software have been helpful to ABE students working on their vocabulary and writing development, and the effect such technologies have on increasing adult students' motivation to persist in their studies.

In chapter 5, Perrine Robinson-Geller of Rutgers University reviews the history of individualized group instruction and its prevalence as an instructional model for ABE and GED preparation. After presenting an extensive literature review and interviews with a number of stakeholders in the field familiar with this model, she discusses the factors that contribute to the continued use of this model, including the structure of adult education programs as they try to respond to the needs of adult students with busy lives and barriers to participation.

In chapter 6, Rima E. Rudd and colleagues at the Harvard School of Public Health present an update of the research on health literacy. In the first volume of the *Annual Review of Adult Learning and Literacy*, research up through 1999 on the connection between health and literacy was reviewed. In this chapter, the authors review the new literature from 2000 through 2005. They review the policy-related efforts to increase funding for initiatives to improve health literacy skills in the United States, and summarize the major research in the areas of print and nontext materials and measures of health literacy, and the research on health outcomes for people at different reading levels. The authors note a change in perspective in recent years, from an emphasis in the literature on how reading deficits of adults contribute to health problems, to an emphasis on the shared responsibility of public health and educational practitioners to understand "the communication process and literacy-related barriers in the health care environment."

In chapter 7, Cristine Smith, NCSALL deputy director based at World Education, and Marilyn Gillespie, senior educational researcher at SRI International, review the research on professional development and teacher change, including the research from both K–12 and adult education that outlines what makes traditional and "job-embedded" models of professional development most effective. They continue with the research related to professional development in the context of standards-based reform. The authors outline needed research for better understanding the role of professional development in teacher quality and student achievement, and a set of changes in policy and practice that could improve the preparation and support of ABE teachers within the current system.

In chapter 8, Rosie Wickert from University of Technology, Sydney, along with Jean Searle, Beth Marr, and Betty Johnson, describes the evolution of the adult learning and literacy system in Australia, using the history of adult numeracy instruction as an example of the major policy and practice issues. Throughout this article, the authors highlight "how purposeful actions by literacy and numeracy advocates helped ensure that adult literacy and numeracy survived and grew through a volatile Australian policy environment over the last 15 to 20 years."

In chapter 9, Veronica McKay of the University of South Africa discusses the efforts to increase literacy education provision since the end of apartheid. After describing the effects of apartheid—lack of education and continuing poverty of Blacks—she outlines the government's policies for supporting ABE and training. She argues that although the government has developed numerous policy statements and multipronged efforts to improve both literacy and livelihood skills, many of which have successfully reached thousands of illiterates, the lack of funding has contributed to a gap between adult education policy and practice.

In chapter 10, Connie Nelson of the Massachusetts Worker Education Roundtable defines workplace education, as distinct from workforce development, and discusses the changes in the U.S. economy that have led to the need for ever-higher levels of literacy skills and the motivations of both workers and employers to see that employees achieve these levels. She then reviews some lessons about implementing quality workplace education programs, drawn from the research, and provides an annotated outline of key resources for practitioners and policymakers that can help them learn more about the issues related to workplace education.

This volume of the *Review of Adult Learning and Literacy* is likely to be the last in the current series because NCSALL's funding formally ended in July 2006. Over the course of these seven volumes, we have covered the research and theory on a wide range of issues in adult learning and literacy, from practical articles about reading, writing, numeracy, and oral language skill instruction to theoretical articles about critical literacy theory and the meaning of evidence-based practice. The *Reviews* have described the adult learning systems in England, Canada, Ireland, New Zealand, Australia, and South Africa. Our authors have outlined key resources related to technology, adult learning theory, metacognition, community organizing for literacy, organizational development, family literacy, and workplace education. Many have used the articles in the *Review* as reading material in graduate courses and in professional development for adult literacy practitioners and we have seen numerous citations and references to *Review* articles in other research publications, Web sites, newsletters, and reviews over the years in our field. NCSALL's goal was to contribute to the knowledge base about teaching adults in a rigorous, clear, concise, and interesting way for those who are dedicated to helping adults learn, and we hope we have met that goal. We also hope that the *Review* will be revived in the future, with new funding from either government or private sources, so that the ongoing work of building a base of research, theory, and professional wisdom in our field will continue.

—*John P. Comings*
—*Barbara Garner*
—*Cristine Smith*
EDITORS

List of Tables and Figures

Tables

Table 1.1	Adult Education and Even Start Appropriations for FY 2005	5
Table 1.2	Adult Education and Even Start Appropriations for FY 2006	8
Table 1.3	State Grant Funding and Enrollments for Program Years 2002–2003 and 2003–2004	16
Table 2.1	Summary of Major Scholarly Works Informing Our Current Understanding of Persistence	28
Table 3.1	National Adult Education Professional Development Consortium (NAEPDC) Electronic Survey Responses	58
Table 7.1	Models of Professional Development	215

Figures

Figure 3.1	The AIDDE program improvement process.	62
Figure 3.2	Baldrige Framework for Excellence.	70
Figure 3.3	Expanded model of the theory of action of standards-based reform: An educational improvement system.	75
Figure 4.1	Dragon Naturally Speaking.	104
Figure 4.2	Co:Writer word prediction with word processor also open.	107
Figure 5.1	ABE enrollment, 1965–1974.	142
Figure 8.1	The National Framework of Adult English Language, Literacy and Numeracy Competence.	260
Figure 8.2	The relationships between the aspects, stages, and phases of the National Framework of Adult English Language, Literacy and Numeracy Competence.	261

1

The Years 2004 and 2005 in Review

Noreen Lopez

This review covers both 2004 and 2005 because more of the public policy issues that affected the field occurred in 2005. Adult educators were challenged as never before in 2005 and successfully met that challenge. It is an important story to tell.

President Bush's Fiscal Year (FY) 2005 budget proposal included a stable level of funding for adult education, so it was a surprise when his budget the following year (FY 2006) included a devastating cut in funding. Due to the work of the National Council of State Directors of Adult Education (NCSDAE) and others, a newly formed advocacy network of adult educators used the speed of the Internet to disseminate quickly to teachers, learners, program staff, and others a set of recommendations for action. This network was highly responsive and very effective in convincing representatives and senators to maintain level funding for adult education.

The field was also involved in advocacy efforts related to authorizing legislation in Congress that would affect the National Institute for Literacy, the integrity of structure and funding for adult basic education programs, and educational services for welfare recipients. Congressional staff indicated that the concerns of those advocating on these issues had been heard and addressed in one or more versions of the pending bills on the Workforce Investment Act (WIA) and welfare reform.

Although there was a significant amount of research on adult literacy taking place, the future of new research was in doubt. The U.S. Department of Education's (USDE) Institute of Educational Sciences indicated they would no longer be funding a national research center for adult education. With the adult education field's attention focused on defeating the proposed funding cuts, many practitioners were not aware of this loss until late in 2005.

Two catastrophic hurricanes in 2005 (Katrina and Rita) dramatically changed the landscape of the geographic areas they hit and the lives of the people affected. They also caused a huge drain on the financial and emotional resources of the United States. In addition, the ongoing war in Iraq and tax cuts by the Bush administration led to an increase in the national debt. These factors had a direct effect on the U.S. economy and education policy: In February 2005, the Bush administration proposed to reduce the national debt by cutting funding for discretionary programs such as adult education and Even Start. By December 2005, the pressure on Congress to further cut funding was exacerbated by the ever-growing costs of hurricane relief. These economic and social pressures on the federal budget serve to highlight the significance of the eventual budget success achieved by the adult education field.

POLICY

Federal Budget and Appropriations

Before discussing the appropriation levels for FY 2005 and FY 2006, it is helpful to understand some basic procedures in the federal budget and appropriations process. Although the president is required by law to present his budget to Congress after the first Monday of January but not later than the first Monday of February, the process of developing the budget actually begins more than 6 months earlier. The USDE works with the Office of Management and Budget (OMB) during the prior spring, summer, and fall to establish USDE funding priorities. For example, for the FY 2006 budget presented to Congress by the president in February 2005, the USDE began its internal work on recommendations for education program funding around May 2004. About August 2004, USDE submitted its FY 2006 budget request to OMB with detailed justifications. Over the next few months, OMB submitted questions about the budget to USDE, which then responded to the questions. Revisions to the proposed budget took place based on the latest fiscal information on expenditures from the previous year (FY 2004) and current congressional action on the FY 2005 budget. Some time in November or December 2004, the OMB notified the USDE of its final decision on the FY 2006 budget, along with any program policy changes and legislative directions. During December 2004 and January 2005, USDE prepared various materials to justify and explain the budget. The President used these materials as part of the budget document for distribution to Congress and as information for the public. Finally, in early February 2005, President Bush presented his FY 2006 budget request to Congress. This budget specified an amount for each program, rather than just a total amount for education.

Congress has its own process for developing a budget and does not have to accept the president's budget. Both the House and the Senate have a budget committee, which set their own self-imposed ceiling for spending. The budget committees further break down their budgets into spending targets for several categories of expenditures, such as education, national defense, agriculture, and so on, but not for specific programs within those categories. The budget committees must arrive at a concurrent budget resolution adopted by both houses, generally by mid-April of 2005 for the FY 2006 budget. This budget serves as the congressional guideline for spending, but does not become law. The budget committee in each house gives the various appropriations subcommittees the maximum amount they can spend on programs under their jurisdiction. For education programs, this is the Labor, Health and Human Services, Education and Related Agencies (Labor/HHS) Subcommittee in both the House and Senate.

From mid-May through June, the House acts on these bills, moving from the subcommittee level to the Appropriations Committee to the House floor. The bills can be amended at any of these stages. House floor action is supposed to be completed by June 30. Generally in July, the Senate appropriations bills follow a similar path, moving from subcommittee to full committee to Senate floor action. (It is important to remember that, unless specified by law, many of these dates are flexible and actions are often delayed for several months beyond those indicated here.) In most cases, the House and Senate appropriations are different and must therefore go to a conference committee to reconcile the differences. Later, the appropriations are brought back to both the House and Senate for final floor action. This should be completed by the end of September to begin the new federal fiscal year on October 1. (For a more thorough explanation of the timeline for federal and state fiscal years, refer to *The Review of Adult Learning and Literacy,* Vol. 6, chap. 1.) When there is no final budget by October 1, Congress must enact a continuing resolution to provide temporary funding to allow federal programs to continue operating. In fact, continuing resolutions have almost become standard practice in Congress.

2005 Appropriations. With a significant federal budget deficit and a slow economy, the President's budget for FY 2005 recommended funding adult education state grants at the same level as FY 2004. Although 2004's level was an increase of $3 million over FY 2003, it still did not restore adult education to the level of funding in FY 2002. Maintaining the same level of funding was equivalent to a cut because it did not keep pace with inflation. The President presented his FY 2005 budget to Congress on February 2, 2004. The amount requested for adult education was $574.4 million, and the president proposed eliminating the Even Start program.[1] With adult education funding looking fairly secure, various adult education organizations contacted relevant committee staff and provided rationales for increasing support for adult education, but did little to involve adult education teachers, program directors, other staff, and learners in advocating on a federal level. With Even Start funding jeopardized, the Family Literacy Alliance (FLA), an initiative of the National Center for Family Literacy (NCFL), made a significant effort to involve local constituencies in contacting members of Congress to restore its funding. The March 2004 issue of the FLA online quarterly publication *Connecting* included more than a page devoted to advocacy efforts.[2] Information was also sent out on the FLA mail list. In a November 2004 policy update,[3] Tony Peyton of NCFL credited the Even Start community with flooding Capitol Hill with calls, letters, and e-mails, resulting in the continued funding of the program and defeating its proposed elimination. The House had passed its appropriations bill with $574.4 million for adult education

---

[1]Even Start is a program that provides education and related services jointly to disadvantaged parents and their young children. Services include early childhood education, adult education, parent–child activities, and parenting skills.

[2]http://www.famlit.org/loader.cfm?url=commonspot/security/getfile.cfm&PageID=15338.

[3]http://www.famlit.org/PolicyandAdvocacy/UpdatesandAlerts/108thcongress.cfm.

TABLE 1.1
Adult Education and Even Start Appropriations for FY 2005
(Amounts in Thousands)

Program	FY 04	FY 05 President	FY 05 House	FY 05 Senate	FY 05 Conference	FY 05 Final
Adult education state grants	$574,372	$574,372	$574,372	$574,266	$574,266	$569,672
National leadership activities	9,169	9,169	9,169	9,169	9,169	9,096
National Institute for Literacy	6,692	6,692	6,692	6,692	6,692	6,638
Even Start	246,910	0	226,910	0	226,910	225,095

and $226.9 million for Even Start (a cut of $20 million from the previous year). The Senate had reduced the adult education line item by $106,000 and eliminated Even Start in its appropriation bill. The final decision came when the conference committee accepted the Senate's cut to adult education and the House's proposal for Even Start. Then, all discretionary programs received an across-the-board cut of .8% to arrive at a final appropriations level (see Table 1.1).

2006 Appropriations. Because the national debt continued to climb and the financial demands of the war in Iraq never abated, adult educators anticipated that there could be another reduction in funds for FY 2006. However, nothing had prepared the field for what was actually proposed. On February 7, 2005, President Bush presented his FY 2006 budget to Congress. His proposal once again included the complete elimination of the Even Start program, but to adult educators' dismay, it also included a devastating reduction of 66% in the adult education state grants program. At a USDE meeting the same day, held to discuss the proposed education budget, officials were asked why adult education had been cut so drastically. The response included four justifications:

1. The president's high school initiative would eliminate the need for adult education.
2. OMB had judged the adult education program as "not accountable" for its funding.
3. The budget retained the $69 million for EL/Civics programs, thus addressing the needs of the limited-English-speaking population.

4. A proposed increase in Pell Grants would compensate for cuts in adult education.

As bad as a 66% cut sounded, it would actually be worse, particularly in the states with larger populations, because the funds are allocated in a two-step process. First, every state or area receives a base amount; second, of the remaining funds, dollars are allocated based on the number of people in the state who are over 16 without a high school diploma. As a result, individual states would lose anywhere from 54% to 76% of the previous year's funding. Large states with populations that had declined under the most recent census would be hit the hardest because they would experience a reduction in funds based on loss of population in addition to the reduction based on the funding cut.

All adult educators felt a true sense of urgency. NCSDAE had been working on establishing a single point-of-contact system for legislative action in each state, in which one person in each state is responsible for sending a "call to action" to all stakeholders in his or her state. NCSDAE quickly endeavored to finalize this system, and worked with the National Coalition for Literacy (NCL) and its member organizations to add additional contacts and further disseminate information through their organizations. As a result, adult education quickly developed a mechanism for addressing this budget crisis. Each time Art Ellison, NCSDAE policy co-chair, sent out a message by e-mail to all the single points of contact in each state and the NCL, the message was further disseminated to hundreds of adult educators, as well as to members of the organizations that belong to NCL.

One of the early messages included information prepared by the state directors to counter the justifications offered by the administration through USDE and referred to as myths by adult educators. In summary, they argued the following:

- The high school initiative would not help the adults currently in the workforce who do not have a high school diploma. Further, even if all the graduating high school seniors entered the workforce, annually they would comprise only 2% of the workforce. For the United States to be more competitive, we must upgrade the skills of the current workforce.
- The assessment by OMB rated the adult education program as "results not demonstrated" because OMB required numeric targets for key performance indicators, whereas the USDE negotiated percentage targets

with the states. Adult education has extensive performance data to document the success of its services.
- Although the EL/Civics program was not cut, it served only 12% of the English as a second language (ESL) students. Forty-six percent of the total students served are ESL students, so the 66% cut would eliminate services to many ESL students.
- Pell Grants cannot be used for adult education. They are for postsecondary education. Adult education is limited by law to instruction below the postsecondary level.

Although some messages were strictly informational, most had specific calls to action, including activities such as these:

1. Urging your member of Congress to sign a "Dear Colleague" letter regarding the level of adult education funds needed in the budget.
2. Encouraging your member of Congress to contact members of the Budget Committee to put enough in the education budget to level-fund adult education
3. Appealing to your senator or representative—if a member of the Labor/HHS Appropriations Subcommittee—to support FY 2005 level funding for adult education.
4. Urging all members of the House to support the appropriation for adult education as recommended by the House Labor/HHS Appropriations Committee.

Adult educators and students rose to the demand by generating thousands of letters, e-mails, and phone calls. National organizations involved in adult education disseminated information to the field and to members of Congress addressing the "myths" of nonaccountability and other justifications provided by the Bush administration to support the cut. When public policy staff from the NCL and NCSDAE met with congressional staff, they were told that members of Congress had been hearing from their constituents about adult education. In addition, state directors successfully secured a time slot for their NCSDAE president, Bob Bickerton, to provide oral and written testimony to the House Appropriations Subcommittee, requesting level funding and refuting the administration's justifications for the proposed cut.

By November 2005, it was clear the campaign was successful. Despite the President's proposed cut of almost $370 million in adult education,

TABLE 1.2
Adult Education and Even Start Appropriations for FY 2006
(Amounts in Thousands)

Program	FY 05	FY 06 President	FY 06 House	FY 06 Senate Committee	FY 06 Conference	FY 06 Final
Adult education state grants	$569,672	$200,000	$569,672	$569,672	$569,672	$563,975
National leadership activities	9,096	9,096	9,096	9,096	9,096	9,005
National Institute for Literacy	6,638	6,638	6,638	6,638	6,638	6,572
Even Start	225,095	0	200,000	0	100,000	99,000

both the House and Senate Labor/HHS Appropriations Committees recommended an appropriation of $569,672,000, the same amount as in FY 2005. The final appropriation bill signed into law by President Bush on December 30, 2005, reflected the FY 2005 level with a 1% cut, resulting in a final figure of $563,975,280. The 1% cut was applied against almost all discretionary federal programs to stay within the budget level set by Congress.

Even Start did not fare as well. The President proposed no funding, the House appropriated $200 million, and the Senate Appropriations Committee recommended no funding. The final figure for Even Start was $99 million. The final appropriations for FY 2006 are reflected in Table 1.2. The success of the advocacy campaign to save adult education federal funding was a result of the combined efforts of all the organizations and individuals that took such an active role in contacting their representatives and senators in Congress. Never before had the threat to adult education been so great, and the response so unified and strong.

Authorizing Legislation

Authorizing legislation is the legislation that establishes, changes, or continues (reauthorizes) a federal program or agency. It must be passed by the House and Senate and signed into law by the president. The primary federal authorizing legislation for adult education and family literacy is contained in the WIA. Welfare reform legislation also contains some provisions that affect adult education. Reauthorizing legislation for both WIA and welfare was addressed in the 108th Congress, and carried over into the 109th Congress.

Workforce Investment Act. In 2003, both the House and Senate passed separate versions of reauthorization of the WIA, the federal law that authorizes funding for adult education originally enacted in 1998. The House's version was HR 1261, The Workforce Reinvestment and Adult Education Act of 2003. The Senate's version was S.1627, The Workforce Investment Act Amendments of 2003. A conference committee, scheduled to meet in January 2004 (a continuation of the 108th Congress) to work out the differences in the two bills and bring an agreed-on version for a vote before both the House and the Senate, never convened because the Senate did not appoint members to the committee. As a result, there was no action on the reauthorization in 2004.

By the beginning of the 109th Congress in January 2005, workforce committees in both the House and the Senate listed reauthorization of WIA as one of their early activities. Because it was a new Congress, they could not simply carry over the bills from 2003 and 2004. Each house had to introduce its bill as a new piece of legislation, even though much of the actual content was carried over from the previous bills. There were a few changes from the earlier versions but the Senate bill once again incorporated many of the recommendations proposed by the NCL and included in the 2003 version. As a result, the adult education community was generally more supportive of the Senate version of the WIA reauthorization.

An interesting aspect of the WIA reauthorization goes back to the President's budget release for FY 2006. In the Labor Department budget, the President stated that he would like some changes that would (a) consolidate the WIA Adult, Dislocated Worker, and Youth and Employment Service funding streams into a single grant to states for employment and training services; and (b) give governors the option of consolidating additional federal job training and employment programs. Governors would have the option of consolidating core WIA programs with additional one-stop partner programs—such as Adult Education and the Food Stamp Employment and Training program—into a single, coordinated program funded through one funding stream. This flexibility for funding was called WIA Plus. This block grant funding has consistently led to the elimination of specific programs placed into the block grant and a significant reduction in overall funding. Adult education could be reduced or eliminated in WIA Plus. The administration indicated they would work with Congress to assure that these WIA Plus provisions were incorporated into the reauthorization of the WIA.

In addition to the struggles required to maintain level funding for adult education, there were battles to keep WIA Plus out of the authorizing legislation. Adult educators viewed WIA Plus as a significant threat to the continuation of the program. Many state directors of adult education and members of the NCL Public Policy Committee expressed their belief that governors were likely to divert adult education funds to other, more favored programs, such as vocational training or Job Corps. Adult education organizations and other concerned groups strongly voiced their positions with the House Education and the Workforce Subcommittee on 21st Century Competitiveness, and the Senate Health, Education, Labor and Pensions (HELP) Subcommittee, although neither subcommittee initially seemed inclined to support the President's proposal.

Indeed, the House bill, HR 27, the Job Training Improvement Act of 2005, passed through subcommittee, committee, and the full House without the addition of WIA Plus. The Senate bill, S.9, the Lifetime of Education Opportunities Act of 2005, introduced in January 2005, was replaced in May by S.1021, The Workforce Investment Act Amendments of 2005, which did not contain a WIA Plus provision and which was reported out of committee to the full Senate in September. As of January 2006, the Senate had still not voted on S.1021. The Senate version retained many of the NCL recommendations and received the most support from adult educators. Although the Senate committee's version did not contain the WIA Plus provision, such a provision could be added as an amendment on the full Senate floor. The public policy leaders in adult education acknowledged that this was possible, but not likely. Once the Senate passes the bill, it will go to a conference committee where the members of the committee will have to develop a version acceptable to both houses.

Other pressing matters, such as filling the Supreme Court vacancies of the late Chief Justice William H. Rehnquist and Justice Sandra Day O'Connor, and the issues surrounding the response to Hurricanes Katrina and Rita, took up much of the Senate's time in the last quarter of 2005. WIA reauthorization was therefore carried over into 2006. Because 2006 was still part of the 109th Congress, no new legislation needed to be introduced. Congress was able to pick up action on the bills where they left off in 2005.

The NCSDAE and the NCL prepared documents for members of Congress indicating which provisions they supported and opposed in both versions of the WIA reauthorization. They shared these documents with congressional members and staff in an effort to secure the most desirable piece of legislation. Many of these documents can be found on the NCSDAE Web site at http://www.ncsdae.org.

Welfare Reauthorization. A welfare reform bill was passed initially in 1996 and reauthorization of the legislation should have been completed in 2003, but was not. The House version of reauthorization, HR 4, was passed by the House in 2003 and sent to the Senate for consideration in 2004. There were several differences between the House and Senate versions and, by the end of the 108th Congress, no bill had passed both chambers.

In 2005, new bills were introduced, based on the proposals from 2003 and 2004. The House introduced HR 240, the Personal Responsibility, Work and Family Promotion Act of 2005, and the Senate introduced S.6, Personal Responsibility and Individual Development for Everyone Act. By the end of June 2005, Congress was unable to pass new legislation but passed the 10th short-term extension of the 1996 welfare law. This extension ran through the end of September 2005 and kept the program operating under provisions of the old law, which technically expired in 2002. An additional extension passed Congress in October to operate the program through March 2006.

Although welfare legislation was not a centerpiece for the provision of adult education, it could affect adult education services. Adult educators were concerned with two specific provisions that differed in the House and Senate versions. The proposed legislation specified the length of time that a welfare recipient could spend in full-time adult education and count that time toward meeting the law's work requirements. It also authorized a "superwaiver" for states.

The superwaiver provision allowed the governor of each state to waive almost all provisions of authorizing legislation of eligible programs. (Eligible programs were those specified in the legislation.) Although the superwaiver did not allow the governor to waive the basic purposes or goals of the program, or to transfer the funds from one account to another, it did allow a state to waive application procedures, performance standards, reporting requirements, and eligibility standards. For example, under the superwaiver provisions, a governor could eliminate the competitive "direct and equitable" application process for adult education funds, and allocate funding to local one-stop centers or for-profit institutions to provide all adult education services in the state, or require that all funds be spent only for general equivalency diploma (GED)-level instruction and not basic skills or ESL.

The House version of the superwaiver included adult education as an eligible program and was available to all states. The Senate's version of the superwaiver did not include the adult education program and would only be operated in 10 states. The House version allowed up to a maximum of 4 months in a period of 24 months for full-time adult education or training to count toward work activity. The Senate version allowed an initial 3 months and then another 3 months if called for in the client's self-sufficiency plan.

Adult educators, fearful of having adult education included in the superwaiver provision and supporting a longer time for full-time adult education services, supported the Senate version of the bill rather than the House version. Garrett Murphy, NCL Public Policy Chairperson, provided written testimony to the House Subcommittee on Human Resources of the House Ways and Means Committee on behalf of the NCL and NCSDAE regarding these two provisions and other issues. The Center for Law and Social Policy (CLASP)[4] also supported the Senate provisions on these issues. They published several reports highlighting the research showing that the most effective welfare-to-work programs provide a variety of services to recipients, including education and training. (See the welfare policy section of the CLASP Web site at http://www.clasp.org.)

As of October 2005, both the House and Senate bills remained at the committee level in each chamber. In November, the House Ways and Means Committee added its welfare reauthorization to the budget reconciliation bill HR 4241. During a conference to resolve the differences between the Senate version of a budget reconciliation bill, S.1932, and HR 4241, several changes were made. The conference agreement eliminated both the superwaiver provisions and the time individuals could spend in adult education full time as part of the work requirement. It gave the Secretary of Health and Human Services the responsibility of issuing regulations to govern the welfare-to-work program, including the precise definition of each work activity that applies toward the work participation requirements. The NCL and NCSDAE have stated their intent to meet with the Secretary's representative to promote the inclusion of full-time adult education as a work activity in these regulations.

---

[4]CLASP is a national, nonprofit organization founded in 1968 that conducts research, policy analysis, technical assistance, and advocacy on issues related to economic security for low-income families with children.

Grassroots Activism

In addition to the 2005 grassroots efforts on appropriations through the single point of contact network, there were other notable advocacy endeavors in 2004. The first was a call to adult educators in January 2004 to take an advocacy role in saving the original legislative intent for the National Institute for Literacy (NIFL). The 2003 House- and Senate-passed versions of WIA reauthorization were scheduled to go to a conference committee for resolution in 2004. Language in the House bill changed the role of the NIFL, shifting its focus from adult literacy (broadly defined to include reading, writing, speaking, math, life skills, and workplace literacy) to literacy (defined as reading) across the life span. The language in the House bill also changed the purposes of NIFL; it was authorized to promote and disseminate reading research. The Senate bill retained language from earlier legislation, which included purposes of the NIFL related to coordinating literacy services and policy, and national leadership for literacy. Concerned adult educators set up a Save NIFL Web site (http://savenifl.org) and urged members of the field to contact their congressional representatives to support the Senate version of WIA reauthorization. These concerned adult educators, as well as the NCL, felt the Senate provisions on NIFL were more desirable because they gave NIFL a role in leadership, policy, and coordination of services. The site included information on the issues, links to both versions of reauthorization, tips on contacting legislators, and a feedback feature called the Advocacy Hall of Honor. People from at least 27 states reported back to the Hall of Honor that they had contacted their legislators. Both the House and Senate 2005 versions of WIA reauthorization retained most of the same provisions on NIFL as they had in 2003–2004, although the House bill did broaden its definition of literacy beyond reading. The final role for NIFL will not be clear until WIA is reauthorized.

The second effort, Literacy President, began in April 2004, and was an attempt to collect questions from the field on adult education issues, submit them to presidential candidates, and solicit a response. With the presidential election coming up in November 2004, the purpose of asking candidates to respond to questions about adult education was to raise their awareness of the issues and raise the priority of adult literacy in whatever administration was elected. Through information disseminated on the National Literacy Advocacy (NLA) listserv and the Literacy President Web site (http://www.litpresident.org), a total of 1,467 individuals voted on the questions that had been posed by the field to arrive at the top five questions to be submitted to the candidates. Data from the survey, which closed on June 7, indicated that respondents included practitioners, adult learners, college or university students in adult education, and others. The NCSDAE prepared additional background information for the selected questions, along with two additional questions, and submitted them to the candidates. Senator John Kerry, the Democratic candidate, responded on September 4, 2004, and President George W. Bush, the Republican incumbent, responded on October 12, 2004. Of course, both candidates claimed to support adult literacy.

Answering a question related to training and retraining, President Bush indicated that he wanted to give governors more flexibility to meet their workforce and adult education needs and that he would consolidate WIA's four major training programs into a single flexible grant to states. (This position was later reflected in his proposal for WIA Plus, discussed earlier.) Also of note was Senator Kerry's response regarding intergenerational literacy. The senator indicated his support of intergenerational programs such as family literacy and Even Start, and cited President Bush's 2005 budget proposal to cut all funding for Even Start. President Bush's response on intergenerational literacy indicated he would promote literacy programs through Head Start, Early Reading First, and Title 1. He did not mention Even Start. The full set of questions and responses can be found on the Literacy President Web site.

PROGRAM ACCOUNTABILITY

Despite the criticism of the OMB, accountability efforts in adult education had been growing steadily since the passage of WIA, which specified performance standards for all programs. These standards include students increasing educational functioning levels (12 levels across adult basic education, ASE, and ESL), obtaining or retaining employment, earning secondary credentials (GED or high school diploma), and transitioning to postsecondary education or other training. Each year, every state negotiates with the USDE to set the performance targets for their state. In program year 2002–2003, 43 of the 50 states met or exceeded their performance targets.

The USDE's 2002–2003 Adult Education and Family Literacy Report to Congress[5] included data across three program years (2000–2001

---

[5]The full report is available at http://www.ed.gov/about/offices/list/ovae/resource/index.html#research.

through 2002–2003), reflecting improved program accountability based on these standards.

With an average of 2.7 million adults served each year, over the 3 years:

- 1,509,475 adults advanced one or more education levels in ABE or low ASE (where one education level equates to a minimum of 2 years grade-level equivalency). The actual number of learners increased in each of the 3 program years and there was a modest 1% increase in the percentage of those advancing one or more education levels each year when compared to the previous year.
- 1,169,696 adults advanced one or more education levels of six English-language-acquisition levels. The number of learners increased in each of the 3 program years, and there was a 2% increase in the percentage of those advancing one or more education levels each year when compared to the previous year.
- 547,590 adults earned a high school diploma or GED. Although the number of learners with a high school completion goal who earned a high school diploma or GED decreased each year, the percentage achieving their goal increased each year, from 33% in program year (PY) 2001 to 44% in PY 2003.
- 145,845 adults enrolled in postsecondary education or training. The number of learners with a goal to transition to further education or training decreased each year, but the percentage of those achieving their goal increased each year, from 25% in PY 2001 to 30% in PY 2003.
- 421,862 adults were employed one quarter after program exit. This is the only performance measure that did not increase each year. Both the number of learners with this goal and the percentage achieving it was highest in PY 2002, with a decrease in PY 2003. The percentage achieving their goal from PY 2001 to PY 2003 moved from 31% to 42%, and then 37%.
- 587,910 adults retained employment three quarters after leaving the program. Although the number of learners with this outcome decreased in PY 2002 they increased slightly again in PY 2003. The percentage increased each year from 62% in PY 2001 to 69% in PY 2003.

Although outcome data were not available at the time of writing for PY 2003–2004, enrollment information for the adult education program was available on the OVAE Web site. The data from PY 2002–2003 and PY

TABLE 1.3
State Grant Funding and Enrollments for Program
Years 2002–2003 and 2003–2004

Program Year	State Grants	Total Enrollment	ABE	ESL	ASE
2002–2003	$575,000,000	2,734,186	1,079,386	1,175,531	479,269
Percentage of total			39.5%	43.0%	17.5%
2003–2004	$571,262,000	2,677,028	1,061,772	1,172,569	442,687
Percentage of total			39.7%	43.8%	16.5%

Note. ABE = adult basic education; ESL = English as a second language; ASE = adult secondary education.

2003–2004 showed a decrease in the total number of adults served, but an increase in the percentage of ESL students served. The data did not explain the decline in the total number served, which could be due to any number of factors: States may have served fewer learners, but provided more hours of instruction per learner; other approaches to improving quality may have resulted in fewer adults served; or the decline in adults served from PY 2003–2004 may be a reflection of the decline in federal support. Table 1.3 reflects data from OVAE reports on the numbers served, and USDE budget information on the federal funds allocated for state grants.

TRANSITIONS IN 2004 AND 2005

The National Institute for Literacy

On the recommendation of the NIFL's Advisory Board, the Secretaries of the Departments of Education, Labor, and Health and Human Services appointed Dr. Sandra Baxter as the director of the Institute in August 2005. Dr. Baxter had been serving as the NIFL interim director since October 2001. Dr. Baxter appointed Lynn Reddy as the Institute's deputy director. Ms. Reddy had served as the NIFL communications director since 1999.

The NIFL continued to provide a high-quality Internet-based information and communication system, LINCS, which was operated through a network of partners nationwide. LINCS offered a broad array of literacy-related information and research, as well as public discussion lists and technology training opportunities. Under a contract with NIFL, the RMC Research Corporation conducted a comprehensive, objective evaluation of

LINCS to determine its strengths and weaknesses, to ascertain if the NIFL was fulfilling its congressional mandate regarding an electronic database of information dissemination, and to help the NIFL chart future actions regarding the LINCS network. NIFL also offered hard copies of publications, including research-based products, through their hotline and clearinghouse. The NIFL also continued to provide their online searchable database of adult, child, and family literacy services in U.S. communities through *America's Literacy Directory. Bridges to Practice,* a research-based guide to improving services to adults with learning disabilities was disseminated through a system of trainers. Having invested in the Equipped for the Future (EFF) project for almost 10 years, and with the USDE adult education office initiating its own content standards project, the NIFL Advisory Board recommended that the NIFL cease investing funds in this initiative to develop adult learning standards. The continuing training and implementation of EFF now resides with the EFF Center for Training and Technical Assistance at the Center for Literacy Studies, University of Tennessee, and its EFF partners. The new portal for EFF information and resources can be found at http://eff.cls.utk.edu/.

Reading research continued to be a high priority for NIFL. They invested in the *Effective Practices in Reading* project discussed further in the research section under USDE, disseminated several publications on implementing research-based findings in the adult education classroom, and offered an online reading assessment tool to help adult education teachers understand their students' reading strengths and needs, along with a minitutorial on teaching adults to read (www.nifl.gov/readingprofiles). They also began new work on adolescent reading. More information can be found on these projects and services at www.nifl.gov.

U.S. Department of Education

Margaret Spellings, after nomination by President Bush and confirmation by the Senate in January 2005, took over from Dr. Rod Paige as U.S. Secretary of Education. In August 2005, Susan Sclafani, Assistant Secretary for the Office of Vocational and Adult Education, submitted her resignation, having served in that position for approximately 2 years. Beto Gonzalez, who had joined the Department as Deputy Assistant Secretary for the Office of Vocational and Adult Education on August 5, 2005, was named acting Assistant Secretary to replace Dr. Sclafani in late August. Mr. Gonzalez has experience teaching Spanish and ESL in high schools, as well as ESL in adult education. He also has experience at a community college and the U.S. Department of Labor.

National Coalition for Literacy

Having incorporated and received nonprofit status by the fall of 2003, the new Board of Directors of the NCL, under the leadership of their president, Dale Lipschultz, accomplished several notable goals in 2004 and 2005. The NCL developed its first short-term strategic plan, and then a multiyear plan; received financial support from Harold McGraw, Jr.; and secured funding from Verizon. The Board hired its first staff, a part-time interim director and a part-time public policy director. Along with the challenges of starting a new organization, the NCL was soon faced with the challenge of addressing the major budget cuts proposed by the President in January 2005, and seeking publicity for the findings of the National Assessment of Adult Literacy (NAAL) released December 15, 2005.[6] Having hired a communications firm to assist in disseminating information on the NAAL, the NCL held a press conference and conducted numerous newspaper and media interviews to call more attention to the issue of adult low literacy levels identified in the NAAL. More information on the NCL actions taken around the NAAL can be found on their Web site at http://www.national-coalition-literacy.org.

RESEARCH IN ADULT EDUCATION

Fortunately, the research funding in adult education held steady during 2004 and 2005, even though it was small compared to the level advocated by the NCL and state directors for FY 2005. These organizations had recommended combined funding of $40 million for OVAE's National Leadership Activities and NIFL. Although all of this proposed funding was not only for research, much of the $24 million increase over FY 2004 actual funding was tied to research. In 2005, the NCL and state directors became more concerned about the future of research as they realized that there would no longer be a national research center for adult education and saw the level of funding for National Leadership and NIFL decline slightly.

---

[6]The NAAL is discussed briefly in the research section. Information is available at http://nces.ed.gov/naal/.

This section identifies some of the adult education research released or in progress during 2004 and 2005, and points the reader to sources for more information. The USDE promoted scientifically based research as the standard for accepting research findings and funding research projects. They define scientifically based research as rigorous, systematic, objective, empirical, and peer-reviewed; relying on multiple measurements and observations; and preferably conducted through experimental or quasi-experimental methods.[7] Evidence-based practice, defined by the USDE,[8] is "the integration of professional wisdom with the best available empirical evidence in making decisions about how to deliver instruction" (professional wisdom is the judgment that individuals acquire through their experience or consensus views, and it includes the effective identification and incorporation of local circumstances into instruction).[9] Not all of the research listed here would be classified as scientifically based, but the field attempted to move in that direction.

Council for the Advancement of Adult Literacy

CAAL's focus in 2004–2005 was on adult literacy and the community college. All of the following reports are available on their Web site at www.caalusa.org.

- *To Ensure America's Future: Building a National Opportunity System for Adults*. Eight separate community college studies provided the information for this final report on adult education and literacy in community colleges.
- *Study of Adult ESL/Literacy Instruction and Faculty Development in Selected Community Colleges*. This study examined instructional strategies and staff and faculty development activities at six institutions, as well as contributions or barriers to the creation and success of these strategies and activities.
- *Study of Impact of Corporate Giving on Adult Literacy*. This study examined the impact of corporate philanthropy in the adult literacy field.

---

[7]See http://www.ed.gov/programs/compreform/guidance/appendc.pdf, Appendix 2.

[8]Speech by Institute of Education Sciences Director Whitehurst, "Evidence-Based Education" in October 2002, available at http://www.ed.gov/nclb/methods/whatworks/eb/edlite-index.html.

[9]See http://www.ed.gov/nclb/methods/whatworks/eb/edlite-slide004.html.

National Center for the Study of Adult Learning and Literacy

The National Center for the Study of Adult Learning and Literacy (NCSALL), the only USDE-funded research center focused exclusively on adult education, was in its third and fourth year of its second phase of funding, so most of its current research was not yet completed in 2004 or 2005. However, three studies were available on the NCSALL Web site at www.ncsall.net:

1. *One Day I Will Make It: A Study of Adult Student Persistence in Library Literacy Programs.* This is the final report of a study in library literacy programs that examined the implementation and effects of various strategies to improve student persistence. (This was a joint study by MDRC and NCSALL.)
2. *The Relationship of the Component Skills of Reading to Performance on the International Adult Literacy Survey (IALS).* This study looked at levels of proficiency in reading skills of students at Levels 1, 2, and 3 of the IALS and tried to determine whether levels of proficiency could be used to describe strengths and needs in reading and therefore be useful to guide assessment and instruction.
3. *Evidence From Florida on the Labor Market Attachment of Male Dropouts Who Attempt the GED.* This study looked at the differences in various employment outcomes between men who took the GED and passed and those who did not pass.

USDE

The USDE sponsored several broad studies of adult literacy, including three that released data by the end of 2005. Information is available on the National Center for Education Statistics Web site at http://nces.ed.gov/. These studies include the following:

- *The 2003 International Adult Literacy and Lifeskills Survey (ALL).* This was an international comparative study of the skills of the participating adult populations.
- *The Adult Education Program Study.* This study provided national-level information about adult education programs and their participants.
- *The 2003 National Assessment of Adult Literacy (NAAL).* This was a nationally representative assessment of literacy skills of adults aged 16 and older.

The OVAE funded several other initiatives in research, ranging from case studies to experimental designs, and translating research findings to practice. The OVAE Web site, at http://www.ed.gov/about/offices/list/ovae/pi/proginit.html#adulted, has more information on most of these projects, or visit the Web sites listed here. These initiatives included the following:

- *Adult Education to Community College Transitions Project.* This initiative identifies programs, practices, and policies that help adult basic education or GED graduates to enroll and succeed in community college programs (http://www.ed.gov/about/offices/list/ovae/pi/hs/factsh/cctrans.html).
- *Effective Practices in Reading.* This is a 5-year project, begun in 2002, in cooperation with other federal agencies, including NIFL, to fund an Adult Literacy Research Network comprised of six institutions that received reading research grants. The grantees use rigorous methodology to test various approaches for increasing reading comprehension in adult education and family literacy programs (http://www.ed.gov/about/offices/list/ovae/pi/AdultEd/readingabs.html).
- *National Technology Laboratory for the Improvement of Adult Education (TECH21).* This initiative developed a system to analyze and implement high-quality instructional technology applications in learning and instruction in adult education (http://www.TECH21.org).
- *Project IDEAL: Improving Distance Education for Adult Learners.* This initiative enables states to participate in experiments using technology-enabled or Web-enhanced distance education to deliver instruction to adult learners who chose not to attend classroom-based programs (http://projectideal.org).
- *Student Achievement in Reading Program (STAR).* This initiative is a partnership with six states to translate and disseminate evidence-based reading practices through training and technical assistance to states and to adult basic education reading teachers and programs (http://www.ed.gov/about/offices/list/ovae/pi/AdultEd/reading.html).

CONCLUSION

Adult educators and the organizations that represent them faced a number of challenges in 2004 and 2005. They addressed those challenges by taking an active role in shaping public policy in several areas: defining the role of the NIFL, promoting adult education services for welfare recipients, fighting for level funding under pressures to cut funds, and opposing attempts to consolidate programs. We know the field was successful in retaining level funding and in having the Senate include favored positions in WIA reauthorization and welfare reform. At the time of this writing, we still do not know the final outcome of the efforts for reauthorization.

The challenges posed in 2005 helped forge a stronger bond among all the national organizations, and united them and the field as never before in defeating the President's dire budget cuts to adult education and winning the support of Congress. The NCSDAE established an effective network for advocacy across all the states, and the NCL developed into a viable national organization poised to provide significant leadership in policy and communication.

As 2006 unfolded, the public policy committees of the NCL and state directors had already identified unfinished and new business that needed attention. This included the loss of a national center for research in adult education, the reauthorization of WIA, the rules to be promulgated for welfare reform, the dissemination of information on the NAAL and its policy implications, and the 2007 appropriations for adult education and Even Start.

What the future holds is impossible to predict. It is likely that the economic strains of Hurricanes Katrina and Rita and the subsequent rebuilding efforts, along with the federal deficit and the costs of the war in Iraq, will place pressure on the President and Congress to find other areas in the budget to cut. Too often in the past, those areas have included funding for adult education. However, a strong case for support was made in the 2006 appropriations battle, and Congress may be ready to recognize the important role that adult education plays in the economy.

Many in the field hope that the experience of fighting for FY 2006 appropriations for adult education will keep adult educators and learners united, and spur them on to greater action on the FY 2007 budget and beyond, to move rapidly toward the goal of increasing funding to a minimum of $1 billion for adult education state grants.

2

Persistence: Helping Adult Education Students Reach Their Goals

John P. Comings

Unlike children, who participate in schooling because of legal mandates and strong social and cultural forces, most adult students choose to participate in educational programs. Adults must make an active decision to participate in each class or tutoring session and often must overcome significant barriers to participate in educational services. Although some adults come to adult education[10] programs with specific or short-term goals, most come with goals that require hundreds, if not thousands, of hours of instruction to achieve (Comings, Parrella, & Soricone, 1999; Reder, 2000). Every adult education program, therefore, should provide its students with services that help them persist in learning long enough to reach their educational goals. This chapter defines persistence, sets out the evidence for why we should pay attention to this issue, and reviews the

---

[10]The term *adult education* includes English for speakers of other language, adult literacy, high school equivalence, and basic skills programs for adults.

persistence research. The chapter concludes by suggesting changes in policy and practice that might support higher levels of persistence, and new research that would provide evidence that these suggestions are useful.

DEFINITION OF PERSISTENCE

Persistence can be seen as being comprised of two parts: intensity (the hours of instruction per month) and duration (the months of engagement in instruction). Persistence rates are reported as hours of instruction during a specific period of months, usually in increments of 1 year. Adult education programs often refer to persistence as *retention*[11] and measure it by recording participation in formal classes or tutoring sessions. Comings and colleagues (1999) proposed the term persistence because adults can persist in learning through self-study or distance education when they stop attending program services, and sometimes return to a program (although not necessarily the same one they dropped out of) after a lapse in attendance. The term retention defines this phenomenon from a program's point of view; the program wants to retain its students. Comings and colleagues (1999) preferred the term persistence because it defines this phenomenon from the point of view of students who persist in learning—inside and outside of a program—until they have achieved their goals. This chapter defines persistence:

> *As adults staying in programs for as long as they can, engaging in self-directed study or distance education when they must stop attending program services, and returning to program services as soon as the demands of their lives allow.*

Persistence is a continuous learning process that lasts until an adult student meets his or her educational goals, and persistence could start through self-study before the first episode of participation in a program. Persistence ends when the student decides to stop learning.

WHY PERSISTENCE MATTERS

The relationship between persistence and learning is supported by several studies. Sticht (1982) and Darkenwald (1986) identified approximately

---

[11] Keeping students engaged in a particular program.

100 hours of instruction as the minimum needed by adults to achieve an increase of one grade-level equivalent on a standardized test of reading comprehension. Comings, Sum, and Uvin (2000) found that, at 150 hours of instruction, adult students in Massachusetts had a 75% probability of making a one (or greater) grade-level equivalent increase in reading comprehension or English language fluency. Porter, Cuban, and Comings (2005) found that 58 hours of instruction led to a .40 grade-level equivalent increase in reading comprehension. Rose and Wright (2006) examined the national reporting system (NRS) data of three states and found that at 100 to 110 hours of participation, 50% of students were likely to show a one NRS level[12] increase or pass the general equivalency diploma (GED) test.

Fitzgerald and Young (1997) analyzed data on the 614 students (out of 22,000) in a Development Associates (1993) study who had both a pretest and a posttest reading score. They found a relationship between hours of instruction and learning gains for immigrants learning English, but not for adult basic education (ABE) and adult secondary education (ASE) students. With a sample of less than 1% of the total students in the study, these results are not conclusive. However, it suggests, as do the studies cited earlier, that adult students might demonstrate gains at specific intervals, 100 hours for example, but the interval may differ depending on such factors as initial test score.

These studies point to 100 hours of instruction as the point at which a majority of adult education students are likely to show measurable progress, and, therefore, it serves as a benchmark that identifies an effective program. That is, if a majority of students are persisting for 100 hours or more, the program is probably having a measurable impact on at least half of its students. The U.S. Department of Education (2003) reported the average time that an adult spends in a program as 113 hours[13] in a 12-month period. However, this figure does not include adults who drop out before they complete 12 hours of instruction, which would lower the

---

[12]A one NRS level increase represents an improvement in a score on a standardized test from one defined level to another. Each NRS level is a range of approximately two grade-level equivalents so an increase could be as little as a single scale score point (a small segment of a grade-level equivalent) to two grade-level equivalents.

[13]134 hours for adults learning English, 103 hours for adults who are improving their literacy and math skills, and 87 hours for adults pursuing a high school equivalency.

average significantly. In addition, these data were influenced by one state (Florida) that reported a mean persistence rate of 258 hours and enrollment at more than 400,000 students, which is more than 15% of the national total. Only three other states reported a mean persistence rate of more than 100 hours: California (138 hours), Massachusetts (121 hours), and North Carolina (102 hours). Seven states reported an average persistence rate of less than 50 hours, and 36 states reported less than 80 hours. A large portion of the student population who stay at least 12 hours do not persist in their studies for 100 hours.

Even 113 hours of instruction is only about one tenth of the time that a K–12 student spends in class during a year. A one grade-level increase, therefore, is a significant gain within this short period of time. However, few adult students enter programs with goals that can be achieved with only a few hours of instruction. Most adult students express the desire to improve their language, literacy, and math skills; acquire high school credentials; and move on to postsecondary education or skilled job training (Comings et al., 1999; Reder, 2000). Program participation of 100 hours or even 150 hours, therefore, is probably inadequate for most adult students to reach their learning goals. Changes in policies and practices that support increased persistence could lead to more adult education students spending sufficient hours engaged in learning and therefore reaching their learning goals. The research presented here provides the best available evidence on what those changes might be.

RESEARCH ON PERSISTENCE

Some of the literature in this chapter draws on research with adults who have good literacy skills, speak English, have high school diplomas, and participate in short-term courses with defined, limited goals, such as job skill development classes in government employment programs and certificate programs in postsecondary education institutions. Although this research is informative, it may not be directly applicable to ABE students who have low literacy and math skills, do not speak English, or do not have a high school diploma. ABE students usually face a long-term commitment that may involve many different goals that change over time. In addition, some studies look at participation (the decision to join a program) rather than persistence (the decision to continue in a program). These decisions are similar but may not be the same. Finally, some studies help define the problem but do not provide insights into how to help ABE students persist in learning. Even with these limitations, this research is the best available evidence for understanding persistence and identifying ways to improve it. This chapter summarizes the findings of four previous reviews that looked at adult education literature, as well as recent studies that took place after these reviews were published (see Table 2.1 for an overview of the findings). The chapter also describes two connected studies that focused on adults whose goals were improving language, literacy, and math skills, or achieving a high school equivalence degree.

Literature Reviews

Four literature reviews analyze the participation, retention, and persistence literature (Beder, 1991; Quigley, 1997; Tracy-Mumford, 1994; Wikelund, Reder, & Hart-Landsberg, 1992). The authors of these reviews have experience with adult education programs, and this experience helps them translate findings on other populations to ABE students. Although these four reviews draw from a common core of studies, each supplements it with additional studies. All of the studies reviewed by these authors have limitations; as a result, the authors drew on their own experience and came to different conclusions. For a more detailed description and analysis of the four reviews, see Comings and colleagues (1999).

In his literature review, Beder (1991) suggested that motivation is the force that helps adults overcome barriers to participation and then described those barriers. Beder suggested that adult education programs must change their recruitment and instruction practices to be congruent with the motivations and life contexts of adult students; if they do, more adults will enter programs and persist longer. Beder concluded that adults may be weighing the benefits and costs of participation and making decisions based on that analysis. In many cases, a decision to drop out may be justified if the costs outweigh the benefits.

The Beder (1991) review concludes by asserting that the present adult education system only has enough resources to serve those who are eager to enter classes. Beder's review also suggests that the difficulties encountered by adult students could be made more manageable if programs had the resources to fit instruction to the needs and learning styles of adults and if programs looked less like school and more like an activity in which adults would want to participate.

The Wikelund et al. (1992) paper calls for broadening the definition of participation to acknowledge that adults engage in education in many

TABLE 2.1
Summary of Major Scholarly Works Informing Our Current Understanding of Persistence

Researcher	Nature of Inquiry	Key Findings
Beder (1991)	Literature review	• Suggests that adults' decisions to participate are often based on cost-benefit analysis • Emphasizes need for programs to align their services with learner motivations and life contexts
Wikelund, Reder, & Hart-Landsberg (1992)	Literature review	• Emphasizes the need to broaden the definition of participation beyond instructional hours • Challenges conventional notions of "nonparticipants"
Tracy-Mumford (1994)	Literature review	• Outlines the key characteristics of a program's persistence plan, one that supports students and informs instruction • Identifies a range of action steps program can take to directly address persistence issues
Quigley (1997)	Literature review and qualitative study	• Provides evidence for the link between adult learner persistence and previous schooling experiences • Underscores the critical importance of the first 3 weeks of participation in a program
Meder (2000)	Quasi-experimental study	• Found that engaging learners in discussion of motivational issues increased persistence
Quigley (2000)	Quasi-experimental study	• Suggests that negative attitudes toward education affect persistence • Found that intake and orientation are critical to persistence • Recommends that intake and orientation should start with goal setting and students matched to classes that meet their needs
Cuban (2003)	Case studies	• Suggests that programs may need to adapt their program curriculum and schedules to the needs and interests of their students

ways that are not limited to participation in formal classes. It also criticizes the concept of "nonparticipant" because such a concept implies that every adult who has low literacy skills needs to enter a program, which might not be true. The review concludes that research and theory, as well as practice, should focus on alternatives to formal schooling. A new definition of participation would acknowledge that learning, even improvements in literacy skills, could take place outside of formal programs. With this new definition, programs could increase persistence by continuing to support learning at times when students cannot attend classes or participate in other formal arrangements.

In her literature review, Tracy-Mumford (1994) summarized suggestions that came from research and from the reports of practitioners who had tried to improve persistence in their programs. Tracy-Mumford called for programs to develop a commitment to, and a plan for, increasing persistence, a plan that should include a strong message to students that the program is there to help them reach their goals. Because student goals can change, the program must be willing to make adjustments to accommodate new goals as they arise. For the commitment to be meaningful, the program should have a set of criteria for measuring persistence and should implement a set of strategies that reduce dropout, increase student hours of attendance, improve achievement, increase personal goal attainment, and improve completion rates.

Tracy-Mumford (1994) defined an effective persistence plan as one that both provides support to students and improves instruction. From the findings of a large number of studies and descriptions of practice, she presented a list of elements of a student persistence plan that weaves persistence strategies into all aspects of the program structure, including these:

- Recruitment methods should provide enough information for potential students to make an informed decision about enrolling.
- Intake and orientation procedures should help students understand the program, set realistic expectations, build a working relationship with program staff, and establish learning goals.
- Initial assessment tools should provide students and teachers with information on both cognitive and affective needs, should be integrated with instruction, and should form the foundation for measuring progress.
- Programs and teachers should establish strategies for formally recognizing student achievement.

- Counseling services should identify students at risk of dropping out early.
- Referral services should coordinate with social service agencies to ensure that all students are connected to the support services they need.
- The program should have a system for contact and follow-up that helps students who drop out return to the program and solicits information on ways to improve program services.
- Noninstructional activities should help form a bond between the program and its students and their families.
- Program evaluation should involve students in assessing and offering advice on each aspect of the program.
- Child care and transportation assistance should be provided.
- Instruction and instructional staff should be of sufficient quality to support effective learning.
- A student persistence team should coordinate dropout prevention activities, collect data on student persistence, and involve students and teachers in addressing this issue.

Tracy-Mumford's list is useful to program staff because it translates theory into practical advice. Unfortunately, most ABE programs lack the funding required to implement all of these elements, but implementing some of them may contribute to increased persistence.

Quigley (1997) added insights from a research study he undertook in Pennsylvania. He viewed persistence as significantly affected by the negative schooling experiences adults had when they were younger and suggested the need to change programs so that they are different from schools. Quigley saw three major constellations of factors that contribute to drop out, which he referred to as *situational* (influences of the adult's life circumstances), *institutional* (influences of systems), and *dispositional* (influences of experience). He suggested that situational influences are largely beyond the control of adult education programs, although they receive most of the attention in the literature on dropouts. Institutional factors are areas that practitioners could affect and should work on continuously. However, he suggested that dispositional factors, such as negative attitudes toward education as a result of previous failures in school, provide a focus for program reform that might affect persistence.

According to Quigley (1997), intake and orientation processes in the first 3 weeks of participation are critical to improving persistence. He suggested that intake should begin with goal setting and planning for success. Students then need to be matched to classes and teachers that can meet their goals and learning needs. Adult students can take charge of this process, but they may need help in the form of careful questions and useful information for making these decisions.

Recent Studies

A review of journals and online sources identified three studies that were not included in the four reviews already discussed and were focused on adult education as defined in this chapter. Two tested interventions in small-scale quasi-experimental studies and one described and analyzed two case studies.

Meder (2000) found that providing three opportunities for goal setting and discussion of the factors that might support or hinder adults in reaching their goals helped 31 students in her GED-level math course to persist in their studies. She had each student fill out a questionnaire on goals, barriers, and supports to persistence, and then discussed the answers with the students. This was done at 4 weeks and 8 weeks. She compared this treatment group to data available in the previous year's classes (in which these opportunities did not exist). This study suggests that involving students in a process of thinking about their motivation to participate in adult education and ways to sustain that motivation helps them persist in learning.

Quigley (2000) followed 20 students who were judged to be at risk of dropping out in a quasi-experimental study of grouping and classroom size and support that included a control group of 5 students and three treatment groups, each with 5 participants. The control group was placed in a classroom with a total of 15 students (i.e., large-group instruction), and none of this group persisted for 3 months or more. Among the treatment groups, 3 of the 5 adults placed in small-group instruction persisted for 3 months or more, 2 of the 5 adults placed in a learning environment with a teacher and a counselor persisted for 3 months or more, and 1 of the 5 adults who were placed in individual tutoring persisted for 3 months or more. Quigley also administered the Witkin Embedded Figures Test (Witkin, 1971; Witkin, Oltman, Raskin, & Karp, 1971) and the Learning Style Assessment Scale (Flannery, 1993) to all students. He found that they were highly field dependent (needing acceptance by peers) and global learners (who find it difficult to focus on topics that require linear sequencing). He suggested that small-group learning may be more appropriate for adult students who fit this profile.

Cuban (2003) reported on in-depth case studies (i.e., many hours of interviews and observation over many months) of 2 women students in a library literacy program. The detail of the case study makes clear that adult life affects persistence in complex ways. The 2 women were caregivers for their various family members and put those responsibilities before their needs and desires. The students were interested in reading romance literature but this was not the focus of their classes. The study suggests that an approach to persistence support that is the same for all students might have a positive short-term impact but, for long-term persistence, programs may need to adapt their services to the lives of each student. This might require scheduling that can accommodate changing student schedules and reading content that is of interest to students.

PERSISTENCE STUDY

Because the existing literature base was limited, in 1996 the National Center for the Study of Adult Learning and Literacy (NCSALL) began a multiphase study of the factors that support and inhibit persistence. This study began with a review of the literature cited previously (Beder, 1991; Quigley, 1997; Tracy-Mumford, 1994; Wikelund et al., 1992) and then plotted a course that would build on this foundation to develop and test an intervention that might improve persistence. In the first phase of the study, researchers interviewed 150 adults and tracked their persistence in pre-GED classes (Comings et al., 1999). Of the total, 100 students persisted for the 4 months of the study; 50 dropped out. In the second phase, researchers studied the efforts of five library literacy programs as they attempted to increase student persistence over a 3-year period (Porter et al., 2005). The third phase—not yet begun at the time of the writing of this chapter—will undertake an experiment to test whether a model of persistence support developed during the first two phases does, in fact, have an impact on persistence in programs. This section summarizes what has been learned in the first two phases of this research.

First Phase

The first phase of the study employed a force-field analysis as its theoretical model. A force-field analysis places an individual in a field of forces that support or inhibit action along a particular path (Gilbert, Fisk, & Lindzey, 1998; Lewin, 1999). This expands the motivation barriers and cost–benefit models to include a large number of forces on each side of the persistence equation. Understanding the forces, identifying which are strongest, and deciding which are most amenable to manipulation provides an indication of how to help someone move in a desired direction, such as reaching an educational goal.

This study found that the many ways in which adult students are usually classified (by gender, ethnicity, employment status, number of children, and educational background of parents or guardians) do not have a strong influence on persistence. The findings suggest that immigrants, those over the age of 30, and parents of teenage or grown children are more likely to persist than others in the study. The greater likelihood of persistence by immigrant students in English for speakers of other languages (ESOL) classes, compared to ABE and ASE students, is well documented (Young, Fleischman, Fitzgerald, & Morgan, 1994), and the findings of this study suggest that this effect continues as immigrants learn English and move on to pre-GED programs. Adults who are over 30 are more likely to have teenage or grown children than those under 30 and children may encourage their parents to join and persist in a program. These findings suggest that older students persist longer because they benefit from the maturity that comes with age, and they no longer have the responsibilities of caring for small children.

The study also found that previous school experience (among U.S.-schooled students) does not appear to be associated with persistence. Of course, those potential students who are significantly affected by negative school experience may never enter a program or may have dropped out before the research team arrived. However, many of the study's participants did describe negative school experiences, with most of the comments centered on high school. Respondents reported being ridiculed and even struck by teachers, bullied or intimidated by other students, told that they were stupid, and asked by administrators to leave school. Issues of class, race, and sexual orientation contributed to the negative school experience for some. Entering an ABE program may signal that a student has overcome the influences of negative school experiences and is ready to restart his or her education.

Another finding is that prior nonschool learning experiences, particularly self-study focused on improving basic skills or studying for the GED, was related to persistence. Attempts at self-study may be an indication of strong motivation, or some people may need several attempts at learning before they are ready to persist.

Both the students who persisted and those who dropped out talked about the forces supporting and inhibiting persistence in the same way. Students mentioned four types of positive forces: *relationships, goals, teacher and fellow students,* and *self-determination. Relationships* are the support noted by participants from their families, friends, or colleagues; God or their church community; support groups; community workers; mentors or bosses; and their children. *Goals* included helping one's children, getting a better job, bettering one's self, moving ahead in life, attending college or some other academic institution, proving someone's assessment of the student's abilities wrong, or obtaining citizenship. *Teacher and fellow students* involves the support from the people in their classes, and their *self-determination* is the positive attitude needed to succeed.

Students mentioned three types of negative forces: *life demands, relationships,* and *poor self-determination. Life demands* included child-care needs; work demands; transportation difficulties; the student's own, or his or her family's, health issues; age; lack of time; fatigue; bad weather; rules set by welfare and other social programs; unfavorable conditions at home; moving; and lack of income. *Relationships* included family members, friends, colleagues, and community or welfare workers who did not support persistence, as well as fears about letting other people down by failing in a program. *Poor self-determination* included "thinking negative thoughts," "my own laziness," and statements indicating a lack of confidence in participants' own ability to succeed.

Students' mention of specific positive and negative forces did not predict persistence, but these findings are valuable because they give practitioners input from adult students on what might be important. Adults in this study mentioned many more positive forces than negative forces. All the students mentioned at least three positive forces but some did not mention any negative forces, even when they were encouraged to do so. Because negative school experience was not associated with persistence and students described many positive forces overcoming a limited number of negative forces, building positive supports may be more critical to increasing persistence than removing barriers. If this is so, then understanding which positive forces are most important is essential to a model that supports persistence.

The study team summarized the implications of its findings by identifying four supports to persistence:

- **The first support to persistence is to establish the student's goal.** The process of goal development begins before an adult enters a program. An adult who could be classified as a potential ABE student experiences an event in his or her life that motivates him or her to enter an educational program. That event might be something dramatic; for example, a well-paid worker might lose his or her job and find that he or she does not have the basic skills needed to qualify for a new job at a similar pay scale. That event might be less dramatic; for example, a parent may decide he or she needs more education when a first child begins school. That event might be subtle; for example, a school dropout might have always felt the desire to study for the GED but not until his or her children are older and need less attention is there finally some free time available for education. Whatever the event, it provides potential adult students with goals they hope to accomplish by entering an ABE program. The staff of the educational program should help the potential adult student articulate his or her goal and understand the many instructional objectives that must be accomplished on the road to meeting that goal. Teachers should then use those student goals as the basis for instruction. The effort to identify goals must be continual as instruction proceeds because goals may change over time.

- **The second support is to increase a sense of self-efficacy.** The self-determination mentioned by students must build on a foundation of self-efficacy, a feeling that they can reach their goals. The term self-confidence is quite often used in adult education literature, but self-efficacy has a different definition. *Self-confidence* is a global feeling of being able to accomplish most tasks. *Self-efficacy* is focused on a specific set of tasks and represents the feeling of being able to accomplish that set of tasks. Bandura (1986) suggested four ways to help build self-efficacy. Programs should introduce new students to adults just like them who have already been successful at learning, design their curriculum in such a way that it challenges students but does not overwhelm them, help students address their feelings of anxiety about failure or slow progress, and provide students with encouragement that they can be successful.

- **The third support is to help students manage the positive and negative forces that help and hinder persistence.** Students must build positive forces, such as people in their lives who support them to succeed, and address negative forces, such as changing work schedules that sometimes conflict with program participation, to persist in their learning. Programs should help students develop an understanding of the negative and positive forces, such as support or lack of it by family and friends, changing work schedules, and child care, that affect their persistence. Building on that understanding, each student could then make plans to manage these forces so that

persistence is more likely. The plans that come out of such an exercise should include strategies for persistence when the forces that affect peoples' lives cause them to drop out. These plans must be revised as adults persist in their studies and these forces change.
- **The fourth support is to ensure progress toward reaching a goal.** Assuming the goal is important, adult students must make progress toward reaching that goal, and they must be able to measure and recognize that progress. If a student's goal is to learn enough English to improve his or her income, the program should include content that meets that goal and measures student progress toward mastering that content. Programs should provide services of sufficient quality that students make progress, and programs need assessment procedures that allow students to measure their own progress.

Second Phase

During the second phase of the project, the research team observed 10 library literacy programs in California, New York, and North Carolina that were attempting to increase student persistence, and interviewed a total of 30 students in depth (and interviewed another 100 informally) about their history of participation, and supports and barriers to their persistence. The study found that most students reported facing barriers to persistence that were personal (related to the student) or environmental (related to the student's life situation). However, the adult education programs did not have the resources to address these personal and environmental barriers. These barriers included a lack of day care or transportation and personal problems that would require professional counseling. The expense and administrative demands of providing these services were beyond the resources of the programs. The programs sometimes overcame this lack of resources by providing referrals to social service agencies that provided the services students needed.

This study also identified five persistence pathways that are determined by these personal and environmental factors and ways that programs might support students on each pathway. Each pathway describes a pattern of persistence. These pathways are useful for planning ways to help students persist. The five pathways are *long-term, mandatory, short-term, try-out,* and *intermittent.*

Long-term students participate regularly over a long period. Long-term students usually do not express specific goals, but, rather, talk of education as an end in itself. Long-term students have managed the personal and environmental factors that support and inhibit their persistence. Presumably, they will persist in a program that is helping them meet their needs, is convenient for them, and provides an enjoyable experience. In fact, this is the story told to the study team by long-term students. Most long-term students view their program as a comfortable and supportive community and talk about it as a family, a club, or a home base for learning. They refer to the program staff as friends or family members. Long-term students express a strong personal commitment to their programs and to their goal of becoming more educated.

Most of the long-term students identified through interviews were over the age of 30. The long-term persistence of older students may appear to be supported by their emotional maturity, but, in fact, it may be supported by stable personal and environmental factors related to children, partners, and employment. Adults over the age of 30 may no longer have child-care responsibilities and may have a stable income, housing situation, and set of relationships, whereas younger students may not be as stable.

This study found that improving formal instruction (through training of teachers and volunteers, improving curriculum, and other program development inputs) and offering many different types of informal instruction appeared to increase hours of instruction for long-term students. For students on the long-term pathway, a multiplicity of ways to learn (e.g., a class, a tutor, and a computer program) might help increase intensity of instruction and allow these students to reach their goals faster.

Mandatory students must attend a program because they are required to do so by a public assistance or law-enforcement agency. Their participation is usually regular and long term, and their goals are often those of the agency that is mandating their attendance. They look like long-term students while they are under the requirement to participate, but usually leave abruptly once attendance is no longer mandatory and sometimes even when it is still a requirement.

Mandatory students overcome personal and environmental factors that constrain their persistence because they are required to do so. Because factors outside the program support their participation, programmatic improvements may not help these students to stay longer. However, if the program changes its services (making them more convenient, more useful, or more enjoyable), mandatory students might choose to participate for more hours or become long-term students. Counseling—during intake and orientation, and throughout instruction—that focuses on helping mandatory students commit to learning as a way to improve their lives, understand how they learn best, find ways to enjoy learning, and build a support system to sustain their learning might help mandatory students persist after the mandate has ended. Additional hours of participation and persistence after legal mandates for participation have ended are probably good measures of impact for innovations meant to address the needs of mandatory students.

During intake and orientation, programs must help students who are on the mandatory pathway move past the required goals of attendance and begin to see learning as something they choose to do. Building their motivation probably requires identifying goals that are personal and an instructional process that helps students see that they can learn and that learning can be enjoyable. Literacy learning focused on family, work, personal interests, or even the problems that led to their legal or social service status might be a focus of instruction that supports persistence for adults on this pathway. An instructional process that involves discussions among a group of adults might provide a social network that supports persistence for mandatory students, and referral to support services (e.g., counseling, day care, and employment) might be necessary for these students to persist, even while they are under a mandate.

Short-term students enroll in a program and participate intensively for a short period to accomplish a specific goal, such as passing the GED test or a job certification test. For some of these students, the short-term participation in a library literacy program meets their needs; for some, this participation leads to enrollment in another type of program. Although students on a short-term pathway may leave their programs after only a few weeks of instruction, some may persist in another program that more closely meets their needs. Because personal goals determine their length of participation, programmatic innovations may have little impact on the persistence of students on a short-term pathway. Transition into another program and accomplishment of a specific, limited goal are probably good measures of the impact of innovations meant to address the needs of short-term students.

For students who are on the short-term pathway, programs should be careful to identify their specific goal during intake and orientation. When transfer to another program is appropriate for reaching that goal, the program might be able to provide some learning opportunities that prepare these students to be successful in a more appropriate program. When new students have a specific short-term goal, programs should try to focus on it, possibly with an individual tutor, or make that goal the focus of their instruction in a more general learning environment.

Try-out students have barriers to persistence that are insurmountable and have goals that are not yet clear enough to sustain their motivation. These students end an episode of program participation quickly, with neither goal achievement nor transfer to another program. Students on the try-out pathway are motivated to learn, and their decision to join program services is a positive step. However, they are not ready to make a commitment to program participation.

Program staff members believe that every new student can succeed and are usually opposed to counseling students to defer participation. However, admitting students who are likely to fail, particularly because most of these students have failed in education previously, is probably not helpful to the student. Students on the try-out pathway who leave a program with a plan for how to address the personal and environmental barriers constraining their participation so that they can return some time in the future probably provide a good measure of impact for innovations meant to address their needs.

Helping try-out students make a decision to postpone program participation during intake could improve program persistence rates by both lowering the number of students who drop out after very little participation and by providing more program resources to students who are on a different pathway. To do this, programs would have to design intake processes that help students self-identify as on the try-out pathway, counsel them to delay entry, and help them design a plan that would lead to successful participation some time in the future.

Intermittent students move in and out of program services. During the time that they are not attending program services, intermittent students may stay in contact with their programs, and their episodes of participation and nonparticipation may reoccur several times and take place in more than one program. Programs do not always know that a student is on the intermittent pathway and assume he or she has dropped out. Belzer (1998) found that students identified as dropouts by adult education programs often see themselves as "stopouts" who are still connected to the program but temporarily unable to attend.

These students may have broad goals (e.g., improving language or basic skills ability) or specific goals (e.g., passing a citizenship test); whichever type, their goals require a long period of engagement to achieve. However, personal and environmental factors limit their ability to attend on a regular basis. Programs can probably have only limited impact on the limiting factors, but programs can adapt to them by helping students link episodes of program participation and self-study into a coherent learning experience. Programs that adapt to the needs of intermittent students would redefine participation as connection to the program, rather than hours of attendance in program services. This connection would have to be meaningful, not just a name in a database. An example of a meaningful connection could be monthly discussions between a program staff member and a student during which they review progress on a self-study plan. Programs would define as participation any form of learning activity that serves the goals of the program and the student. These activities would include classroom instruction or tutoring but might also include guided self-study at home or at the program venue. Length of continuous connection to the program and cumulative hours of engagement in learning might be good measures of impact for innovations meant to address the needs of intermittent students, regardless of whether they are formally participating in program activities.

The intermittent pathway may be the only one open to most students. Personal and environmental factors are always going to present barriers to long-term persistence, and most students have goals that require a good deal of study to achieve. Programs should accept this reality and look at ways to redesign their services to provide connected episodes of participation that use a multiplicity of learning resources. Program staff also need ways to help students maintain contact with the program and to continue to think of themselves as students.

These five pathways provide guidelines for the kinds of program changes that might be useful to different types of students. Practitioners know that a single approach to services will not help all students persist and learn, but programs generally do not have the resources to provide an individual approach for each student. However, programs could provide supports based on the understanding of these five pathways to help students achieve their goals.

IMPLICATIONS FOR PRACTICE, POLICY, AND RESEARCH

Although the relationship between persistence and learning gains has not been proven, evidence suggests that students could benefit from longer instruction. How do we accomplish that?

The literature reviewed already provides insights for changes in adult education practice that might lead to higher persistence rates and perhaps higher learning gains as well. However, these changes in practice will take place only if the policies that govern funding support them. The advice that comes out of the existing literature is untested, but rigorous research could test the efficacy of the recommendations and also lead to better suggestions. This section offers advice on what programs could do to improve persistence, suggests policies that would be supportive of changes based on that advice, and outlines research that could both test and improve these recommendations.

Implications for Practice

This literature suggests two approaches to improving program practice with the aim of increasing persistence. The first approach adds persistence supports to existing programs, whereas the second requires programs to change participation in ways that make it easier for adults to pursue episodes of program participation and self-study to achieve their learning goals. This section describes a set of persistence supports and changes in participation for three chronological phases of program participation: entrance into services, participation in program services, and reengagement in learning.

Entrance into services includes recruitment, intake, and orientation. This is the time when programs prepare students to be successful in learning. If identifying each student's pathway on entrance into a program proves difficult, program staff might assume that all students are intermittent. That is, that students are prepared to participate in an episode of learning that, if it is short, might lead to additional episodes of learning that continue until they reach their goal.

The first step in this phase would be to help students express clear goals that represent their motivation for participation. The second step would be to develop a learning plan that includes both instruction and the support services a student needs to persist in learning to reach those goals. For tryout students, this phase would lead to their postponement of participation, but they would leave the program with a plan for how to prepare to reenter services later. The program would identify this student as successful, because the program provided the student with the best possible outcome, even though he or she demonstrated no learning gains. For other students, intake and orientation would lead to a plan for participation in the program. That plan would assume that students would engage in episodes of participation that lead to accomplishment of a specific goal, transfer to another program, or departure from the program followed by another episode of participation. Of course, students on a long-term pathway may only have a single long episode of participation.

The plan would be a written document that sets out the goals each student is trying to reach, the skills and knowledge each student needs to learn to meet those goals, and the services each student needs to successfully complete that learning. These services would include instruction, self-study, and support services. The plan would also include a process that would allow the student to judge his or her own progress.

During this period, students would have a chance to meet other adults who are like them in most ways and have been successful in reaching their learning goals. Some of these successful students might be paid employees of the program who can help students build their self-efficacy. Program staff would make clear that an intermittent approach to participation is not only accepted but also the expected pattern of participation.

Participation in program services includes both instruction and support services. General improvements in instruction and expansion of support services probably help support learning and persistence, but most students need more than just good services. They need instruction that fits their pattern of participation and support services that help them address their particular persistence needs.

A multiplicity of instructional modes (e.g., classes, tutoring, peer learning groups, technology or distance education, and print and media materials) provides students with ways to participate that do not always demand adherence to a regular schedule. However, these alternative modes would be more effective if they fit into a plan that is followed by both the student and the tutor or teacher. Helping students and instructional staff follow a plan that uses several modes of instruction and that builds toward the attainment of specific goals is not easy. This chapter can only support this approach, not define it. The development of this approach requires collaboration between practitioners and program development experts.

The individual plan would allow a student who must stop instruction to continue learning (either at home or at the library) through self-study. When that student is ready to return to regular attendance, any tutor or teacher should be able to look at the student's progress on his or her plan and start instruction there. Program services should include regular counseling that helps students meet their own needs for support services and identify the times when they will not be able to meet the instructional schedule and so begin the self-study part of their plan.

During instruction, teachers and tutors can use student goals and their supports and barriers to persistence as the content of learning activities that build language, literacy, and math skills. Out of these activities may come student needs that cannot be met by the program, but students might be able to meet those needs on their own, or the program staff may be able to offer advice or referrals.

Reengagement in learning includes procedures for staying in contact with students who are not attending and encouraging them to return to services. Most students do not tell their program or tutor that they are stopping participation; they just stop attending. During interviews with students, many reported that they believe that once they stop attending they cannot return (Porter et al., 2005). Program staff must help students build an understanding that reengagement is acceptable and encouraged. Former or even current students might be the best people to play this role as they may have addressed the same personal and environmental factors as the students who have dropped out. These new procedures require resources that are now being used to support instruction. However, if these procedures were successful, students who now drop out permanently would make learning gains after they return to continue learning.

Implications for Policy

The literature suggests a number of supports that might lead to increased persistence rates, but programs that add supports to persistence would be more expensive than those that do not, and additional resources are not easy to find. Policymakers must identify persistence supports as an essential part of program design and provide the necessary resources. The first step in policy implementation, therefore, would require programs to limit enrollment as a way to increase per-student spending. Once persistence and achievement rates increase, programs would have to argue for additional funds to expand services.

If funding for supports to persistence is available, policymakers could use persistence rates as a measure of program quality and a surrogate measure of learning gains for students who leave before sitting for a test of progress. However, if funding guidelines do not differentiate among groups of students, programs will find ways to discourage participation of adults who face barriers to persistence or learning gains to meet accountability standards. Policymakers might look at the list of persistence pathways and develop program approaches and accountability criteria that are different for each group. Then programs can meet their accountability goals while serving a full range of students.

The literature reviewed in this chapter suggests that supports to persistence within the existing program structure, which requires attendance at a specific time and place, may have value but may have an upper limit on impact. A profitable approach to increasing persistence might be to add some supports to programs and then to help programs develop ways to assist students in continuing their learning when they cannot attend services and then return to the program as soon as possible. These self-study options might involve technology that employs computers and the Internet, or might take a traditional approach that employs written materials. Policymakers could support program experimentation with new ways to deliver services by providing funding and allowing programs to count hours of self-study in their accountability reports.

Implications for Further Research

No research has yet tested with experimental or quasi-experimental methods whether practice and policy recommendations would indeed have an impact on persistence and help more students reach their learning goals. Although further study into the nature of persistence and the forces that support and inhibit it would add valuable knowledge, now may be the time to test program models that incorporate the existing research. If these models prove to be sound, practitioners and policymakers could feel assured in making changes based on them, and further research could begin to build on this foundation.

Three models could be tested. One would add persistence supports that would help students continue to attend existing programs. A second model would redesign services to more closely fit the lives and needs of students that attend intermittently. A third model would combine both.

More research is always valuable, but now is probably the time to accept that, for adults, support to persistence and self-study are essential components of any instructional approach. The existing research provides some good advice on how to design these components. Researchers should now put this advice into an intervention that could be tested. If the intervention proves effective, researchers, practitioners, and adult students could work together to develop improvements on that intervention and test those improvements. This approach would allow the field to move forward quickly, at the same time putting in place a process that would lead to continuous improvement.

REFERENCES

Bandura, A. (1986). *Social foundations of thought and action: A social cognitive theory.* Englewood Cliffs, NJ: Prentice-Hall.
Beder, H. (1991). *Adult literacy: Issues for policy and practice.* Malabar, FL: Krieger.
Belzer, A. (1998). Stopping out, not dropping out. *Focus on Basics, 2*(A), 15–17.
Comings, J., Parrella, A., & Soricone, L. (1999). *Persistence among adult basic education students in pre-GED classes* (NCSALL Rep. No. 12). Cambridge, MA: NCSALL.
Comings, J., Sum, A., & Uvin, J. (2000). *New skills for a new economy: Adult education's key role in sustaining economic growth and expanding opportunity.* Boston: Massachusetts Institute for a New Commonwealth.
Cuban, S. (2003). "So lucky to be like that, somebody care": Two case studies of women learners and their persistence in a Hawai'i literacy program. *Adult Basic Education, 13*(1), 19–43.
Darkenwald, G. (1986). *Adult literacy education: A review of the research and priorities for future inquiry.* New York: Literacy Assistance Center.
Development Associates. (1993). *National evaluation of adult education programs: Profiles of client characteristics.* Arlington, VA: Author.
Fitzgerald, N., & Young, M. (1997). The influence of persistence on literacy education in adult education. *Adult Education Quarterly, 47*(2), 78–92.
Flannery, D. (Ed.). (1993). *Applying cognitive learning theory to adult learning.* San Francisco: Jossey-Bass.
Gilbert, D., Fisk, S., & Lindzey, G. (1998). *Handbook of social psychology* (Vol. I, 4th ed.). Oxford, UK: Oxford University Press.
Lewin, K. (1999). *The complete social scientist: A Kurt Lewin reader* (M. Gold, Ed.). Washington, DC: American Psychological Association.
Meder, P. (2000). The effect of continuous goal setting on persistence in math classrooms. *Focus on Basics, 4*(A), 7–10.
Porter, K., Cuban, S., & Comings, J. (2005). *One day I will make it.* New York: MDRC.
Quigley, B. (1997). *Rethinking literacy education: The critical need for practice-based change.* San Francisco: Jossey-Bass.
Quigley, B. (2000). Retaining adult learners in the first three critical weeks: A quasi-experimental model for use in ABE programs. *Adult Basic Education, 10*(2), 55–69.
Reder, S. (2000). Adult literacy and postsecondary education students: Overlapping populations and learning trajectories. In J. Comings, B. Garner, & C. Smith (Eds.), *The annual review of adult learning and literacy* (Vol. 1). San Francisco: Jossey-Bass.
Rose, S., & Wright, M. (2006). *Using state administrative records for analyses of student attendance, student achievement, and economic outcomes: A three-state study.* Washington, DC: U.S. Department of Education.
Sticht, T. (1982). *Evaluation of the reading potential concept for marginally illiterate adults.* Alexandria, VA: Human Resources Research Organization.
Tracy-Mumford, F. (1994). *Student retention: Creating student success.* Washington, DC: NAEPDC.
U.S. Department of Education. (2003). *Report to Congress on state performance.* Washington, DC: Author.
Wikelund, K., Reder, S., & Hart-Landsberg, S. (1992). *Expanding theories of adult literacy participation: A literature review.* Philadelphia: University of Pennsylvania, National Center on Adult Literacy.
Witkin, H. A. (1971). *The Embedded Figures Test.* Palo Alto, CA: Consulting Psychologists Press.

Witkin, H. A., Oltman, P. K., Raskin, E., & Karp, S. A. (1971). *A manual for the Embedded Figures Tests.* Palo Alto, CA: Consulting Psychologists Press.

Young, M., Fleischman, H., Fitzgerald, N., & Morgan, M. (1994). *National evaluation of adult education programs: Patterns and predictors of client attendance.* Arlington, VA: Development Associates.

3

Achieving Adult Education Program Quality: A Review of Systematic Approaches to Program Improvement

Mary Ziegler and Mary Beth Bingman

The success of efforts to improve the quality of programs that provide adult education has a direct impact on adult students' abilities to meet their educational goals. Since 1991, policymakers in the United States have taken two approaches to improving program quality: focusing on the elements of a quality program that lead to anticipated student outcomes or focusing on student outcomes as the measure of a program's quality.

Taking the first approach, the National Literacy Act of 1991 mandated the development of program quality indicators (PQI); the majority of which focused on program processes as a way to evaluate the effectiveness of adult education programs. PQI defined the processes that should be in place at the program level. For example, Indicator 7 states, "Program successfully recruits the population in the community identified in the Adult Education Act as needing literacy services" (Office of Vocational and Adult Education, 1992, p. 14). PQI did not provide a systematic and consistent way to either measure the process or the result of the indicators at the state or national level, making it impossible to track improvement across states. The Workforce Investment Act of 1998, on the other hand, mandated a systematic way of measuring results through a comprehensive performance accountability system. The National Reporting System (NRS) requires states to set performance levels and collect information on particular student outcomes, but does not suggest a specific approach to improve the quality of educational services that lead to these outcomes. These two approaches are not mutually exclusive, and most states and adult education programs apply elements of both without necessarily establishing a link between the two.

For either approach to be successful in improving program quality, positive change must occur at the program level. To bring about change, states and programs, including teachers and students, must engage in a process of examination of their data—about student outcomes, program processes, or both—and then identify and implement plans for change based on these data. This change process may happen haphazardly when individual teachers or directors make changes as they see fit. For example, a teacher might notice that a particular instructional approach does not seem to be working and therefore abandon it, or a program director might experiment with giving fast-food coupons in an effort to improve attendance. At the other end of a continuum, program improvement may be carried out systematically in an effort that includes (a) explicit statement of goals, (b) systematic data collection that shows whether these goals are being achieved, (c) identification and implementation of changes needed to better meet goals (including professional development and other necessary supports for change), and (d) evaluation of results of the changes. Although program improvement occurs at the local program level, state adult education agencies often guide these systematic efforts when multiple programs are involved. In this chapter, we examine efforts of adult education agencies to work with local programs statewide to systematically improve program quality.

The emphasis on program quality and accountability mandated by the 1991 and 1998 legislation for adult education programs is part of a larger focus on quality and accountability in the private sector and government. In this chapter, we begin by situating adult education programs in this larger arena and reviewing the national efforts to improve program quality in adult education. We then review approaches that states are taking to systematically improve program quality and performance and examine more closely case studies of three states. Finally, we draw conclusions from state approaches and consider implications for practice, policy, and research.

QUALITY AND ACCOUNTABILITY EFFORTS

Interest in adult education program improvement parallels the private-sector quality movement. Quality emerged as a foundational concept in the 1980s when the superiority of Japan's products threatened U.S. markets. Since then, *quality* has become the "term generally used to encompass the multiple outcomes, effects, and processes that organizations must pursue in order to achieve success" (Winn & Cameron, 1998, p. 492). W. Edwards Deming contributed perspectives that increased the scope of quality from a focus on manufacturing processes to the present-day focus on the management of an organization as a complex system (Walton, 1986). Quality management emphasizes continuous improvement through organization-wide participation, customer satisfaction, management based on fact (or measurement), continuous improvement, and learning.

Private Sector

Quality as an overall management strategy proliferated in the United States as manufacturers addressed increasing competition from Japan and the need to produce higher quality products more efficiently. Improving the quality of U.S. products drew national attention in 1987 with the passage of the Malcolm Baldrige National Quality Improvement Act and the establishment of a national quality award for companies in the private sector. The Act, administered by the U.S. Department of Commerce, mandated the development of a common framework on which to base judgments about quality processes and outcomes. According to Winn and Cameron (1998), the framework, referred to as the Baldrige Framework for Excellence, integrated the majority of philosophies and techniques espoused by quality theorists in North America and Asia. They point out that quality, in the scholarly literature on organizations, is the term used most often to encompass the multiple outcomes, effects, and processes that organizations pursue to achieve their goals. With the inception of the Baldrige Award program in the private sector, quality concepts had gained momentum in government.

Government

In government, rising costs, decreased quality of services, and entrenched bureaucracies created fertile ground for the need to adopt quality concepts. Building on the work of Deming, Osborne and Gaebler (1992) presented what they termed "a new paradigm" for reinventing government. They argued that U.S. bureaucracy, appropriate in the industrial era, was no longer effective for the postindustrial information age. By focusing on compliance with regulations, government had lost sight of the results, which made management of public monies difficult. The authors proposed that government must become entrepreneurial to meet citizen demands to increase quality, lower costs, and improve efficiency. Osborne and Gaebler's book appeared at the same time the Clinton administration began the *National Performance Review* (1993) (later named *National Partnership for Reinventing Government*) spearheaded by Vice President Albert Gore. The Clinton administration initiative convened an interagency task force of federal employees to focus on ways to make the government "work better and cost less" (Peckenpaugh, 2001).

The following year, Congress passed the Government Performance and Results Act of 1993 (GPRA) to reduce waste and inefficiency in federal programs. Quality concepts are embedded in the legislation's language; for example, Section 2, "Findings and Purposes," lists the following three purposes (we have added explanatory comments in brackets):

- Promote a new focus on results, service quality, and customer satisfaction [this gave rise to the use of the word *customer* instead of *client* in many social-service agencies].
- Help federal managers improve service delivery by . . . providing them with information about program results and service quality [this describes the feedback loop proposed by Deming].
- Improve Congressional decision making by providing more objective information [an example of management by fact or measurement].

The GPRA legislation also called for strategic planning, performance targets, and measurement of performance over time. "Management by fact" introduced objectivity into decision making and led to a plethora of measurement initiatives to help agencies define which results should be measured and develop ways to measure them (GPRA, 1993). The language of quality—particularly the focus on meeting the needs of the customer, use of data and measurement for decision making, and continuous improvement—then spilled into education at all levels.

Education

Over the last decade, educational agencies have faced increasing criticism for the failure of U.S. schools. The purpose of the Goals 2000: Educate America Act, which became law in 1994, was to "improve the quality of education for all students by improving student learning through a long-term, broad-based effort to promote coherent and coordinated improvements in the system of education throughout the Nation at the State and local levels" (Goals 2000: Educate America Act, 1994). Arif and Smiley (2003) examined the history of accountability in education and the steps that ultimately led to the demand to improve quality. They reviewed a series of federal reports from the early 1980s that were sharply critical of education, beginning with the maelstrom generated by *A Nation at Risk: The Imperative for Educational Reform* (National Commission on Excellence in Education, 1983), which proclaimed that falling educational achievement was endangering the strength of the United States in commerce, technology, and science. Other reports, such as *Academic Preparation for College: What Students Need to Know and Be Able to Do* (The College Board, 1983) and *America's Competitive Challenge: The Need for a National Response* (American Council on Education, Business-Higher Education Forum, 1983) emphasized the need for improving the quality of education. Arif and Smiley (2003) traced the link between public policy, the application of total quality management in education beginning in the 1980s, and its expansion over the years into the Baldrige Award. In 1998, President Clinton signed legislation allowing the educational sector to apply for the Baldrige Award, previously available only for business and industry.

The literature from the past 20 years is replete with anecdotal evidence describing the implementation of quality initiatives at individual K–12 schools (Bonstingl, 1992; Borsum & Francke, 1998; Wiedmer & Harris, 1997) or in higher education sites (Boyle & Bowden, 1997; Messner & Ruhl, 1998; Satterlee, 1996). Many academic programs refer to *continuous quality improvement* (CQI) in reference to their application of quality concepts. Depending on the individual site, the emphasis might vary from a focus on performance accountability to a focus on system improvements. According to Winn and Cameron (1998), "The most notable characteristic of the scholarly literature on quality is the dearth of empirical investigations" (p. 492). This lack of research has not diminished the interest in or demand for quality education. The focus on quality in industry, K–12 education, and higher education preceded the growth of quality and accountability in adult education.

LEGISLATION TO IMPROVE QUALITY IN ADULT EDUCATION

As in business, government agencies, and K–12 and higher formal education, legislation for adult education sought new ways to assure ever-increasing productivity. In the past 15 years, the field has shifted its focus from serving adults to counting the outcomes adults achieved.

National Literacy Act of 1991

As noted in the introduction, the National Literacy Act of 1991 emphasized quality as a value for adult education programs to "ensure that educational services supported with federal funds are quality services" (Office of Vocational and Adult Education [OVAE], 1992, p. 4). To ensure quality services, the National Literacy Act authorized the development and implementation of PQI for use in evaluating whether programs funded under the Act were effective in recruiting, retaining, and improving literacy skills of individuals they served. The OVAE, in a participatory process (with subject-matter experts and practitioners in the field), developed eight PQI and measures as models for states to use as a guide in developing state-specific quality indicators.

The resulting guide, *Model Indicators of Program Quality for Adult Education Programs* (OVAE, 1992), placed more emphasis on the quality of program process and content than on outcomes. Six indicators addressed program components, such as program planning, curriculum and instruction, staff development, support services, recruitment, and retention. Only two indicators addressed student outcomes: progress in attaining basic skills and advancement and completion of educational credential.

Although the OVAE guide outlined each quality indicator, measures for both process and outcome indicators were state-specific. For example, the first PQI (an outcome indicator) was, "Learners demonstrate progress toward attainment of basic skills and competencies that support their educational needs." The guide only suggested ways to measure this indicator, such as standardized test score gains, teacher reports of gains, or portfolio assessments. Individual states created measures they deemed relevant for their programs. Because one state might have used a standardized test to measure progress and another might have used portfolio assessment, it was difficult to make comparisons at the state or system level. Although the process of developing and using PQI led to numerous positive benefits for program improvement at the state and local level, the process failed to provide the basis for evaluating adult education because it was voluntary and focused on improving program processes without an accompanying framework for performance accountability.

WIA, NRS, and Related Mandates (1998)

The Workforce Investment Act of 1998 (WIA) replaced the National Literacy Act of 1991 and changed the emphasis to performance accountability, rather than program processes. Section 212 of the WIA established a performance accountability system to assess the effectiveness of adult education programs in achieving continuous improvement of adult basic skills and family literacy to optimize the return on the investment of federal funds. Core indicators of academic performance included (a) measurable improvements in basic skill levels in reading, writing, speaking the English language, and basic math; (b) receipt of a secondary school credential; (c) placement in postsecondary education; and (d) employment. As part of their education plans, states established levels of performance for each core indicator.

To fulfill the requirements of the WIA, OVAE—as the administrator of the adult education portion of the Act—established the NRS for Adult Education. The NRS defined six functional literacy levels, performance targets, and reporting procedures for individual states. In addition to the four indicators of performance already described, states could set optional measures, such as community or family measures, to evaluate the performance of local programs (U.S. Department of Education, 2001). The NRS focused on outcomes rather than on program processes, and only addressed program quality indirectly. Although continuous improvement is an expectation of the WIA legislation, a systematic approach to achieve it is not one of the Act's mandates. The NRS provides training materials for using NRS data for continuous improvement (Condelli, Seufert, & Coleman, 2004) but does not recommended a particular approach. These decisions have been left to the states and the efforts of other national initiatives.

NATIONAL EFFORTS TO IMPROVE PROGRAM QUALITY IN ADULT EDUCATION

Various national adult education organizations, such as the Association for Community-Based Education (ACBE) and the National Institute for Literacy (NIFL), made efforts to develop approaches that would support states in the implementation of quality processes. Some of these efforts continue today and we examine these more closely in the state case studies. Others are important as precursors of current efforts.

Association for Community-Based Education Framework for Assessing Program Quality

The ACBE developed a program quality framework in response to the 1991 legislation's requirements that states provide direct and equitable access to federal adult education funds for nonprofits based on their past effectiveness in providing services. The purpose of the framework was to assist nonprofit providers of adult basic education (ABE) to define and measure program quality (Stein, 1993). There were three sections to the framework:

1. What the Program Does to Support Planning, Evaluation, and Change.
2. Demonstrated Improvements in Learner Achievements, Program Quality and Community Development.
3. Process and Structures for Program and Learner Development. (p. 10)

For each section, the framework suggested indicators and measures.

The introduction of the ACBE Framework made explicit the influence of total quality management on adult education program management, and identified three Baldrige Award values as its "philosophic underpinning" (Stein, 1993 p. 7) with an emphasis on customer satisfaction, continuous improvement, and full participation. Rather than focusing on outcomes, the framework emphasized systematic data collection about performance and change.

Members of the ACBE used the framework for program improvement. A former program director who had been active in ACBE said that it was very useful for some programs because it was comprehensive; however, smaller programs that had scarce resources did not have the capacity to implement it (P. McGuire, personal communication, October 14, 2004).

National Institute for Literacy—Performance Measurement Reporting and Improvement System

In 1995, the NIFL developed the Performance Measurement Reporting and Improvement System (PMRIS), a framework to establish statewide accountability systems for adult literacy that would lead to a national accountability system. The purpose of PMRIS was to move adult literacy forward from a "patchwork quilt of services" to a "quality system" (Condelli & Kutner, 1997) by focusing on results from a systemic perspective. "An effective statewide accountability system must be customer-focused, results-oriented, and quality-driven" (Swadley & Ziolkowski, 1996, p. 12). PMRIS advocated the establishment of an interagency accountability system for adult literacy programs that had four key goals. The first was to form interagency groups that would focus on the national adult literacy goal outlined in the Goals 2000: Educate America Act (1994) that by the year 2000, every adult American would be literate and possess the knowledge and skills necessary to compete in a global economy and exercise the rights and responsibilities of citizenship. Second, states would measure progress in achieving the goal by measuring results, not process. Third, states that participated in PMRIS would establish an interagency working group to plan and implement an information management system that would provide a consistent reporting framework for local programs and enable state agencies to streamline reporting, share information, and eliminate duplicate record keeping. The final goal was to ensure continuous improvement because participating agencies would have data from the system that would enable them to identify strengths and weaknesses at the program level.

The NIFL awarded five states—Alabama, Hawaii, Kentucky, New York, and Tennessee—grants to establish interagency accountability systems for adult literacy in their states. Participating agencies were different in each state but generally included representation from state employment agencies, human services, and state libraries that had a stake in increasing adult literacy. A key contribution of PMRIS was viewing adult literacy from a "system" perspective. This perspective shifted from defining success as "inputs," such as increasing the number of individuals enrolled in a program, to defining success as "outputs," such as the number of individuals who increased their literacy skills, and ultimately to "outcomes," which it described as the goals adults achieved as a result of increasing their skills, such as enrollment in postsecondary education or advancement to a better job. The PMRIS change to a systemic view of adult literacy shifted the responsibility for :

achieving outcomes from individual programs to a shared responsibility of the system as a whole. For example, by taking an interagency perspective, adults would receive not only educational services, but support and transitional services if these were needed. Outcomes achieved by students translated to a program's performance, implied by the name of the system itself. In the 2-year time period of the grant, states achieved mixed results. Although an evaluation of PMRIS showed that states were not able to complete a functional, interagency statewide performance measurement system before their grants ended, states made progress in developing a more collaborative and strategic approach to adult literacy and recognizing the link between data requirements and outcomes (Swadley & Ziolkowski, 1996). Condelli and Kutner (1997) recommended that the lessons learned by the states during the PMRIS project be considered during the development of a national outcome reporting system.

Professional Development Network Competencies

In 2000, the U.S. Department of Education, Division of Adult Education and Literacy, sponsored the Professional Development Network (Pro-Net). Pro-Net developed three sets of competencies for instructors, program managers, and professional development specialists in adult education. The purpose of developing the competencies was to improve program quality by identifying the skills and knowledge that individuals would need to be effective in their roles (Sherman, Tibbetts, Dobbins, & Weidler, 2001). Each competency had a set of corresponding performance indicators that illustrated how the competency could be demonstrated. For example, a leadership competency for managers stated, "demonstrates effective interpersonal and communication skills." One of the four indicators was "seeks input from all levels of staff, listens attentively, demonstrates fairness and consistency, and conveys information fully and clearly." Pro-Net suggested various ways that states could use the competencies, such as developing credentialing systems for managers or for evaluation of local programs (Sherman et al., 2001). Materials, such as a self-assessment instrument, were provided to help practitioners and state staff use the competencies (see Pro-Net at http://www.pro-net2000.org/). Local programs could use the competencies for professional development. Pro-Net competencies, although informative about effective practice, focus on discrete skills and do not tie these skills back to a systematic program improvement effort that includes the state, program, staff, learner goals, or expected outcomes.

3. ACHIEVING ADULT EDUCATION PROGRAM QUALITY   57

These national efforts to provide frameworks for improving accountability and program quality—ACBE framework, the PMRIS focus on performance measures, and the Pro-Net competencies—increased the information that was available to state administrators and local programs, but none of these efforts was implemented nationally. In the next section, we examine models that are currently being used in our case studies of the states where they are being applied.

STATE EFFORTS TO IMPROVE PROGRAM QUALITY

Under the WIA, the states make decisions about what particular program improvement approach to use. For this chapter, we wanted to identify the states that had systematic approaches to improving program quality and the model, if any, they used. The following section describes the methods we used to identify state approaches.

Review of Web Sites

We began to identify states that had systematic approaches for improving program quality by reviewing the Web sites (in spring 2003) of publicly funded state ABE programs. Most states mentioned quality and program improvement in their state plans and related it to the language in the NRS. Only a limited number of states described a specific program improvement process on their Web sites. These included the Equipped for the Future (EFF) initiative in Delaware, Hawaii, Maine, Virginia, and Washington; Pennsylvania's Project Educational Quality in Adult Literacy (Project EQuAL); Tennessee Quality Award using Baldrige Criteria for Performance Excellence; and the Horizon Project in Maine. We were not able to determine if the information on the state Web sites was current, or if all of the states that had systematic program improvement processes in place described them on state-related Web sites.

Survey of State Directors

To augment the information we found on the Web sites, we conducted a brief survey of state ABE directors (see Appendix). In September 2004, the National Adult Education Professional Development Consortium (NAEPDC) distributed the survey and a letter of explanation in its monthly

TABLE 3.1
National Adult Education Professional Development Consortium
(NAEPDC) Electronic Survey Responses

State	Statewide Initiative?	Include Use of NRS Data?	Based on a National Model?	If So, Which One?	What % of Programs?	When It Began?
A	Yes	Yes	No	—	100%	2004
B	Yes	Yes	Yes	AIDDE	100%	2000
C	Yes	Yes	Yes	NAEPDC Going to Scale	—	2004
D	Yes	Yes	No	—	100%	1996
E	Yes	Yes	No	—	100%	2000
F	Yes	Yes	Yes	Baldrige	20 per year	2001
G	Yes	Yes	Yes	EFF, NAEPDC Going to Scale	13%	1986
H	Yes	Yes	No	—	100%	2004
I	No	Yes	Yes	—	—	—
J	No	Yes	Yes	—	—	—
K	No	—	—	—	—	—
L	Yes	Yes	No	—	5%	2004
M	No	—	—	—	—	—
N	Yes	Yes	Yes	Baldrige	100%	2003
O	Yes	Yes	Yes	AIDDE	100%	2002
P	Yes	Yes	Yes	Baldrige	100%	1998
Q	Yes	Yes	No	—	100%	2004
R	No	Yes	Yes	—	—	—
S	Yes	Yes	Yes	EFF	100%	2003
T	Yes	Yes	No	Some Baldrige	100%	2002
U	Yes	Yes	No	—	100%	1998
V	Yes	Yes	No	—	100%	2004

Note. AIDDE = Analyze Program Practices and Data, Identify Possible Practices and Procedures, Design an Implementation Plan, Document Practice or Procedure, Evaluate Implementation; Baldrige = Baldrige Education Criteria for Performance Excellence, part of the Malcolm Baldrige National Quality Award Program; EFF = Equipped for the Future; NAEPDC = National Adult Education Professional Development Consortium.

newsletter to state directors of adult education; 14 states responded. As a reminder, we sent the survey in an e-mail message to state directors and received 10 additional responses, for a total response of 22 states (see Table 3.1 for results).

Approximately 14 states had statewide initiatives that involved close to 100% of the programs. Nine of these were based on one of four national models: Analyze, Identify, Design, Document, and Evaluate (AIDDE); Baldrige; EFF; and NAEPDC's Going to Scale. Only four began the initiative before 2000. We used the results of this survey to guide our selection of states to use for case studies of program improvement. The following criteria were used to select states for case studies:

- Type of systematic approach being used—we wanted to represent a variety of approaches.
- Extent to which local programs are involved in the approach—we wanted approaches that were in use across the state, not in just a few programs.
- Duration of the approach—we wanted approaches that have been in use long enough for states to have some sense about their success.
- Geographic region of the state—we hoped to examine cases across the country.
- State director's willingness to have a case study written about his or her state.

Based on the results of the survey and on these criteria, we developed case studies about program improvement efforts in Oregon, Tennessee, and Vermont.

CASE STUDIES OF PROGRAM IMPROVEMENT EFFORTS

The state agencies that agreed to participate in the case study differ in their department affiliation. Adult education in Oregon is affiliated with the Oregon Community College system. In Tennessee, adult education is part of the Department of Labor and Workforce Development. Vermont's adult education program is part of the Department of Education.

Data for the case studies were collected through telephone interviews with either the state director, or an individual assigned by the state director who had worked directly with the program improvement model. One of the authors conducted an initial interview with either the state director or individuals recommended by the state director and then wrote notes from the interviews and e-mailed the notes back to the respondents. To clarify the notes, we conducted additional interviews or exchanged e-mail messages until the respondent or respondents agreed that the data described the way the state applied the model.

The models of program quality improvement used by the states vary, but their overall purpose is to improve program quality, including processes and results. However, states define processes and results differently. The following section describes the model used in each state, the state's story (including how the initiative began), related professional development activities, results achieved, and lessons learned.

Oregon and the AIDDE Model

In Oregon, ABE is part of the Oregon Community College system. Instructors are referred to as faculty, and program managers are referred to as program directors. Oregon began its statewide program improvement strategy in 2001 when it volunteered to be part of the Northwest Quality Initiative (NQI). The NQI is a research and demonstration project to create, pilot test, and refine a process for developing leadership and carrying out program improvement in adult education at the state and local levels (Alamprese, 2003). Abt Associates, Inc., a large for-profit government and research consulting firm, established the NQI with funding from the U.S. Department of Education. The model used was AIDDE, which stands for the initial letter in the steps of the improvement process: analyze, identify, develop, document, and evaluate.

Two underlying assumptions guided the project: (a) continuous program improvement is an integral component of adult education program operations, and (b) a systemic approach to program improvement involves state adult education staff, local program directors, and program instructors and other staff.

To develop the model, Abt Associates reviewed the research on program improvement, program reviews from a variety of settings, and PQI. In addition to these reviews, researchers conducted case studies in six northwestern U.S. states to identify common components of adult education. From a systems perspective, each of the components influences the other components. The 12 identified components of the system are:

- Community environment.
- Institutional capacity.
- Program management.
- Program improvement.
- Interagency collaboration.
- Program recruitment and intake.
- Assessment and instruction.
- Program exposure.
- Support services.

- Learner transition.
- Learner personal development.
- Learner outcomes.

Each system component has accompanying illustrative criteria for program quality. For example, one component of the system is program recruitment and intake. Criteria for determining quality for student intake include using multiple instruments for assessment (one being a standardized assessment) and the use of a formal referral process to other services or programs. Another component is program management. A criterion for quality of this component is communication between the program director and the staff showing that the director communicates with staff regularly, meets with staff on substantive issues, and obtains feedback.

The Program Improvement Process: Analyze, Identify, Develop, Document, and Evaluate

The AIDDE model is a series of action steps for improving any aspect of the 12 components of the adult education system at the classroom, program, or state level. The model has its roots in problem-based learning (analyzing issues and identifying solutions) and the scientific method (collecting, analyzing, and interpreting data). The AIDDE model is based on the premise that all levels of the adult basic skills (ABS) system must participate in change initiatives to see sustainable program improvement.

The AIDDE pilot was conducted in six states (Alaska, Idaho, Montana, Oregon, Washington, and Wyoming) beginning in 2001. Partners in the pilot were the six state offices and local programs in each state. State office staff provided leadership, support, technical assistance, reporting, and feedback to local program directors. Local program directors implemented the improvement process, planning and resource identification, data collection, and support and feedback for staff. Instructors and other staff participated in planning and identifying instructional resources, data collection, and dissemination within and beyond programs.

In addition to developing the model, Abt Associates provided professional development for applying the model to practice in three phases. In the first phase, local program directors and instructors identified "instruction" and "intake" for improvement. Following this was training for program directors to learn to use the AIDDE model to analyze and improve program management and program operations. The final phase involved state staff in three states that wanted to use the model for statewide program improvement.

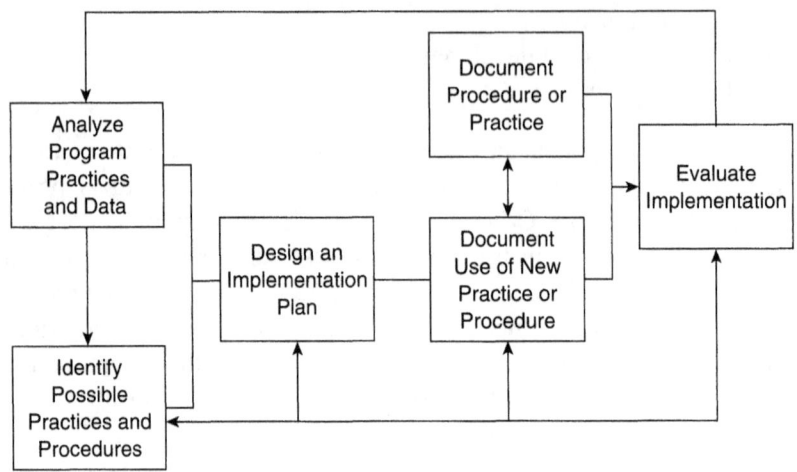

FIG. 3.1. The AIDDE program improvement process.

The AIDDE model has five main steps. Each initial letter of the acronym AIDDE describes an action—analyze, identify, develop, document, and evaluate—that is a step in the systemic change process, as outlined in Fig. 3.1.

Each of the arrows in Fig. 3.1 demonstrates how the individual components work together as a system. Evaluation influences each step of the process. Because the model is applicable at all levels of the system, individuals or groups might carry out the steps for improving instruction, programs, or the state system. In Oregon, for example, program directors focused on student orientation and intake. Once they identified the area for improvement, they followed the steps of the AIDDE process:

- *Analyze* data, current practices, and research to identify areas of instruction, program operations, or state operations requiring change; set priorities for improvement. This step includes identifying current activities in each program operation component, including relevant data, issues, or pressures that staff must address. Staff (instructors, program administrators, state staff, teachers, or all groups working together) prioritize expected outcomes that may lead to improvement.
- *Identify* new practices or procedures for improving current practice. In this step, staff develop new practices using resources, strategies, and techniques from multiple sources, including research.
- *Design* a plan for new practices or procedures and implement the plan by using the new practice or procedure. The planning process

includes outlining the new practice or procedure, identifying the target population for the new procedure, and pilot testing.
- *Document* in two phases. First, describe current practices. Second, document new practices and procedures. These steps include making records of personnel, materials, and resources that currently exist and what resources are needed. After the procedure or practice has been implemented, staff identify its potentially successful aspects and barriers encountered.
- *Evaluate* outcomes from program or instructional improvement. The final step is for staff to evaluate the practices or procedures they used, what worked, what did not work, and the reasons for success or failure. Evaluation includes determining if the outcomes of the practice or procedure lead to program improvement.

Using the model effectively in any of the components of an ABE program requires professional development to learn how to apply the model in practice.

Specific Objectives in Oregon

Oregon has used the AIDDE process over 4 years with two primary goals: program improvement and leadership development. The first, program improvement, includes continuous improvement at the instructional, program, and state levels. The second goal, leadership development, focuses on instructional and program leadership. According to the state director, "We identified this as a strategic planning process the state could use to target system improvement, build a common language for the system, and develop existing and emerging leadership." This was the first time AIDDE was systematically implemented at all levels in Oregon.

Program Improvement. There were four key program improvement activities over the course of 3 years, initiatives that focused on improving (a) instructional practices, (b) program operations, (c) program management, and (d) state system alignment. Oregon's participants in the NQI during the first 2 years included six instructors and program directors from three local programs and a state representative. They focused on identifying and piloting new instructional practices. Instructors identified a key question or problem they wanted to address in their individual classes and followed the AIDDE process to: (a) analyze data, including their current practices and their assumptions about these practices;

(b) identify and plan new practices; (c) document the use of the new practices; and (d) evaluate their activities for effectiveness. During Year 1, each instructor developed one question. In Year 2, all instructors focused on the same topic, factors that affect student success in transitioning to college. By working on the same topic across three programs, instructors had greater opportunities to collaborate and learn from one another. Programs were also able to see that many of the factors were common to all instructional programs. According to the state director, "Our instructors who took part in the project found it beneficial as a way of helping them become more deliberate about how they target instructional content, activities, and evaluate instruction."

During the NQI's second year, Abt Associates conducted a pilot training for two to three program directors from each state to apply the AIDDE process to improve the program operations of their ABE programs. Oregon's second program improvement activity was for two of Oregon's program directors to participate in this training and pilot process. Meanwhile, instructors from three of Oregon's programs continued their AIDDE improvement activities (described previously).

A third key improvement activity based on the AIDDE model in Oregon has been the focus on program management. This initiative trained local program directors who make up the Oregon Council of Adult Basic Skills Development (OCABSD), an association of Oregon program administrators, to use the AIDDE process as a program management and operations improvement tool. State staff asked for volunteers from the OCABSD to attend the third phase of the AIDDE training on how to use the continuous improvement model in program management; every director of the OCABSD volunteered. Directors received an initial training and two follow-up training sessions over 2 years. During this time, directors implemented the AIDDE model focusing on one or two areas for improvement. The majority of directors focused on student orientation and intake. The other programs focused on improving partnerships through joint collaborations, such as developing vocational ESL programs. The involvement of all of the directors has been pivotal to the success of the AIDDE implementation throughout the state. The state director explained, "The local directors' involvement is critical if we hope to see effective professional training and instructional improvement at the classroom level. We are striving to build a stronger link with directors that connects to instructors and state staff and that aligns state and local priorities with each other."

The fourth program improvement activity focused on aligning priorities of the state system as a whole, and on methods of evaluation. An interagency group of partners, including instructors, directors, council leadership, state staff, and external agency partners, followed the AIDDE process to conduct a thorough system evaluation; make recommendations on how to better connect the multiple policies, procedures, and activities of the system; and better align the system priorities with those of external partners. One of the results of the process was an annual joint planning session between the state office and the OCABSD that links priorities of key stakeholder groups.

Leadership Development. In addition to program improvement, the state also had a goal to develop leadership within local programs, the director's council, and at the state level. The state focused on three primary leadership activities: (a) creating a council leadership scholarship, (b) ensuring that the Oregon Professional Development System (OPDS) participated in the national Leadership in Action project, and (c) supporting the state staff to continue to participate in the NQI.

The state expanded an established professional development scholarship for the outgoing OCABSD chair to include a second "leadership" scholarship for the vice-chair. The state director explained, "Last year the scholarship sent both the past-chair and the vice-chair to the national meeting of state directors to gain a broader field perspective that would contribute to stronger council leadership and integration of federal, state, and local priorities." Additionally, in 2005, Oregon and Washington state directors explored ways for cross-state collaboration and leadership development by having state and council leaders participate in each other's state spring council meetings.

The OPDS became a focus of the systemic improvement efforts in 2002–2003 when the state director participated in the Leadership in Action project that was funded by the U.S. Department of Education. The Leadership in Action Project included two training sessions on the use of the AIDDE model in designing and managing a professional development system. As a part of the training, Oregon's project was a comprehensive needs assessment of directors and the OPDS.

Participation in this national initiative led the state to develop more purposeful and clear professional development expectations for all staff. For example, when faculty engage in the statewide instructional practices project, the state develops a participation agreement that details state and instructor responsibilities, and describes how the director will support the faculty in carrying out the project and integrating the knowledge and skills into the program. The state staff member, instructor, and local director must agree to specific responsibilities to participate and receive the financial support from the state. This helps assure that projects are not undertaken with insufficient resources at the local level. The expectation is that what is learned by one group of instructors and directors will be documented and passed on to others. The outcome has been stronger commitment to priorities for system improvement on the part of all involved.

Currently, Oregon is one of four states continuing to participate in the NQI. In anticipation of reauthorization of the federal legislation, the states are using the AIDDE model for developing a new state plan and process for grant proposals. State staff are also continuing to apply what they have learned in their training as they explore ways to "go to scale" with the instructional practices project across their states, and investigate ways of providing further support to sustain local directors and state councils as they continue to work on leadership development and system improvement strategies.

Results

According to the state director, the AIDDE model has reinforced Oregon's commitment to supporting program improvement and leadership development at many levels—with faculty, directors, partners, and state staff. She said that using the AIDDE process helped everyone understand the critical pieces for a continuous improvement model—analyzing data and information, identifying areas for improvement, developing and implementing new activities, and documenting and evaluating practices.

A critical step in the AIDDE model is analyzing data and information that reflect program practices because this process identifies areas for improvement. This step in the process is often overlooked because it is challenging to locate and compile the appropriate data and analyze it. In Oregon, this step was the foundation of a solid framework for improvement. OCABSD reviews state and local program data quarterly and identifies factors that affect program performance. Faculty participate in the data analysis and all other facets of the AIDDE process at the program level. They work as a team to set priorities, interpret data, and identify what is and is not working.

Using the AIDDE model also requires program managers at local and state levels to identify internal and external pressures from federal, state, community, and institutional levels to the program level. A common understanding and foundation make the system more manageable and increase participation from all stakeholders. Staff can see it as both sustaining and improving a system over time.

The AIDDE steps were integrated into the end-of-the-year program grant reporting requirements and applications for continued funding, requiring programs to clearly state program improvement priorities, proposed outcomes, and how they plan to achieve their goals. Oregon has also added a requirement that programs report statistics and analyze their data to assess past—and inform future—practices. The state office also revised Oregon Indicators of Program Quality and integrated the AIDDE model into the state program review process.

Results in Oregon include the alignment of the multiple components of the adult education system with the overarching principles of quality and continuous improvement, and implementation of a systematic process for evaluating data and information that then lead to a purposeful strategic planning process. The state director explained that Oregon is doing a better job at the following activities:

- Building a common foundation for the adult education system: "We're not just thinking about today or this year, but where we want to be as a system, long-term, and how continuous improvement, planning, and evaluation help get us there."
- Connecting processes, procedures, and activities at all levels: "No one wants to be given one more thing to do and everyone sincerely wants to understand how the work connects across programs and with the state system. Implementing the AIDDE model does not add work. Instead it supports the work by connecting the components of the system in a clear and manageable framework that requires continual evaluation and improvement of existing and new practices."
- Creating a broader understanding of the system for local leaders.
- Aligning local, state, and national priorities: "Identifying pressures is an important part of building awareness of the complexity of the basic skills system. For a system to continually evolve and improve, we must be able to understand each partner's expectations and investments in the system and assess the consequences of meeting or not meeting expected outcomes."
- Connecting local, council, and state planning.
- Communicating more effectively with internal and external partners.
- Increasing credibility and investment both internally and externally.
- Using a systematic process for identifying and piloting new instructional practices: "We all try to understand and analyze our data so we can apply it to program evaluation and planning."

- Expanding involvement of all staff in program operations and management.
- Developing leadership that will support the system in the long term.

The adult education programs in Oregon have always worked well together and as a group have built strong collaborative relationships with other state and local partner agencies. The AIDDE model helped make existing collaboration more systematic and intentional. This model has been an effective tool for helping the state staff work with partners within their agency, as well as in other agencies. It has provided a more systematic approach to evaluating and improving programs, which in turn has led to stronger partner support and program representation. Using the AIDDE model as a strategic planning process has enabled the state to "better align adult basic education with broader state initiatives such as workforce readiness and career pathways," according to the state director. The most significant result of implementing the AIDDE model has been improvement in the way that adult education operates in the state.

Lessons Learned

- *Positive sustainable change requires leadership and involvement.* Staff at both the state and local level made an investment in the AIDDE process, established clear expectations, a system for accountability, and a vision for making this process a part of ongoing program management and operations.
- *Implementing an improvement process takes time.* Identifying specific areas for improvement and then following up on the steps of the process requires time for talking and thinking together, and time for practicing and documenting the process.
- *Evaluation provides focus.* Although implementing program improvement in a systematic way has its challenges, ongoing reflection and evaluation helped provide the clarity and focus necessary to ensure that implementing new processes would lead to continuous improvement.
- *Focus on key areas to improve.* Program directors selected orientation and intake as a common area of improvement and then stayed with it. Although getting sidetracked is common, staying with the initial questions about improvement is important.
- *Stay the course.* As different procedures and practices became part of the improvement process, state and program staff considered

how to go to scale within programs and across the state and how to maintain ongoing training and technical assistance in the reality of limited resources and staff turnover. Program improvement was not a one-time activity; rather, it became the way the state has decided to "do business."

Tennessee and the Baldrige Criteria for Performance Excellence

Tennessee bases its systematic program improvement on the Baldrige Criteria for Performance Excellence developed as part of the National Quality Award. Any organization can use the criteria as a self-study process to develop business processes and improve organizational performance. In 1999, federal legislation extended the Baldrige Award to education and health care organizations, and the criteria were revised slightly to make the language more appropriate for these new contexts. The underlying assumptions, however, come from a business perspective, such as seeing the adult learner as a "customer." Use of the Baldrige Criteria for Performance Excellence is growing in the education sector. By 2004, four educational organizations (three local school systems and one university) in the United States had received the Malcolm Baldrige National Quality Award after applying the criteria for performance excellence. Many states have established quality awards at the state level that use the same criteria for performance excellence as the national quality award. Tennessee, for example, offers a Tennessee Quality Award at four increasingly challenging levels—interest, commitment, achievement, and excellence—to encourage participation in the state's quality program.

The Program Improvement Process: Baldrige Education Criteria for Performance Excellence

Baldrige National Quality Program's (2005) *Education Criteria for Performance Excellence* are the basis of an organizational self-study guide to help educational organizations use an integrated approach to organizational performance management. The guide includes more than 200 questions in seven major categories of organizational performance. According to the guide, the purpose of the criteria is "to serve as a working tool for understanding and managing performance and for guiding organizational planning and opportunities for learning" (Baldrige National Quality Program, 2005, p. 1). Figure 3.2 describes the key categories of the Baldrige framework.

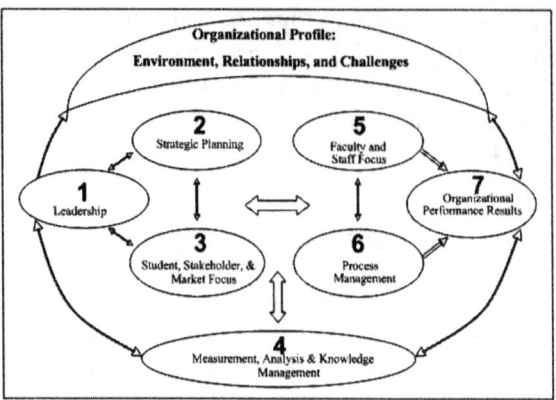

FIG. 3.2. Baldrige framework for excellence.

Each category of criteria is listed here:

- *Leadership* asks how senior leaders guide an organization, including the plan for governance (ethical, legal, and community responsibilities).
- *Strategic planning* asks how an organization develops and implements strategic objectives and action plans.
- *Student, stakeholder, and market knowledge* asks how the organization determines the requirements, expectations, and preferences of students and stakeholders and how it creates an overall climate for learning.
- *Measurement, analysis, and knowledge management* asks how an organization selects, gathers, analyzes, improves, and makes available its data to stakeholders.
- *Faculty and staff focus* asks how an organization's work systems, faculty and staff learning, and motivation lead to high performance and how it builds a work environment and support climate conducive to performance excellence and personal and organizational growth.
- *Process management* asks about key organizational processes for educational programs and services that create value for students and other stakeholders.
- *Organizational performance results* asks about outcomes in key areas, including student learning and satisfaction, stakeholder satisfaction, budgetary and market performance, faculty and staff results, operational performance, leadership, and social responsibility.

More than 40 states have created public–private partnerships to encourage quality at the state level, using the Baldrige criteria and the self-study for evaluation and recognition. In Tennessee, for example, the Center for Performance Excellence annually presents qualifying organizations with awards at four incremental levels of achievement: interest, commitment, achievement, and excellence. According to the Web site of the Tennessee Center for Performance Excellence (2005), these four levels are not "a competition against another organization, but rather . . . a competition against increasingly difficult criteria . . . ." The process of applying for the award is similar to the Baldrige process at the national level. For example, if an ABE organization wants to apply for the award, the first step would be to develop an organizational profile that describes the program's mission, goals, and challenges. The next step would be to conduct a self-study using the questions under each major category of Baldrige criteria. Finally, quality examiners (generally volunteers from business and industry) visit each candidate organization to evaluate whether the organization has adequately met the performance criteria for receiving an award and, after the evaluation, provide written feedback on ways the organization can improve.

In Tennessee, ABE is administered by the Tennessee Department of Labor and Workforce Development with local programs in more than 90 counties. Most managers are referred to as supervisors and work full time. The majority of teachers are part time. Programs are located in local school systems, community colleges, and local career centers.

Tennessee formally adopted the Baldrige criteria as its program improvement strategy in 2002. The state's goal is for all 94 adult education programs in the state to receive the Tennessee Quality Award (TQA) at the commitment level by 2009. According to the assistant state director, "We wanted a systematic approach to continuous improvement that had a proven track record. We thought Baldrige was the best approach because it has been tested in education and business. In addition, we thought it would help us connect with business and industry in their language. And it has."

Tennessee began using the Baldrige criteria for improving adult education programs in 1997, when a pioneering program manager learned about the Baldrige criteria from a new staff member who had taught the application of quality principles when he was a trainer in the military. "Our new staff member introduced us to the Malcolm Baldrige Education Criteria for Performance Excellence. These criteria take the total quality management principles originally used in the private sector and apply them to educational institutions" (Cody, Ford, & Hayward, 1998, p. 3).

Use of the Baldrige criteria spread to other programs in three ways. One way was through state conference presentations that program staff made about the way they applied the Baldrige criteria in their programs. A second way was ongoing professional development for program managers interested in applying quality principles in their programs. The Center for Literacy Studies at the University of Tennessee[14] (CLS) provided professional development with the support of the Tennessee Director of the Division of Adult Education. Third, CLS invited local program staff to help facilitate a Leadership Institute for other program managers based on the knowledge they had gained at both the program and classroom level; eventually the local program staff member who initiated the process joined the CLS staff. As programs completed the self-study process and received the state's quality award, their "effective practices" were integrated into the training and training materials for other supervisors.

Based on what was learned in the field about using the Baldrige criteria, the state office adopted the Baldrige process as the basis of the state's performance improvement plan in 2002. From 1998 through 2004, of the 95 programs in Tennessee, 97% had achieved the state quality award at some level. As of January 2005, 77% (or 71 programs) had received the TQA at the interest level, 12% (or 11 programs) had achieved the commitment level award, and 1% (or 1 program) received the achievement level award.

Specific Objectives in Tennessee

From the start, Tennessee's approach has been to focus on program managers, with the understanding that once program managers undergo the self-study process, they will spread their efforts to teachers and other staff, and eventually to program participants. The Baldrige model requires that stakeholders (e.g., learners, teachers, and volunteers) must participate by the time the program reaches the commitment level. As a part of the state's support of the Baldrige process, the state office conducted a self-study of its own operations and received the TQA at the commitment level in 2005. According to the state director, "We didn't want to ask the programs to do anything that we weren't willing to do ourselves."

---

[14]M. B. Bingman currently serves as Associate Director of the CLS and M. F. Ziegler is the former director.

With support from the state office, CLS has offered professional development on the Baldrige program model to both managers and teachers since 1999. The state director also appointed a staff member to provide support to programs that were applying the Baldrige criteria. In addition to an annual Leadership Institute, program supervisors participated in workshops that help sustain their interest and build their skills in areas such as interpreting data, making data accessible to stakeholders, and identifying the "vital few" program areas to improve. Sessions at the annual state conference focus on how teachers can use quality principles in the classroom. In addition to providing formal learning experiences, CLS offers one-on-one support at the program's site as they are conducting the self-study process. An electronic discussion list enables managers who are going through the process to ask questions and provide support to each other. Programs that successfully complete the self-study process receive the TQA in a public ceremony.

Results

A key result of using the Baldrige model, according to the Tennessee state associate director, has been the integration of various adult education initiatives into a cohesive system. For example, the state is merging the Baldrige criteria with PQI and will use these new criteria for evaluation of local adult education programs. By using common criteria in conjunction with the Baldrige self-study process, local program staff members will be able to prioritize their goals, then decide on and use the strategies they believe will help achieve the goals, and evaluate their performance based on data they collect. All programs will be using the same criteria to identify the particular program components that need improvement. The common criteria will also enable the state to more easily measure progress consistently across programs and more effectively plan for professional development.

The purpose of engaging in the Baldrige process was to improve the overall system's processes and results. The state is tracking results based on the broader definition of the Baldrige framework, which includes student learning, customer and stakeholder satisfaction, operational performance, and leadership. The state's data show an increase in customer satisfaction, measured at all levels, which the associate director attributes to an increased emphasis on listening to students and other stakeholders. Because programs are adopting the Baldrige process in waves, the link between improving program quality and results is not yet consistent across the state. The program that has been using the Baldrige model for the longest period of time, and that has received the TQA at achievement level, reports an increase of student learning of more than 20%, based on advancement from one NRS level to another. In addition, the program reports that retention and GED attainment have increased, and instructional hours have decreased. Other programs are reporting increased retention, improved rates of pre- and posttesting, more effective intake and orientation processes, and "a much better sense of knowing what works."

Lessons Learned

- *Listen to stakeholders and meet their needs.* Stakeholders in the Tennessee adult education system include adult learners, teachers, local program directors, state staff, and partners from other state agencies and business and industry. As customers, adult learners regularly evaluate the services they receive from local programs and local programs regularly evaluate state services. These multilevel evaluations become part of the continuous improvement process.
- *Use a recognized program-improvement model.* The TQA has been recognized by the governor, agency leaders, and leaders from business and industry. The increased visibility has amplified the adult education program's credibility among its partners and led to broader support for the goal of adult education.
- *Integrate system components.* Tennessee has integrated the criteria from the Baldrige model with the Tennessee PQI. These coordinated criteria are used at both the state and program level for evaluation, setting goals, and developing a continuous improvement plan.
- *Present the real experiences of programs using the process and incorporate them into professional development for others.* State professional development staff documented effective practices used by local program staff and added them to professional development materials. As a part of professional development, program directors participate in an electronic discussion about their experiences with program improvement and with applying for the TQA.

Vermont and Equipped for the Future

Vermont has taken a standards-based approach to improving program quality, using the EFF standards to frame their adult education programs.

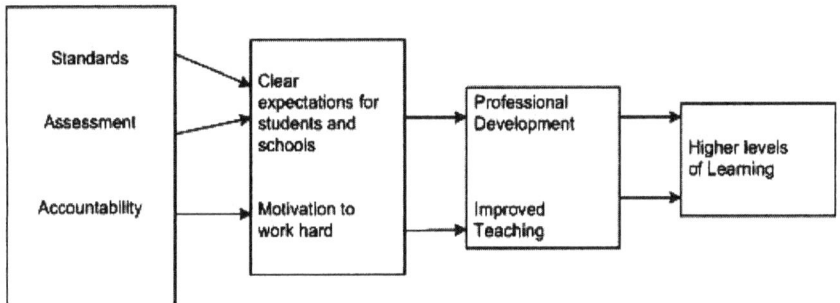

FIG. 3.3. Expanded model of the theory of action of standards-based reform: An educational improvement system (National Research Council, 1999, p. 20).

The basic assumption of standards-based improvement is that content standards with aligned assessments and accountability mechanisms will provide "clear expectations for learning" and "will lead to continually higher levels of learning and achievement" (EFF Assessment Consortium, 2004). The National Research Council (1999) model for standards-based educational improvement starts with content standards, assessment, and accountability requirements in alignment to provide clear expectations for what students should be learning. Figure 3.3 shows that for this model to be effective in building quality (defined here as higher levels of learning), information about expectations defined by standards and about how to teach to meet those expectations must be distributed throughout the system.

The Program Improvement Model: Equipped for the Future

EFF was developed as an initiative of the NIFL to improve the quality and results of the U.S. adult learning system. Through a process of collaborative research, EFF developed 16 content standards that define what adults need to know and be able to do to meet the National Adult Literacy and Lifelong Learning Goal that "Every adult American will be literate and possess the knowledge and skills necessary to compete in a global economy and exercise the rights and responsibilities of citizenship" (Goals 2000: Educate America Act, 1994). The 16 EFF standards define the skills adults use in their roles as workers, family members, and community members, and include communication skills, decision-making skills, interpersonal skills, and skills for lifelong learning. The standards are:

- Read with understanding.
- Convey ideas in writing.
- Speak so others can understand.
- Listen actively.
- Observe critically.
- Use math to solve problems and communicate.
- Solve problems and make decisions.
- Plan.
- Cooperate with others.
- Advocate and influence.
- Resolve conflict and negotiate.
- Guide others.
- Take responsibility for learning.
- Reflect and evaluate.
- Learn through research.
- Use information and communications technology.

The standards include, but go beyond, academic skills, to define integrated skills processes that describe what is involved in using skills for the purposes in adults' lives. So, for example, the components of the standard *Read With Understanding* are:

- Determine the reading purpose.
- Select reading strategies appropriate to the purpose.
- Monitor comprehension and adjust reading strategies.
- Analyze the information and reflect on its underlying meaning.
- Integrate it with prior knowledge to address reading purpose (Stein, 2000).

The standard describes what an adult does when reading a text.

In 1994, NIFL began developing the standards through a process that included adult students; stakeholders from a wide variety of groups including employers, trade unions, civic organizations, governmental bodies, and parents' groups; and experts on educational standards. NIFL identified adult students' purposes for participating in adult education. Three "role maps" described the broad range of activities that adults perform in their roles as workers, family members, and citizens and community members. NIFL worked with field development partners from adult education programs in 13 states and an expert review panel to develop the EFF content standards describing the skills adults use in these three roles. Additional field research and expert review has led to performance continua describing performance of the EFF standards with increasing levels of complexity.

The NRC standards-based model requires assessment aligned with standards. The EFF staff determined that performance-based assessments were best suited to evaluating the integrated skills defined by the standards, and they developed continua of performance and accompanying level descriptors for 11 of the standards. These continua describe performance on the standards in terms of knowledge base, fluency, independence, and range. For example, an adult performing at Level 1 on the read with understanding performance continuum can "read and comprehend words in short, simple texts slowly and with some effort but with few errors, to independently accomplish simple, well defined, and structured reading activities in a few comfortable and familiar settings" (EFF Center for Training and Technical Assistance, n.d.), for example, to read store or product names.

An EFF quality model describes research-based program practices that support use of EFF standards, including "A systematic approach to accountability and program improvement based on meeting student and national goals" (Bingman & Stein, 2001). However, although adult education programs should be able to use the EFF standards and aligned performance assessments in their efforts to be accountable for meeting student goals and particular local goals such as building student leadership, EFF standards and assessments have not been approved for purposes of reporting on national goals for the NRS.

Vermont was involved in the early field development of EFF and uses EFF as the model on which statewide program improvement is based. Their Web site states:

> The Department of Education and the adult education and literacy providers have adopted Equipped for the Future as the primary framework for standards, student goal setting curriculum, instruction, and assessment. The EFF Framework aligns with Vermont's collective philosophy and vision for how education can support adult learners to function in their roles as workers, citizens, and family members. (State of Vermont, Department of Education, n.d.)

Specific Objectives in Vermont

In 2001, when the Adult Education and Literacy Programs staff at the Vermont Department of Education decided to move to a standards-based system, they determined that EFF met their needs as a framework of adult standards. Although the decision to adopt standards was to some extent driven by the need to be aligned with the standards-based K–12 system, the state staff had other reasons to use standards and, in particular, the EFF standards. They were interested in broadening the curriculum to include a wider range of skills, such as problem-solving and interpersonal skills. The state staff found that teachers involved students in "wonderful activities" but did not take advantage of these activities systematically as a way to build a range of skills. The purpose of the learning activities was not always clear. State staff wanted teachers to be more intentional about what was happening in their classes and with their students, and for students to be clear about what they were learning. The state staff was also interested in moving toward performance assessment as a way for students to demonstrate competency in skills. They expected EFF to support both state and student goals.

The state staff took into account the structure of adult education in Vermont when implementing the EFF framework and standards. The Vermont Department of Education, Adult Education and Literacy Programs, contracts with a single provider, Vermont Adult Learning, to offer adult education services across the state. These services, including instruction in literacy and essential skills, English language learning, preparation for the GED, and an adult diploma program (ADP), are provided through 10 full-service adult education learning centers across the state. Vermont Adult Learning (and its three subcontractors) hire the teachers, 85% of whom work full time, and a statewide professional development team plans and contracts to provide professional development.

Because Vermont's program improvement efforts have focused primarily on teachers and teachers' instructional practice, professional development has been the primary approach Vermont has used to implement the EFF standards. Professional development in support of EFF has included workshops, but has moved toward more on-site efforts such as teacher inquiry, curriculum development, and having staff developers coteach with local teachers. The professional development has focused on helping teachers move from teaching sets of discrete skills to using the EFF standards to integrate skills instruction into learning projects that address issues in adults' lives. For example, a class might have concerns about how to make decisions as a consumer. The teacher plans a series of learning activities that address this concern: comparing advertisements to choose a product, identifying unsupported statements in advertising claims, or writing a consumer complaint letter. The EFF standards help the teacher focus on the elements of the skills that are used in these activities, such as observe critically, which includes the component "analyze the accuracy, bias, and usefulness of the information" (Stein, 2000, p. 33). Students learn to read critically, to write clear paragraphs, and other "academic" skills as they use them.

In addition to ongoing professional development on using the EFF standards to frame project-based instruction, the state has also developed performance-based assessments that are multistep activities or projects that allow students to demonstrate competence on a set of standards. For example, a student might be asked to research and summarize the positions of Vermont legislators in preparation for a conversation with the legislators on a particular issue of concern to the student. Their work is compiled in a student portfolio. The Vermont ADP has crosswalked, or identified the congruency of, the EFF standards with the state high school standards for this assessment development process. Assessors for the ADP examine portfolios of student work based on six performance-assessment activities as a "capstone assessment." When their performance assessments are sufficiently reliable, the state hopes that all adult students will work toward the ADP based on EFF standards.

When the state introduced the performance assessments, teachers saw them as a useful way to structure teaching and asked to use them for instructional purposes. The state and Vermont Adult Learning are now working to involve teachers in developing assessment activities that can be used as an element of classroom instruction while they continue to develop performance assessments to be used as measures of achievement of the standards.

Although the state's primary focus has been on the quality of instruction, in 2004, Vermont instigated a process of annual "quality visits" to each of the 10 learning centers. During the visits, a team of community members, teachers, and managers meet with program staff and students to examine how the center is meeting local goals, EFF standards, and NRS data collection. After the initial quality visit, the program develops an improvement plan, and the next year's visit focuses on targets from these plans.

One major hurdle in the implementation of the EFF framework in Vermont has been the requirements of the federal accountability system and the NRS. Because programs cannot use performance on the EFF standards to report the learning gains required by the NRS, they continue to use standardized assessments for reporting purposes. It has not been possible for the programs or the state to align content standards, assessment, and accountability, the premise of the standards-based educational improvement approach.

Results

Professional development and the introduction of performance-based assessments encouraged some teachers to adopt EFF, but others were "a little reluctant to give up their traditional skills-based teaching methods and approaches." When the ADP became standards-based, the state staff saw that "a pretty dramatic shift" had occurred as teachers became more willing "to shift their thinking and teaching strategies to support students in the ADP." In 2005, the state staff estimates that as many as 75% of the 110 adult education teachers used the EFF standards in some way, but as few as 5% to 10% used the standards in a systematic way to design curriculum, plan instruction, and assess performance. They imagine that program managers are not using it to "a great extent," so the program improvement is beginning at the classroom level and then may move to a programwide process.

Lessons Learned

EFF and a standards-based system are not yet fully implemented in Vermont, but the state staff has identified lessons they have learned to date. These are:

- *Assessment drives practice.* When assessment for the ADP was tied to the EFF standards, teacher interest in using EFF as the basis for instruction increased markedly. Having tangible performance tasks that led to something (the ADP) that teachers and students valued both lent credibility to EFF and helped teachers better understand how to use the EFF standards in instruction.
- *Manager support is critical.* Because the teachers have been the ones implementing the programs, managers may not understand EFF well enough to provide support to their teachers' efforts. State staff are exploring ways to address this.
- *Provide teachers support over time.* The state has found that professional development that takes place with teachers in their classrooms working on projects over time has been more effective than single-session workshops in leading to change.
- *Performance assessment is difficult.* Developing assessments and training assessors to use them consistently has been more difficult than the state anticipated. Although they have been effective in "focusing teachers more on applied learning," the assessments have been expensive to develop and the state is not yet satisfied with their validity and reliability.

APPLYING PROGRAM IMPROVEMENT MODELS IN ADULT EDUCATION

All three of the states in the case studies are applying different models for systematic improvement to better serve the adults who participate in their adult education programs. Although each state adopted a model that suits its particular purpose, we found commonalities in practice across the models. For the sake of discussion, we write about these commonalities separately, but in fact, they are interrelated.

Improving Quality Within Different State Structures

Where adult education is located within a state structure may influence the type of improvement process the state adopts. Adult education in Oregon is a part of the Department of Community Colleges and Workforce Development system and has 26 programs. Program directors work full time and the majority of teachers work part time. In Tennessee, adult education is administered by the Department of Labor and Workforce Development, which aligns its goals with the needs of business and industry. The state has more than 90 programs; most have full-time directors and primarily part-time teachers. Vermont is structured very differently. Adult education is in the Department of Education and is aligned with the K–12 system. The state has one main program provider and offers services at 10 sites; each site has a local program director. Teachers and administrators are primarily full time.

The impetus for program improvement was different in each state. Oregon began its implementation of the AIDDE model as part of a pilot project to improve instruction. The pilot led to the realization that teachers need the support of program managers to make significant changes in instruction, and eventually led to the state's adoption of the AIDDE model for comprehensive system improvement. In Tennessee, program supervisors took the lead in applying the Baldrige criteria to their programs. Use of the model began with one manager who wanted to improve her management skills so her program could be more effective. Her efforts spread to other managers and eventually their successes led to the state's adoption of the Baldrige model for all adult education programs because not only had the model been tested in the field, but it was also valued by business and industry. Tennessee teachers have been involved only if they were part of local program-improvement teams. Vermont, on the other hand, focuses its efforts by using standards to guide instruction because the standards support the state's values and goals. Teachers have been participating since the development of the EFF standards and recently, program directors have become involved. The state structure may have influenced not only the choice of a particular model, but the way the model is applied to practice.

Developing a Common Language

Each program improvement model has a particular language that provides a way to think and talk about improvement in concrete terms. In Oregon, for example, the AIDDE model focuses on process, making it applicable to addressing a wide range of program components at local and state levels. Regardless of the action, those who are using it over time develop a shared understanding of what it means to "design an implementation plan" or "evaluate implementation." In Tennessee, the language of the Baldrige criteria is widely accepted among state agencies, business, and industry. Adult education program staff who engaged in the self-study process have developed a shared understanding of the criteria as applied to adult education. Program staff know what types of improvement activities apply to "program leadership" or "faculty and staff focus." Use of the EFF framework in Vermont has provided the same type of common language that reinforces the state's focus on supporting adult learners in their roles as workers, citizens, and family members. Teachers who are applying the standards to instruction can use the EFF language to both think about their practice in new ways and develop a common understanding of standards as they apply them with learners and talk about them with other teachers. The common language makes the improvement process more accessible, enables those in roles at different levels of the system to share information, and provides a way to communicate more effectively with stakeholders outside the system.

Collaborating Across Boundaries

As in other types of organizations, adult education programs have numerous boundaries between different stakeholder groups. For example, professional development staff may design training based on national trends, whereas teachers want professional development based on local needs.

A boundary surrounds each of these groups and without intentional connections, professional development staff and teachers may each believe the other group is out of touch with what is needed. This can lead to a type of silo effect, in which staff members from one part of the program become disconnected from staff in other parts (Watkins & Marsick, 1993). These boundaries develop because the roles of learners, teachers, volunteers, local administrators, professional development staff, and state administrators are different. Crossing these boundaries as part of a program improvement process means that a member of a particular group participates in the activities of another group. As administrators, teachers, and learners cross boundaries, they gain a broader perspective of the system as a whole.

In Oregon, local program staff became more involved in state program operations and management. For example, state staff and program directors held a joint planning session. In Tennessee and Vermont, professional development staff invited staff from local programs to contribute to professional development because of their experience in practice. The Baldrige criteria require the involvement of all key stakeholders in the self-study and improvement process. This requirement leads naturally to teams that cross administrative and instructional boundaries. From an instructional perspective, the EFF model crosses the typical teacher–learner boundary as learners become involved in instruction based on their own goals. In the three states we studied, boundary crossing increased people's awareness of the system as a whole and reduced the silo effect because individuals had a reason to move out of their particular area and engage with others.

Learning and Sharing Knowledge at Different Levels

Stakeholders at all levels have learned from these improvement processes. As local and state staff have gained more experience in applying the models, they have begun to develop a knowledge base about program improvement; sharing this knowledge base makes it available to the system as a whole.

Oregon focused improvement efforts on "going to scale"; in other words, as teachers or administrators engage in potential program improvement efforts, they explore ways to take what they have learned and apply it on a larger scale. In Tennessee, program managers who have conducted a successful self-study process share their knowledge with others by contributing materials to training or engaging in an online discussion about quality improvement. In Vermont, instructors are coteaching with professional development staff. Rather than adding new work, program improvement models are intended to provide a clearer and more effective way of working. Although this may ultimately be the case, understanding a particular model and how to apply it takes considerable time and presents a steep learning curve for many. A key challenge for adult education program staff who engage in learning for ongoing continuous improvement is the limitation of resources (e.g., time for many part-time staff, and financial resources for many states).

Providing Professional Development

A model is only a guide. How to apply a model in a particular context, especially when the model suggests practices that are very different from those commonly used, is not self-evident. Most continuous-improvement models require translation from the language of the model to everyday practice in an ABE program (Ziegler, 2005).

In all three states, professional development was a key strategy for encouraging adoption of the model and its use in practice. Professional development in this instance was more than an occasional workshop. In Oregon, state staff received training from Abt Associates, and when the association of program directors was asked for volunteers to receive professional development, all members volunteered. In Tennessee and Vermont, programs received on-site support from professional development staff in their respective states. Although both time and cost intensive, on-site support provides more opportunities for inquiry and practice than single-session workshops. Each of the three states selected a model that had support from a larger federal organization. Staff who were knowledgeable about the model and had expertise in applying it were available to provide professional development. These states had the resources to obtain the education and training that they wanted.

Using Data Strategically

Each model stresses the importance of using data as either a strategic management tool or a strategic instructional tool. In the past, data in adult education traveled one way, from the local program to the state and on to the federal government. The purpose of collecting data was to report them, not use them (Merrifield, 1998). The emphasis on quality in the public sector changed the meaning of data from a reporting and monitoring mechanism to a program-improvement mechanism. At the federal level, programs are still reporting their data to the state and the states input the data in the NRS system. However, Oregon and Tennessee are using data strategically at the administrative levels; the AIDDE and Baldrige models rely on data to identify program components that need improvement and to determine whether improvement has occurred. Oregon program directors, as a collective, set aside time for data analysis at meetings. Tennessee program directors receive specific training in interpreting data and making them meaningful and accessible. In Vermont, improvement of instruction also relies on data. By aligning the EFF standards with the ADP, the state has a quantitative measure that can be reported on the NRS and is aligned with their state standards represented by EFF.

Aligning Program Processes

All three states used the improvement models to align administrative processes, priorities at the state and local level, and instructional processes. States in the case studies saw a relationship between improving program processes and results; however, each state defined results more broadly than program outcomes, such as an increase in the number of participants advancing an NRS level. Results might have included greater involvement of staff in planning, increased customer satisfaction, or more teachers applying standards. In the case studies, state staff did not make a direct link between improving a particular program process and increasing a particular program outcome.

Becoming More Deliberate and Systematic

All three states became much more deliberate and systematic about program improvement, but in varying ways. The AIDDE model is process oriented. It does not suggest what program component to improve; rather, it provides a process (analyze, identify, develop, document, and evaluate) that can be applied to instruction or administration at local or state levels, and by any member of the system. The Baldrige framework defines categories for both processes and results but organizations must identify areas for improvement and address these in different ways. For example, the category of strategic planning must be addressed as part of the self-study process; however, each program might answer questions about strategic planning differently. Although measuring results is part of the model, programs might have varied results, including those collected by the NRS, depending on the outcome of their self-study processes. Use of the EFF framework for program improvement is based on a set of established standards.

By using a particular model, program staff consider not only the instructional areas they will address and how they will address them, but also what resources they will need, the data they will need before they start, how they will measure success, and how the learner will know that success has been achieved. By using a systematic process, program improvement becomes more proactive than reactive. Being proactive by engaging in inquiry and reflection leads to the type of planning and decision making that supports a long-term view of improvement.

IMPLICATIONS FOR PRACTICE, RESEARCH, AND POLICY

Although the systematic program improvement models described in the three case studies were different from one another, their commonalities suggest that a systematic approach has merit. Looking across these case studies, we can see implications for practice, research, and policy.

Practice

Meaningful Data

The program improvement models described in this chapter have the potential to strengthen widespread access to information and learning that results from sharing and interpreting information. Using a framework highlights the importance of making data more transparent and accessible and therefore open to scrutiny by broad stakeholder groups (Cervero & Wilson, 1994). A corresponding challenge is making data available for program improvement, particularly data that may not be captured by state systems designed to collect NRS data. Collecting these data requires resources that may be beyond the capacity of small states, or states that do not receive money from the state for adult education.

Professional Development

Each of the three states has used professional development to learn to apply the model, because improvement approaches are likely to require changes in practice. This requires aligning professional development activities to meet both program needs and instructional needs. Programs can also use a program-improvement model as an inquiry method for professional development. In this way, the model itself becomes integrated into practice.

All three states used their model to improve practice in both administration and instruction and stimulated learning and changes in practice.

Research

Connecting Program Performance and Program Processes

The relationship between systematic improvement of program processes and student performance as measured by NRS outcomes is unclear. Although standards-based models appear to have relevance for improving instruction, it is not clear whether these improvements lead to greater learning gains and if they do, how this happens. We do not really know which changes affect which outcomes because research has not focused on this relationship. What is the relationship between particular program components and student outcomes? Research that sheds light on this connection can help us understand whether one program component, such as intake, influences a particular performance indicator, such as learning gains.

Program Improvement at the System and Instructional Levels

In what ways does the use of a statewide program improvement model influence instruction? Although numerous anecdotes in the literature suggest that applying program improvement models leads to positive change, few studies have actually investigated this process. Those that have been conducted in K–12 and higher education focus mainly on administration and question how process-oriented models might influence instruction (Xue, 1998). Teachers traditionally enjoy professional autonomy in making decisions about the most effective ways to help individual students. Further systemization, which may be an asset to administrative functions, may limit teachers in their responses to student needs. Research is needed to better understand teacher change and what supports teacher change.

Policy

Resources

Ongoing, comprehensive program improvement takes resources, including time, funding for professional development, and collection of data not gathered by the federal performance accountability systems. States may have multiple funding sources for adult education—or only one funding source—to dedicate to program improvement. States with limited resources may not have the capacity to engage in a systematic improvement process. If a policy for program improvement is established, the federal agency supporting adult education must consider these implications for state structure and budgets.

Program Quality Indicators

The PQI that were in place attempted to balance improving program results with improving program processes. Although the PQI measures were not nationally defined, and therefore not comparable across states, many states believed the PQI had merit, and in fact, they are still in use in two of the case study states. Rather than starting over, policymakers could build on what states learned as they implemented the PQI. These lessons could help align federal, state, and local goals so that neither states nor local programs get caught between competing stakeholder needs.

Measuring Outcomes—The Limitations of Standardized Assessments

The NRS relies on standardized assessments to have comparable quantitative data across states and programs. However, the adult education system has a limited number of standardized assessment instruments that local programs can use. For example, Vermont used the EFF standards-based system for instruction and performance assessment but also uses standardized tests that are not aligned with their standards for the external accountability system. However, not all of the assessments being used by states were designed to be used for instruction. Most instruments define learning gain narrowly, to make it more measurable. Although standardized assessment can be compared, one danger is that assessment instruments drive the whole system. Those who are at lower literacy levels or those who are native speakers of languages other than English may have goals that are not measured by the NRS and they may achieve gains that cannot be measured with current standardized tests. States that define assessment more broadly may need a parallel system to use assessments not accepted by NRS. Policymakers must find ways to broaden the assessment instruments and options available to states.

Achieving Adult Education Program Quality

In their efforts to take a systematic approach to improving program quality, Oregon, Tennessee, and Vermont each took a different approach that helped state and local staff gain clarity about the meaning of program quality. Each state has in place a process that it believes will move it toward quality. However, as more states adopt improvement models, they face ongoing demands for increasing performance outcomes and the constant threat of fewer resources. A disjuncture may occur between their conceptions of quality and the implied federal definition of quality as ever-increasing performance on a narrow set of measures. Although current policies have addressed the need for adult education to have aggregate performance data that demonstrate their effectiveness, the system still needs to develop a national accountability system that can also serve to increase the quality of services for adult learners. All stakeholders, including agencies at the federal level, need to be involved in a meaningful, integrated process of program improvement.

REFERENCES

Alamprese, J. (2003). *Implementing program quality adult basic education programs: Systemic change strategies.* Paper presented at the Twentieth Annual Rutgers Invitational Symposium on Education, Bethesda, MD.

American Council on Education, Business-Higher Education Forum. (1983). *America's competitive challenge: The need for a national response.* Washington, DC: Author.

Arif, M., & Smiley, F. (2003). Business-like accountability in education: Commentary on Morrill to Baldrige. *Education, 123,* 741–762.

Baldrige National Quality Program. (2005). *Education criteria for performance excellence.* Retrieved December 18, 2004, from http://www.quality.nist.gov/Education_ Criteria.htm

Bingman, M. B., & Stein, S. (2001). *Results that matter: An approach to program quality using Equipped for the Future.* Washington, DC: National Institute for Literacy.

Bonstingl, J. J. (1992). The quality revolution in education. *Educational Leadership, 50*(3), 4–9.

Borsum, L. A., & Francke, C. A. (1998). *Baldrige Award application to education: A case study.* Paper presented at the Annual Quality Congress Proceedings, Milwaukee, WI.

Boyle, P., & Bowden, J. A. (1997). Educational quality assurance in universities: An enhanced model. *Assessment and Evaluation in Higher Education, 22,* 111–122.

Cervero, R. M., & Wilson, A. L. (1994). *Planning responsibly for adult education: A guide to negotiating power and interests.* San Francisco: Jossey-Bass.

Cody, J., Ford, J., & Hayward, K. (1998). A story of improvement. *Focus on Basics.* Retrieved December 18, 2005, from: http://www.ncsall.net/?id=393

The College Board. (1983). *Academic preparation for college: What students need to know and be able to do.* New York: Author.

Condelli, L., & Kutner, M. (1997). *Quality indicators for adult education programs: Lessons learned from other programs.* Washington, DC: Pelavin Associates.

Condelli, L., Seufert, P., & Coleman, S. (2004). *NRS data monitoring from program improvement.* Washington, DC: US Department of Education.

EFF Assessment Consortium. (2004). *Improving performance, reporting results: The guide to using the EFF Read with Understanding assessment prototype.* Washington, DC: National Institute for Literacy.

EFF Center for Training and Technical Assistance. (n.d.). *Assessment resource collection: Read with understanding performance continuum.* Knoxville: University of Tennessee, Center for Literacy Studies. Retrieved October 17, 2004, from: http://eff.cls.utk.edu/assessment/read5.htm

Goals 2000: Educate America Act, 20 U.S.C. § 5801 (1994). Retrieved November 18, 2004, from http://web.lexis-nexis.com/congcomp/document?_m=5d170f2db659314f0c87921084ac9686&_docnum=14&wchp=dGLbVtz-zSkSA&_md5=0151f84c11dc2acb922c6a32d2f49a76

Government Performance and Results Act, 31 U.S.C. § 1101 (1993). Retrieved November 18, 2004, from http://web.lexis-nexis.com/congcomp/document?_m=a40eb707b5a71d34395ef8789325a16b&_docnum=13&wchp=dGLbVtz-SkSA&_md5=e9d0902bdd9ac52eda0267a8baed32ff

Malcolm Baldrige National Quality Improvement Act, 15 U.S.C. § 3711a (1987). Retrieved October 20, 2004, from: http://web.lexis-nexis.com/congcomp/document?_m=4297610ffd1f084bf5829fbf8db6ba7c&_docnum=2&wchp=dGLbVlz-zSkSA&_md5=9db433c40c2c9f3587d9b625b1928d7f

Merrifield, J. (1998). *Contested ground: Performance accountability in Adult Basic Education* (NCSALL Rep. No. 1). Cambridge, MA: The National Center for the Study of Adult Learning and Literacy.

Messner, P. E., & Ruhl, M. L. (1998). Management by fact: A model application of performance indicators by an educational leadership department. *International Journal of Educational Management, 12,* 23–27.

National Commission on Excellence in Education. (1983). *A nation at risk: The imperative for educational reform.* Washington, DC: U.S. Government Printing Office.

National Literacy Act, 20 U.S.C. § 1201 (1991). Retrieved November 18, 2004, from http://web.lexis-nexis.com/congcomp/document?_m=590fd49a97c533c37476527d83ae091f&_docnum=9&wchp=dGLbVtz-zSkSA&_md5=119674c761878fe192b74f8647c9ebfb

National Performance Review. (1993). *From red tape to results: Creating a government that works better and costs less.* Washington, DC: U.S. Government Printing Office.

National Research Council. (1999). Testing, teaching, and learning: A guide for states and school districts: Committee on Title I testing and assessment. In R. F. Elmore & R. Rothman (Eds.), *Board on testing and assessment, commission on behavioral and social sciences and education.* Washington, DC: National Academy Press.

Office of Vocational and Adult Education. (1992). *Model indicators of program quality for adult education programs* (Rep. No. TAC-B-290). Washington, DC: U.S. Department of Education. (ERIC Document Reproduction Service No. ED 352499)

Office of Vocational and Adult Education, Division of Adult Education and Literacy. (2001). *Measures and methods for the National Reporting System for adult education: Implementation guidelines.* Washington, DC: U.S. Department of Education. Retrieved November 18, 2004, from http://www.nrsweb.org/reports/implement.pdf

Osborne, D., & Gaebler, T. (1992). *Reinventing government.* Reading, MA: Addison-Wesley.

Peckenpaugh, J. (2001, January 18). Clinton administration claims management success. *Government Executive.* Retrieved July 9, 2004, from http://www.govexec.com/dailyfed/0101/011801p2.htm

Satterlee, B. (1996). *Continuous improvement and quality: Implications for higher education.* Lake Wales, FL: Warner Southern College. (ERIC Document Reproduction Service No. ED 399845)

Sherman, R., Tibbetts, J., Dobbins, D., & Weidler, D. (2001). *Management competencies and sample indicators for the improvement of adult education programs.* Washington, DC: Pelavin Research Institute.

State of Vermont, Department of Education. (n.d.). *Programs & services: Adult education & literacy.* Retrieved October 17, 2004, from http://www.state.vt.us/educ/new/html/pgm_adulted.html

Stein, S. (1993). *Framework for assessing program quality: A community based approach to literacy program evaluation.* Washington DC: Association for Community Based Education.

Stein, S. (2000). *Equipped for the Future content standards: What adults need to know and be able to do in the 21st century.* Washington, DC: National Institute for Literacy.

Swadley, R., & Ziolkowski. (1996). *The National Institute for Literacy performance measurement, reporting and improvement system final report.* Washington, DC: National Institute for Literacy.

U.S. Department of Education. (2001). *National Reporting System for adult education: Implementation guidelines.* Retrieved June 26, 2005, from http://www.nrsweb.org/reports/implement.pdf

Walton, M. (1986). *The Deming management method.* New York: Perigree.

Watkins, K. E., & Marsick, V. J. (1993). *Sculpting the learning organization.* San Francisco: Jossey-Bass.

Wiedmer, T. L., & Harris, V. L. (1997). Implications for total quality management in education. *The Educational Forum, 61,* 314–318.

Winn, B. A., & Cameron, K. S. (1998). Organizational quality: An examination of the Malcolm Baldrige national quality framework. *Research in Higher Education, 39*(5), 491–512.

Workforce Investment Act, 20 U.S.C. § 9201 (1998). Retrieved November 18, 2004, from http://web.lexis-nexis.com/congcomp/document?_m=de47ea0a29393a53cc4c766f721053a3&_docnum=26&wchp=dGLbVtzSkSA&_md5=b1dbf1d4c3d4e2513e594534a36225a7

Xue, Z. (1998). *Effective practices of continuous quality improvement in U.S. colleges and universities.* Unpublished dissertation, University of Massachusetts, Amherst, MA.

Ziegler, M. (2005). "It opens your eyes": Transforming management of adult education programs using the Baldrige criteria for excellence. *Adult Basic Education, 15,* 169–186.

APPENDIX: E-MAIL SURVEY INSTRUMENT

1. Name of state
2. Does your state have a statewide initiative that focuses on program improvement, i.e., does your office involve programs in a systematic statewide process of program improvement?
3. If you answered "yes" to Question 2, please continue. If you answered "no," thank you for your help!
4. Does the process include use of NRS data? Yes or No
5. Is the process based on a national model, e.g., EFF, NAEPDC Going to Scale, Baldrige?

If so, which one:

6. About what percent of programs are involved: a few, about half, most, all?
7. Approximately when did you begin this process?
8. Please provide contact information for a staff member who could give us more information by phone:

If you complete this survey, we appreciate your consent to participate in this study. Thank you!

4

Assistive Technology and Adult Literacy: Access and Benefits

Heidi Silver-Pacuilla

This chapter focuses on the role that assistive technology (AT) can play in improving the literacy acquisition and motivation of struggling adult students who have mild reading disabilities. Mild reading disabilities may be the result of learning, attention, memory, cognitive, or sensory impairments, and these categories often overlap. For example, Schulte, Conners, and Osborne (1999) found that attention deficits (AD) and learning disabilities (LD) co-occur at rates greater than can be predicted by chance. Although the main difficulties associated with the two disorders are distinct (LD is associated with language-based disorders and AD with executive-function disorders), the combination of the two disabilities often contributes to poor school performance and achievement.

Providing access to assistive technologies to supplement classroom instruction can address students' needs for additional tutoring and small-group instruction, as well as support their literacy learning by making studying and reading easier. Students could then begin to engage in more effective self-study activities, thus boosting their learning, classroom performance, and sense of competence and motivation.

The range of AT is vast and addresses many different types of functional limitations, but in this chapter I focus on only a few categories of computer-based AT that support literacy development. I first review services provided for adults with LD in the adult basic and literacy education (ABLE) field, followed by a brief overview of the elements of adult literacy learning. Then I present specific AT tools and their functions and uses, followed by two case studies of how literacy learners benefited from supplemental instruction with AT. In the fourth section, I look at the research and discuss the use of computer-based technologies to support youth and adult engagement with literacy tasks. Finally, I explore the practice, policy, and research implications of integrating these technologies into services for adult literacy students with mild reading disabilities.

PROVIDING SERVICES

As young people leave the K–12 educational system when they graduate, reach the maximum age (22) for special-education services, or drop out, they leave behind the entitlement program and legal mandates of the special education system, which is governed by the Individuals with Disabilities Education Improvement Act (IDEA, 2004). They enter abruptly into the legal standing of individuals with the right to claim disability protection under the Americans with Disabilities Act (ADA) and Section 504 of the Vocational Rehabilitation Act of 1973. However, most youth and adults with disabilities do not understand this right, or how to claim it (Mull & Sitlington, 2003; Stodden & Conway, 2002).

The ABLE field must comply with legal mandates to accommodate students with disabilities and to provide appropriate services to benefit students with disabilities. The policies and effective practices associated with such services, however, are less than clear-cut. The capacity to provide such services—among practitioners, programs, and communities—is still sorely lacking (Corley & Taymans, 2002).

Postsecondary institutions and employers are required to maintain physical environments that are universally accessible, provide nondiscriminatory services, and respond to an individual's self-disclosed disability. Postsecondary institutions and employers must provide "reasonable" accommodations when requested. The government does not mandate universally accessible services and products. Rather, these must be provided in nondiscriminatory formats in a manner that is timely, accurate, and appropriate to the material accommodated, as well as to the individual with the disability (Grossman, 2001). For example, scheduling information for a program should be available in multiple formats (large print, online or on disks for those who use computer readers, or recorded); a "discriminatory" format would be a complicated printed schedule, with the only arrangements made for accommodation being a receptionist reading the schedule aloud to a student in a lobby.

The Bridges to Practice initiative funded by the National Institute for Literacy from 1993 to 1999 provided guidance to the ABLE field. Through professional development and technical assistance, the project provided resources and training to practitioners and program managers to evaluate whether curriculum and policies effectively met the needs of adults with LD. Programs were urged to adopt screening policies and instruments to identify students at risk for LD and forge community coalitions for obtaining appropriate diagnoses. Five years after the publication of Bridges materials (National Adult Literacy and Learning Disabilities Center [NALLDC], 1999), Corley and Taymans (2002) suggested the field still has a way to go to realize improved outcomes for students with learning disabilities.

Although the research base on teaching students with mild disabilities within adult education is exceedingly slim, there is a substantial database of research addressing the instructional needs of elementary and secondary students with LD. In a review of several meta-analyses and syntheses of research on intervention strategies for K–12 students with LD, Vaughn, Gersten, and Chard (2000) identified several guiding principles. Their review found that effective instruction requires the following:

- Visible and explicit components (expectations and examples demonstrated clearly and through multiple sensory channels).
- Managed task difficulty and sequence (complex tasks taught in logical steps and sequence).
- Interactive dialogue and thinking aloud (lots of teacher–student conversation and probing questions).
- Opportunities for guided practice and directed feedback (practice activities completed in class with immediate and focused feedback).
- Small-group settings (either for practice or differentiated instruction based on group needs).
- Peer-mediated activities (peer tutoring or cooperative-learning activities).
- Both a skill- and strategy-level focus (building and practicing skills, as well as learning how to problem solve in a discipline).

These findings were consistent across elementary and secondary studies reviewed over a 30-year period representing the research on LD. The authors concluded that although the findings are not revolutionary, the practices are not widespread in U.S. classrooms, leaving students with LD to languish due to ineffective instruction.

In fact, students with mild disabilities are resisting this ineffective instruction and curriculum. In 2000, an estimated 3.8 million youth and young adults (ages 16–24) were high school noncompleters, a full 10% of their age group (Kaufman, Alt, & Chapman, 2001). As is true historically, students from low-income families drop out in greater numbers—28.9% in October 2000 as compared to the national average of 10.9% (Kaufman et al., 2001). Statistics on special-education students' dropout rates include recent rates as high as 29.4% (Office of Special Education Programs, 2000). Leading the trend are students diagnosed with serious emotional disturbance (51.4%), specific LD (27.6%), mental retardation (26%), speech or language impairments (24.6%), and other health impairments (22.4%).

For youth and adults with mild disabilities in search of educational improvements, ABLE and family literacy programs are some of the few places they can turn to for affordable services. Yet the programs are not prepared to serve them well. Scanlon and Lenz (2002), in a national survey of adult education completed by program directors and practitioners from 34 states, sought open-ended responses to questions about literacy areas emphasized in interventions for adults with LD, and specific interventions and materials used in programs. The survey findings demonstrate the eclectic nature of ABLE practice and the gaps in research conducted with adult literacy students with LD. Notably, respondents did not cite any common practices or materials representing any field-based knowledge of best practice. What respondents did cite was a range of practices and materials that reflected a skills-based, functional literacy curriculum and a philosophy of LD as a set of deficits. Whereas skills-based practices may be appropriate as a component of a curriculum for youth and adults with LD, adult LD researchers (Scanlon & Lenz, 2002; Sturomski, Lenz, Scanlon, & Catts, 1998) caution that adults in ABLE settings may resist skills-based or functional pedagogies and deficit-model philosophies.

Furthermore, adult education programs that focus solely on functional literacy and skill development may be missing some of the higher order thinking and problem-solving strategy instruction strongly recommended for youth and adults with LD in ABLE programs (Corley & Taymans, 2002; NALLDC, 1999). This type of strategic instruction is also documented as best practice for youth with LD through encompassing reviews (Swanson & Hoskyn, 1998; Vaughn et al., 2000) and without LD (Hinchman, Alvermann, Boyd, Brozo, & Vacca, 2003–2004; National Institute of Child Health and Human Development, 2000).

Adult literacy practitioners should choose pedagogies based on research, but most research takes place in secondary or postsecondary schools. Nevertheless, research representing secondary and college students with mild disabilities may be the closest body of knowledge from which to make inferences for our practice. In the next section, I explore adult literacy development from two perspectives: LD research and new literacies theory.

ADULT LITERACY DEVELOPMENT

Adult reading research (Kruidenier, 2002) sees literacy development as the improvement of a set of component skills. Learners with LD struggle with basic phonological awareness (the ability to hear and manipulate individual sounds and clusters of sounds within words) and with how sound and visual patterns comprise the foundational blocks of learning English literacy (phonics). Many learners with LD struggle with visual perception, finding the two-dimensional, black-on-white presentation of text difficult to keep in focus or discern, causing fatigue, frustration, and an inability to concentrate on text. Attention deficits may also interfere with the level of attention, persistence, and memory learners are able to bring to literacy learning. Readers who have difficulty with any of these basic skills are bound to struggle with fluency (the ability to do these tasks smoothly and quickly; Kruidenier, 2002). Slow, laborious decoding, guessing at unknown words based on superficial clues, and fatigue from the reading process are hallmarks of the reading efforts of adults with low literacy.

How adults with LD acquire vocabulary is also a concern. Their phonologic and orthographic difficulties make teaching and learning vocabulary a complex challenge that interferes with success on the general equivalency diploma (GED), in further education, and in employment. Readers' acquisition of, or even exposure to, interesting and content-appropriate reading instruction or materials can be blocked by these difficulties, in varying combinations and prominence. Higher order and critical comprehension strategies are often left off the instructional, and even research, agenda with adult new readers with mild disabilities.

Critical literacy or new literacies theorists (Lankshear & Knobel, 2003; Luke, 2000; Luke & Freebody, 1997) would likely cast most of this research as woefully and unhelpfully individualistic. Reading, they maintain, is a social, transactional act that cannot adequately be understood by studying a single person or classroom, but rather requires a social context and critique to be understood adequately. The New Literacy Studies model shares much with the Freirian model of literacy that embeds literacy learning and use in praxis of naming powers and working openly toward social justice. This model also includes a strong critique of the assumption that facility with print literacy is central to identity and personal development, an essential assumption underpinning skills-based and literacy-practice theory. New and critical literacy theories remind us to question the materials and approaches we employ and the outcomes we watch and measure in adult literacy instruction. The questions raised by critical literacies help us frame questions such as "Access to what, for what, and for whom?"

Adult reading instructors and researchers must keep these multiple and overlapping theories in mind when working with students and when designing research and instruction, and remember that theories show us the same phenomenon—literacy—from various perspectives (Leu, Kinzer, Coiro, & Cammack, 2004). None of the perspectives alone can provide a full understanding. Balancing perspectives and goals for literacy learning is a challenge that can only be met by involving the adult learner in setting goals, identifying his or her developing needs and hopes, and exploring—and more important—creating options and access to new materials.

The use of AT to create options for literacy learners requires a creative and strategic approach that pairs the functions of the technology with the needs of the student and the demands of the literacy task. The next section explores types of AT in more detail.

CATEGORIES OF ASSISTIVE TECHNOLOGIES

AT is a subfield of educational technology, and for youth and adults, it is associated with rehabilitation practice and research (Watts, O'Brian, & Wojcik, 2004). AT was defined in the 1988 Technology-Related Assistance Act as "any item, piece of equipment, or product system acquired commercially off-the-shelf, modified, or customized, that is used to increase, maintain, or improve the functional capabilities of individuals with disabilities"

(Technology-Related Assistance for Individuals With Disabilities Act of 1988). This definition was used in the 1997 reauthorization of the IDEA, which mandates pre-K through 12th-grade special education services. Although this definition has proven to be too broad to guide educational practice (Edyburn, 2000), it remained unchanged in the 2004 reauthorization of IDEA (H.R. 1350) and of the AT Act of 2004 (H.R. 4278).

Special educators have used several applications of computer-based technologies effectively to meet the literacy needs of students with mild disabilities, such as learning, attention, memory, or mild sensory impairments. Although the research base is still small, it is growing; new studies with sophisticated designs and outcome measures are emerging. There is a complementary growing database of practical knowledge, which explains how technologies are used and modified to meet needs in instructional, employment, and daily-living situations.

Drawing on this emerging knowledge base for secondary and postsecondary students with mild disabilities, in this section I examine three of the most readily available categories of software: text readers, voice recognition, and predictive word processors. The functions, range of applications, and demands on the user are discussed, as well as how the software–user interactions may meet literacy development needs. How these technologies can supplement adult education instruction for learners with disabilities will be shared in two brief anecdotes.

Text Readers

Text-to-speech (TTS), or speech-synthesis technology, refers to the conversion of digital information into synthesized speech. In other words, the computer reads the text aloud. TTS engines[15] can be an optional feature combined with other software programs or configured as stand-alone specialized text readers.

Functions, Applications, and Demands. Speech engines vary in the quality of the "voices" they use to read aloud and the range of customizable features they offer, such as text and background colors and contrast, reading rate, or highlighting and masking. Dynamic highlighting—a feature that colors a single word or phrase—emphasizes the text being

---

[15]Two free TTS engines are ReadPlease (http://www.readplease.com) and Microsoft Reader (http://www.microsoft.com).

read. Dual highlighting is a related software feature, sometimes called masking, in which the context (sentence or paragraph) is highlighted in one color while the spoken word is highlighted in a second color, making it easier for readers to stay in sync with the spoken text.

These features are digital versions of the window cards (index cards with a slot cut out of the middle) teachers have relied on to assist struggling readers to keep their place on a line of text. The dynamic digital version brings the reader's attention to a word and its placement on the line without a loss of peripheral vision of the rest of the text (a drawback of index cards, rulers, and blank paper used to track reading). TTS with dynamic highlighting, therefore, offers simultaneous auditory and visual input. When users read along, or even subvocalize (lip sync), their speech muscles add proprioceptive (mouth and throat muscle) input to the experience, making it truly multisensory.

There are specialized tools that read only some files, such as talking Web browsers[16] or a program that reads Adobe Acrobat files.[17] Other TTS engines read text from multiple software applications (word processors, spreadsheets, database, Web pages, e-mail, etc.).

Comprehensive software programs designed to help learners with disabilities combine TTS with other powerful capabilities—such as optical character recognition (OCR), embedded resources, and word processors—include programs such as several versions of the Kurzweil readers,[18] WYNN readers,[19] programs from the Premier Assistive Suite,[20] and Read and Write Gold.[21] According to a national survey of postsecondary institutions (Michaels, Prezant, Morabito, & Jackson, 2002), these AT devices are some of the most commonly provided, available on 78% of campuses, and considered by survey respondents to be among the top five most useful AT devices[22] for college students with disabilities.

---

[16]Such as Web Talkster (http://www.code-it.com), or BrowseAloud (http://www.browsealoud.com)—both are free TTS engines that navigate Internet Web pages.

[17]Such as PDF Aloud (http://www.texthelp.com/PDFaloud.asp?q1=products&q2=PDFaloud).

[18]See http://www.kurzweiledu.com/.

[19]See http://www.freedomscientific.com/LSG/index.asp.

[20]See http://www.premier-programming.com/.

[21]See http://www.texthelp.com/home.asp.

[22]Other useful devices identified in the survey include recorded textbooks, real-time captioning, screen magnification software, and specialized tape recorders.

OCR is scanning software that digitizes print from a piece of paper and converts scanned images into document files. These scanners do not simply make a picture or image of a page of scanned text, but actually decode the print and turn it into an electronic document, which can then be read aloud by the TTS. OCR can recognize standard text fonts, but accuracy depends on clear, crisp print and high-quality scanners. Proprietary scanners preserve the layout of the scanned page on the computer screen and are capable of reading text that continues across multiple columns, reading tagged graphics (those with a linked description), and preserving navigational markers such as chapter breaks. This can be an advantage if a student is using an OCR program in a classroom in which instruction often references textbook features.

All of these comprehensive programs (Kurzweil, WYNN, the Premier Assistive Suite, Read and Write Gold) are highly customizable. The programs have elaborate TTS engines, often with a wide variety of voices of differing pitches, tones, and even accents. Readers can select preferences such as reading rate, the amount of text visible at a time on the screen, the size of the font, the colors of the presentation (background, text, highlighting), the text segment that is highlighted or masked (sentence, phrase, or word), the toolbar icons visible, and so on. These preferences can be set as defaults for a particular learner (as a user profile), eliminating the need to reset them at each session.

These top-of-the-line programs offer many resources and features to enhance studying, such as multiple dictionaries, syllabication and pronunciation guides, thesauruses, text highlighters (static highlighters that replicate highlighting on a paper text), and annotation options such as digital sticky notes or margin notes into which the reader can copy and paste definitions from the dictionary or glossary, type comments, or (in the Kurzweil 3000) speak a voice note (saved as an audio file). These annotations attach to a line or word in the text, but are not visible until opened. Most programs allow users to extract (copy) the text annotations. For example, a learner could extract all of her annotations of definitions to a word processor and create a personal glossary for later use.

Literacy Supports and Learning Opportunities. OCR software and TTS engines have opened the world of print to users with mild visual disabilities. Sophisticated TTS engines that navigate the Web have done the same for Web-based materials. Comprehensive programs create a working environment modeled after master students' habits, with tools and resources at the ready. However, OCR and TTS are not perfect tools. TTS engines often mispronounce homographs (words that are spelled the same but pronounced differently, such as *read* as a past- or present-tense verb). Not all Web pages are designed to be compatible with TTS engines, rendering them incomprehensible. Print scanned into OCR often needs to be edited to clean up any misrecognitions caused by poor print copies, unusual fonts, or scanner software glitches.

The imperfections in the tools, however, are opportunities to examine how the tools function. When literacy learners notice incorrect pronunciation and are coached to spend time exploring them, they have an opportunity to compare what they had expected with what was pronounced. Looking for the cause of the mispronunciation of the verb *to read,* for example, can lead to a minilesson on verb tense, homographs in general, or quality of scanned print and how to correct misrecognitions. When literacy learners are given supported access to AT (in the form of a literacy coach or tutor), the novelty of the tools and the situation create an environment in which literacy is made visible and open for exploration, analysis, and mastery.

Voice Recognition

The converse of text readers is speech or voice recognition software, which can process spoken language into digital text.[23] Industry increasingly uses such software as a front-line service option for over-the-telephone reservations, requests, and routing. This technology has a long history of intense research and is still receiving research and development attention from companies such as AT&T, Microsoft, and IBM (Kanellos, 2003; Kelly, 2004) in an effort to improve accuracy of recognition, range of recognized speech-pattern variations (tone, pitch, rate, volume, dialect, idioms, specialized vocabularies, etc.), and ease of training. Improvements in any one of these areas involve trade-offs in other areas of the program. For example, accuracy for a single user can be greatly enhanced, but for a commercial software package to be programmed to recognize an unknown buyer, software companies have to maximize the range of voices that can be recognized. Portability of voice files that would allow a user to dictate and word process on multiple machines and with multiple microphones, for example, is an urgent area for future development so that users can use the

---

[23]Such as IBM ViaVoice (http://www.scansoft.com/viavoice/), Dragon Naturally Speaking (http://www.scansoft.com/naturallyspeaking/), and SpeakQ (http://www.wordq.com/speakqenglish.html).

program on more than one computer. Cross-disciplinary research, including linguistics, speech and hearing sciences, the science of sound and microphones, artificial intelligence, and computer science, is contributing improvements as well, and the next generation of these products promises great improvements in usability.

Functions, Applications, and Demands. These programs are widely utilized by individuals with motor and physical impairments that make using a keyboard difficult or impossible. Individuals who struggle with spelling and handwriting are now using voice recognition to bypass those tasks.

Voice recognition can be included with software programs performing other functions (e.g., in the Apple and Microsoft operating systems), or it can be the central feature of a software application, such as Dragon Naturally Speaking. Even dedicated software programs, however, now combine several functions into a seamless user interface (both programs working simultaneously in one "window") so that the voice recognition capabilities are available for multiple applications. With Naturally Speaking, for example, users can dictate into a variety of word processing programs, database programs, spreadsheets, e-mail, and operating systems.

Accuracy is a still a major hurdle. The software requires a quiet location and a high-quality microphone dedicated to a powerful and fast computer. Users must train the computer to recognize their voice and, although initial training can now take as little as 10 minutes, for literacy learners, reading scripts aloud for voice training is a process that requires support and patience. Some voices are more easily recognized by the technology than others, and other voices require additional and sometimes extensive training. SpeakQ is a new program that is dedicated to improving accuracy for users with voices that are difficult to recognize, users who stutter, and students with literacy difficulties. As users train and dictate to the program, their "voice file," or what the program knows about recognizing the user's voice and pronunciation as well as specialized vocabulary, continues to grow, thus improving accuracy.

Users need to tell the computer how to format what they dictate. Therefore, they must learn the formatting commands (here referenced to Naturally Speaking commands) such as Indent, New Paragraph, Flush Left, and so on, and the vocabulary of punctuation. They must command the program with these exact phrases, or, instead, format their composition using the keyboard and mouse.

Dictation must be performed with clear enunciation and an even rhythm, volume, intonation, and conventional phrasing. Users must discipline

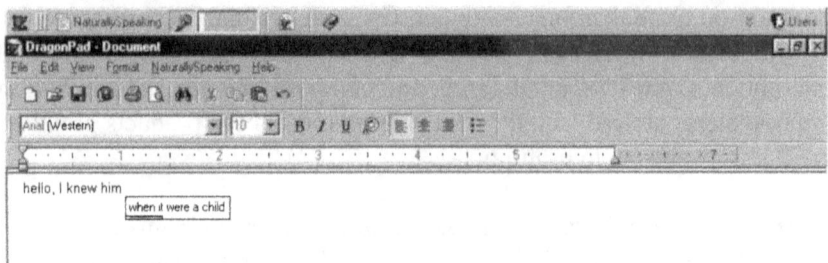

FIG. 4.1. Dragon Naturally Speaking. Note that the Results Box is processing the second phrase dictated and errors are appearing ("it" for "I" and "were" for "was").

themselves not to add extraneous verbal input that will distort the recognition process, such as "uhms," sighs, tongue clicks, throat clearing, and so on. As a user dictates, the Results Box on the screen displays the way the program recognizes the speech. The Results Box is a window into the workings of the linguistic and artificial intelligence predictions the program makes based on context clues and the user's voice file data (see Fig. 4.1).

Even under the best conditions, perfect accuracy is not possible, and users must expect recognition errors (*I scream/ice cream*). A user must decide how to handle misrecognitions, such as whether to pay attention to accuracy or to continue dictating and work on revisions, edits, and corrections later. Alternatively, a user can decide to pay attention to accuracy during the dictation process, starting with reading the text as it appears in the Results Box. Writers can correct recognition errors through multiple means, each with advantages and disadvantages. For example, by keyboard or voice command (Scratch That), they can delete dictated phrases that contain errors and then redictate. None of these actions "teaches" the program about the error or improves the voice file.

A third option is for users to correct errors through a process that actually improves the accuracy of their voice file, with correction procedures and further training on each misrecognition. When the user chooses a word or phrase for a Correct That process, a box appears on the screen with several choices based on semantic context or alternative formatting (e.g., a variety of ways to represent dates). If the correct recognition is on the list, a user can simply choose the correction by commanding, "Choose #," or by entering the shortcut key. Programs that pair with TTS engines can read these choices aloud. Naturally Speaking also includes a Train That option, a further word-by-word or short-phrase dictation that will train the voice file to recognize a user's particular pronunciation of a word. Each correction, whether done during the dictation process or later during editing, then, requires strategic planning and a high level of engagement with the print.

Literacy Supports and Learning Opportunities. In education and employment settings, voice recognition has provided computing access to individuals with physical impairments that limit their ability to use a keyboard. With the vast improvements in accuracy and cost reductions in the past decade, voice recognition has gained a growing user base among individuals with LD.

For students for whom writing is slow, laborious, or torturous due to their spelling, handwriting, and composition difficulties, voice recognition software opens new opportunities to express themselves and complete writing assignments. Voice recognition software employs a user's oral vocabulary and expression strengths to capture the intended message while bypassing many of the most common barriers to writing.

Voice recognition, however, does not do all the work. The cognitive demands when using voice recognition are high for users with language disabilities and LD, limited literacy, or AD. Using voice recognition software requires writers to constantly engage and monitor the text produced. Users must compare the actual results with their expected results to determine accuracy. They must determine the most strategic response to correct any errors (e.g., delete the mistake and redictate the phrase with more attention to enunciation, go through a correction procedure, ignore the mistake and edit later, incorporate the unexpected words into the flow of the text), command the program to format the text, and simultaneously maintain their train of thought to continue composing.

Several features support users in their efforts to utilize voice recognition software successfully. TTS engines included with the software read the dictated text and the text given as correction alternatives. Dictating into a word processor that has embedded tools, such as a spelling and grammar checker, alerts users when an incorrect word or sentence has been accepted. Automatic formatting tools in word processors also perform some basic formatting tasks, such as indentations, capitalization, or aligning and numbering lists. Writers can use predefined templates to minimize formatting, and, for enterprising users and instructors, customized templates and macros (abbreviation expanders) can be created to structure users' interaction with the software.

For example, a user could program his or her address to be automatically finished after typing only a few starter letters.

Word Prediction

Word prediction programs and phonetic spell checkers[24] have opened access to word processing and composing for those with severe spelling disabilities. Like many other forms of AT, word prediction technology was originally designed for a specific category of disabled students (in this case, those with physical disabilities for whom typing was highly problematic), but has since become a crossover technology for the larger population of students with spelling difficulties. Research from linguistics was used in the design of the word prediction tools, providing the writer a practical set of words, in a choice box similar to a spell-checker box, that logically completes a phrase, a sentence, or word that the writer started. For example, if a writer types, *I need to buy milk at the st. . .* , the prediction box would likely include nouns such as *store* and *street* as alternatives, and if one of these were chosen by shortcut key or mouse, the program would automatically finish typing the word into the sentence.

Phonetic spell checkers, a similar technology, are designed to accommodate the common errors made by dyslexic writers. Instead of providing options of words with sequences of letters similar to the incorrect entry (as a typical spell-checking program does), these spell checkers are built based on research on the actual spelling attempts made by writers with dyslexia. For example, if a writer types *dragon* as *jragun*, ordinary spell checkers will suggest or autocorrect to the word *jargon*, but phonetic spell checkers would include *dragon* as an alternative.

Functions, Applications, and Demands. There are stand-alone word prediction and phonetic spell checker software programs that work with a user's word processor, simply displaying a second or an alternative results box and small toolbar in the open program window. Other word prediction and phonetic spell checker functions are included with word processing applications, such as those available in the comprehensive text reader packages of Kurzweil, WYNN, and Read and Write Gold. The word prediction

---

[24]Such as WordSmith (http://www.texthelp.com/wordsmith.asp?q1=products&q2=wordsmith), Co:Writer (http://www.donjohnston.com/catalog/cow 4000d.htm), and WordQ (http://www.wordq.com/products.html).

4. ASSISTIVE TECHNOLOGY AND ADULT LITERACY

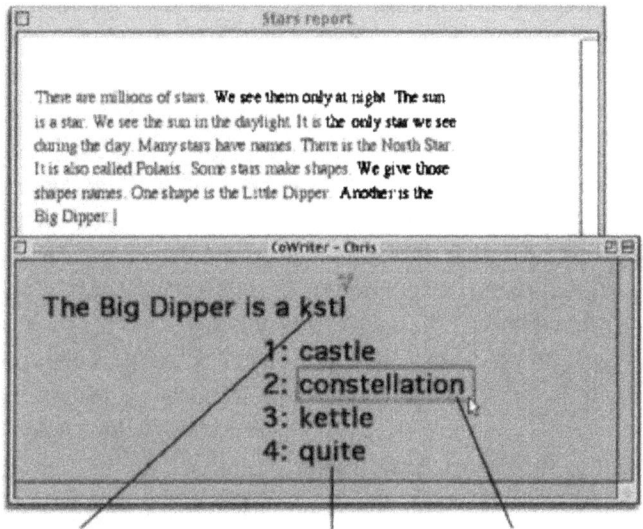

FIG. 4.2. Co:Writer Word Prediction with Word Processor Also Open. Note the student spelling attempt, the alternatives suggested, and the shortcut keys that will auto-type the choice.

program Co:Writer can be paired with Write:OutLoud[25] to create a seamless application, in which all functions appear in one workspace or window. WordQ is a program designed to work within Microsoft Windows. Most word processors are paired with a TTS engine to read aloud the alternatives as well as the composed text. TTS support can be set to read each letter as it is typed, each word, or a sentence once it is completed. Users can choose from the suggestion list by either typing the word or simply pressing the shortcut key (see Fig. 4.2). The choice then appears in the document, finishing a word that was only partially typed, replacing a word that was misspelled, or adding a new word or phrase to a text. Shortcut keys reduce the number of keystrokes necessary to type a word or phrase and the amount of typing and spelling necessary for composition.

Most word prediction programs also build in homophone (e.g., pair–pear) and homonym (there–their) checkers, which prompt (through TTS) the user to choose a correct option based on a quick definition. For example, if a user types *their,* the program can alert him that "This is the

---

[25]See http://www.donjohnston.com/catalog/writecover/writecoverfrm.htm.

their that is possessive." Similarly, if a user types *pair,* the alert could be "This is the pair that means two of the same thing." (See Fig. 4.2 for an example of a word processor with the prediction tool activated.)

Literacy Supports and Learning Opportunities. Word prediction software, like voice recognition, imposes a heavy cognitive demand on a user. The ever-changing results box, offering alternative word choices for each typed word, can be a distraction. Programs such as WordQ, which can be customized to appear continuously on screen or only when called up with a shortcut key, can help a user manage this distraction. TTS engines in the word processors also help students listen to their own writing as they compose, edit, and proofread. Nevertheless, word prediction requires a strategic approach to composing, spelling, and editing. Learning and applying such a strategic approach to writing for most students requires coaching and practice. Students with severe spelling difficulties, however, can benefit by being able to produce writing assignments that are legible and more complete than those they are able to produce without the technology.

Word prediction is particularly appropriate for students who have good keyboarding skills. Such students may choose to work with word prediction software rather than voice recognition and make use of a more thorough and helpful spell checker without overtly changing the way they interact with the computer.

CASE STUDIES

ABLE instructors have long supported students' literacy development by being scribes to students' dictation or assisting comprehension by reading aloud in class and digressing to define words, demonstrate annotations, consult resources, and model monitoring strategies. When students are empowered to do these activities themselves during class or self-study time, the responsibility for understanding the literacy process is transferred to them. The equipment does not replace instruction; rather, it provides an enriched environment so that students can engage in their own study and practice. The two cases shared here are taken from a participatory action research project conducted with adult students with mild disabilities at an adult education program (discussed later). This project investigated the role small group or peer-assisted access to AT could play in supplementing regular class instruction.

Case 1: How Voice Recognition Works as a Language-Experience Activity

One older African-American man, John (a pseudonym), recently retired from a career as a city employee, was returning to reading classes determined to finally learn how to read and spell. He was attracted immediately to voice recognition and found that the process of dictating to the computer gave him new insight, "new light," into the literacy learning process:

> I'm more enthusiastic in trying to pronounce my words and understand them. Because if we learn how to pronounce them, and read them, eventually we should learn how to write them. You know, 'cause if . . . the writing and reading goes side by side so you're like, you know, if you don't know how to read, you really don't know how to write. So but if you conquer both of them, you got your reading and your writing there . . . [Dictation is] opening up some new light, you know, in my vision. And . . . makes you want to strive a little farther and see how much . . . how far you can go.

John's use of the software helped him understand the connections between speech and writing. He watched as his spoken words were recognized or misrecognized and discovered that the accuracy of the program improved when he paid attention to enunciating his words more distinctly. He learned to use the Mute button on the microphone to manually filter out extraneous utterances, such as sighs and self-talk ("Let me see . . ."), which was easier than changing his natural speech patterns. He learned about writing mechanics by watching the word processor (Microsoft Word) automatically format his document (e.g., with capital letters) or prompt him with underlining to include ending punctuation. Because he used a casual, African-American dialect that was not recognized well by the software, he naturally explored the differences between oral and written language conventions. He used the capacity of the built-in TTS feature to command the program to Read That, as well as the digital recording feature (which captures a brief segment of a user's dictation) to Play That Back. By listening to two auditory models and comparing them to the recognition results, he could determine where errors had occurred and strategically decide how best to fix them.

At the end of each dictation session, which lasted approximately 1 hour, John saved his voice file and the document, and printed out the document for reading practice. He improved the document in later sessions. These are the elements of a classic language experience activity lesson: dictation, production, reading, and revising. The intervention of the software, however, demanded much more from the student. No longer was the "scribe" an already literate and compassionate tutor, responsible for correct spelling, legible handwriting, determining word boundaries, and disregarding misarticulations. The student and the computer now shared these literacy component tasks, with the student assuming responsibility to monitor the developing document.

Case 2: Reading With Embedded Resources

From the same study, Emma (a pseudonym), a Hispanic young woman with LD and attention deficit disorder (ADD) made use of supported access to a computer equipped with the comprehensive text-reading program Kurzweil 3000. She was attending a fast-track GED class, which met for 4 hours a day, covered one subject every 2 weeks, and expected students to complete copious amounts of reading and homework. Despite her commitment, drive, and persistence, she struggled with limited vocabulary skills that hindered her reading comprehension, had difficulty organizing and spelling writing assignments, was distractible, and had extreme test anxiety.

Emma identified reading comprehension, concentration, and anxiety as her immediate struggles. She talked a great deal about the visceral feelings of being overwhelmed by the volume of text and homework, and by her test anxiety. She said that as soon as her eyes touched a page of text, her stomach knotted, her shoulders clenched, and her spirits flagged. "If it's like a big passage, I get overwhelmed and I get more focused on how big it is than on reading each step," she said in her initial interview.

By working on assignments scanned into the Kurzweil 3000 program from her GED book, Emma was able to read along with the TTS, use the dictionary, learn the definitions, make annotations, and highlight the words and phrases necessary to her assignment. She could print out personal glossaries, built from her extracted annotations and definitional notes. She no longer felt overwhelmed by volume. She realized that her listening vocabulary was much greater than her reading vocabulary (she often said, "Oh, is *that* what that word is?!"), and felt empowered to deal with that disparity by using electronic dictionaries that eliminated frustrating and time-consuming searches through paper dictionaries.

Additionally, Emma talked about how the auditory input allowed her to visualize what she was reading, and that even listening once would help when she took the printed passage home:

> Yes, I think for me there is [transfer of learning], because like last night, I reread the story [on paper] and I was actually visualizing it! Usually I'm like, "Oh my goodness" [sigh] [rolling her eyes]. . . . But it actually worked for me, I was actually in there [the story], visualizing them walking on the beach or talking on the rock, things like that, and I finished it . . .

The responsibility for learning was transferred to Emma, and she gladly accepted it. She was empowered by access to the equipment that made her efforts at self-study effective. Supported access to OCR helped her better understand the content of her class and reference materials. She maintained her motivation and persisted, passing her GED tests and entering community college where she sought disability support services, such as access to AT and testing accommodations.

RESEARCH AND PRACTICE ON ASSISTIVE TECHNOLOGY FOR STUDENTS WITH MILD DISABILITIES

Disability advocates and technology researchers have touted AT as the "fix" for disabilities through the explosion of computerized technologies over the past decade. Networks and newsletters, such as Closing the Gap (http://www.closingthegap.com) and Quality Indicators for Assistive Technology (http://www.qiat.org), have sprung up to discuss the benefits of AT for those with functional limitations, offering practical and technical advice on how to match needs with applications. For all of the "wow" factor of what AT can help people achieve, however, there is a strikingly small research base on how or whether these devices and the integration of AT into education improves learning or participation outcomes (Edyburn, 2004).

Reviewed here are findings about what is assistive about AT for literacy learning and independent studying for secondary and postsecondary students with mild disabilities. This review focuses on the literature published on secondary and postsecondary students with LD. Strategic use of these tools in the ABLE curriculum requires understanding how these technologies support information processing and learning needs.

This section presents five themes from the research demonstrating the promising practices of AT:

1. Pairing text with speech.
2. Text enhancements.
3. Writing supports.
4. Motivation and persistence.
5. Integration into a well-designed curriculum.

Each section explains the theme, provides the evidence and pedagogies that support the practice, describes how the practice adapts to a digital environment, and presents available research documenting effectiveness for students with mild disabilities.

Pairing Text With Speech

Highlighting words and sentences as the computer reads them aloud is a powerful updating of a proven approach to presenting information to two senses: hearing and vision. When students read aloud or even subvocalize, they add a third sense: proprioceptive, or speech muscles. The simultaneous presentation of auditory and visual supports taps into long-standing teaching methods for students with LD (Fernald, 1943; Orton, 1932/1966), which emphasize multisensory input and expression. Two reading methods that enact this principle are repeated reading (RR) and the neurologic impress method (NIM). RR is an effective instructional strategy for students with reading disabilities. It develops reading fluency and increased comprehension (Allinder, Dunse, Brunken, & Obermiller-Krolikowski, 2001; Meyer & Felton, 1999). When teachers guide students through rereading the same passage, the number of word recognition errors decreases, reading speed increases, and oral reading fluency and expression improve (Dowhower, 1994; Meyer & Felton, 1999; Reitsma, 1988; Samuels, 2002). NIM is a strategy that presents a fluent reader as a model in very close proximity to the student. Traditionally, this strategy has been used by a teacher–student pair reading in unison, with the teacher sitting behind and to the side (reading in the student's ear), setting the pace and tracking the text with a finger. This multisensory method builds readers' fluency skills and diminishes dysfunctional reading habits while building positive ones (Heckelman, 1986).

Both of these strategies adapt easily to technological applications to create an individualized, multisensory, and intense experience with print. For example, digital text is available for endless repetitions, dynamic highlighting tracks the text, and TTS (preferably through headphones to mimic the teacher's reading into the student's ear) provides a fluent oral model and elicits proprioceptive input when readers read along aloud or subvocalize.

Several studies report the positive effects of TTS for struggling readers. Dawson, Venn, and Gunter (2000) studied the effects of a fluent model reader for students with mild disabilities in three conditions: no model, a teacher model reading through the passage one time while students followed along, and a TTS model that presented the text on the screen while it was read (without dynamic highlighting). Students' reading performance was measured for rate and accuracy. Students in the teacher model performed best, and the TTS model group outperformed the no-model condition. This study shows that hearing a fluent model read a passage, even one time through, can help orient students with reading difficulties to the vocabulary and rhythm of the passage and set them up to succeed in their own decoding efforts.

Montali and Lewandowski (1996) conducted a detailed investigation on dynamic highlighting with middle school students (Grades 8 and 9). Their study looked at two groups of students (students with LD and normally achieving students) in three conditions: visual only (text on the computer screen), auditory only (listening to recorded text with no text on screen or paper), and bimodal (visual highlighting of text with simultaneous TTS). They found that students with LD who were given text passages with bimodal input performed as well on the comprehension questions as the average reader control group with visual input alone. Additionally, they found that students with LD received no benefits from the auditory-only condition. They relate their findings to the well-established psychology literature that shows the power of multimodal input versus single modal input on attention and memory.

Summary. TTS is now available free of charge to anyone with Internet access. If the reading material can be scanned or is digital, it can be read by a TTS engine. Research studies such as those cited here have demonstrated that the multisensory presentation of text boosts students' subsequent reading efforts. Digital text and a TTS engine not only provide access to content, but to literacy benefits, as students' skills improve with the practice.

Text Enhancements for Vocabulary Development and Comprehension

Enhancements are resources such as digital highlighters, electronic references (e.g., dictionaries, glossaries, or encyclopedias), and annotation options that are embedded within comprehensive literacy software programs.

Although all students need to learn how to use reference resources effectively, for students who struggle with alphabetical listings, distractibility, memory, and persistence, traditional print-based references can present a barrier, not a support (Edyburn, 1991). Similarly, comprehension and study strategy instruction (Nist & Holschuh, 2000) emphasize reader interaction with text through annotations, vocabulary inquiry, question posing, and strategic highlighting. For students who struggle with note taking, spelling, and comprehension, such annotation tasks can also present a barrier.

The relationship between vocabulary and comprehension is reciprocal throughout the literacy acquisition process (Jitendra, Edwards, Sacks, & Jacobson, 2004); reading increases vocabulary, which in turn improves comprehension. Although oral language is a relative-to-self strength (a strength compared to other weaknesses, such as literacy acquisition) for adult literacy learners, their vocabularies are often limited. Moreover, adults with low literacy can have difficulty expanding their vocabularies and recognizing word-family relationships (Greenberg, Ehri, & Perin, 1997).

Recent reviews of the research on teaching vocabulary to youth with LD (Bryant, Goodwin, Bryant, & Higgins, 2003; Jitendra et al., 2004) and developmental college students (Simpson & Randall, 2000) reveal that effective practices for vocabulary instruction include the following:

- Direct instruction, with explicit teaching followed by guided practice.
- Emphasis on both definitional and contextual knowledge.
- Words chosen in clusters related to a discipline or content-area theme.
- Peer learning and peer tutoring activities and practice.
- Language-rich environments and wide reading.
- Activity-based instruction that is intense, multisensory, and hands-on.
- Computer-assisted instruction with a variety of software programs.

All of these instructional practices elicit deep cognitive processing by students as they make word-family connections and put their growing vocabulary to use. They also require interaction and discussion of the text between teachers and students. When teachers engage students in such interactive learning, their learning demonstrates improved long-term recall of vocabulary and improved reading comprehension (Bos & Anders, 1990).

Adapting these vocabulary and study strategies to a digital learning environment is possible with comprehensive software programs that link digital text with enhancements such as reference materials or annotation features. E-dictionaries, for example, can show and read definitions, syllabication and pronunciation guides, sample sentences, and further definitions of words within a complex definition—all at the click of a mouse or command prompt without having to retype the word or laboriously sort through paper dictionaries. Students can use annotation features of software programs to write questions, margin notes, notes to an instructor or tutor, or to attach definitions to new vocabulary words. Programs that offer extract features enable users to copy their annotations to a word processing document where they are then available for further study, such as the creation of a personal glossary or set of study questions.

The roles of the instructor, tutor, or coach and peers should not be overlooked or underemphasized. Best practices already cited emphasize that the learning environment needs to be dynamic, language-rich, and dialogic to excite the deep processing that enables transfer and recall.

Studies that investigated the impact of digital enhancements have struggled to isolate the impact of the enhancements from the full digital learning environment in which they are embedded. Two projects—at the Center for Electronic Studying (CES) and the Center for Applied Special Technology (CAST)—have created student tracking software with which to monitor students' use of enhancements. CES (http://ces.uoregon.edu/) creates and investigates technological enhancements for instructional materials and activities. CES describes the digital learning environments they create and use with secondary students with and without mild disabilities as *"supported text* to refer to electronic documents in which the text has been enhanced with various types of media for the purposes of expanding or improving student comprehension" (Anderson-Inman & Horney, 1999, p. 129). With software tracking students' interactions or paths through the text and resources, CES researchers have been able to document how students access and use enhancements. They have found that students use the embedded resources in purposeful ways that can best be described as "studying the text." They define studying as being "actively engaged in constructing meaning, struggling to comprehend unfamiliar vocabulary, or determinedly trying to assimilate and accommodate new concepts into their cognitive schemas" (p. 163). This documentation shows that students are not passive users of the technology, but utilize collateral resources that boost their comprehension. CES hosts a library of Web-based textbooks and materials that have embedded enhancements to promote comprehension (http://ces.uoregon.edu/intersect/default.html), and although these do not include TTS, they can be read by a TTS engine.

CAST (http://www.cast.org) is a leader in the field of AT and universal design for learning, a set of principles that guide the development of accessible learning materials, environments, and assessments (Rose & Meyer, 2002). CAST has recently developed a product called Thinking Reader (distributed by Tom Snyder, Inc.), developed for middle-school language arts students. This is a set of digitized versions of popular Newbery Award-winning books. The e-books are supported with TTS, have embedded comprehension strategy prompts, e-resources such as glossaries and dictionaries, note-taking and journaling capabilities, and an avatar or animated navigational aide (similar to the "paper clip guy" in Microsoft Word). Thinking Reader software includes student progress monitoring features that track a user's progress as well as alert an instructor to trouble spots. Researchers compared two groups of middle-school students; one group was given paper copies of the books, the other received the enhanced digital books through Thinking Reader. Both groups were taught the same comprehension strategies in whole-class instruction. Struggling students (those performing at or below the 25th percentile) who used the digital versions showed significantly more gains on the reading achievement tests than those who used the paper copies (Dalton, Pisha, Eagleton, Coyne, & Dysher, 2001).

Elkind and colleagues (Elkind, 1998; Elkind, Black, & Murray, 1996; Elkind, Cohen, & Murray, 1993; Hecker, Burns, Elkind, Elkind, & Katz, 2002) have reported several studies over the past decade on the use of computer readers' effects on reading comprehension for youth and postsecondary students with mild disabilities. Findings from their work emphasize the importance of matching student profiles of strengths and weaknesses to strategic uses of the software. For example, OCR programs (specifically, Kurzweil 3000) provided to college students with LD and attention deficit hyperactivity disorder (ADHD) were found to help students decrease distractibility, complete assignments with less stress and fatigue, and persist longer on reading tasks. Comprehension measures reveal greater improvement for students with weaker decoding skills, but much less improvement for students who were more proficient readers already (Hecker et al., 2002).

Summary. Readers cannot comprehend text they cannot decode, or text that has too much unfamiliar vocabulary. At the same time, struggling readers need explicit instruction on and prompting to develop effective comprehension strategies. Providing text with embedded resources to support readers' acquisition of vocabulary and strategies is a transformative use of technology, facilitating contextualized learning and providing access to more complex materials.

Writing Supports

In this section I describe the research on effective practices for improving the writing performance of struggling students. Youth and adults with LD struggle with "the physical demand and conventions of writing and . . . have difficulty coordinating the complex cognitive processes of setting goals, generating content, organizing their writing, and evaluating and revising their text" (MacArthur, Ferretti, Okolo, & Cavalier, 2001, p. 345). Add difficulties with spelling and vocabulary (discussed throughout the chapter), and writing assignments can present major barriers for students with mild disabilities. Engaging adult students who struggle with the acquisition of writing skills and confidence requires a well-designed instructional model that supports their literacy learning—reading and writing—in strategic ways.

A "gradual release model" recommended for secondary students struggling and at risk for dropping out (Fisher & Frey, 2003) will sound familiar to adult educators. Beginning with language experience activities, students see their oral language transformed into print. Groups or tutor–student pairs can then move into an interactive writing activity, during which they share the pen and compose a text together, making literacy "visible" (Luke, 2000); risks and mistakes are used as teachable moments. Teachers can then provide writing models, such as sentence starters or poetry models ("I am . . ." or "Somewhere in the world today . . ."), to structure and elicit students' responses. Generative sentences, taken either from students' work or from literature, can provide material to analyze and teach mechanics and grammar concepts. Power writing, also known as free writing, is a fluency activity that encourages students to write as much as they can (without editing) in a short, intense burst. Independent writing is, of course, the ultimate goal. This will be facilitated most effectively for students with mild disabilities if they are taught strategies to use when writing. For example, when students face a blank page and an essay question, they can call on an internalized strategy to talk themselves through creating a model or sentence starter out of the words in the essay question.

There are many ways mainstream technologies and AT can support a gradual release model of writing development for students who struggle with the many aspects of writing. The first case study shared earlier demonstrates how speech recognition can help students bridge their oral language to digital print, which is inherently flexible and modifiable. Digital text can then be edited, revised, read aloud, printed out, and so on. Small groups, or pairs of students with a tutor or coach, can "share the pen"—or in this case, the keyboard—and participate in interactive writing and writing models. Sentences are easily available for analysis in a generative sentence activity. Power writing could be done either on voice recognition or with keyboarding. (Keyboarding skills are obviously a great asset to working on word processors and using these technologies. Adult literacy students should be encouraged to work on typing tutorial software programs[26] to gain facility with keyboarding and formatting.)

The research on supporting the writing of students with mild disabilities with technology has a fairly long history. MacArthur and his colleagues conducted several studies investigating the use of mainstream technologies to support the writing processes and products of middle school and high school students with LD (see review in MacArthur, 2000). Their early work investigated the introduction of the current technologies (word processors, spell checkers) for students with LD receiving standard (nonexperimental) instruction. The bulk of these short-term, technology-focused studies found little significant advantage for students with LD. Later, more sophisticated studies matched specific strategy instruction taught explicitly in whole-group settings with particular technology features. For example, Graham and MacArthur

---

[26]Tutorials include commercial programs such as Mavis Beacon Teaches Typing (http://www.mavisbeacon.com/), and free Web sites that offer drills such as Learn2Type (http://www.learn2type.com/) and Touch Typing (http://www.senselang.com/).

(1988) found significant positive impact on students' writing from providing both instruction on revising strategies and on word processing revision strategies in the same class, in effect doubling the instructional intervention. They found that the number of revisions, the length and quality of compositions, and students' self-efficacy were positively affected.

Spell checkers, similarly, have been shown to be more effective when paired with strategy instruction on their uses. Although MacArthur, Graham, Haynes, and De La Paz (1996) found that middle school students with LD improved their error finding rate from 9% to 37% with the assistance of a spell checker, the compositions still had many errors not caught by the spell checker or the student (e.g., real—but incorrect—words). McNaughton, Hughes, and Ofiesh (1997), however, explicitly taught strategies to secondary students with LD to back up the spell checker, such as trying a phonetic typing of a misspelled word, proofreading a paper copy, or asking a peer to edit the paper copy. They found students were able to catch as many errors as their nondisabled peers. Lewis (1998) reported similar benefits of a "SpellCHECK" strategy for secondary students with LD. This set of strategies includes (a) check the beginning sound of the word, (b) hunt for correct consonants, (c) examine the vowels, (d) consult changes in the word list for hints, and (e) keep repeating each of the steps. Paper dictionaries, a word list, a peer, and a teacher were consulted as last resorts.

Other studies have focused on the impact of more specialized AT such as voice recognition programs. In an article called "Speaking to Read," Raskind and Higgins (1999) reported on their investigations of the effects of voice recognition software (Dragon Dictate, a "discrete" or word-by-word dictation version) to enhance basic reading skills for youth with LD. They found that students who used speech recognition software showed significantly more improvement than their control peers (taking a computer basics class) on word recognition, spelling, and reading comprehension. Additionally, their analysis found that improved phonological processing was associated with significant differences in all of the academic measures: word recognition, spelling, and reading comprehension.

Higgins and Raskind (2000) found that correction procedures in the voice recognition software were one of the most powerful learning experiences in their original study and were the focus of a follow-up extension study (Higgins & Raskind, 2000) that added an experimental group who used a then newly released continuous speech recognition program that allows more natural spoken input in phrases (Naturally Speaking). These students also showed significant gains in word recognition and reading comprehension, although the word-by-word dictation group showed stronger gains in spelling and phonological awareness measures. The continuous dictation group showed greater gains in working memory, discussed as a possible effect of dictating longer utterances. Correction procedures, wherein users are intensely comparing similar words (both on orthographic and phonologic features) to determine and train the program about their intended choice, are posited as key to the boost in literacy skills. They suggest, following Ehri (1984), Leong (1991), and Olson and Wise (1992), that multisensory print exposure, in this case provided by the visual, auditory, proprioceptive, and kinesthetic experience of using voice recognition, can enhance phonological awareness growth. Their work highlights the reciprocal relationship between reading and writing development.

Voice recognition software was recently studied as a viable accommodation on standardized tests for high school students. Traditionally, students who cannot write tests due to physical or writing disabilities are provided scribes, either a human scribe or a tape recorder into which the student speaks his or her text. MacArthur and Cavalier's (2004) investigation looked at how secondary students with ($n = 21$) and without LD ($n = 10$) performed on assigned writing prompts under three conditions (all students tried each option): handwriting, dictation to a human scribe, and use of voice recognition software. All students received 8 hours of training on the use of the software and voice training, as well as strategic use of graphic organizers and planning strategies for writing a persuasive essay. All but three students achieved recognition accuracy levels above 80%. Essays dictated to a human scribe were scored as being the highest in quality of composition, followed by those completed with the software, and then the handwritten essays. Dictation to a human was also considerably faster than either of the other two conditions; it was concluded that the time gained by avoiding spelling and handwriting with the software was balanced out by time spent on correction procedures. Overall, the students responded very positively to the voice recognition software and judged it to be helpful and worth using for future assignments. MacArthur and Cavalier concluded that the software can indeed be a valid accommodation, if—as is recommended for any accommodation to a test—students have trained to a level of comfort with the software and equipment prior to taking the test.

Summary. Identifying the roles technology can play in supporting struggling writers is an ongoing process because technology is quickly changing the nature of writing tasks, expectations, and practices for youth and adults; for example, correct spelling or mechanics in text messages in which the goal is to send as few characters or digits as possible and still be understood is quite different from standard writing. The research is clear, however, that technological features must be taught as part of a strategic, supported approach to writing for struggling students and those with mild disabilities. Adopting a gradual release model (Fisher & Frey, 2003), supplemented with technology, offers real promise.

Motivation and Persistence

Motivation is a crucial element for students who must work hard to succeed at literacy tasks. Such students have no (more) time to waste (Allington, 2000) and energizing their motivation and persistence early in their reentry into education is critical to their persistence in literacy programs (Quigley, 1998).

Although motivation is difficult to quantify, it is an important factor to study. Regardless of the literacy skill benefits found in the research, there is nearly unanimous enthusiasm among researchers about the potential of AT to affect the motivation of students with mild disabilities. Across age groups and settings, researchers and practitioners document the positive motivation generated among students with mild disabilities using technology. Features of the technological learning environment that students report enjoying include the novelty, the customizable interface (the unique way each person can use the technology), interactive features that allow them to explore and follow their own interests, newfound avenues for self-expression, the nonjudgmental nature of the interaction, the sense of boundless challenges, and the sense of independence and self-determined engagement.

The NCSALL Persistence Study (Comings, Parella, & Soricone, 1999) defines persistence among adult students as "staying in programs for as long as they can, engaging in self-directed study when they must drop out of their program, and returning to programs as soon as the demands of their lives allow" (p. 3). This definition recognizes the critical role motivation plays for adult literacy learners who might find the need to "stop out" of programs when their lives make regular classroom attendance difficult. Motivation is the force we draw on to persist and to surmount barriers that might interfere with achieving our goals. We need more research about the role access to technology can play in an adult's self-study.

Persistence on a particular task is important as well. Students who struggle and find literacy study stressful and exhausting are less likely to complete assignments or persist in class. As mentioned earlier, Elkind (1998) and others have found TTS and OCR technologies can provide a tremendous boost in speed (fluency), accuracy, and persistence or endurance for secondary and postsecondary students whose decoding skills are weak, thereby making it possible for them to keep up with reading requirements.

The participatory action research study from which the preceding case studies are drawn (Silver-Pacuilla, 2004) indicates that small group tutoring with AT for students with mild disabilities can be an enabling and empowering learning environment. Data are reported on 10 native English-speaking students who participated in the full project, representing wide ranges on many factors:

- Age: 19 to 62 years old.
- Time in the adult education program: 3 months to more than 10 years, with an average of 2 years.
- Ethnicity: 2 African American, 3 Hispanic, 5 White.
- Gender: 8 women, 2 men.
- Literacy levels: Preliteracy skills to GED test takers.
- Computer literacy: Complete novice to quite experienced (using e-mail and word processors daily).
- Time in formal schooling: 1 had not attended high school at all, 5 had completed 10 or 11 years of school, 4 were high school graduates.
- Cooccurrence of disabilities: 8 were diagnosed with LD, 7 of these had at least one other diagnosis including depression, bipolar disorder, ADHD, ADD, and epilepsy.

Assessments were given pre- and postparticipation, including the Test of Adult Basic Education, as well as standardized assessments of phonological awareness—Lindamood Auditory Conceptualization Test (LAC; Lindamood & Lindamood, 1979)—decoding, and spelling—Wide Range Achievement Test-3 (Wilkinson, 1993).

Participants attended 90-minute sessions with AT and a literacy coach once or twice a week while they were enrolled in a class at the adult education program, averaging 16 hours per semester with the AT and coach. Like Reder and Strawn's (2001) survey findings, the participants in this study recognized the necessity of self-study in addition to their classroom instruction. The participants began early in the investigation to talk about the benefit of study time in the AT lab. They related home environments that were noisy and interruptive and literacy skills and strategies that were unproductive. "I just read it and read it and read it," one woman said, "I just can't get anywhere with it by myself." When they came to the AT lab, they were able to study as the serious and motivated students they wanted to be. They were able to work through their class assignments or personal literacy tasks in an organized and strategic manner, effectively using the technology, electronic references, and resources. They relied on the coach equally as a "frustration buffer" for technology glitches and as a tutor to explain and demonstrate computer and software features as well as literacy tasks and assignments.

Even students with the lowest literacy skills were able, with coaching, to learn how to access personally motivating and relevant materials. They demonstrated this learning by making use of their new skills and confidence on home or library computers, away from the coaching support. One woman pursued an interest in classical art, visiting museums online and listening to the descriptions of the art and biographies of the artist through a TTS engine. Another woman began journaling with voice recognition software, fulfilling a desire to write about her parenting experiences with an emotionally challenged child. After one session, she held the printed paper in her hand in amazement, marveling at how professional it looked, and reflected:

> I feel really good because it's . . . I mean I could not have done this on my own . . . I'm like looking at it and it's like . . . I'm still not sure [about] commas and where you have to have your periods and stuff. I'm still a little confused on that. But other than that I think I really did a really good job on it . . . I definitely have learned that you could go back and fix it and then it teaches you how to say it right. And it fixes the mistakes I've done. But you know, without any of this, I would not be able to write this the way I did, you know, and . . . So like with this, I could actually show my son and it's spelled right.

She was proud to be able to take this paper home and show her son, who often sneered at her spelling and handwriting. As she looked at the printed text, she commented that it felt as if it was and it wasn't her work: "I mean, it's like my own words, but the bad . . . like, the bad is not in there." She gestured shaking a sieve, as if she had filtered out her spelling difficulties or her learning disabilities. "It just . . . I don't know, makes me feel like I do have intelligence."

Students' posttest results showed that, by increasing their active engagement with print, they had improved their fundamental understanding of oral-to-print connections so crucial to future literacy learning. Phonological awareness and spelling abilities showed the most significant growth, increasing by an average of more than three grade levels for phonological awareness (on the LAC) and an average of one grade level in spelling (on the WRAT-3). This jump in phonological awareness represents students' change from preschool-equivalent levels of ability to articulate whatever phonological awareness they had, to being able to segment, blend, and identify sounds within words on an assessment that uses colored blocks to represent sounds.

Moreover, these participants reported that the supported access to mainstream technology and AT helped them envision even greater goals and means of achieving them, and enhanced their sense of self-determination through promoting feelings of competence and self-efficacy. Dormant dreams of college and careers were reignited, and students reported feeling more empowered in their roles as parents and workers. They even reported that their new technology-supported study habits seeped into the fabric of their family life with children, spouses, and extended family members who became intrigued with what the technology could do to support learning and inquiry.

Summary. Self-determination is a critical element for adult education students with mild disabilities (Corley & Taymans, 2002). Because they have experienced years of school failure or discouragement, is it important to engage them early in practices that can nurture both literacy learning and self-determination. Mainstream technology and AT provide a new avenue for literacy practitioners and researchers to study persistence, motivation, self-determination, and the role of self-study in adult literacy learning.

Integration Into a Well-Designed Curriculum

Research indicates that AT does not reach its full potential as an add-on or literacy patch. Technology must be integrated into a well-designed instructional effort and transformed curriculum (Leu et al., 2004; MacArthur et al., 2001; Maccini, Gagnon, & Hughes, 2002). Several themes emerge from these reviews:

- The use of the AT tool or application must be presented through effective teaching strategies for adults with LD, which include explicit and multisensory guided practice, interactive small group and peer group settings, and a focus both on skills and strategies.

- The particular tool or application and the features it offers must be thoughtfully matched with the individual's cognitive profile and the specific literacy task; for example, a student with fairly strong keyboarding skills may prefer word prediction over voice recognition to support composition efforts.
- AT tools and applications have the potential to "collapse" the levels and stages of literacy inherent in learning to read print-based text (McKenna, 1998); for example, TTS supports decoding and fluency processes simultaneously.
- The full potential of the AT and the features embedded within programs cannot be realized unless the standard or traditional instruction and curriculum is transformed; that is, the program should not just add on time for activities using technology but must specifically integrate them throughout the lesson and through all instructional activities.

An instructive example of technology used to supplement a full curriculum comes from developmental education programs in community colleges. Developmental education programs at community colleges focus on retaining students who are underprepared for college-level classes and provide wraparound student support services (e.g., tutoring, child care referrals, transportation vouchers, etc.; Casazza, 1998). These programs increasingly share much of the content and many of the same students as adult education programs (Morest, 2004; Reder, 1999). According to *What Works* (Boylan, 2002), the summative evaluation of a national network on developmental education, and a literature review of the use of technology in college reading programs (Caverly & Peterson, 2000), technology is best used as a supplement to course instruction.

Supplemental instruction, in fact, is a cornerstone of effective developmental education. Supplemental instruction provides a content-knowledgeable coach along with alternative means to explore the course content, such as related Internet resources or course materials, and allows the student to engage in effective study sessions. Accessible technologies and peer learning opportunities are posited as the keys to participants' success in these supplemental classes.

Unfortunately, a great number of developmental education advisors and faculty remain uninformed about the instructional and institutional ramifications of the Americans with Disabilities Act, technology uses and innovations, and the disability rights movement (Doña & Edmister, 2001; Leyser, Vogel, Wyland, & Brulle, 1998; Roessler & Kirk, 1998), thereby limiting the full potential of supplemental education.

Summary. A reevaluation of the curriculum and teaching methods must accompany supplemental access to technology to realize significant benefits for students. Access must be accompanied by strategic instruction in the use of the features and tools. Teaching the features within the curriculum of the class deepens the learning of both and shifts the responsibilities to students for their own studying. Creative scheduling and community partnering as well as the use of peer and near-peer tutors and coaches can open opportunities to provide supplemental instruction that meets these needs.

IMPLICATIONS FOR PRACTICE, POLICY, AND RESEARCH

AT can play many roles in literacy development for adult students. However, this chapter is not a definitive review of all of those roles: There are other types of software and devices for literacy development; other ways that technology can be used to support content areas such as English as a second language, mathematics, science, social studies, and so on; and there will be new technologies and improved versions by the time this volume reaches readers. However, this chapter joins a growing dialogue (Askov, Johnston, Petty, & Young, 2003; Ginsburg, 2004; Stites, 2003) on the use of mainstream technology and AT in adult education as a part of a transformed and transformative literacy pedagogy. The following are some suggestions and implications for practice, policy, and research.

Practice

Just as Freire (1970), Purcell-Gates, Degener, Jacobson, and Soler (2002), and Purcell-Gates and Waterman (2000) emphasized in their literacy work, this review demonstrates that there is no "lower limit" on literacy levels, both for traditional print and computer literacy, for those who can benefit from increased access to literacy. There is no doubt that the level of incoming literacy and computer literacy affects how easily and confidently students approach learning to use computer-based AT and how quickly they are able to assimilate the technologies into their understanding of literacy practices, but students at even the lowest levels of literacy can benefit. As emphasized earlier, the role of the coach, instructor, tutor, or peer remains crucial in the success of students with mild disabilities.

A two-pronged approach is necessary to address the "performance gap" for students with disabilities; they need to develop learning strategies for independence as well as build their foundational skills (Deshler et al., 2001). Such an approach requires us as adult educators and researchers to shift our perspectives beyond scrambling to provide accommodations to poorly designed curriculum materials or methods, or insisting that learners with low-level skills master ABE materials before allowing them access to GED and college preparatory content. Instead, we must imagine, demand, and create materials and learning environments that provide access and benefits to students at multiple levels and for multiple purposes. Supplemental instruction, including supported access to mainstream technology and AT for struggling students, holds tremendous potential to be an enabling and empowering learning environment.

Participants in the action research study (Silver-Pacuilla, 2004) encourage instructors and tutors to "try it"—engage with students as colearners of the technology. The free TTS engines ReadPlease[27] and Microsoft Reader[28] require only Internet access, patience, and curiosity to download and explore with students. Free e-books to download into Reader can be found through the University of Virginia's e-library,[29] Project Gutenberg,[30] and increasingly through a simple Internet search. Subscribing to a free, online journal that addresses educational technology practice (see several listed in the Appendix) can help teachers and tutors learn more about how to integrate technology into the teaching and learning environment. Sharing these journals and explorations with colleagues can help bridge the gap from research to practice as teachers work to relate the practices to their particular situations.

Policy

Students with disabilities have the right to accessible learning environments and experiences. Programs are mandated to provide accommodations. Too often, the traditional adult education classroom, teaching, and materials do not meet the needs of students with disabilities, even when basic accommodations are provided. Reconceptualizing literacy practices and services for students with mild disabilities includes examining the roles and benefits mainstream technology and AT can bring to their learning.

---

[27]See http://www.readplease.com.
[28]See http://www.microsoft.com/reader/default.asp.
[29]See http://etext.lib.virginia.edu/.
[30]See http://www.gutenberg.org/.

Programs grapple with resource issues related to technology integration such as hardware and software costs, maintenance, and upgrading. Physical spaces are not always prepared or appropriate for the installation of technology. Teachers and tutors need professional development to gain confidence to integrate technology into their instruction strategically. Addressing these concerns and realities will require creativity, funds, and collaboration.

Program administrators and policymakers can reach out to other programs in the community that serve adults with disabilities. Vocational rehabilitation agencies are important partners for adult education programs. Their mission is to assist adults with disabilities to gain employment and independence and they have a vast network of support and resources—including AT—that can be made available to eligible students. AT centers in communities across the country are available for information, demonstrations, and referrals (check local directories and a national association of AT centers at http://www.ataccess.org). Starting a community conversation can lead to a sharing of resources, knowledge, and commitment. As always, involvement of students in the process leads to more collaborative planning, service, and evaluation.

Federal- and state-level leadership and funds should address this issue. Legislation for federally funded programs needs to include language that recognizes the importance of AT for adults with LD, and the government should provide funds for specialized equipment, software, and professional development. Additionally, the need for more flexibility and availability of accommodations on standardized tests and the GED should be a strong point of advocacy. As more research is published validating the use of accommodations on standardized assessments for secondary and postsecondary students, pressure should be applied to the government to make similar policy adjustments to the provision of accommodations for GED test takers.

Research

A research base documenting the impact of AT in adult education is sparse. Therefore, we need a research agenda that builds on what is currently known about both adult learning and the effectiveness of AT for secondary and postsecondary students with mild disabilities.

The adult education field should outline a research agenda to learn how students benefit from electronic and supported text, how the features of computer-based technologies help users—both native and nonnative speakers of English—learn about language, and how education programs can best integrate their teaching with technology. Furthermore, this agenda needs to investigate how AT can assist youth and adults with mild disabilities to become more self-determined and persistent in their studying, learning, and goal setting. This agenda most likely needs to start with more participatory action research and situated case study analyses of the integration of technology into literacy instruction, designs that can capture incidental and hidden effects and "offer signposts" (Miller & Olson, 1998, p. 357) of the complexities and the possibilities to other educators and researchers. Such signposts could help practitioners apply and generalize research findings from other postsecondary and community settings.

At the same time, the evaluation of technology integration needs to heed the tenets of adult learning principles and include the voices and reflections of adult learners (Kasworm & Londoner, 2000; Stites, 2003). Students need to be empowered to participate in, conduct, and report research on their own learning, including how technologies affect their literacy practices in and out of the classroom.

Summary. Much more work needs to be done to understand how students benefit from electronic and supported text, how the features of computer-based technologies help users teach themselves about language, and how adult education instructors and programs can best integrate their teaching with technology. The reality that many adult education students with mild disabilities are not succeeding in existing programs and that programs report they are not prepared to teach them raises difficult questions of access and accommodations. If "who we are and how we act is as much a function of what is at hand as of what is in head" (Lemke, 1998, p. 286), then a key concern should be to get more appropriate materials, tools, and learning environments in place for students. Accessible mainstream technology and AT represent an opportunity to transform our literacy instruction in ways that put much more creative control in the hands—and heads—of the students with mild disabilities.

REFERENCES

Allinder, R. M., Dunse, L., Brunken, C. D., & Obermiller-Krolikowski, H. J. (2001). Improving fluency in at-risk readers and students with learning disabilities. *Remedial and Special Education, 22,* 48–54.
Allington, R. L. (2000). *What really matters for struggling students: Designing research-based programs.* New York: Longman.

Anderson-Inman, L., & Horney, M. A. (1999). Electronic books: Reading and studying with supportive resources. *Journal of Adult and Adolescent Literacy, 40,* 486–491.

Askov, E. N., Johnston, J., Petty, L. I., & Young, S. J. (2003). *Expanding access to adult literacy with online distance education.* Cambridge, MA: National Center for Adult Learning and Literacy. Retrieved September 23, 2004, from http://www.ncsall.net/index.php?id=26

Assistive Technology Act (2004). H.R. 4278.

Bos, C. S., & Anders, P. L. (1990). Effects of interactive vocabulary instruction on the vocabulary learning and reading comprehension of junior-high learning disabled students. *Learning Disabilities Quarterly, 13,* 31–42.

Boylan, H. R. (2002). *What works: Research-based best practices in developmental education.* Boone, NC: Continuous Quality Improvement Network with the National Center for Developmental Education.

Bryant, D. P., Goodwin, M., Bryant, B. R., & Higgins, K. (2003). Vocabulary instruction for students with learning disabilities: A review of the research. *Learning Disability Quarterly, 26,* 117–128.

Casazza, M. (1998). Who are we and where did we come from? *Journal of Developmental Education, 23,* 2–7.

Caverly, D. C., & Peterson, C. L. (2000). Technology and college reading. In R. F. Flippo & D. C. Caverly (Eds.), *Handbook of college reading and study strategy research* (pp. 291–320). Mahwah, NJ: Lawrence Erlbaum Associates, Inc.

Comings, J., Parella, A., & Soricone, L. (1999). *Persistence among adult basic education students in pre-GED classes* (NCSALL Rep. No. 12). Cambridge, MA: National Center for the Study of Adult Learning and Literacy.

Corley, M. A., & Taymans, J. M. (2002). Adults with learning disabilities: A review of the literature. In J. Comings, B. Garner, & C. Smith (Eds.), *Annual review of adult learning and literacy* (Vol. 3, pp. 44–83). San Francisco: Jossey-Bass.

Dalton, B., Pisha, B., Eagleton, M., Coyne, P., & Dysher, S. (2001). Engaging the text: Strategy instruction in a computer-supported reading environment for struggling readers (OSEP Project Final Rep.). Retrieved May 18, 2004, from http://www.cast.org/udl/downloads/EngagTextResearchRept_12-02.pdf

Dawson, L., Venn, M. L., & Gunter, P. L. (2000). The effects of teacher versus computer reading models. *Behavioral Disorders, 25,* 105–113.

Deshler, D. D., Schumaker, J. B., Lenz, B. K., Bulgren, J. A., Hock, M. F., Knight, J., et al. (2001). Ensuring content-area learning by secondary students with learning disabilities. *Learning Disabilities Research and Practice, 16,* 96–108.

Doña, J., & Edmister, J. H. (2001). An examination of community college faculty members' knowledge of the Americans with Disabilities Act of 1990 at the 15 community colleges in Mississippi. *Journal of Postsecondary Education and Disability, 14*(2). Retrieved July 5, 2004, from http://www.ahead.org/jped/JPED/vol14-2-a.html

Dowhower, S. (1994). Repeated reading revisited: Research into practice. *Reading & Writing Quarterly: Overcoming Learning Difficulties, 10,* 343–358.

Edyburn, D. L. (1991). Fact retrieval by students with and without learning handicaps using print and electronic encyclopedias. *Journal of Special Education Technology, 11*(2), 75–90.

Edyburn, D. L. (2000). Assistive technology and students with mild disabilities. *Focus on Exceptional Children, 32*(9), 1–24.

Edyburn, D. L. (2004). Measuring assistive technology outcomes in reading. *Journal of Special Education Technology, 19.* Retrieved June 21, 2004, from http://jset.unlv.edu/19.1/asseds/edyburn.html

Ehri, L. (1984). How orthography alters spoken language competencies in children learning to read and spell. In J. Downing & R. Valtin (Eds.), *Language awareness and learning to read* (pp. 119–147). New York: Springer-Verlag.

Elkind, J. (1998). Computer reading machines for poor readers. *Perspectives, 24*(2), 9–13.
Elkind, J., Black, M., & Murray, C. (1996). Computer-based compensation of adult reading disabilities. *Annals of Dyslexia, 46,* 159–186.
Elkind, J., Cohen, K., & Murray, C. (1993). Using computer-based readers to improve reading comprehension of students with dyslexia. *Annals of Dyslexia, 42,* 238–259.
Fernald, G. (1943). *Remedial techniques in basic school subjects.* New York: McGraw-Hill.
Fisher, D., & Frey, N. (2003). Writing instruction for struggling adolescent readers: A gradual release model. *Journal of Adolescent & Adult Literacy, 46,* 396–405.
Freire, P. (1970). *Pedagogy of the oppressed* (M. B. Ramos, Trans.). New York: Continuum.
Ginsburg, L. (2004). *Adult literacy practitioners' readiness to use technology in the classroom: A five state survey in 2002–2003.* Philadelphia: National Center on Adult Literacy. Retrieved September 22, 2004, from http://www.tech21.org
Graham, S., & MacArthur, C. (1988). Improving learning disabled students' skills at revising essays produced on a word processor: Self instructional strategy training. *Journal of Special Education, 22,* 133–152.
Greenberg, D., Ehri, L., & Perin, D. (1997). Are word-reading processes the same or different in adult literacy students and third-fifth graders matched for reading level? *Journal of Educational Psychology, 89,* 262–275.
Grossman, P. D. (November–December 2001). Making accommodations: The legal world of students with disabilities. 87 Academe. *Bulletin of the American Association of University Professors,* pp. 41–46.
Heckelman, R. G. (1986). N.I.M. revisited: An update on the Neurological Impress Method and the presenting technique. *Academic Therapy, 21,* 411–421.
Hecker, L., Burns, L., Elkind, J., Elkind, K., & Katz, L. (2002). Benefits of assistive reading software for students with attention disorders. *Annals of Dyslexia, 52,* 243–272.
Higgins, E. L., & Raskind, M. H. (2000). Speaking to read: The effects of continuous vs. discrete speech recognition systems on the reading and spelling of children with learning disabilities. *Journal of Special Education Technology, 15,* 19–30.
Hinchman, K. A., Alvermann, D. E., Boyd, F. B., Brozo, W. G., & Vacca, R. T. (2003–2004). Supporting older students' in- and out-of-school literacies. *Journal of Adolescent and Adult Literacy, 47,* 304–310.
Jitendra, A., Edwards, L., Sacks, G., & Jacobson, L. (2004). What research says about vocabulary instruction for students with learning disabilities. *Exceptional Children, 70,* 299–347.
Kanellos, M. (2003). Talking computers nearing reality. Cnet News.com. Retrieved May 15, 2004, from http://news.com.com/2104-1008-1023966.html?tag=bigpic
Kasworm, C. E., & Londoner, C. A. (2000). Adult learning and technology. In A. L. Wilson & E. R. Hayes (Eds.), *Handbook of adult and continuing education* (pp. 224–242). San Francisco: Jossey-Bass.
Kaufman, P., Alt, M. N., & Chapman, C. D. (2001). *Executive summary of the statistical analysis report of dropout rates in the United States: 2000.* Washington, DC: U.S. Department of Education, National Center for Education Statistics.
Kelly, J. (2004). Why speech now? *Speech Technology Magazine, 9*(2). Retrieved April 7, 2004, from http://www.speechtechmag.com/issues/9_2/
Kruidenier, J. (2002). *Research-based principles for adult basic education reading instruction.* Portsmouth, NH: RMC Research.
Lankshear, C., & Knobel, M. (2003). *New literacies: Changing knowledge in the classroom.* Buckingham, UK: Open University Press.
Lemke, J. L. (1998). Metamedia literacy: Transforming meanings and media. In D. Reinking, M. C. McKenna, L. D. Labbo, & R. D. Kieffer (Eds.), *Handbook of literacy and technology: Transformations in a post-typographic world* (pp. 283–302). Mahwah, NJ: Lawrence Erlbaum Associates, Inc.

Leong, C. K. (1991). From phonemic awareness to phonological processing to language access in children developing reading proficiency. In O. J. Sawyer & B. J. Fox (Eds.), *Phonological awareness in reading: The evolution of current perspectives* (pp. 217–254). New York: Springer-Verlag.

Leu, D. J., Jr., Kinzer, C. K., Coiro, J. L., & Cammack, D. W. (2004). Toward a theory of new literacies: Emerging from the Internet and other information and communication technologies. In R. B. Ruddell & N. J. Unrau (Eds.), *Theoretical models and processes of reading* (5th ed., pp. 1570–1613). Newark, DE: International Reading Association.

Lewis, R. B. (1998). Musing on technology and learning disabilities on the occasion of the new millennium. *Journal of Special Education Technology, 15.* Available online at http://jset.unlv.edu/

Leyser, Y., Vogel, S., Wyland, S., & Brulle, A. (1998). Faculty attitudes and practices regarding students with disabilities: Two decades after implementation of Section 504. *Journal of Postsecondary Education and Disability, 13*(3). Retrieved July 5, 2004, from http://www.ahead.org/jped/JPED13-3-a.html

Lindamood, C. H., & Lindamood, P. C. (1979). *Lindamood Auditory Conceptualization Test–Revised.* Austin, TX: PRO-ED.

Luke, A. (2000). Critical literacy in Australia: A matter of context and standpoint. *Journal of Adolescent and Adult Literacy, 43,* 448–461.

Luke, A., & Freebody, P. (1997). The social practice of reading. In S. Muspratt, A. Luke, & P. Freebody (Eds.), *Constructing critical literacies: Teaching and learning textual practice* (pp. 185–226). Cresskill, NJ: Hampton.

MacArthur, C. A. (2000). New tools for writing: Assistive technology for students with writing difficulties. *Topics in Language Disorders, 20,* 85–100.

MacArthur, C. A., & Cavalier, A. R. (2004). Dictation and speech recognition technology as test accommodations. *Exceptional Children, 71,* 43–58.

MacArthur, C. A., Ferretti, R. P., Okolo, C. M., & Cavalier, A. R. (2001). Technology applications for students with literacy problems: A critical review. *The Elementary School Journal, 101,* 273–300.

MacArthur, C. A., Graham, S., Haynes, J. A., & De La Paz, S. (1996). Spelling checkers and students with learning disabilities: Performance comparisons and impact on spelling. *Journal of Special Education, 30,* 35–57.

Maccini, P., Gagnon, J., & Hughes, C. (2002). Technology-based practices for secondary students with learning disabilities. *Learning Disabilities Quarterly, 25,* 247–261.

McKenna, M. D. (1998). Electronic texts and the transformation of beginning reading. In D. Reinking, M. C. McKenna, L. D. Labbo, & R. D. Kieffer (Eds.), *Handbook of literacy and technology: Transformations in a post-typographic world* (pp. 45–59). Mahwah, NJ: Lawrence Erlbaum Associates, Inc.

McNaughton, D., Hughes, C., & Ofiesh, N. (1997). Proofreading for students with learning disabilities: Integrating computer use and strategy use. *Learning Disabilities Research and Practice, 12,* 16–28.

Meyer, M. S., & Felton, R. H. (1999). Repeated readings to enhance fluency: Old approaches and new directions. *Annals of Dyslexia, 49,* 283–306.

Michaels, C. A., Prezant, F. P., Morabito, S. M., & Jackson, K. (2002). Assistive and instructional technology for college students with disabilities: A national snapshot of postsecondary service providers. *Journal of Special Education Technology, 17*(1), 5–14.

Miller, L., & Olson, J. (1998). Literacy research oriented toward features of technology and classrooms. In D. Reinking, M. C. McKenna, L. D. Labbo, & R. D. Kieffer (Eds.), *Handbook of literacy and technology: Transformations in a post-typographic world* (pp. 343–360). Mahwah, NJ: Lawrence Erlbaum Associates, Inc.

Montali, J., & Lewandowski, L. (1996). Bimodal reading: Benefits of a talking computer for average and less skilled readers. *Journal of Learning Disabilities, 29,* 271–279.

Morest, V. S. (2004). *The role of community colleges in state adult education systems: A national analysis.* New York: Council for the Advancement of Adult Literacy. Retreived July 5, 2004, from http://www.caalusa.org/

Mull, C. A., & Sitlington, P. L. (2003). The role of technology in the transition to postsecondary education of students with learning disabilities: A review of the literature. *Journal of Special Education, 37,* 26–32.

National Adult Literacy and Learning Disabilities Center. (1999). *Bridges to practice: A research-based guide for literacy practitioners serving adults with learning disabilities.* Washington, DC: National Institute for Literacy.

National Institute of Child Health and Human Development. (2000). *The report of the National Reading Panel: Teaching children to read. An evidence-based assessment of the scientific research literature on reading and its implications for reading instruction.* Washington, DC: U.S. Government Printing Office.

Nist, S. L., & Holschuh, J. L. (2000). Comprehension strategies at the college level. In R. F. Flippo & D. C. Caverly (Eds.), *Handbook of college reading and study strategy research* (pp. 75–104). Mahwah, NJ: Lawrence Erlbaum Associates, Inc.

Office of Special Education Programs. (2000). *Annual report.* Washington, DC: U.S. Department of Education. Retrieved July 1, 2004, from http://www.ed.gov/about/reports/annual/osep/2002/index.html

Olson, R. K., & Wise, B. W. (1992). Reading on the computer with orthographic and speech feedback. *Reading and Writing: An Interdisciplinary Journal, 4,* 107–144.

Orton, S. T. (1966). *Word-blindness in school children and other papers on strephosymbolia.* Baltimore: Orton Dyslexia Society. (Original work published 1932)

Purcell-Gates, V., Degener, S., Jacobson, E., & Soler, M. (2002). Impact of authentic adult literacy instruction on adult literacy practices. *Reading Research Quarterly, 37,* 70–92.

Purcell-Gates, V., & Waterman, R. A. (2000). *Now we read, we see, we speak: Portrait of literacy development in an adult Freirian-based class.* Mahwah, NJ: Lawrence Erlbaum Associates, Inc.

Quigley, A. B. (1998). The first three weeks: A critical time for motivation. *Focus on Basics,* 2(Issue A). Retrieved September 25, 2004, from http://www.gse.harvard.edu/~ncsall/

Raskind, M. H., & Higgins, E. L. (1999). Speaking to read: The effects of speech recognition technology on the reading and spelling performance of children with learning disabilities. *Annals of Dyslexia, 69,* 251–282.

Reder, S. (1999). Adult literacy and postsecondary education students: Overlapping populations and learning trajectories. In J. Comings, B. Garner, & C. Smith (Eds.), *The annual review of adult learning and literacy* (Vol. 1). Cambridge, MA: National Center for the Study of Adult Learning and Literacy.

Reder, S., & Strawn, C. (2001). Program participation and self-directed learning to improve basic skills (Focus on Basics, Vol. 4). Cambridge, MA: National Center for the Study of Adult Learning and Literacy.

Reitsma, P. (1988). Reading practice for beginners: Effects of guided reading, reading-while-listening, and independent reading with computer-based speech feedback. *Reading Research Quarterly, 23,* 219–235.

Roessler, R. T., & Kirk, H. M. (1998). Improving technology training services in postsecondary education: Perspectives of recent college graduates with disabilities. *Journal of Postsecondary Education and Disability, 13*(3).

Rose, D., & Meyer, A. (2002). *Teaching every student in the digital age: Universal design for learning.* Alexandria, VA: Association for Supervision and Curriculum Development.

Samuels, S. (2002). Reading fluency: Its development and assessment. In A. Farstrup & S. Samuels (Eds.), *What research has to say about reading instruction* (pp. 166–183). Newark, DE: International Reading Association.

Scanlon, D., & Lenz, B. K. (2002). Intervention practices in adult literacy education for adults with learning disabilities. *Journal of Postsecondary Education and Disability, 16,* 32–49.

Schulte, A., Conners, C., & Osborne, S. (1999). Linkages between attention deficit disorders and reading disability. In D. D. Duane (Ed.), *Reading and attention disorders* (pp. 161–184). Baltimore, MD: York Press.

Silver-Pacuilla, H. V. (2004). *Assistive technology and adult literacy: Bridging the gap for adults with learning disabilities: Final report.* Washington, DC: National Institute for Disability and Rehabilitation Research (NARIC Accession No. 015274).

Simpson, M. L., & Randall, S. N. (2000). Vocabulary development at the college level. In R. F. Flippo & D. C. Caverly (Eds.), *Handbook of college reading and study strategy research* (pp. 43–74). Mahwah, NJ: Lawrence Erlbaum Associates, Inc.

Stites, R. (2003). Implications for new learning technologies for adult literacy and learning. In J. Comings, B. Garner, & C. Smith (Eds.), *The annual review of adult learning and literacy* (Vol. 4). Cambridge, MA: National Center for the Study of Adult Learning and Literacy.

Stodden, R., & Conway, M. (2002). Supporting youth with disabilities to access and succeed in postsecondary education. *National Center on Secondary Education Transition (NCSET) Issue Brief, 1*(5). Retrieved July 3, 2003, from http://www.ncset.org/publications/default.asp#issue

Sturomski, N., Lenz, K., Scanlon, D., & Catts, H. (1998). The National Adult Literacy and Learning Disabilities Center: Standards, criteria, procedures, and strategies for screening and teaching adults with learning disabilities. In S. Vogel & S. Reder (Eds.), *Learning disabilities, literacy, and adult education* (pp. 93–106). Baltimore: Brookes.

Swanson, H. L., & Hoskyn, M. (1998). Experimental intervention research on students with learning disabilities: A meta-analysis of treatment outcomes. *Review of Educational Research, 68,* 277–321.

Technology-Related Assistance for Individuals With Disabilities Act of 1988 (1988). P.L.100-407 and 103-218.

Vaughn, S., Gersten, R., & Chard, D. J. (2000). The underlying message in LD intervention research: Findings from research syntheses. *Exceptional Children, 67,* 99–114.

Watts, E., O'Brian, M., & Wojcik, B. (2004). Four models of assistive technology consideration: How do they compare to recommended educational assessment practices? *Journal of Special Education Technology, 19.* Available online at http://jset.unlv.edu/

Wilkinson, G. (1993). *Wide Range Achievement Test-3.* Wilmington, DE: Wide Range.

APPENDIX

RESOURCES

Information on Learning Disabilities

LDOnLine: http://www.ldonline.org
and
SchwabLearning.org: http://www.schwablearning.org/index.asp

Both sites contain articles (new and archived, some in Spanish), chat rooms, book reviews, artwork, experts on call, and free monthly e-newsletters. Both sites pay attention to common cooccurring difficulties, such as ADHD. The focus is on children, but both sites cover adult issues well.
Dyslexic Adult Link (DAL): http://www.dyslexia-adults.com/index.htm
DAL features articles (new and archived), links to news articles, book reviews, and areas of interest e-bulletin boards. It focuses on adults with dyslexia.
The National Organization on Disability (NOD): http://www.nod.org/
The NOD Web site offers articles, news, and advocacy for adults and children with disabilities. It includes updated statistics, surveys, legislation, and so on.
The National Association for Adults with Special Learning Needs (NAASLN): http://www.naasln.org/
This is a site for advocates, educators, and adult learners.

Technology and Teaching

Contemporary Issues in Technology and Teacher Education (CITE): http://www.citejournal.org/
This journal covers many areas of technology and teacher education. It is a refereed, free online journal.
International Society for Technology in Education (ISTE): http://www.iste.org/
The ISTE publication *Learning and Leading With Technology* features articles on curriculum studies, equity in technology, telecommunications, computer science, and multimedia. It is an editor-reviewed journal.
T.H.E. Journal: http://www.thejournal.com/
This journal reports on curriculum studies, education management and administration, and educational technology systems.
The Center for Applied Research in Educational Technology (CARET): http://caret.iste.org/
CARET provides online articles, frequently asked questions, resources, an annual conference, and more.
Adult Literacy and Technology Network (ALTN): http://www.altn.org
ALTN is an association of adult educators dedicated to improving adult education through technology. It holds workshops and preconference sessions at major adult education conferences.

Assistive Technology

ABLEDATA: http://www.abledata.com/
ABLEDATA is a clearinghouse of AT information, links, and products.
Assistive Technology Industry Association (ATIA): http:// www.atia.org/
The ATIA Web site features links to member businesses and offers an online journal.
The Alliance for Technology Access (ATA): http://www.ataccess.org
The ATA is a member organization of community or statewide AT training and information centers. The Web site features the Hub—a search engine of AT devices, manufacturers, and product information, including many online demonstrations or video tours of products.

5

Individualized Group Instruction: A Reality of Adult Basic Education

Perrine Robinson-Geller

Observations of classes suggest that English for speakers of other languages (ESOL) programs typically employ group instruction and volunteer programs use one-on-one instruction, but adult basic education (ABE) and general educational development (GED) programs use a hybrid model of instruction (Beder, Tomkins, Medina, Riccioni, & Deng, 2006), in which students gather in a group with a teacher but work independently on individualized assignments while the teacher assigns work, corrects student work, keeps records, and assists students as needed. In this chapter, we refer to this hybrid model of instruction as individualized group instruction (IGI).[31] In IGI, a group of students has a set time and place for class and a specific teacher. In other words, it is a setting that could be run as a traditional teacher-led, whole-group class. However, the students work independently, on individually assigned work, although one-on-one interactions with the teacher occur as students need help.

---

[31] John Comings coined this term in a meeting at Rutgers University in 2003.

Teachers alternate between helping students, correcting, and assigning new work.

In the 1960s and early 1970s, the adult education field referred to this type of instruction as *individualized instruction* but this term does not distinguish either self-study or one-on-one tutoring from *in-class* individualized instruction. The benefit of using a specific term (IGI) for individualized in-class instruction is that it describes more clearly a common type of instruction practice. This article describes IGI; the factors that led to and perpetuate IGI; the prevalence of IGI in the ABE field now; what is known about the effectiveness of IGI; and implications for policy, practice, and research related to IGI.

> **Terminology**
>
> ABE programs generally divide their classes into three major groups: ABE (adult native speakers reading at the 0-8 level), adult secondary education ([ASE], often GED students reading at the 9-12 level), and ESOL. ABE is further divided into low-level adult literacy students (nonreaders and very low-level readers at the 0-4 level), and the pre-GED students (adults reading at the 5-8 grade level). IGI is commonly found in ABE, pre-GED, and GED classes, but not in ESOL classes, which are usually grouped by oral language level (beginning, intermediate, and advanced), and learner-to-learner interaction is considered essential to oral language acquisition. This chapter uses ABE to encompass ABE, pre-GED, ASE, and GED classes, but it excludes volunteer one-on-one tutoring programs. Because the focus of this chapter is on ABE classes, I refrain from using the broader term adult education, which covers everything from literacy learners to professional continuing education and leisure learning.

METHODOLOGY

Because little has been written about IGI, our research team at Rutgers University conducted a comprehensive literature review about the history of IGI. The team also conducted an informal e-mail survey of state directors of adult education regarding the incidence of IGI in their state. In addition, the team conducted 19 interviews with people who have been involved in adult literacy education for many years. To locate interviewees who were involved in ABE when IGI became an accepted model of instruction, we posted a request on national ABE listservs; from those who responded, we selected participants who had both long tenure in the field and extensive backgrounds in ABE instruction. The respondents averaged 25 years of experience in ABE, with a range from 3 years to more than 50 years of experience. Respondents were current and former teachers, staff developers, program administrators, state-level administrators (including former state directors), researchers, and instructional-materials vendors. We used the data from the literature and the interviews to identify themes and issues about the use of IGI in ABE classrooms.

Description of IGI

IGI is not generally found in the K–12 or higher education context, but it has been a part of ABE since the modern era of ABE began in the late 1960s and early 1970s. IGI appealed to ABE practitioners because it was a manageable solution to the difficulties of serving the unique needs of adult students who are not required to be in classes, who fit classes in and around their busy schedules, who read at many different levels, and whose education competes with many other demands of life for their attention and energy. Although IGI is a very common approach to dealing with these unique needs, it is nearly invisible in the research and practitioner literature.

There are few descriptions of IGI in the ABE literature. Quigley (1997) presented a fictionalized account of a typical adult student's initial encounter with a classroom, which is in fact an IGI class. The student arrives at an ongoing class, with intake test results in hand, and a teacher assigns a workbook based on a review of the student's scores. The student is told to sit at a table, read a passage, and then try to answer the questions at the end. The teacher tells the student that she will be back to check on her in a while and then works with other students, eventually coming back to the new student to correct her work.

Beder and Medina (2001) conducted an observational study of 20 ABE classrooms in eight states. Their description of classrooms provides a picture of an IGI setting:

> Learners in classes practicing individualized instruction were typically assigned folders or portfolios to hold their work. When students came to class, they picked up their folders, which often contained work the teacher had corrected since the last class. The learners then worked independently on sequenced materials that were commercially published. When learners had

difficulty with an exercise, they called on a teacher or aide for assistance, and help was given, sometimes in the form of a one-on-one mini-lesson. (p. 47)

IGI takes several forms. In some IGI classes, students never work in groups and structured interaction between students is minimal; students work individually through their workbooks or textbooks. In other IGI classes, students sometimes gather in impromptu small groups for mini-lessons, or the teacher may gather them for a short whole-group activity followed by individual tasks. Another form of IGI is the learning center, usually a computer lab where students come in on their own schedule and work primarily on computer-assisted instruction, getting assistance from an instructor as needed. In general, IGI is characterized by the following:

- Dependence on materials (usually commercially produced, sequential, and leveled by difficulty).
- Initial placement, by the teacher, into leveled instructional materials by means of diagnostic testing.
- Students working independently, with teachers assisting as needed.
- Progression through the materials monitored by teachers correcting students' work and by testing, with teachers then assigning additional or different work based on students' progress.

In IGI classes, teachers may assign instructional materials from different workbook series from different publishers, and they may include some non-commercial teacher-designed materials as well. The materials used in IGI are not necessarily materials that were designed for use by individual students working independently. When students turn to a teacher for assistance with their learning, the teacher may provide direct instruction, or may decide that the materials do not suit that student and change the materials or provide additional instructional materials to ensure that the student understands the concept before progressing. In an IGI classroom, the student is responsible for learning the content, primarily from the materials, and the teacher functions as the "educational manager" (Hickok & Moore, 1978).

FACTORS THAT LED TO AND PERPETUATE INDIVIDUALIZED GROUP INSTRUCTION

In this section, we cover a range of factors that provided the rationale for using IGI, and contributed to the incidence and persistence of IGI in ABE over the past three decades, including the following:

- The nature of federal funding, which had an enormous influence on initial development of the ABE field through the provision of money and guidance for teacher training, and material and resources development.
- The popularity of programmed instruction, which used self-paced, self-study materials based on the ideas of behaviorist psychology in which learning is broken down into small pieces.
- The adult learning theories of the time, which emphasized the independent student.
- The availability of materials, which were initially scarce, increased during this time. Many sets of instructional materials were designed for individualized instruction and self-paced learning.
- The structural nature of ABE, in which programs needed to recognize the realities of a student population with differing needs and busy lives, leading to mixed-level classes and sporadic attendance patterns.

The combination of these factors is characterized succinctly by one of our interview respondents, Beth[32] (who has 25 years of experience in ABE, including state-level staff development):

> My impression is that it [IGI] was there from the start. It's a kind of chicken and egg situation. . . . Nobody told me that they consciously went over to this model, which they call the learning lab model. . . . It coincided with a philosophy in adult education about individualized instruction, seeing adults as self-motivated people whose individual goals needed to be the driving force for the instructional plan and the curriculum. Most of that research came from higher education, Malcolm Knowles and the like. Also, that whole movement at the time, the learning lab, the emphasis on skills, the whole behaviorist sort of mindset about learning and the fact that learning could be reinforced by sitting and encountering content and so on. So, I think it just happened that various things coincided at the time adult basic education began to be publicly funded.

Federal Funding

The federal government, which was influential in the development of the ABE field (Radwin, 1984), adopted and strongly supported individualized instruction, as IGI was known then. In 1964, the federal government apportioned ABE funds as a part of President Johnson's War on Poverty.

---

[32] All interview respondents' names are pseudonyms.

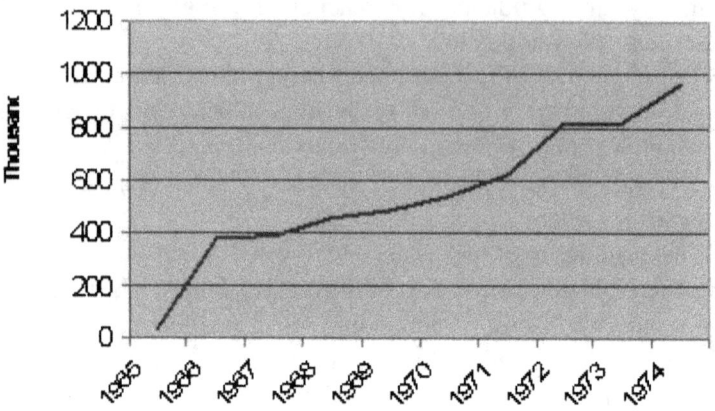

FIG. 5.1. ABE enrollment 1965–1974 (From Radwin, 1984).

The funds were provided as grants to states on a formula basis to provide classes to low-literate adults. The money was used to support local ABE programs run by public elementary, secondary, or adult schools; in 1968, private not-for-profit agencies were added as eligible grant recipients (Eyre, 1998). The newly available federal funds led to the modern era of the ABE field (Hunter & Harman, 1979; Leahy, 1991; Mangano, 1969; Mezirow, Darkenwald, & Knox, 1975; Ulmer & Dorland, 1981). Prior to 1965, only 8 states had significant ABE programs, but by 1967, all 50 states and the territories had programs in place (Comptroller General of the United States, 1975). According to Mezirow and colleagues (1975), "Almost half of the largest cities in the country used the federal funds to establish ABE classes for the first time" (p. 114).

The impact of the 1964 Adult Education Act on the delivery of ABE was explosive. In the first 2 years, enrollment jumped tenfold, going from 38,000 in 1965 to 389,000 in 1967 (Comptroller General of the United States, 1975). The rapid increases in enrollments continued (see Fig. 5.1) and by 1975, enrollment was just over 1 million (General Accounting Office, 1995).

During this era of explosive growth, programs, teachers, and administrators, needed methods and approaches that would work best with the adult population. The federal government was aware that developing an ABE system rapidly required more than direct funding of programs. Section 309 of the 1966 Adult Education Act provided the federal government with discretionary funds for professional development, and materials and resources development (Radwin, 1984). Professional development training institutes run by the federal government were the major sources of information, training, and guides for ABE practitioners.

The professional development activities initially took the form of summer teacher training institutes, which were a continuation of federally organized but privately funded (Ford Foundation) institutes that ran from 1964 to 1966 (Leahy, 1991; Radwin, 1984). These institutes provided training to teachers and administrators, and produced materials, such as training and curriculum guides. The institutes were expensive to run, costing as much as $1,200 per person in 1971, and the investment was lost when participants left the ABE field (Leahy, 1991).

In 1972, the federal government instituted a regional approach to staff development with the goal of training people more efficiently. This regional approach included supporting postsecondary institutions to create credit classes in ABE and increase the number of graduate adult education programs. The goal was to establish a group of experts and professionals in the field (Radwin, 1984). The university-driven approach was not sustained once federal control of staff development ended, and only a few universities currently prepare ABE teachers.

In 1974, Section 309 grants ended, and new federal legislation required that states set aside 15% (later 10%) of their allocation for staff development and special projects, thus effectively ending federal control of ABE professional development. At this point, ABE teacher training became the responsibility of the states, and each state handled it differently (Leahy, 1991; Radwin, 1984). States continue to be responsible for providing professional development to enhance the practice of teachers and administrators. However, many states do not provide initial training for new ABE teachers (Smith & Hofer, 2003).

The impact of the federal staff development effort was strong. According to Radwin (1984), from 1967 to 1974, approximately 83,000 ABE teachers and administrators participated in federally sponsored training activities. By providing funding and training, the federal government established the structure and operation of the ABE field, including the types of curriculum offered and instructional delivery methods employed. The training institutes covered the nature and characteristics of adult students and how best to work with this population. They also placed an emphasis on programmed instruction and the use of the technology of the time (e.g., filmstrips, tape recorders, and controlled-reader machines) in instruction. According to Leahy (1991), the 1967 overview seminar for state directors included a presentation on "programmed instruction and learning (including a discussion of teacher attitudes toward both).... Some sessions were designed to 'model' individualized instruction...." (p. 9). These were the early seeds of the establishment of IGI as a classroom model in ABE.

Programmed Instruction

In the late 1960s and early 1970s, programmed instruction, based on the work of the psychologist B.F. Skinner, was a new and promising approach to instructional delivery and curriculum development. In programmed instruction, subject matter is broken into a series of small steps with clearly defined goals. Students work their way through the material individually and at their own pace. They receive immediate feedback on the accuracy of their responses, and mastery of a lesson is required prior to continuing on to the next step (Martin, 1966). The role of the teacher is significantly different from the role played in traditional classrooms. The teacher assigns the starting point and monitors progress, functions as a coach and an administrator, and does not, generally, directly impart information. The burden of actual instruction is on the programmed materials (Lane & Lewis, 1971; Martin, 1966; Mocker & Sherk, 1970; Teachey & Carter, 1971).

The newly forming ABE field was interested in programmed instruction. For example, the North Carolina community colleges used programmed instruction for adult education, establishing learning labs throughout the state (Teachey & Carter, 1971). These learning labs used programmed instructional materials, with a teacher present to provide help, guidance, and direct instruction as needed. This was unlike pure programmed instruction, which was often a self-study approach with minimal instructor interaction. New York quickly followed North Carolina's example, starting with a few initial pilot programs that eventually spread across the state (Kacandes, 1969). By 1971, at least 10 states had adopted North Carolina's model of learning labs utilizing programmed instructional materials as part of their adult education program (Teachey & Carter, 1971) and eventually this model was commonplace throughout the country. The advantages of programmed instructional materials for ABE, according to experts at that time, included:

- Individualization, which addressed the needs of a heterogeneous population (Mocker & Sherk, 1970; Murphy, 1969).
- Promotion of active rather than passive learning (Sepede, 1972).

5. INDIVIDUALIZED GROUP INSTRUCTION

- Improvement of attendance for students who attended erratically or who dropped out and then returned; such students could pick up where they left off and neither held back the class nor were left behind by it (Teachey & Carter, 1971).
- Continuous reinforcement and mastery of a concept before moving on to the next one (Lane & Lewis, 1971; Martin, 1966).
- Initial diagnostic testing and assignment of appropriate modules addressed specific student needs (students who tested into the same level but had different patterns of errors could be better served; Murphy, 1969).
- Students working at their own pace to complete their modules (Teachey & Carter, 1971).

Adult Learning Theories

Knowles's (1970) work on adult education and andragogy (ways of thinking about working with adult students) was influential in the development of IGI. Although the concept of andragogy later came under criticism and was modified, it made an enormous contribution to the way the adult student was taught and viewed (Merriam & Brockett, 1997). Knowles (1970) proposed four tenets about adult students:

1. *Self-concept*: Adults are self-directed persons able to, and insistent on, making their own decisions and resentful of being treated as dependent persons.
2. *Experience*: Adults come to learning with a foundation of experience that can be a resource for learning. If that experience is not valued and respected, the adults feel rejected.
3. *Readiness to learn*: Adults are most interested in learning that is connected to their social roles.
4. *Orientation to learning*: Adults expect to immediately apply what they learn to their lives.

Tough's work (reviewed in Merriam & Brockett, 1997) in the early 1970s showed that adults generally planned, implemented, and evaluated learning projects themselves; they were self-directed. The ideas of Knowles and Tough supported the use of IGI, which requires students to be independent. Sepede (1972) described how adult learning theory is a justification for individualized instruction in which learners work independently but a teacher is present to help:

If self-direction is a goal of an ABE project, and it should be, adults must be given the opportunity to develop self-direction. They must have a chance to experience it through independent study on an individual basis. The learning packets can provide a viable learning experience. The learning packet is a self-contained set of teaching-learning materials designed to teach a single concept and designed to guide the learner through various independent study materials for individual and independent use. (p. 289)

A stated goal of ABE teachers is to meet students' needs (Beder & Medina, 2001). IGI practitioners believe that IGI is suited to accomplishing that goal because each student is treated individually and learning plans are established based on each student's ability level. In this way, IGI is considered student-centered. The following comment from an interview respondent illustrates this view:

It's very difficult to teach a room full of people the same issues when they don't all need the same issues. So, you necessarily have to break it up, and apply a more individualized approach to whatever that person needs. So it's more student centered than one would think. (Tom, 20 years ABE experience)

Availability of Materials

In IGI, instructional materials are crucial. Students primarily learn the content from the materials rather than the teacher, so teachers are able to simultaneously handle many students working on entirely different content. Without suitable materials, IGI would not have become an established part of ABE.

Initially, appropriate instructional materials were scarce. In 1964, the U.S. Department of Education charged a task force, under the direction of the Director of the Adult Education Branch of the U.S. Office of Education, with evaluating the then currently available instructional materials for use in the newly legislated ABE programs. The task force assessed the materials for clarity, accuracy, aptness of illustrations, general usefulness, and various technical characteristics. The task force found that "One of the most critical problems in adult basic education is the dearth of suitable instructional materials" (Montclair State College, 1970).

In 1966, Greenleigh Associates made a more detailed effort to evaluate the relative merits of the four existing, commercially available adult learning systems (Brown & Newman, 1970). The Greenleigh study was a 1-year,

5. INDIVIDUALIZED GROUP INSTRUCTION

three-state project in which teachers with varying levels of education and professional preparation used four adult learning systems in classes for adults on public assistance. Students were randomly assigned to the different classes. The purpose of the study was twofold: to assess the effectiveness of the materials and to discover the optimal level of education and professional preparedness of ABE teachers. The four systems included one with a lock-step, choral-reading, whole-group approach; two that assumed a heterogeneous class with some whole-group and some small group work; and one that employed programmed instruction and assumed self-paced, individualized work. The study assessed each learning system according to specific criteria, including the following:

- Ability to teach low literates to read in a short time.
- Ability to help low literates qualify for jobs or job training.
- Ability to work with the "least possible skill on the part of the teachers" (p. 9).
- Ability to accommodate students at different levels.
- Feasibility in terms of cost and administration (Greenleigh Associates, 1966).

No particular learning system emerged as significantly better than the others. All four taught some people how to read but none were judged to be particularly effective in quickly teaching adults how to read or meeting all of the other criteria. However, the study tested only the four adult learning systems that existed at that time.[33] By the completion of the study, additional systems that would have met the criteria of cost and feasibility were available (McCalley, 1966), an indication that materials developers had recognized and were making efforts to correct the problem of limited materials suitable for ABE instruction.

The efforts by government, publishing companies, and ABE programs—such as Job Corps, Adult Performance Level, and the Cherry Hill Conference—to create materials for use in ABE classrooms contributed to the establishment of IGI.

The government funded or implemented several projects to develop materials that were designed for, or eventually used for ABE. For example,

---

[33]The initial design called for selecting the best 4 systems out of the approximately 20 the researchers believed to exist. However, at the initial phase of the study only 2 systems existed and 2 more were available by the time data collection started.

the Civilian Conservation Centers (part of the Job Corps program) run by the Department of Agriculture and Interior, had a uniform ABE curriculum, which they designed as an individualized instruction model, but, as described by LaPlante (1969), was an IGI model. A task force, headed by Douglas Porter from Harvard University, designed an individualized program of graded self-instructional materials, which were assigned based on results of placement tests and were accompanied by frequent comprehension and mastery checks. Teachers were responsible for initial diagnostic testing and assignment, as well as monitoring progress and providing assistance as needed. The higher level materials (above Grade 3) were primarily graded-reading selections on a variety of topics. Eventually, Job Corps found that the reading selections (about 2,000 of them) were too limited, and they engaged a publisher to develop additional materials. This unknown publisher was allowed to make these new materials commercially available; by 1969, 2,000 school systems had purchased the materials for their remedial reading programs (LaPlante, 1969). Additionally, in the late 1960s, the Job Corps disseminated their techniques and materials to community action programs, the Department of Defense, and urban school districts, by training teachers and sharing materials. In this way, their system of individualized instruction moved into the general ABE field.

Job Corps was not the only large-scale program to develop a self-paced system for ABE instruction. The military had programs—such as Project 100,000—that it used to educate low-literate recruits. The basic skills instruction component was based on intensive, self-paced, individualized instruction (Montclair State College, 1970).

Commercial publishers also played an important role in developing materials for IGI. In the mid-1960s, publishers had initially responded to the newly mandated ABE programs by examining the materials that were already in their catalogs, suggesting that these would suffice. However, it quickly became clear (from the task force report and the Greenleigh evaluation) that these existing materials were not sufficient to meet the needs of a varied ABE student population, and by 1970 the publishers had begun to develop profitable materials that would meet the needs of the ABE field (McCalley, 1966; Montclair State College, 1970).

The Cherry Hill Conference in 1970, funded by a Section 309 grant, brought together commercial publishers, ABE personnel, university researchers, and federal officials to establish cooperation and communication aimed at encouraging the creation of additional commercially available materials for ABE instruction (Montclair State College, 1970;

Radwin, 1984; Ulmer & Dorland, 1981). This conference was an opportunity for the publishers to hear from the field, and for publishers to describe their development efforts and challenges. Presentations from people in the ABE field varied in their vision, and in some cases disagreed with each other, but they were universal in claiming that traditional instructional approaches would not work. Many advocated for an individualized, flexible, self-paced, learning lab approach with programmed materials. One of the final recommendations from the Cherry Hill Conference was "the production and use of program learning material," urging publishers and authors to "design and adapt materials which lend themselves to the adult learning laboratory concept" (Montclair State College, 1970, p. 98). In the closing speech, Paul Delker, at that time the director of the Division of Adult Education, said:

> My priorities would go for training teachers to be knowledgeable about materials, giving them the skills to interpret an individual's needs in relation to existing materials and would go into developing systems more along the line of individually prescribed instruction; a system for integrating existing materials and new materials as they are developed. (Montclair State College, 1970)

According to Radwin (1984), Delker and the Division of Adult Education were strong forces in shaping the nascent ABE field. They considered it their job to help develop and define the ABE field, and they wielded a great deal of power through direct oversight and control of Section 309 funds.[34] Therefore, these comments carried significant weight as the publishers left the conference and prepared to develop materials for ABE. Teachers and ABE programs also created materials appropriate for IGI classes. For example, in 1972, an article in *Adult Leadership* (at that time a major practitioner journal) advocated individualizing ABE instruction through the creation of learning "packets." Practitioners were urged to create individualized, self-paced learning packets that included the following:

- The concept to be covered.
- Instructional and behavioral objectives.
- Pretests.

---

[34]As mentioned earlier, Section 309 of the Adult Education Act of 1966 provided federally controlled discretionary money for teacher training and special projects of both national and local importance.

- Sequential learning activities to implement the content.
- Diverse methodologies for motivation and presentation.
- Independent study projects for further depth and breadth of learning.

The packets were not to be too broad or they would intimidate the student, and they were not to be too narrow or they would not provide sufficient learning (Sepede, 1972). In a field with part-time teachers who were paid only for teaching time, creation of such packets was impractical.

However, a few programs used Section 309 monies to create curriculum materials. Most, but not all, of these materials had a limited distribution (Radwin, 1984). Section 309 also funded the Adult Performance Level (APL) project at the University of Texas at Austin, the beginning of a large movement toward competency-based education in ABE. The idea behind competency-based education is that students should be competent to perform certain life skill activities proficiently, such as filling out a job application. Curricular decisions and evaluations are thus tied to the desired competencies. Initially, the APL project's goal was to define the competencies that adults needed to be successful (Beder, 2003). The APL project was enormously influential: By 1980, two thirds of ABE programs were using competency-based models, with about one third using the APL approach specifically (Young, 1980).

Competency-based education is not an instructional delivery method. Rather, it is a concept of the purpose of literacy education as functional; that is, one attends literacy education to become more successful in one's life by being better able to perform the functions required by society. It is also an approach to placement, assessment, curriculum development, and evaluation. Crandall et al. (1984) called it an "instructional management system." However, any method of instruction can be used to teach the desired competencies, and the APL project developed different styles of competency-based instructional materials, including materials for IGI classes. The APL project designed a series of modules for the individualized ABE classroom. The modules covered diagnosis, prescription, instructional activities, and evaluation for specified APL goals and objectives.

In describing the rationale for creating their modules Hickok and Moore (1978) described what is essentially an IGI class, and they pointed out the difficulties of running such a class without access to materials. They said that individualized instruction contains four elements: diagnosis, prescription, instruction and classroom management, and evaluation. They asserted that:

All four elements must be complete before individualized instruction is complete and all four steps must be performed for and with every learner. Each learner will approach each phase of the process at a different rate and time. Each learner will be prescribed different materials and activities to match his/her diagnosed needs. Learners will use the materials in different ways, in varying amounts of involvement with the teacher (who is the educational manager of the learner's prescription). Finally, each learner can demonstrate mastery by a variety of means. Since it's rather exhausting to think about all of this, much less do it, the APL staff determined to structure modules to meet as many instructional situations as possible. (Hickok & Moore, 1978, p. 41)

Due to time and resource constraints, modules were not completed for all of the APL goals and objectives. At the conclusion of their article, Hickok and Moore called for "forward looking" commercial publishers to continue their work. Commercial publishers had resources to create instruction materials based on the perceived needs of the field.

Commercial materials for ABE did become increasingly available through the 1970s and into the early 1980s. According to one of our interviewees, some commercial publishers worked with adult educators, paying them to be consultants and adapting materials they wrote. In one northeastern state, the state department of education encouraged this by recommending people to the publishers as possible consultants. By 1984, Crandall and colleagues surveyed 213 adult literacy programs across a variety of provider types (state/LEA, CBO, corrections, postsecondary, military, and employment and training) and found that the majority of materials used were commercially produced (Crandall et al., 1984). The ABE field was established with an understanding that individualized instruction within a group context was a desirable and efficient approach to teaching basic skills and literacy to the many adults who needed to be served and whose enrollment patterns were irregular. For many, IGI became (and still is) the way in which ABE is taught. Initially there was top-down pressure that encouraged IGI as a preferred model. One of our interview respondents remembers it this way:

> When I first came into this work, there was a lot coming from the state level that supported that approach [IGI] because there was a lot of emphasis on individual goal setting, customized individual learning plans for students. . . I also have a feeling that the whole idea of the lab and the scientific approach to having little pieces of knowledge available to students either through technology or workbooks was very much considered state of the art. (Beth, 25 years ABE experience)

As those who were trained in the federally funded institutes went out into the field and started to administer and teach in ABE programs, they put many of the ideas from the institutes into practice and others learned from them. Interview respondent Rebecca, who has 30 years of experience in ABE, described the process as she remembers it:

> It was THE model even for part-time evening classes. . . . They were proposing that this is the way you might do it. [My] state . . . is very local controlled, always has been. And so it was offered as a model. . . . [T]here was . . . some dissemination of the model through [federally funded regional teacher training institutes] . . . [and] lots of discussion about it. I don't know if I would use the word advocated but it was definitely out there. And most programs that were just coming up were looking to their neighbors to see how [they] were doing this and what's working and it proliferated that way. In fact, it's still out there big time.

Once the staff development efforts became regionalized, the importance of individualizing instruction became, in some cases, codified in the state professional development plans. For example, the 1971 state plans for both North Carolina and South Carolina list having their ABE teaching staff individualize instruction as a professional development goal (Southern Regional Education Board, 1971). In 1975, North Carolina reported that, "Individualized materials programmed to the student's educational level are used frequently" (North Carolina State Department of Community Colleges, 1975). New York established a system of adult learning labs that were used either in conjunction with traditional classes or in lieu of them. These learning labs were a form of IGI in that students came in and worked on their assigned materials individually. Instructors were available for assistance, assignments, assessment and reassessment, and encouragement (Kacandes, 1969; Murphy, 1969; New York State Education Department, 1971). One interview respondent from New York remembers transitioning his small literacy program to a larger program funded by the Adult Education Act. For the first year, the program ran with traditional whole-group instruction. Then the New York State Department of Education heard about the work being done in North Carolina with mobile learning labs using an IGI model and instituted similar learning labs in New York (although from the beginning New York advocated a model that included informal, small group work). According to our interview respondents, and supported by Kacandes (1969), IGI and learning labs became standard in New York (except in New York City) due to top-down pressure, the idea being that this model would better suit the characteristics of the ABE students.

The Last Gamble on Education study (Mezirow et al., 1975) found that some variant of the learning lab was present in two out of three cities in their study. Among the final recommendations of this highly influential work was the suggestion that an increase in individualized instruction within classrooms and an increase in the number of learning laboratories would be helpful for ABE students. In 1980, an evaluation of programs funded by the Adult Education Act found that much of the instruction in these programs was individualized (especially in non-ESOL programs). Although it is not clear exactly what is meant by individualized instruction, it is also reported that teachers worked with an average of 48 students per year, so it is unlikely that the model used was direct one-to-one tutoring (Young, 1980).

The federal and state efforts to increase the use of IGI had an effect. IGI became ingrained in ABE to the point where it was often the custom rather than a choice. Interview respondent Beth, who does staff development that encourages teachers to move away from IGI, saw it this way:

> [O]ne of the issues is that it is hard for teachers to break [away from IGI], even though they get information from us and training in teaching a course that requires working with larger groups. It's hard for them to get out of this because there is the heavy weight of custom and routine and it has always been done this way. (Beth, 25 years ABE experience)

The Structure of Adult Education

IGI also became—and remained—prevalent due to its ability to handle the pressures caused by the specific practices of ABE. This chapter now examines these pressures and how IGI relieves them.

Enrollment and Participation. Open enrollment, in which students enter and leave programs at any time, has been part of ABE since its inception in the 1960s. This is, in part, due to the nature of the students in adult education classes. Adult students have pressures such as jobs and child care requirements that often make it difficult to attend class regularly. Students can choose to either drop out entirely or take a break from (stop out of) programs for reasons such as family, job, or health pressures. Students also leave programs when they have met their short-term goal or found that the particular program is not a good match for their needs and goals (Fingeret & Drennon, 1997; Quigley, 1997). In 1993, the National Evaluation of Adult Education Programs (NEAEP) found that ASE students participated for a median of 28 hours and ABE students for a median of 35 hours, and that 19% of all students (ABE, ASE, and ESOL) leave before 12 hours of instruction (Development Associates, Inc., 1993). Although it peaks in September and January, demand for ABE services occurs year-round (Young, Fleischman, Fitzgerald, & Morgan, 1995). The empty seats left by dropouts or stopouts are often filled immediately, leading to the very common pattern of open-entry/open-exit continuous enrollment, in which students enter or leave the class at any time during the year (Beder, 1996; Quigley, 2000). Programs have an incentive to maintain open-entry policies because funding is often based on enrollment figures, and they wish to retain and assure future funding.

However, the classroom situation created by open-entry policies is difficult for teachers to manage: "Evidence from the teacher survey and interviews suggest that continuous enrollment of new students is seriously detrimental to effective teaching and learning" (Mezirow et al., 1975, p. 146). Nearly 30 years later, Smith and Hofer (2003), in their study of ABE teachers, observed, "Teachers grappled with class groupings (individualized instruction versus class instruction), which were complicated by enrollment policies in the majority of programs that allowed students to enter and exit at any time during the semester or cycle" (p. 24). For each class session, teachers do not know if they will have new students in the class, and they do not know which of their enrolled students will attend that day. Additionally, if students are absent, teachers do not know if they plan to return or if they have left the program, making planning sequenced group instruction difficult and frustrating. IGI is a pragmatic approach to this situation; whether or not a student is present does not affect the learning activities of the rest of the class. There is no penalty for absent students, as they can continue from where they left off when they return to class. Teachers can integrate new students into the class as they arrive, as returning students continue to work on their individual assignments.

One of our interviewees described the connection between IGI and fluctuating enrollment and participation:

> Another strength is the need to accommodate the nature of the population, which really sort of drops in and drops out on odd schedules. It's hard enough to get a classroom full of students without also saying, you all have to start on this date in order to keep our class full. I mean that's just not how

this population works. Their lives are very complex ... and they have multiple responsibilities and multiple barriers and so, they can't start on the first day of the quarter and go until the end of the quarter. They're in the middle of the quarter [and] suddenly they get laid off and want to come back to school and only have a few weeks to try to do something and so I think that accommodating the unique nature of the population is something that's a little bit easier in an individualized model. (Cheryl, 25 years ABE experience)

Multilevel Classes. In ABE classes, students frequently are at widely differing reading, writing, math, and background knowledge levels. It is possible, even common, to have low-level ABE students mixed with GED students in the same class, particularly in smaller programs that cannot offer a large number of different classes. Even when students test into similar levels, they may have different academic needs (i.e., one may need help with math, another with reading, and a third with writing) and yet they are all in the same class.

Mixed levels have been an issue in ABE for many years. In 1975, Mezirow found "variation in skill and ability levels" to be one of the most significant factors impeding teaching and learning (Mezirow et al., 1975).

Open-entry/open-exit continuous enrollment contributes to mixed levels because it is hard to keep a particular class at the same level as students move in and out. In rural areas, programs may not have enough students at a particular level and must combine levels to fill a class.

The following quotes from our interviews demonstrate the ways in which mixed-level classes seem to drive the use of IGI.

> At first, I remember being totally overwhelmed, and I lost a lot of students because I was trying to teach everybody the same thing, which wasn't what they needed. (Sharon, 15 years ABE experience)

> The only way you can gather together 20 students for a class is to have students at a variety of levels with a variety of needs. And so, administratively this kind of an approach [IGI] allows you to create "classes" where you might not be able to do it if it had to be a specific group type experience. (Cheryl, 25 years ABE experience)

> They have to maintain a certain number of students to keep the class open and you've only got 20 ABE students, then, you have all levels and that sort of drives the individualized instruction. (Pam, 34 years ABE experience)

Staffing. ABE teachers are generally part time, many with experience teaching in K–12, have limited (frequently unpaid) opportunities for professional development; pay is low and many teachers receive few or no benefits

(Smith & Hofer, 2003; Young et al., 1995). Young and colleagues (1995) found that slightly more than half of the instructors in their study were teaching in more than one area (e.g., ABE and GED) rather than specializing. Smith and Hofer (2003) found that many teachers were isolated from both their program directors and from other teachers in their program, and had few opportunities to share ideas and experiences. Additionally, some teachers work at sites that are physically removed from the main program site, and they may be the only teachers at their location. Smith and Hofer (2003) also found that only 54% of the teachers in their sample received any paid preparation time. The preparation time that teachers did receive varied greatly, with some receiving as little as 1 hour of paid preparation for every 5 hours of teaching, and others receiving 1 hour of paid preparation for every hour of teaching. Young and colleagues (1995) found that half of the part-time staff in ABE had been teaching for less than 3 years.

An IGI teacher, in a strictly IGI setting, does not plan traditional whole-class lessons, nor individual tutoring sessions. Rather, these teachers oversee the topics and levels for each learner, basing their decisions on what they know of the learner's skills, previous work, and diagnostic testing. If they choose to enhance the IGI model with small group work or whole-group work, they must also plan and organize it. This style of teaching differs from standard K–12 or higher education instruction. None of our interviewees reported receiving staff development or preservice training specifically in how to conduct IGI classes. Rather, they were socialized into running their classes this way:

> I think I got about an hour's orientation from the other teacher who was leaving. (Ann, 17 years ABE experience)

> Back in '87 or '88, when I [began volunteering] . . . they had a small community oriented program run by a church, and they were open two nights a week for a couple hours, and I went there to volunteer my services as a tutor, and they just turned me loose on the room, and said, just wander around and help whoever needs help. They were all doing worksheets and writing, math, it was probably about 15, 20 people in the room. (Tom, 20 years ABE experience)

> Well, I think I was a pretty typical adult educator. You just show up and nobody tells you . . . what to do, and you just kind of figure it out on your own. I think the very, very, very first thing I did was working at an off-site GED classroom, and we just had GED workbooks. . . . In college, I was a psych major and I had taken some teaching courses, but I didn't really, until that point, consider myself a teacher, and nobody had ever really told me

how to do it, and so I just started by using workbooks and that's how everybody in the program did it. Their program, at that time, [had about] seven different teachers and they all taught the same way, and I think some of them still do even now. So, I didn't know there would be any other way to do it, and that's how I did it. (Tony, 20 years ABE experience)

With a teaching staff that often has little training, little or no preparation time, and limited experience teaching adults, IGI—through programmed instruction in workbooks—provides a consistency of instruction that might otherwise be missing. IGI does not require teachers to invest much in preparation. As one interview respondent put it:

[IGI] doesn't take a lot of skill, and it doesn't take planning. And that's key, because most of us in adult [education] are part time and a lot of [us] don't get paid for prep time.... And it's something that you can do without having to plan. (Nancy, 20 years ABE experience)

However, IGI neither requires nor excludes extensive planning and preparation; in a recent study involving IGI instruction, researchers observed examples of both minimal and extensive planning and teaching in IGI classrooms (Beder et al., 2006).

By being responsive to individual curricular and participation needs without placing an undue burden on either the teacher or the other students, IGI both allows and supports an instructional setting in which open-entry/open-exit enrollment, sporadic participation, mixed-level classes, and part-time teaching staff continue to exist.

THE PREVALENCE OF IGI

There is almost no information about the prevalence of IGI in ABE programs nationwide, and many of the studies that investigated classroom practices in ABE did not distinguish what we call IGI from one-on-one tutoring, individualized instruction, or self-study. Since the 1970s, the number of references to "individualized instruction" has decreased in the research literature, perhaps because practitioners in the field no longer felt the need to differentiate this type of instruction from other types. IGI had almost become synonymous with ABE instruction.

Young (1980) conducted a national study describing the state-administered programs of the federal Adult Education Act. This study surveyed and interviewed state directors, local program directors, teachers, and students.

The study found that mode of instruction—*individualized, self-study or small group,* and *classroom* (p. 152)—was one of the variables that could be used to differentiate between ABE, ASE, and ESOL teachers: ABE and ASE teachers were more likely to use individualized instruction, whereas ESOL teachers were more likely to use classroom (group) instruction. However, the paper detailing the findings of the study did not provide definitions of each of the modes of instruction, did not make clear why self-study and small group were considered a single instructional mode, or whether individualized implied one-to-one tutoring. The study found that slightly more than half of the ABE (57%) and ASE (52%) teachers used individualized instruction, and given that the lowest student–teacher ratio was 13 to 1, these instructors were probably using IGI.

Crandall and colleagues (1984) investigated effective literacy practices across six provider types (state/LEA, employment and training, corrections, postsecondary, community-based organizations, and the military). One of the eight major components of each program studied was instructional methods and materials. This study defined individual instruction as a one-to-one learning experience, and group instruction as a teacher presenting a designated topic to the entire class with the students expected to work at the same pace on the same materials (Crandall et al., 1984). Based on their findings, the researchers argued that a program could be successful regardless of which grouping strategy programs use, but no information specific to IGI can be deduced from this study.

In 1990, Kutner and colleagues published a study that was intended to be an overview of how ABE programs work. The purpose was to identify areas of interest for further nationally representative research. The study compiled data from a literature review, informal interviews with eight state directors of adult education, and in-depth case studies of nine programs. They found that "individualized instruction has become the principal format in basic skills classes" (Kutner, Furey, Webb, & Gadsden, 1990, p. 20). However, this study does not distinguish between tutoring and IGI.

Solórzano (1993), in a review of effective practices in adult literacy programs, addressed instructional group size briefly, simply drawing distinctions among one-on-one tutoring, small group instruction, and classroom-based teaching, and it is unclear which of these might represent IGI. Because the entire discussion is less than one page in a hundred-plus page report, it is also unclear whether the effectiveness of IGI can be deduced.

In 1992, the NEAEP conducted two surveys: a universe survey that collected data from 2,619 programs (93% of the local programs receiving federal basic state grants funds in 1990) and a program profile survey that collected more detailed data from a nationally representative sample of 131 programs. Program profile surveys, completed by program directors, addressed program-level, rather than the class-level, factors. For example, the survey asked, "To what extent does your program use each of the following learning environments: . . ." and provided eight choices as a response, including: individualized instruction (e.g., one-on-one tutoring), individualized self-study with no instructor or tutor present, and classroom style instruction with 1 or more aides (Development Associates, Inc., 1992, Appendix C). None of these choices directly describes the IGI model. However, the item pertaining to individualized instruction offers tutoring as an example of one type of individualized instruction. More than half of the nationally representative sample of 131 programs (57%) reported that they used individualized instruction. However, only 20% of those programs reported that none or almost none of their clients received instruction in a group setting (implying that up to 80% of their clients received instruction in some kind of a group setting). These two statistics—57% using individualized methods and 80% providing group settings—suggest that IGI was a common mode of instruction.

To gain an understanding of the prevalence of IGI, my colleagues and I at Rutgers sent an e-mail to all state directors of education defining IGI, asking how common it was in their state. We received replies from 14 states; because none of the states kept formal statistics on this, these replies included only estimates of the prevalence of IGI. Two of the state directors replied with commentary but did not indicate prevalence in their state. Two other directors indicated that this was a common practice but did not provide an estimate of prevalence, responding with words such as "many" and "a significant number." Of the remaining 10 states, 5 indicated that IGI was used in 75% or more of their programs, with 2 of these indicating greater than 95% of their programs used IGI. An additional 3 states indicated that 40% to 50% of their programs used IGI. Two states estimated that IGI was used in 25% or less of their programs, with 1 of those indicating that they estimated the use at less than 15%. Although informal and general, these results do suggest that IGI is highly prevalent in ABE and that its prevalence may vary significantly by state.

THE EFFECTIVENESS OF IGI

We found no studies of the effectiveness of the IGI model as we have defined it; however, one small study looked carefully at students in classrooms that appeared to be IGI. Venezky, Sabatini, Brooks, and Carino

(1996) undertook three student case studies to gauge what was learned directly from adult literacy instruction. The researchers presented a profile of each of the students' coursework and their academic strengths and weaknesses. The instructional settings for two of the three students clearly followed an IGI model, with individual workbooks assigned based on students' performance on initial mastery tests. The study was conducted in Delaware, which required that programs employing individualized skill instruction use an individualized skills program called Learning Unlimited. According to the authors, these materials were used in the majority of state-funded programs (Venezky et al., 1996). None of the students had major learning breakthroughs during the time that they participated in this study; they exhibited slow and sometimes uneven progress. The authors stated that the classroom work was focused on specific academic skills, with little time for building strong fluency in any one of them. Also, all the students had difficulty with more complex tasks (e.g., organization in writing), which were not well addressed in the instruction. Additionally, the diagnostic information available to the teachers was task specific and did not address broader issues such as level of phonological awareness or logical reasoning. The main conclusion reached by this study was that although students may make some progress with this approach (individualized self-paced instruction, with an emphasis on basic skills), it is flawed and might not be a good use of resources. There is a real limitation to generalizing the results of this study because it is based on only three case studies.

If the goal of literacy instruction is to pass the GED, one might surmise that IGI, with its focus on basic skills and worksheets, would be effective. If, however, the goal of literacy is to master social practices related to literacy, one might hypothesize that IGI would be less effective: "Although literacy requires knowledge of the technical skills of forming letters, spelling words, decoding and so on, these technical skills are useless without social knowledge that attaches meaning to words *in context*" (Fingeret & Drennon, 1997, p. 62). IGI classes, with their emphasis on commercial materials, may offer some simulated rehearsal in the social practices of literacy, such as filling out a sample job application or driver's license form. However, rehearsing, although necessary and helpful, is not the same as the actual performance.

The effectiveness of IGI was a key issue emerging from the interviews with our informants in the field, and their comments indicate some common questions about the effectiveness and quality of instruction, including questions about skills learned, amount of instruction received, time on task, and learning style in IGI. The questions are discussed in the sections that follow.

What Is the Range of Skills Addressed and Learned in IGI?

Tony, who has 20 years of experience in ABE, explained the issue this way:

> I think another weakness is that [IGI is] very narrow, in that it presents a really narrow focus on what success is. So success would be just considered getting through the pages or getting to the next stage and the next stage, whereas to be successful in the world, there's a whole lot more to it. You have to . . . be able to work with others. You have to be able to work on a team. And you have to be able to negotiate, cooperate, plan, and all those other things. And all of that is not part of this type of instruction. So I think by trying to do things more in a group, where all those other skills are brought in, it's really going to be much better for the student.

Because IGI is dependent on commercially available materials, and teachers determine assignments, it is likely that the majority of IGI classes might fall into the decontextualized discrete skills instruction category, rather than the meaning-making category, of Beder and Medina's (2001) typology of ABE classes. *Discrete skills instruction* classes place an emphasis on the development of isolated skills in traditional subject areas such as reading and mathematics. Assuming that IGI classes are focused on discrete basic skills, we do not know the extent to which IGI classes address the broader and more complex skills needed to integrate and transfer the discrete skills from the workbook to more demanding academic tasks and then to life tasks. This is consistent with the findings of Venezky and colleagues (1996), who suggested that learners in an IGI-like setting struggled with more complex issues, such as organizing information for writing. It is also unknown the extent to which IGI helps students develop "soft skills," such as the ability to work with others and participate as a member of a team, skills that are considered necessary for the modern workforce (Equipped for the Future, 2005; Kane, Berryman, Goslin, & Meltzer, 1990).

Discussion and incorporation of metacognitive techniques in ABE instruction can help learners become stronger and more able literacy learners (Paris & Parecki, 1993). Metacognition—learners thinking and learning about how to learn—is a powerful tool. It involves reflection on the learning tasks and appropriate strategies needed to accomplish those tasks, as well as reflection on one's own abilities and motivation. Mikulecky and Lloyd (1997) found that adult students in workplace literacy programs that incorporated metacognition into instruction—with regularly planned discussions about learner beliefs and plans regarding literacy—demonstrated increased self-efficacy in both literacy tasks and plans for future literacy activities and education. Although IGI has the potential, through intensive teacher–learner interaction, to offer instruction in metacognition, it is unlikely that the commercial ABE materials provide much guidance in metacognition, as they generally require short factual answers rather than reflective activities.

How Much Actual Instruction Is Happening in IGI?

In IGI classes, a teacher might rotate among learners to see who needs help and then deliver significant one-on-one instruction throughout the class session; or a teacher might sit behind a desk and announce that learners should come up if they have a question (Beder et al., 2006; Mezirow et al., 1975). Several of the interviews illustrate the range of teacher behavior in IGI:

> I went around to every student because a lot of times the ones who needed the help most would never ask you so I just continually circulated around the room. I could even tell what problem on the page [that] student was going to miss. If you really get to know your students then all that comes naturally. (Sharon, 27 years ABE experience)

> What I see a lot is Not-teaching . . . I see teachers circulating around saying, "If you need any help give me a call," and the students don't know if they need help or not. And, so, they become much less effective. I would see a lot of teachers sitting at the desk reading the newspaper. Bored. Students are also bored because all they have is the workbook and they don't know each other. You wonder why people leave? . . . I have very little good to say about the "here's your workbook . . . call me if you need me." And that's what it turned into unfortunately. (Pam, 30 years ABE experience)

> I've seen it overdone, where teachers just pointed to the materials and said, "Work on that." (Darryl, 40 years ABE experience)

Although IGI teachers determine what the learner will be working on, they are not the primary transmitter of information as they might be in a traditional class; rather, it is mainly the materials that transmit information.

In the IGI model, the teacher is supposed to help each student to attain the desired skills, if and when the student needs help, but it is primarily through the interaction between the student and the materials that the learner acquires basic literacy skills.

When one of our interview respondents ran a staff development project that asked teachers for lesson plans, one teacher sent a list of names with the workbook page number that each learner was on (Beth, 25 years ABE experience). The idea of the materials "doing the teaching" comes out of the programmed instruction movement (Martin, 1966; Mocker & Sherk, 1970; Teachey & Carter, 1971). This does not mean that IGI teachers never provide direct instruction. However, there is the potential for such instruction to be largely responsive and reactive, which can be quite stressful for the teacher, as illustrated by the following interview response:

> I came out of K–12 as a high school English teacher for a couple of years and to go into this center where it was very individualized was a huge switch for me from working with groups of students, all kind of at the same level, to going to a center where I literally within minutes would switch from teaching somebody decoding at a very basic level to teaching someone trigonometry.... It was very well organized and so I felt confident about how to follow students' progress and how to know what I needed to work on with a student. I felt pretty supported in terms of what I needed to do, but it was also a little bit daunting and challenging to have the immediate switch. You're just "click, click, click, click" all day long from one subject to another, from a young high school student to an older reentering vocational student, to a single parent who had some emotional issues, to somebody who had learning disabilities ... just constant moment by moment switching of ways of interrelating with the students. I remember at the end of the day, I was always exhausted. (Cheryl, 25 years ABE experience)

How Much Time on Task Happens in IGI?

Waiting is a problem in IGI that affects both teachers and learners. Teachers have the pressure of knowing that someone always needs their attention, and learners have the frustration of being stuck and not being able to continue without teacher intervention and assistance. Venezky and colleagues (1996) identified the same problem in their case studies, finding that instruction in which the teacher switches from one student to another, and from one topic to another, created a situation in which the teachers were unable to provide the level of individualized instruction needed by each student, a situation mirrored in comments from our interviewees.

> [IGI] means that students can . . . get exactly the help that they need. But sometimes it's not possible to do that if you've got six people lined up waiting for your help, five of them are going to be sitting there twiddling their thumbs. I mean, they may well get to a point where they're just so stuck that they can't do anything without some assistance and so, that part of it can be frustrating for the teacher who has this sense that people are just waiting and waiting, and for the student who gets the sense that everyone else is coming before him. (Cheryl, 25 years ABE experience)

> For the teacher, [IGI] poses a real class management challenge if you have a few students who are a lot more needy than everybody else. And they tend to preempt all your time, and then the other students get very resentful. Like the students who are so very needy get very resentful if you are not there all the time, because they can't proceed without you. (Ann, 17 years ABE experience)

A common solution to the problem of students who have to wait for teachers is to form impromptu small groups of learners who are struggling with the same topic and provide a minilesson to the group. It is not known the extent to which learners' waiting for teacher attention affects the quality and effectiveness of instruction.

For What Profiles of Learners Does IGI Work Best?

One of the purported benefits of IGI is that it is individualized to each student—the students work at their own pace on what they need to do to accomplish their educational goals. However, ABE students are highly diverse in measures of socioeconomic status, age, race, ethnicity, gender, educational history (including special education and learning difficulties), learning style, and native language. One question about IGI's effectiveness, therefore, is whether IGI works equally well for all adult students. For example, some of our interviewees felt that the skills level of students—particularly students with low levels of basic skills—could impact how independently a student could work in the IGI model. Other interviewees felt that the students' approach to learning could interact with IGI instruction, and they hypothesized that students who are less self-directed and do not ask for help might be less successful in the IGI model.

> Another drawback is that when adults are working on an individual basis, the more aggressive [students] will ask for assistance but the more passive individuals will not. Although they might need some assistance they won't seek that out. (Beth, 24 years ABE experience)

I think a real weakness of the model is if you have a student who is inclined to drift it really lets them drift. You know if you have a student who is inclined to not have a sense of the steps in this learning task. And they've got that whole book in front of them. And they get bored with this one so they try a different one, several pages over. Or they like that story in the first chapter so they go back to it. It's not very efficient in that sense for those students. (Ann, 17 years ABE experience)

A student who is not real oriented toward independent reading has a real problem with [IGI]. (Ann, 17 years ABE experience)

Is There a Cohort in IGI and Does That Improve Retention and Learning?

Another issue raised by the interviews was that of community and cohort. Strict IGI provides minimal opportunities for the formation of cohorts, which recent research has shown to be important to adult students. Cohorts provide both emotional and academic achievement support. Additionally they can help broaden the perspectives of the students within the group (Drago-Severson et al., 2001; Fingeret & Drennon, 1997; Kegan et al., 2001).

I think that if somebody is just working [alone] they don't develop . . . the social cohort. The people aren't really getting a social experience when they come, and they're not making friends, and they don't have other people to support, and they don't maybe realize [that] they feel isolated. They won't realize that they're not the only person in this predicament, so those will feel dumb and maybe think they're the only ones. (Nancy, 20 years ABE experience)

The interviews not only illuminated problems and concerns of community and cohort but also potential problems in the relationship between the teacher and student.

Now the weakness that I have encountered is that [IGI] eliminates any kind of group cohesiveness, and that's a big issue because if there is a lack of socialization the individuals don't get to know each other and it is much easier for them to drop out of a program. They won't be noticed by anyone else. They might be noticed by the instructor that has come to know them and talk to them but . . . if the instructor has as many as 10–15 students in a program, she or he will only get to the students once during the course of the time the student is working. And so, that might not be enough connection,

> enough human connection to make a difference for that individual to think, "Yes I am doing the right thing, I am committed to this and I've got the assistance that I need." (Louise, 24 years ABE experience)

> I think that it allows ... you to connect very directly with students... working with that person one on one. The student ... knows you. The students can't hide in the back of the classroom and just slide. ... So I think that the understanding of exactly where students are and the ability to target instruction very specifically are two good things. (Cheryl, 25 years ABE experience)

It is not known what the social relationships are in an IGI setting. It is possible that certain IGI variations, such as classes that include some group work, may foster cohort formation, and this may affect student academic achievement (Kegan et al., 2001). It is also possible that the potential for a close relationship with the teacher may somehow change or have an effect on the need for a cohort. The interviews hint at the complexity of the issue of social relations in the ABE IGI classroom, which may make future research difficult but also of great importance.

How Effective Are the Materials?

Materials—books, software, video, or other types—are vital to the IGI model. However, little is known about the efficacy of the commercially available materials in terms of their ability to teach reading and other basic skills. Rigg and Kazemek (1985) highlighted a number of concerns with commercially available ABE materials. They argued that the reading passages are generally short and use artificial language that conforms to readability formulas. This precludes real character or plot development, or even simple clarity. They went on to say, "The compression forced on the writer means that the reader must supply an enormous amount of background knowledge and must apply this knowledge quickly and effectively with only minimal clues from the page. That is, the materials require a quite proficient reader, just the opposite of the adult students actually trying to use these texts" (Rigg & Kazemek, 1985, p. 727). It is likely that these problems still exist in current materials; they generally have short passages that are at specified reading levels. One experienced ABE teacher raised a related issue regarding the commercial material she used in an IGI class:

> We were using mostly instructional materials that kind of mimic the GED. Using the IGI model with those materials, I believe left our students with a really, really, choppy view of the world. Pages 3 through 7 would be a piece

about the American Revolution and then pages 9 through 12 would be a piece about World War II. (Ann, 17 years ABE experience)

Other studies have raised problems of bias, and racial and gender stereotyping in ABE materials (Coles, 1977; Quigley & Holsinger, 1993; Sandlin, 2000).

The use of authentic materials has been shown to increase literacy practices outside of the classroom (Purcell-Gates, Degener, Jacobson, & Soler, 2000). Therefore, this is an area in which IGI may not be as effective because authentic materials (items directly from, and connected to, students' lives) are unlikely to be widely used in an IGI context. This is because to use such materials requires planning, input from students (on what is connected to and important in their lives), and less dependence on commercial products.

What Kinds of Variations Are There in IGI and Which Ones Are Beneficial?

Not all IGI classes are what I have referred to as "pure IGI." Teachers may group students for a variety of purposes, even in an IGI setting. These reasons may include providing minilessons or enrichment activities. There is no research about which types of variations in IGI classes are the most beneficial for helping students achieve the goals of their educational experience.

IMPLICATIONS FOR RESEARCH, POLICY, AND PRACTICE

Research

The difficulties we encountered when trying to find information for this study of classroom practice in ABE have broader implications for further research in ABE. The model of classroom instruction is an important variable that needs to be more carefully considered and controlled for. An ABE class that uses IGI may be very different from one that uses group instruction. Therefore, assumptions made about one type of class will not necessarily carry over to another. More research needs to be done at the classroom level, looking at all models of instruction in ABE. Currently, studies tend to be done either at the individual student level, or at the program, state, or national level.

The main question for research related to IGI that emerged from this review is how effective IGI is, as compared to classroom or group instruction (either small or large group) or compared to one-on-one tutoring, in helping adult students acquire basic literacy skills and proficiencies, expand literacy practices, develop critical thinking and metacognitive skills, and increase "soft skills" such as the ability to work in teams and solve problems. Is IGI more effective with one particular population of adult student than another?

The research that would answer this question would, of necessity, be complicated. Would it, for example, be possible to find and match a large enough sample of adult students and classes, some of which participated in IGI, some in classroom or group instruction, some in one-on-one tutoring, some who engaged in self-study, and some who did not participate in adult education at all? Additionally, the groups would have to be able to sustain the high attrition rates, common in adult education, and still yield solid data. Such a study boggles the mind, and might in part explain why there is so little research into the effectiveness of IGI. However, given the concerns that many of our interviewees had about the quality and efficacy of IGI, research on such a prevalent form of instruction seems warranted.

Policy

Current policies, at all levels (federal, state, and local), contribute to an ABE culture that preserves the structures—such as open enrollment, mixed levels, and underprepared teaching staff—that drive and underlie the IGI model. For example, many teachers do not have any formal coursework in ABE prior to teaching; in many states only K–12 certification is required (Smith & Hofer, 2003). It appears from our informal survey of state directors of adult education that state policies, in particular, may have a significant role in the instructional models used in the classroom. Currently, we do not know if policies should encourage or discourage IGI because we have no outcome or efficacy data. Until such data are available, policymakers should consider policies that do not force an IGI situation, but rather encourage choice and innovation on the part of programs and teachers, allowing them to design programs they believe will best foster student learning and retention. For example, policies that provide greater funding and opportunities for teacher training and professional development, and program funding policies that take into account enrollment patterns of students who stop out (Belzer, 1998), as demands of their life and time require, would be helpful.

Practice

An ABE class can mean a traditional group instruction model, an IGI model, or some other model. Making distinctions between tutoring and IGI when using the terms *individualized instruction,* and between class and classroom instruction when using the term *group instruction* would be helpful. Clarity of terms could lead to improved communication and understanding among researchers, policymakers, administrators, and practitioners, which might make discussing its prevalence and effectiveness easier.

CONCLUSION

IGI has become so ingrained in the practice of ABE that it is rarely reflected on, discussed, or even acknowledged. At the outset of this project, several very knowledgeable adult education researchers did not expect us to uncover any sense of where IGI came from; their impression was that it was always part of ABE. They did not think that it had developed out of any thoughtful tradition. Instead, what we found is that, at the beginning, IGI was considered state-of-the-art teaching for the ABE population. There was a conscious effort to promote IGI as the preferred method of ABE instruction. However, over time, it has become an established practice, particularly in adult literacy and ASE instruction, partially because it addresses several unique features in the delivery of education to adults, including continuous enrollment, mixed levels, sporadic attendance, and part-time teaching staff.

What I have tried to do here is to deconstruct this established—and yet nearly invisible—classroom model to acknowledge and identify it. The hope is that this will initiate a dialogue within the field about the pros and cons of using this method, that using IGI (or not using it) will become a considered choice, not just "the way it's done," and that the field will consciously look at methodologies that address the realities of the classroom. Freire (1970) spoke of "naming the word to name to world"; that is to give the forces in our lives names, so that they can be examined, understood, and reflected on, and then action can be taken to transform them into something better. Here we have taken the first step by naming, describing, and beginning to examine IGI. Hopefully this will spark discussion and research into IGI and this will help us to teach more effectively and therefore foster more student success.

ACKNOWLEDGMENTS

I thank Christine Bradley-Rodriguez for her help with initial data collection, and Hal Beder for insight and guidance.

REFERENCES

Beder, H. (1996). *The infrastructure of adult literacy education: Implications for policy* (National Center on Adult Literacy Tech. Rep. TR96-01). Retrieved October 4, 2004, from http://www.literacyonline.org/products/ncal/pdf/TR9601.pdf

Beder, H. (2003, October). *Quality instruction in adult literacy education.* Paper presented at the Rutgers Invitational Symposium on Education: Defining and Improving Quality in Adult Basic Education: Issues and Challenges, Camden, NJ.

Beder, H., & Medina, P. (2001). *Classroom dynamics in adult literacy education* (NCSALL Rep. No. 18). Retrieved October 21, 2004, from http://gseweb.harvard.edu/~ncsall/research/report18.pdf

Beder, H., Tomkins, J., Medina, P., Riccioni, R., & Deng, W. (2006). *Learners' engagement in adult literacy education* (NCSALL Rep. No. 27). Boston: National Center for the Study of Adult Learning and Literacy.

Belzer, A. (1998). Stopping out, not dropping out. *Focus on Basics, 2*(A), 15–17.

Brown, D. A., & Newman, A. P. (1970). Research in adult literacy. *Journal of Reading Behavior, 2,* 19–46.

Coles, G. S. (1977). Dick and Jane grow up: Ideology in adult basic education readers. *Urban Education, 12*(1), 37–54.

Comptroller General of the United States. (1975). *The adult basic education program: Progress in reducing illiteracy and improvements needed: Report to the Congress.* Washington, DC: U.S. General Accounting Office. (ERIC Document Reproduction Service No. ED 110682)

Crandall, D. P., Lerche, R. S., Marchilonis, B., Turner, J. C., Jenzer, J., Swartz, J. P., et al. (1984). *Guidebook for effective literacy practice.* San Francisco: Far West Lab for Educational Research and Development. (ERIC Document Reproduction Service No. ED 253776)

Development Associates, Inc. (1992). *National evaluation of adult education programs: Profiles of service providers first interim report.* Arlington, VA: Author. (ERIC Document Reproduction Services No. ED 354371)

Development Associates, Inc. (1993). *National evaluation of adult education programs: Profiles of client characteristics, second interim report.* Arlington, VA: Author. (ERIC Document Reproduction Service No. ED 364125)

Drago-Severson, E., Helsing, D., Kegan, R., Popp, N., Broderick, M., & Portnow, K. (2001). The power of a cohort and of collaborative groups. *Focus on Basics, 5*(B), 15–22.

Equipped for the Future. (2005). *Equipped for the Future: Worker role map.* Knoxville, TN: EFF Center for Training and Technical Assistance. Retrieved January 7, 2005, from http://eff.cls.utk.edu/fundamentals/role_map_worker.htm

Eyre, G. (1998). *History of the Adult Education Act.* Washington, DC: National Adult Education Professional Development Consortium, Inc. Retrieved November 9, 2005, from http://www.naepdc.org/issues/AEAHistort.htm#FedLeg

Fingeret, H. A., & Drennon, C. (1997). *Literacy for life: Adult learners, new practices.* New York: Teachers College Press.

Freire, P. (1970). *Pedagogy of the oppressed.* New York: Seabury.

General Accounting Office. (1995). *Adult education: Measuring program results has been challenging report to congressional requesters.* Washington, DC: U.S. General Accounting Office, Health, Education, and Human Services Division. Retrieved November 1, 2004, from http://www.gao.gov/archive/1995/he95153.pdf

Greenleigh Associates. (1966). *Field test and evaluation of selected adult basic education systems.* New York: Author. (ERIC Document Reproduction Service No. ED 011090)

Hickok, D. S., & Moore, C. S. (1978). ABE, APL and individualized instruction. *Adult Literacy & Basic Education* (Winter), pp. 37–51.

Hunter, C. S. J., & Harman, D. (1979). *Adult illiteracy in the United States: A report to the Ford Foundation.* New York: McGraw-Hill.

Kacandes, J. G. (1969). Innovation in reading instruction: An adult learning center. In J. A. Mangano (Ed.), *Strategies for adult basic education.* Newark, DE: International Reading Association.

Kane, M., Berryman, S., Goslin, D., & Meltzer, A. (1990). *The Secretary's Commission on Achieving Necessary Skills: Identifying and describing the skills required by work.* Washington, DC: U.S. Department of Labor Employment & Training Administration. Retrieved January 7, 2005, from http://wdr.doleta.gov/SCANS/idsrw/idsrw.pdf

Kegan, R., Broderick, M., Drago-Severson, E., Helsing, D., Popp, N., & Portnow, K. (2001). *Toward a new pluralism in ABE/ESOL classrooms: Teaching to multiple "Cultures of Mind" executive summary* (NCSALL Rep. No. 19a). Boston: National Center for the Study of Adult Learning and Literacy. Retrieved January 2, 2005, from http://gseweb.harvard.edu/~ncsall/research/report19a.pdf

Knowles, M. S. (1970). *The modern practice of adult education.* New York: Association Press.

Kutner, M. A., Furey, S., Webb, L., & Gadsden, V. (1990). *Adult education programs and services: A view from nine programs.* Washington, DC: Pelavin Associates. (ERIC Document Reproduction Service No. ED 334456)

Lane, C. W., & Lewis, R., B. (1971). *Guidelines for establishing and operating an adult learning laboratory.* Raleigh: North Carolina State University, School of Education. (ERIC Document Reproduction Service No. ED 052436)

LaPlante, W. (1969). The reading program—Civilian Conservation Centers. In J. A. Mangano (Ed.), *Strategies for adult basic education.* Newark, DE: International Reading Association.

Leahy, M. A. (1991). *The Adult Education Act: A guide to the literature and funded projects* (Information Series No. 347). Columbus, OH: ERIC Clearinghouse on Adult, Career, and Vocational Education. (ERIC Document Reproduction Service No. ED 341876)

Mangano, J. A. (Ed.). (1969). *Strategies for adult basic education.* Newark, DE: International Reading Association.

Martin, W. T. J. (1966). *Fundamentals learning laboratories in industrial education centers, technical institutes and community colleges in North Carolina.* Unpublished doctoral dissertation, Duke University, Durham, NC.

McCalley, H. (1966). *Basic education for adults: Are special tools and techniques needed. Panel and Workshop VI.* Paper presented at the National Conference on Manpower Training and the Older Worker, Washington, DC. (ERIC Document Reproduction Service No. ED 017787)

Merriam, S. B., & Brockett, R. G. (1997). *The profession and practice of adult education: An introduction.* San Francisco: Jossey-Bass.

Mezirow, J., Darkenwald, G. G., & Knox, A. B. (1975). *Last gamble on education: Dynamics of adult basic education.* Washington, DC: Adult Education Association of the USA. (ERIC Document Reproduction Service No. ED 112119)

Mikulecky, L., & Lloyd, P. (1997). Evaluation of workplace literacy programs: A profile of effective instructional practices. *Journal of Literacy Research, 29,* 555–585.

Mocker, D. W., & Sherk, J. (1970). Developing a learning center in ABE. *Adult Leadership, 19*(2), 48–50, 61–62.

Montclair State College. (1970). *Curricular-instructional materials and related media for the disadvantaged adult in the 1970's: Conference Proceedings.* Cherry Hill, NJ: Author. (ERIC Document Reproduction Service No. ED 041218)

Murphy, G. (1969). Individualizing instruction in adult basic education programs. In J. A. Mangano (Ed.), *Strategies for adult basic education.* Newark, DE: International Reading Association.

New York State Education Department. (1971). *Functions of the New York State learning laboratories.* Albany: New York State Education Department. (ERIC Document Reproduction Service No. ED 052468)

North Carolina State Department of Community Colleges. (1975). *Report to the North Carolina State Board of Education on adult basic education.* Raleigh: North Carolina State Department of Community Colleges, Division of Adult Services. (ERIC Document Reproduction Service No. ED 120531)

Paris, S., & Parecki, A. (1993). *Metacognitive aspects of adult literacy.* Philadelphia: National Center on Adult Literacy.

Purcell-Gates, V., Degener, S., Jacobson, E., & Soler, M. (2000). *Affecting change in literacy practices of adult learners: Impact of two dimensions of instruction.* (NCSALL Tech. Rep. No. 17). Boston: National Center for the Study of Adult Learning and Literacy. Retrieved January 6, 2005, from http://www.gse.harvard.edu/~ncsall/research/report17.pdf

Quigley, B. A. (1997). *Rethinking literacy education: The critical need for practice-based change.* San Francisco: Jossey-Bass.

Quigley, B. A. (2000). Retaining adult learners in the first three critical weeks: A quasi-experimental model for use in ABE programs. *Adult Basic Education, 10*(2), 55–68.

Quigley, B. A., & Holsinger, E. (1993). "Happy consciousness": Ideology and hidden curricula in literacy education. *Adult Education Quarterly, 44,* 17–33.

Radwin, E. (1984). *Promoting innovation and controversy in adult basic education: Section 309 of the Adult Education Act.* San Francisco: Far West Lab for Educational Research and Development.

Rigg, P., & Kazemek, F. E. (1985). For adults only: Reading materials for adult literacy students. *Journal of Reading, 28,* 726–731.

Sandlin, J. A. (2000). The politics of consumer education materials used in the adult literacy classroom. *Adult Education Quarterly, 50,* 289–307.

Sepede, J. H. (1972). Individualizing ABE programs through learning packets. *Adult Leadership, 20,* 289–290.

Smith, C., & Hofer, J. (2003). *The characteristics and concerns of adult basic education teachers* (NCSALL Rep. No. 26). Boston: National Center for the Study of Adult Learning and Literacy. Retrieved April 27, 2004, from http://www.gse.harvard.edu/~ncsall/research/report26.pdf

Solórzano, R. W. (1993). *Reducing illiteracy: Review of effective practices in adult literacy programs: Vol. I. Research report.* Princeton, NJ: Educational Testing Service. (ERIC Document Reproduction Service No. ED 390885)

Southern Regional Education Board. (1971). *The professional staff development plans of Region IV.* Atlanta, GA: Author. (ERIC Document Reproduction Service No. ED 060441)

Teachey, W. G., & Carter, J. B. (1971). *Learning laboratories: A guide to adoption and use.* Englewood Cliffs, NJ: Educational Technology Publications.

Ulmer, C., & Dorland, J. (1981). Modern adult basic education: An overview. In L. Y. Mercier (Ed.), *Outlook for the 80's: Adult literacy* (pp. 1–22). Washington, DC: U.S. Department of Education. (ERIC Document Reproduction Service No. ED 211701)

Venezky, R. L., Sabatini, J. P., Brooks, C., & Carino, C. (1996). *Policy and practice in adult learning: A case study perspective.* (National Center on Adult Literacy Tech. Rep. TR96-06). Retrieved March 18, 2003, from http://www.literacyonline.org/products/ncal/pdf/TR9606.pdf

Young, M. B. (1980). *An assessment of the state-administered program of the Adult Education Act: Final report.* Arlington, VA: Development Associates, Inc. (ERIC Document Reproduction Service No. ED 195700)

Young, M. B., Fleischman, H., Fitzgerald, N., & Morgan, M. (1995). *National evaluation of adult education programs executive summary.* Arlington, VA: Development Associates, Inc. (ERIC Document Reproduction Service No. ED 385762)

6

Health Literacy: An Update of Medical and Public Health Literature

Rima E. Rudd
With Jennie Epstein Anderson, Sarah Oppenheimer, and Charlotte Nath

Health literacy has been commonly defined as "the degree to which individuals have the capacity to obtain, process, and understand basic health information and services needed to make appropriate health decisions" (U.S. Department of Health and Human Services [HHS], 2000). However, subsequent discussions of research in health literacy have highlighted the importance of moving beyond a focus on individuals' skills to consider health literacy as an interaction between the demands of health systems and the skills of individuals (HHS, 2000; Institute of Medicine, 2004). Health literacy now represents a substantive area of research in public health and medicine and has been recognized as an important element in the nation's health agenda. This chapter provides an overview of the health literacy literature that appeared between 2000 and mid-2005. We begin where "Health and Literacy: A Review of Medical and Public Health Literature," published in Volume 1 of the *Annual Review of Adult*

Learning and Literacy (Rudd, Moeykens, & Colton, 2000), left off. First, we provide a short history of the growth of the academic field of health literacy. Next we describe the methods we used to select articles, and then we discuss key research issues drawn from publications in the field.

HISTORY OF THE FIELD

The field of inquiry commonly referred to as health literacy has grown considerably since 2000 when "Health and Literacy: A Review of Medical and Public Health Literature" was published (Rudd et al., 2000). At the time of publication, information related to the 1992 National Adult Literacy Survey (NALS) was still new to many in the health fields and the dissemination of findings was still under way. Of primary interest to health researchers and practitioners was the principle finding that 47% to 51% of U.S. adults were limited in their ability to use print materials to accomplish everyday tasks. This statistic drew the attention of those concerned about implications for health activities and health outcomes.

Several decades of health studies in the United States, Britain, and Europe had already established strong links between health status and educational attainment or income, both commonly used as markers of socioeconomic status. However, the NALS findings highlighted the fact that literacy influences one's ability to access information and to navigate in the highly literate environments of modern society. Analyses of health materials published before and subsequent to the NALS findings indicated a mismatch between the reading level of health materials and the average reading skills of adults. Studies in the latter half of the 1990s yielded statistically significant differences in health-related knowledge and behaviors between those with strong reading skills and those with limited skills (Rudd et al., 2000). By the turn of the century, literacy and its implications for health outcomes was the focus of a growing number of research studies in health. At the start of the new century, the National Institutes of Health called for research proposals examining components of education for possible pathways to health.

Publications in peer-reviewed journals in medicine, health education, and public health indicated interest in the health-related implications of limited literacy skills along four strands or research themes. One strand focused on assessments of the readability of print communication and the match between health materials and the skills of intended audiences. Another strand of research focused on differences between patients with strong reading skills and patients with limited reading skills related to knowledge of disease and medical regimen, hospitalization, a variety of health behaviors, and physical markers of health status. A third strand included a growing number of studies focused on the promise for improving communication through the use of new technologies, as well as the use of icons. Finally, a fourth strand, not as fully developed as the others, focused on the development and, in some cases, the evaluation of programs designed to improve health literacy. Many of these programs considered literacy skills of the intended participants and then shaped materials or program design to more appropriately fit their needs. Some of the studies in this area focused on the effects of improvements to materials, such as substituting everyday words for medical language and jargon, and using short sentences and highlighting key points. These changes represent critical components of what is known as *plain language*.[35] Other studies focused on building communication and knowledge-exchange skills and capacity within communities and among patients and providers. New research efforts are focused on numeracy[36] and the listening and speaking skills so critical to public health communication and to the dialogue between clients or patients and a variety of health providers.

The number of studies and editorials addressing health literacy published between 2000 and the end of 2004 was more than double the number published between 1970 and 1999. A preliminary examination indicates that, to date, well over 200 articles can be found in the 2005 literature alone. Overall, the body of literature with some consideration of health literacy now consists of close to 1,000 articles. Furthermore, researchers from a broad spectrum of health fields—now including those from the oral health (dental health) and mental health fields—have published findings related to health literacy.

National conferences, white papers, and reports from prestigious agencies and academies have put health literacy on the national agenda. The growing interest in health literacy during the 1990s led to an articulation of improved health literacy as a national objective for Healthy People 2010, the 10-year health goals and objectives for the nation (HHS, 2000). Subsequently, HHS assembled scholars and practitioners to develop action plans and communication strategies for the six health communication

---

[35]*Plain language* is defined as a clear, simple, conversational style—one that presents information in a logical order.

[36]*Numeracy* is defined as "the knowledge and skills required to effectively manage the mathematical demands of diverse situations" (from http://www.ets.org/Media/Tests/ETS_Literacy/ALLS_NUMERACY.pdf).

objectives and issued a full report, *Communicating Health: Priorities and Strategies for Progress,* in 2003 (HHS, 2003a). One chapter of that report focuses on an action plan for health literacy. The Institute of Medicine (IOM) formed a committee on health literacy in late 2002 to study the field and produce an analytic report with research, practice, and policy recommendations entitled *Health Literacy: A Prescription to End Confusion,* published by the National Academies of Sciences in the spring of 2004 (IOM, 2004). Two other important publications were issued at the same time. The Agency for Healthcare Research and Quality (AHRQ) supported an inquiry into the quality of research in this nascent field and also published its report, *Literacy and Health Outcomes,* in the spring of 2004 (Berkman et al., 2004). Researchers, one of whom was involved in the development and analysis of the NALS (Kirsch, Jungeblut, Jenkins, & Kolstad, 1993), released *Literacy and Health in America* (Rudd, Kirsch, & Yamamoto, 2004), an examination of U.S. adults' literacy skills in health contexts based on the 1993 NALS data. By the end of 2004, the American Medical Association published *Understanding Health Literacy: Implications for Medicine and Public Health,* a text for medicine and public health professionals, with many of the health literacy researchers responsible for key publications in the 1990s through the present day serving as section editors and chapter authors (Schwartzberg, Van Geest, & Wang, 2005). White papers from professional working groups in oral health (NIDCR Workgroup Report, 2005) and in hospital and health care oversight (Workgroup on Health Literacy and Patient Safety, planned completion in 2006) offer calls to action and delineate research opportunities.

Many governmental, professional, and local health literacy initiatives began between 2003 and 2005. For example, in 2003, the National Institutes of Health (NIH) issued requests for research proposals for more in-depth explorations of the pathways connecting literacy and health. In 2004, 13 of the NIH institutes worked together to issue and support requests for proposals specifically addressing health literacy. The Health and Human Services Office of Disease Prevention and Health Promotion convened a cross-agency workgroup on health literacy that brings together staff from across HHS, including the NIH, the Centers for Disease Control and Prevention, the Food and Drug Administration (FDA), AHRQ, Health Resources and Services Administration, Centers for Medicare and Medicaid Services, and the Indian Health Service (IHS). The purpose of the workgroup is to address health literacy, which includes developing strategies to reduce literacy-related barriers to vital health communication.

The scope of health literacy inquiry has expanded as researchers and practitioners move beyond the medical encounter to consider health-related activities at home, at work, in the community, in the policy arena, and within health systems. The HHS action plan, the IOM report, and the Educational Testing Service (ETS) analysis of health literacy all called for such an expanded inquiry. Multiple national, state, and citywide health literacy initiatives have begun, some funded by the private sector. For example, the health literacy initiative led by the Literacy Assistance Center of New York City with the Mayor's Office of the City of New York focuses on skills adults need as they address health-related tasks at home, in the workplace, in the community, and in health care settings (Tassi, 2004).

The ETS report, *Literacy and Health in America*, offered a first look at health literacy skills through an analysis of existing health-related items drawn from large-scale surveys conducted before 2003 (Rudd, Kirsch et al., 2004). However, the 2003 National Assessment of Adult Literacy (NAAL) included a small purposive sample of health-related items, developed in cooperation with HHS. NAAL findings indicate no improvement in overall literacy skills of U.S. adults over the 1992 NALS (Kutner, Greenberg, & Baer, 2005) and even lower scores for health literacy proficiencies (Kutner, Greenberg, Jin, & Paulsen, 2006). Analyses in two different time periods indicate that large numbers of U.S. adults do not have health literacy skills that enable them to effectively use health materials to accomplish the many challenging and complex health-related tasks they encounter.

METHODS

To collect articles for this review update, we ran a computer-based search for relevant literature, using the PubMed, PsycINFO, and ERIC databases. We began with combinations of terms: *health, medical, functional* with *literacy, literate, illiteracy, readability, reading level,* and *health literacy*. We included articles from English-speaking industrialized nations. We also reviewed materials drawn from the Library of Medicine bibliography and from manual searches of journals that had published literacy and health or health literacy articles but were not yet included in the computer databases. We read the array of articles and sorted them into the four categories used in the earlier literature review:

- National reports. These reports analyze and add to previous research (covered in Rudd et al., 2000) and offer recommendations for research and policy change in the public and private sectors.
- Research on print text materials and measures.
- Research on nontext materials and measures.
- Research on health outcomes for people with different levels of reading skills.

This review, originally planned as a 5-year update, primarily offers citations from the years 2000 through 2004. However, the review was expanded into the sixth year and includes a review of articles published during the first half of 2005. Articles from 2005 are referenced insofar as they address a new area of inquiry or represent a new focus.

Analytic Reports

Traditionally, reviews of the literature in public health and medicine focus on articles published in peer-reviewed journals. However, this review begins with analytic reports, most of which were developed by request of governmental or national agencies and each of which report on policy implications. The purview of each of the reports, all published between the end of 2003 and the early months of 2004, is different. The HHS report presents an action plan for the health literacy objective noted in Healthy People 2010, the statement of goals and objectives for the health of the nation. The IOM report offers an assessment and overview of a newly emerging field and offers concrete recommendations for action to be taken by both governmental and nongovernmental agencies. The AHRQ report reviews and assesses the research linking literacy to health outcomes as the foundation for policy decisions. The ETS policy report provides a measure of literacy skills in health contexts and discusses implications for the education and health sectors.

Healthy People 2010 and Communicating Health: Priorities and Strategies for Progress. Healthy People 2010 sets forth a delineation of the national health goals and objectives for the nation covering a 10-year period (HHS, 2000). For the first time, Healthy People 2010 includes an objective to "improve the health literacy of persons with inadequate or marginal literacy skills" and action plans for the health literacy objective and the five other health communication objectives (HHS, 2000). *Communicating Health: Priorities and Strategies for Progress* (HHS, 2003a) offers an articulation of action plans for the health communication objectives.

The chapter focused on the action plan for the health literacy objective highlights the need to address characteristics of health systems, including the communication skills of professionals, institutional protocols, and print materials in common use such as health history forms, informed consent, discharge instructions, and patient education materials. The discussion of the health literacy action plan notes the mismatch between institutional assumptions and documented literacy skills of adults accessing and using health systems. Consequently, the health literacy action plan identifies key stakeholders and suggests a variety of action steps for government departments and agencies, private sector organizations, and professional associations. These include efforts to improve education, study and improve print materials, enhance communication skills among professionals, remove barriers to information and services, and decrease the complicated bureaucratic processes of health systems. Finally, the report suggests that new inquiries in health literacy expand beyond health care settings and include health actions and decisions at home, in the community, in the workplace, and in the policy arena (HHS, 2003a).

Institute of Medicine: Health Literacy—A Prescription to End Confusion. Over the course of the traditional 18-month work schedule, the IOM's Health Literacy Committee heard testimony from a wide variety of stakeholders and addressed definitions of terms, health contexts, measurement, research findings, culture, new media, and financial implications. The report (IOM, 2004) reflects the committee's analysis of the published research and programs, its review of the conceptual underpinnings of health literacy, and its considerations of implications for education and health policies. The report's premise is that health literacy is an interaction between social demands and skills of individuals, and that health literacy can be improved through a combination of more realistic demands and improved skills. Consequently, the report encourages researchers and practitioners to understand, measure, and modify both the demands of health systems and the skills of professionals, as well as the skills of the public.

The IOM report also stresses the need for attention to the array of health activities within multiple health contexts, and to the broad spectrum of literacy skills that include oral exchange, numeracy, and access to and accrual of background information related to health (IOM, 2004). The IOM committee report notes that current measures do not offer a sufficient assessment of health literacy, are too narrowly focused on the ability of individuals to use the written word (rather than on a full complement of skills, which include oral communication), and do not fully capture cultural nuances or the experiences of people with limited proficiency in English. The report highlights 18 findings and offers 15 recommendations for action that address program, policy, and research priorities directed toward various federal departments, health agencies and institutions, and the academic and private sectors.

Agency for Healthcare Research and Quality: Health Literacy and Health Outcomes. The AHRQ commissioned a report (Berkman et al., 2004) to review and assess the state of the art in health literacy and health outcome research studies. The researchers examined health literacy studies that used some measure of literacy skills and examined specific health outcomes.[37] The review covered methods and findings of close to 50 outcome studies, many of which were published before 2000. The findings from the AHRQ report indicated that limited literacy level, as measured by approximations of reading skills, is associated with a range of adverse health outcomes, such as knowledge and comprehension (e.g., Lindau et al., 2002), hospitalization (Baker, Gazmararian, Williams, et al., 2002), global measures of health (Kalichman & Rompa, 2000; Ross, Frier, Kelnar, & Deary, 2001; Schillinger et al., 2003), and management of chronic diseases (e.g., Arnold et al., 2001; Conlin & Schumann, 2002; Kalichman & Rompa, 2000; Miller et al., 2003; Schillinger et al., 2003). However, the report recommends that covariates such as education or socioeconomic status be more thoroughly explored and notes that cross-sectional studies do not provide needed insight into change over time. Furthermore, the analysis indicates that as intervention research increased over time, further work in this area is warranted (Berkman et al., 2004).

Educational Testing Service Policy Report: Literacy and Health in America. This analysis of health literacy skills among U.S. adults (Rudd, Kirsch, et al., 2004) was based on all the health-related tasks from large-scale surveys of adult literacy. These large-scale surveys, including the NALS and the International Adult Literacy Surveys (IALS) in the United States and in Canada, were all based on the concept of functional literacy as assessed through adults' ability to use print materials to accomplish mundane tasks. All items identified as health-related were coded as belonging to one of the following groupings of health activities: health

---

[37]Findings from this review were also published in a journal article (Dewalt, Berkman, Sheridan, Lohr, & Pignone, 2004).

promotion, health protection, disease prevention, health care and maintenance, and navigation of health systems. The resulting 191 items were assembled as the Health Activities Literacy Scale and then linked to the demographics of the 26,000 adults participating in the NALS. Mean health literacy scores were calculated by gender, education, minority status, nativity, age, and access to resources through a link to the NALS database. The report, *Literacy and Health in America* (Rudd, Kirsch, et al., 2004), indicates that approximately 47% to 51% of U.S. adults have low or limited literacy skills. Limited literacy proficiency is generally associated with lower educational attainment, presence of health-related restrictions (health problems that limit participation in work or school), minority or immigrant status, and lack of access to resources. Findings indicate that large percentages of vulnerable or at-risk groups do not have adequate skills to meet many of the health-related demands they are likely to encounter. The differences within and among various population groups with different levels of literacy proficiencies indicate powerful effects of social factors (Rudd, Kirsch, et al., 2004). The report, a first look at health literacy based on a national assessment, suggests changes in the education and health sectors and notes the importance of a collaborative effort between the two.

Common Issues

Each of the reports addressed issues related to the scope and measurement of health literacy, all noting the promise of early studies in health literacy that linked reading skills and health outcomes. All call for a broader scope of inquiry and for studies that continue to include—but also move beyond—the doctor–patient encounter, including investigations into health-related activities at home, in the workplace, in the community, and in a range of health systems and care settings.

In addition, each of the reports notes the importance of attention to the broad range of literacy skills, and highlights the need to examine math skills as well as the oral and aural language skills that are so important for public health announcements, media communication, and patient–provider exchanges. All of the reports concur that measures of health literacy now commonly used in research settings do not actually measure health literacy, but instead offer approximations of reading skills. Consequently, each report calls for the development of health literacy measures that address reading, writing, basic math, and oral language skills. The analyses also suggest that researchers more closely examine patients' information-seeking skills, consider the importance of background knowledge for health-related activities, and study the value of new technologies such as interactive computer programs, touch-screen technologies, voice components, DVDs, and the Internet. Furthermore, the IOM report urges researchers and practitioners to pay attention to culture and cultural differences and to prevailing and, perhaps, faulty assumptions about adults' background knowledge and experience. Finally, all of the reports identify issues related to policy, regulations, and research procedures and offer recommendations for change or new developments.

TEXT

The health literacy literature from 2000 through early 2005 includes examinations of health-related texts, print materials used for research tools and instruments, and health information posted on Web sites. The research findings indicate that health information continues to be written at levels of complexity that exceed the skills of average high school graduates. This mismatch has been documented for educational materials, instructions, informed consent, research instruments, and public health information and warnings about known dangers and hazards. Research findings also indicate that neither medical nor public health materials adequately prepare people to take needed action or to make informed decisions.

Most studies of print materials report use of a small variety of tools to assess the readability of materials. These tools include those for assigning a reading level to print materials, such as the SMOG Readability Formula (McLaughlin, 1969), FRY Formula (Fry, 1977), and the Flesch Reading Ease Formula (Flesch, 1948). Broader assessment tools, such as the SAM (Doak, Doak, & Root, 1996), look at reading-level calculations, as well as the organization and design of text, such as use of headings, font, white space, visuals, and cultural appropriateness. A few published assessments include the PMOSE/IKIRSCH (Mosenthal & Kirsch, 1998), a tool for assessing the level of complexity of the structure of "documents"—those materials formatted as lists, charts, and graphs.

New Assessment Measures and Focus

Most of the published studies in health literacy focus on assessments of health materials. These inquiries set the foundation for health literacy studies and, starting from the mid-1960s, provided evidence of the "high demand" of health materials on literacy skills (Rudd et al., 2000). Such studies continue to be published as researchers examine literature from a wide range of health-related fields. In addition, researchers are expanding the analysis of materials to include examinations of research and survey instruments and commonly used psychosocial measurement scales, as well as a variety of information posted on Web sites. Findings remain consistent and indicate that health information continues to be written at levels of complexity that exceed the skills of average high school graduates. For the most part, this body of literature uses a reading grade level as an indicator of the level of difficulty of existing text. One study reports on the process of assessing materials (Harvey & Fleming, 2000), and another on the process of assessing and rewriting materials (Rudd, Kaphingst, Colton, Gregoire, & Hyde, 2004). Two studies focus on processes and tools for assessing materials posted on the Internet (Bernstam, Shelton, Walji, & Meric-Bernstam, 2005).

Research Instruments

The well-documented mismatch between the reading levels of health-related materials and NALS findings of adults' ability to use text found in everyday life spurred interest in medical and research concepts, instruments, and processes.

Literacy-related barriers could influence participation in research studies and compromise data, as well as confound analysis. For example, informed consent is linked to all research efforts. Studies indicate a long-standing mismatch between the reading demand of consent forms and the reading skills of average high school graduates. Kubba (2000) found that the reading skill level of otolaryngology patients under study was lower than the reading level of information leaflets, admission notification letters, and surgical consent forms in use. Cox (2002) found that patients did not understand the informed consent materials for a cancer clinical trial. Conlin and Schumann (2002) found that the reading skill levels of open-heart-surgery patients were lower than the reading level of informed consent forms and discharge instructions. Gausman Benson and Forman (2002) found that informed consent forms were too complicated for affluent geriatric patients in their study. Finally, an examination of materials provided by institutional review boards indicated that they commonly provide text for informed consent materials that is written at reading levels that are too high and do not meet their own readability standards (Paasche-Orlow, Taylor, & Brancati, 2003).

Several studies indicate that many types of research instruments should be examined for literacy-related barriers. For example, Sentell and Ratcliff-Baird (2003) found less comprehension of the Beck Depression Inventory[38] among those with limited reading skills. Woloshin, Schwartz, Moncur, Gabriel, and Tosteson (2001) found that those with limited reading skills were less likely to understand risk–benefit analyses. These studies indicate that health measures that assume critical concepts are being widely understood may be assessing literacy skills instead of the main variable of interest.

New Technologies

A number of studies looked beyond booklets and pamphlets to explore new communication approaches, including the Internet, multimedia computer software, and the use of touch-screen technology to communicate health information to patients with low health literacy skills. The use of a computer and access to the Internet must still be considered print material and would not, of course, increase access to information if the materials are written at levels beyond the average reading skills of the public.

Several studies reported on the readability and accessibility of health-related information on the Internet and indicate that sophisticated reading skills are needed to access and comprehend Web-based health information (Berland et al., 2001; D'Alessandro, Kingsley, & Johnson-West, 2001; Friedman, Hoffman-Goetz, & Arocha, 2004). Birru and colleagues (2004) discussed the importance of having health information on the Internet written at low reading levels, and with culturally appropriate references. Furthermore, studies do not yet indicate whether use of computers enhances or diminishes people's ability to locate needed information.

Some researchers have experimented with the use of touch-screen technology to bypass some of the difficult aspects of computer use. Hahn and colleagues (2004) discussed the use of a "talking touch screen" as a practical, user-friendly data acquisition method that allows providers to measure self-reported outcomes in patients with a range of literacy skills.

---

[38]The Beck Depression Inventory (BDI, BDI-II), created by Dr. Aaron T. Beck, is a 21-question multiple-choice survey that is one of the most widely used instruments for measuring depression severity (http://en.wikipedia.org/wiki/Beck_Depression_Inventory).

Lobach, Arbanas, Mishra, Campbell, and Wildemuth (2004) reported on the development of a computer system that uses touch-screen technology to gather health information from patients with low literacy skills and has implications for both educating patients and research applications. This computer system is being used in an academically affiliated family medicine clinic and in an indigent adult medicine clinic; study findings are not yet available.

Beyond the Printed Word

A small but accumulating body of literature includes the study of materials that use symbols, cartoons, and pictograms for communicating critical health and medical information. Approximately 20 studies have examined outcomes associated with specific low-literacy materials that include use of pictographs, videos, and interactive multimedia software, as well as comic books. For example, a number of studies indicate that pictographs used in medicine labels and medical instructions have helped patients increase their knowledge (Houts, Witmer, Egeth, Loscalzo, & Zabora, 2001). Mansoor and Dowse (2003) reported that pictograms on medicine labels and patient information leaflets had a positive effect on patients' acquisition and comprehension of drug information. Leiner, Handal, and Williams (2004) reported on the increased effectiveness of using cartoons over text-based materials for delivering information about polio vaccinations to patients. However, Hwang, Tram, and Knarr (2005) found that commonly used illustrations on medicine labels were of little or no use in improving patients' comprehension of the medication for patients under study.

Examinations of the use of videos indicate increased understanding among patients viewing videos compared to patients using print materials. These studies include use of videos or interactive software products for prostate cancer treatment (Diefenbach & Butz, 2004; Rovner et al., 2004), for breast cancer screening among Latinas (Borrayo, 2004), for sleep disorders (Murphy, Chesson, Walker, Arnold, & Chesson, 2000), and for polio vaccines (Leiner et al., 2004).

MEASURES OF LITERACY SKILLS

Most of the researchers in the published literature linking patient or client skills to health outcomes use one of two commonly used measures: the Rapid Estimate of Adults' Literacy (REALM) or the short form of the Test of Functional Health Literacy in Adults (TOFHLA). Both of these instruments, developed in the 1990s, were discussed at length in the first review of the literature (Rudd et al., 2000). The REALM is based on a word recognition test and the short form of the TOFHLA on a cloze-style reading comprehension test. Both tests can be administered in a brief period of time in medical and research settings. In addition, both tests correlate well with each other and with other tests of reading skills and have been used effectively to distinguish between groups of patients with varying levels of reading skills and a variety of health outcomes. However, the IOM, AHRQ, and ETS reports concur that these tools offer approximations of reading skills and do not test health literacy.

ETS developed a computer-based test, the Health and Literacy Survey, a 30-minute assessment of adult literacy skills in health contexts (ETS, 2005). They developed this tool in late 2004 after the publication of the ETS report. It is based on items from the large-scale assessments of adult literacy, including the NALS, IALS, and the NAAL, and can be linked to national measures. Most recently, Weiss (2005) announced the development of a new and short tool, *The Newest Vital Sign,* resembling the material and question format used in the NALS and NAAL. The instrument allows a researcher to determine a patient's document literacy skills.

HEALTH OUTCOME STUDIES

New developments in examinations of health outcomes over the course of the past 5 years include measures of differences between those with more limited reading skills and those with strong reading skills (as assessed by the REALM or the short form of the TOFHLA) for knowledge and understanding of a variety of health-related concepts such as risk, probability, or chronicity (Arnold et al., 2001). Similarly, several studies document that an understanding of chronic diseases and of associated treatment protocols is related to reading skills (Gazmararian, Williams, Peel, & Baker, 2003; Kalichman et al., 2000; Kalichman & Rompa, 2000; Van Servellen, Brown, Lombardi, & Herrera, 2003). Two studies found that patients with poor reading skills had poorer physical and mental health compared to those with stronger skills (Gazmararian, Baker, Parker, & Blazer, 2000; Sentell & Shumway, 2003). Findings indicate that participants with lower reading skills are less likely than those with stronger skills to engage in health-promoting behaviors (Kaufman, Skipper, Small, Terry, & McGrew, 2001), to engage in screening programs (Davis et al., 2001; Dolan et al.,

2004; Fortenberry et al., 2001; Lindau et al., 2002), or to access appropriate health care (Baker et al., 2004; Pirisi, 2000; Scott, Gazmararian, Williams, & Baker, 2002). In addition, patients with limited reading skills are less likely to follow preoperative instructions (Chew, Bradley, Flum, Cornia, & Koepsell, 2004) or to be compliant with breast cancer treatment protocols (Li et al., 2000), and are more likely to be hospitalized than are those with strong reading skills (Baker, Gazmararian, Williams, et al., 2002; Gordon, Hampson, Capell, & Madhok, 2002).

Study findings link reading skills to biological change and disease burden as well. Several research publications indicate that study participants with poor reading and numeracy skills, compared to those with stronger skills, have worse anticoagulation control (Estrada, Martin-Hryniewicz, Peek, Collins, & Byrd, 2004) and worse control of diabetes (Endres, Sharp, Haney, & Dooley, 2004; Kim, Love, Quistberg, & Shea, 2004; Schillinger et al., 2002). Diabetes research indicates that diabetic children between the ages of 5 and 17 had poorer glycemic control if their parents had limited reading skills (Ross et al., 2001).

Other research studies document decreased cognition (Baker, Gazmararian, Sudano, et al., 2002a; Barnes, Tager, Satariano, & Yaffe, 2004) and increased levels of depression or other mental health issues (Gazmararian et al., 2000; Sentell & Shumway, 2003) among patients with limited reading skills compared to others with stronger skills. Several studies document increased rates of cervical cancer among those with more limited reading skills (Lindau et al., 2002; Sharp, Zurawski, Roland, O'Toole, & Hines, 2002).

Costs associated with literacy are often considered another outcome variable. Three reports indicate an increased cost to the health system (Baker et al., 2004; Howard, Gazmararian, & Parker, 2005; Weiss & Palmer, 2004). Howard and colleagues (2005), for example, concluded that persons with inadequate health literacy incur higher medical costs and use an inefficient mix of services. However, the IOM (2004) report concluded that no studies to date have differentiated costs linked to patient literacy and costs associated with medical errors. Thus, there might not yet be sufficient evidence to associate a particular cost with patient literacy level.

NUMERACY

The national and international surveys of adult literacy included assessments of quantitative or numeracy skills. Policy recommendations in the

HHS and IOM reports, noted earlier, call for attention to a full range of literacy skills in health contexts, including quantitative skills, as do several health researchers (Woloshin et al., 2001; Zarcadoolas, Pleasant, & Greer, 2005). Such skills are needed for day-to-day health-related activities, including comparison shopping, discounting, measuring, calculating, dosing, and scheduling and timing of medicine (Rudd, Kirsch, et al., 2004). Woloshin and colleagues (2001) measured numeracy skills among a group of volunteers and concluded that limited numeracy skills may be an important barrier for patients who are asked to make decisions based on an understanding of risk and probability. One of the mandated responsibilities of public health practice is to alert the public to dangers and hazards based on risk assessments. Practitioners and researchers have been remiss in their ability to provide such information and continue to use problematic texts and complex calculations (J. Hyde, personal correspondence, 2005). Golbeck, Ahlers-Schmidt, Paschal, and Dismuke (2005) proposed a distinct definition of health numeracy to spur additional research in this area.

CONTRIBUTIONS OF VARIOUS DISCIPLINES

Over the past 5 years, research in health literacy has expanded beyond examinations of the medical encounter and now includes more papers from professionals involved in public health, health education, oral health, mental health, and nursing. Attention to health literacy among a broader group of professionals is indicative of how interest in the topic has spread. To date, health literacy research in fields such as public health, pharmacy, occupational health, and social work has been relatively sparse when compared to publications in medicine; however, the numbers of such studies are increasing. In addition, researchers in public health, oral health, mental health, nursing, and pharmacology report testing direct interventions that promote better health communication.

Public Health

Few public health studies, beyond those focused on screening noted previously, examine literacy-related barriers to access of public health information. At the same time, public health literature has traditionally included attention to diffusion of information, communication efforts, and the design of specific messages. Communication failures have been linked to poor design of materials or text, insufficient piloting, and, only recently, to lack of attention to literacy-related issues. Two studies report attempts to assess and reduce the reading demand of public health materials such as brochures about water safety sent to all households in a state (Rudd, Colton, Das, DeJong, & Hyde, 2003; Rudd, Kaphingst, et al., 2004). Another study focused on health alerts concluded there is a need for increased rigor in the development of official announcements. For example, the anthrax-related postcard sent to all households in the country by the Postmaster General, one of only two national household mailings on health, masked critical health information with the use of unnecessarily cumbersome terms. Researchers argue that information provided during times of crisis must be developed and designed with rigor, and in plain language, to assure clear communication (Rudd, Comings, & Hyde, 2003). Zarcadoolas and colleagues (2005) similarly noted the need for clear communication in times of crisis and, most especially, instances of bioterrorism.

Oral Health

The Surgeon General's *National Call to Action to Promote Oral Health* (HHS, 2003b) notes that all stakeholders should work together and use data to enhance oral health literacy. To date, however, the majority of oral health studies pertaining to health literacy have addressed the paucity of educational resources written in plain language suitable for audiences with average or limited literacy skills (Alexander, 2000; Chestnutt, 2004). One study noted that the recognition of oral health problems and directives for oral health care may be linked to adults' ability to understand information provided (Gaston, 2002). Thus far, the published literature linking oral health and literacy is sparse (Williams, 2004). A working group white paper and several articles and editorials published in 2005 do call for more attention to oral health literacy, research, and intervention development and implementation (NIDCR Workgroup Report, 2005; Rudd & Horowitz, 2005a, 2005b).

Mental Health

Literacy research in the field of mental health has been less rooted in materials development and more centered on outcomes-based research, measurement issues, and the effects of mental health literacy. Research includes a focus on the extent to which limited health literacy may serve as a contributor to poor mental health status (Gazmarian et al., 2000; Sentell & Shumway, 2003). Studies have also addressed the extent to which results from existing measurement tools used in mental health research and practice (e.g., the Beck Depression Inventory and the Mini-Mental State Examination) may be confounded or skewed by respondents' limited literacy skills (Baker, Gazmararian, Sudano, et al., 2002; Sentell & Ratcliff-Baird, 2003).

In addition, research in the mental health field introduces the concept of *mental health literacy* as a term used to describe knowledge and understanding of mental health issues specifically (Goldney, Fisher, & Wilson, 2001; Jorm, 2000). The concept of mental health literacy is focused on the content of mental health information and not on the functional skills needed to engage in mental health actions. Mental health literacy, or lack thereof, has been used as a possible factor to explain uncertainties or lack of knowledge about mental health and the ensuing effects on effective treatment and care. The degree to which mental health literacy as a separate and slightly altered concept will be integrated into subsequent research and practice has yet to be seen, and will presumably have significant implications for the tone and direction of future research in this field.

Nursing

Nurses have long played a role in patient education, and the nursing literature has been attentive to issues related to education background and, increasingly, to literacy (Rootman, 2004). Many articles in the nursing literature mentioning education or literacy focus on the suitability of both print (Galloway, Murphy, Chesson, & Martinez, 2003; Winslow, 2001) and Internet-based patient information (Oermann & Wilson, 2000). Some studies have assessed the general importance of lower reading level materials; others link the importance of reading skills for specific health content areas such as cancer prevention or cardiovascular care (Chelf et al., 2001; Conlin & Schumann, 2002; Wilson, Baker, Brown-Syed, & Gollop, 2000). Some research includes a focus on nurse–patient communication and the oral exchange (Alspach, 2004; Glanville, 2000).

Although most health literacy studies conducted by and for nurses have focused primarily on raising awareness, several discussion papers offer insights on how nurses can be involved in more tangible change through materials design (Horner, Surratt, & Juliusson, 2000; Ross, Potter, & Armstrong,

2004) and intervention development (Evers, 2001; Mayer & Villaire, 2004; Wydra, 2001). Given the enormous growth of literature on nursing and health literacy, it is expected that this field will continue to be a major contributor to health literacy and will play an increasingly critical role in translating health literacy research into practice.

Pharmacology

Recent pharmacology research has contributed to the body of literacy focused on the readability levels of printed health resources, specifically, medication package inserts and other direct-to-consumer drug information (Hochhauser, 2002; Kirksey, Harper, Thompson, & Pringle, 2004). Literature in this field highlights the importance of written materials for the proper use of medicine and the ways that the written materials may limit or support treatment and adherence (Koo, Krass, & Aslani, 2003; Mansoor & Dowse, 2003). Several editorials and articles highlight the particular role played by pharmacists and the assistance they could offer in encouraging medication adherence. These articles focus on the critical need for pharmacists to consider health literacy as they talk with patients (Nichols-English & Poirier, 2000; Youmans & Schillinger, 2003).

An article by Rothman and colleagues (2004), for example, addresses the responsibility of pharmacists who can provide a bridge between patients' limited literacy skills and successful medicine use. Findings indicate that diabetes patients educated by pharmacists maintained better glycemic control. However, Praska, Kripalani, Seright, and Jacobson (2005) reported that community-based pharmacists may not be attentive to the needs of patients with limited literacy skills.

The published literature related to pharmacology indicates a growing interest in medicine labels, patient package inserts (PPIs), and advertising. Ross and colleagues (2004) developed and field-tested a PPI for oral contraceptives that the FDA will soon be using. PPIs for oral contraceptives were previously written at 10th- and 12th-grade reading levels; this new PPI is written at a 6th-grade reading level. Emerging research topics in this field include attention to speakers of other languages. For example, Leyva, Sharif, and Ozuah (2005) reported that medicine labels were difficult for Spanish-speaking patients with limited English proficiency to read and understand.

Prescription drug information developed for print format and television advertisements has drawn attention as well. For example, Kaphingst and colleagues examined direct-to-consumer advertisements for prescription medications and found that the available print materials are too complicated for adults with average literacy skills (Kaphingst, Rudd, DeJong, & Daltroy, 2004). This same research team also reported that consumers with limited literacy skills recalled the benefits of drug information presented in television advertisements, but not the risks (Kaphingst, Rudd, DeJong, & Daltroy, 2005).

Efficacious and Innovative Approaches

Researchers have studied brochures and booklets that use plain language and are written at reading grades below high school levels for a wide range of public health issues, such as immunizations (Evers, 2001), hepatitis (Wilson, 2003), breast self-exams (Coleman et al., 2003), and diabetes care (Echeverry, Dike, Washington, & Davidson, 2003). In most instances, materials more appropriately matched with the reading skills of the intended audience have been associated with healthful outcomes, such as decreased emergency department visits (Herman & Mayer, 2004) and decreased anxiety (Coyne et al., 2003).

One study of vaccine information combined videos with the use of brochures and found an increase in the likelihood that patients would talk with providers about vaccines and then receive a vaccination (Thomas et al., 2003). Borrayo (2004) reported on the use of a video in a soap opera format to create awareness about breast cancer and to motivate low-literacy Latinas to have mammograms. Rossi, McClellan, Chou, and Davis (2004) found that ankle fracture surgery patients who watched a video before signing a consent form were more likely to understand the surgery than those who only received a verbal explanation of the surgery. One article focused on the development of an asthma glossary of terms to help patients with asthma access print materials with greater ease and suggests that companion materials such as glossaries may help patients engage more easily in discussions with caregivers (Rudd, Zobel, et al., 2004).

Elkind, Pitts, and Ybarra (2002) reported that a one-act Spanish play in Washington State enacted by a community players' group increased participants' positive knowledge about farm health and safety. In another innovative use of media, Rich (2004) found that videos developed by children and adolescents provide clinicians with insight into patient health issues perhaps beyond what the patients may have been able to offer orally. Communications that use audio and visual components may prove promising for people with limited literacy skills.

Materials developed in Canada and in the United States have been designed to help professionals improve health literacy. Examples may be found in the Canadian National Literacy and Health Program (in association with the Canadian Public Health Association), which offers a Plain Language Service that provides plain language and clear design assessments and revisions, as well as focus testing and workshops for the public, private, and voluntary sectors for health products intended for the general public (Canadian Public Health Association, 2005). In addition, the program's Health Resources Centre continues to publish materials and guidelines that incorporate plain language approaches for work with seniors and others with low literacy skills. In the United States, the American Medical Association used video segments from tapes accumulated in medical practices in Louisiana and Georgia to develop a video and accompanying materials for medical practitioners interested in learning about health literacy and techniques for working with patients who have low literacy skills (Weiss, 2003). Researchers with the National Center for the Study of Adult Learning and Literacy developed professional development programs for adult educators interested in teaching health literacy skills (Rudd et al., 2005). Finally, marking new potentials for greater ease in research studies, Kalichman and colleagues (2005) reported on the use of a visual analog scale, with pictographs, for a measure of medication adherence efficacy.

CONCLUSIONS

The body of literature and research addressing health literacy in the first 5 years of the new century has exponentially expanded the scope and depth of the knowledge base about health literacy. Published studies in health outcomes continue to address important concerns related to comprehension and knowledge, but also include sophisticated physical measures related to disease control or lack thereof. Published studies about materials assessment have moved beyond calculations of reading levels and now include closer examinations of organization, primacy of information, language, sentence structure, and layout and design elements. Researchers and practitioners are examining documents (materials in the form of lists, charts, and graphs) as well as prose (materials in full sentences in paragraph format), and are testing the match between the demands of materials and the skills of the intended audiences. Furthermore, new studies are focusing on materials and communication channels that move beyond the printed word. Similarly, new developments in implementation studies enable educators and clinicians to consider materials as vehicles of information exchange, as well as tools for completing health-related tasks. Studies are also examining the effects of these materials on behaviors of both health professionals and patients as they interact with one another.

Articles now published in a wide variety of professional journals indicate that many health professional groups have begun to pay attention to literacy-related issues and literacy-related barriers to action, care, and services. Professionals from multiple health-related disciplines have been examining the materials they develop and use, the match between the reading level of materials and the skills of the intended audiences, the links between literacy-related skills and a variety of health outcomes, and the links between literacy-related skills and health disparities.

At the same time, gaps are evident. Few studies focus on the communication or understanding of basic math skills related to complex mathematical concepts of risk and probability. Studies to date have not addressed the wider range of literacy skills that include oral comprehension and oral presentation—skills of particular interest for public health communications and for an understanding of the dialogue between clients or patients and service or health providers. Researchers have not yet examined the links between literacy or health literacy skills and documented health disparities among population groups in the United States. Few studies have looked at literacy issues in research settings—either the barriers to be found in the language and structure of commonly used measures or the effect of complex informed consent language for recruitment among minority population groups. Finally, the full potential for innovative use of computers has not been addressed or studied. For example, few, if any, computer programs or Internet sites on health topics include voice options or online glossaries.

The literature does indicate a change in perspective. During the 1990s, many health professionals evinced concern with reading deficits among adults, implying that the lack of reading skills alone explained problems such as lack of comprehension or inability to follow a regimen. Current articles indicate growing awareness of a shared responsibility in the communication process, and of literacy-related barriers in the health care environment (Rudd, 2004). Furthermore, the Healthy People 2010 Action Plans to achieve the health communication objectives (HHS, 2000) note clearly that the skills of health professionals, the use of jargon and technical language, and the complications of bureaucratic processes affect health literacy. Similarly, the IOM (2004) report on health literacy highlights that dual responsibility and indicates that health literacy is a shared function of social demands and individuals' skills.

Improvements in health literacy, suggested by both of these reports, require change within health systems and among health professionals, as well as changes in the skills of U.S. adults. Findings from the 1992 NALS (Kirsch et al., 1993) drew the attention of the health sector. The first publication of findings from the 2003 NAAL at the end of 2005 added additional confirmation of the 1992 findings, indicating little if any change over the course of 12 years. The health literacy literature indicates that improvements in health may well be linked to stronger investments in education in both the K–12 and adult education sectors.

The Healthy People 2010 and IOM reports identify critical stakeholders and partnerships that could be forged to improve health literacy. Links between adult education professionals and health professionals are specifically highlighted. Such partnerships can lead to mutual learning and contribute to improvements in both health literacy skills of the public and literacy-related demands within health systems.

REFERENCES

Alexander, R. E. (2000). Readability of published dental educational materials. *Journal of the American Dental Association, 131,* 937–942.

Alspach, G. (2004). Communicating health information: An epidemic of the incomprehensible. *Critical Care Nurse, 24*(4), 8, 10, 12, 14.

Arnold, C. L., Davis, T. C., Berkel, H. J., Jackson, R. H., Nandy, I., & London, S. (2001). Smoking status, reading level, and knowledge of tobacco effects among low-income pregnant women. *Preventive Medicine, 32,* 313–320.

Baker, D. W., Gazmararian, J. A., Sudano, J., Patterson, M., Parker, R. M., & Williams, M. V. (2002). Health literacy and performance on the Mini-Mental State Examination. *Aging & Mental Health, 6,* 22–29.

Baker, D. W., Gazmararian, J. A., Williams, M. V., Scott, T., Parker, R. M., Green, D., et al. (2002). Functional health literacy and the risk of hospital admission among Medicare managed care enrollees. *American Journal of Public Health, 92,* 1278–1283.

Baker, D. W., Gazmararian, J. A., Williams, M. V., Scott, T., Parker, R. M., Green, D., et al. (2004). Health literacy and use of outpatient physician services by Medicare managed care enrollees. *Journal of General Internal Medicine, 19,* 215–220.

Barnes, D. E., Tager, I. B., Satariano, W. A., & Yaffe, K. (2004). The relationship between literacy and cognition in well-educated elders. *Journals of Gerontology Series A: Biological Sciences and Medical Sciences, 59,* 390–395.

Berkman, N. D., DeWalt, D. A., Pignone, M. P., Sheridan, S. L., Lohr, K. N., Lux, L., et al. (2004). Literacy and health outcomes. *Evidence Report/Technology Assessment, 87,* 1–8.

Berland, G. K., Elliott, M. N., Morales, L. S., Algazy, J. I., Kravitz, R. L., Broder, M. S., et al. (2001). Health information on the Internet: Accessibility, quality, and readability in English and Spanish. *Journal of the American Medical Association, 285,* 2612–2621.

Bernstam, E. V., Shelton, D. M., Walji, M., & Meric-Bernstam, F. (2005). Instruments to assess the quality of health information on the World Wide Web: What can our patients actually use? *International Journal of Medical Informatics, 74,* 13–19.

Birru, M. S., Monaco, V. M., Charles, L., Drew, H., Njie, V., Bierria, T., et al. (2004). Internet usage by low-literacy adults seeking health information: An observational analysis. *Journal of Medical Internet Research, 6*(3), e25.

Borrayo, E. A. (2004). Where's Maria? A video to increase awareness about breast cancer and mammography screening among low-literacy Latinas. *Preventive Medicine, 39,* 99–110.

Canadian Public Health Association. (2005). *National Literacy and Health Program.* Retrieved December 29, 2005, from http://www.nlhp.cpha.ca/

Chelf, J. H., Agre, P., Axelrod, A., Cheney, L., Cole, D. D., Conrad, K., et al. (2001). Cancer-related patient education: An overview of the last decade of evaluation and research. *Oncology Nursing Forum, 28,* 1139–1147.

Chestnutt, I. G. (2004). Internet-derived patient information on common oral pathologies: Is it readable? *Primary Dental Care, 11*(2), 51–54.

Chew, L. D., Bradley, K. A., Flum, D. R., Cornia, P. B., & Koepsell, T. D. (2004). The impact of low health literacy on surgical practice. *American Journal of Surgery, 188,* 250–253.

Coleman, E. A., Coon, S., Mohrmann, C., Hardin, S., Stewart, B., Gibson, R. S., et al. (2003). Developing and testing lay literature about breast cancer screening for African American women. *Clinical Journal of Oncology Nursing, 7,* 66–71.

Conlin, K. K., & Schumann, L. (2002). Literacy in the health care system: A study on open heart surgery patients. *Journal of the American Academy of Nurse Practitioners, 14,* 38–42.

Cox, K. (2002). Informed consent and decision-making: Patients' experiences of the process of recruitment to phases I and II anti-cancer drug trials. *Patient Education and Counseling, 46,* 31–38.

Coyne, C. A., Xu, R., Raich, P., Plomer, K., Dignan, M., Wenzel, L. B., et al. (2003). Randomized, controlled trial of an easy-to-read informed consent statement for clinical trial participation: A study of the Eastern Cooperative Oncology Group. *Journal of Clinical Oncology, 21,* 836–842.

D'Alessandro, D. M., Kingsley, P., & Johnson-West, J. (2001). The readability of pediatric patient education materials on the World Wide Web. *Archives of Pediatrics and Adolescent Medicine, 155,* 807–812.

Davis, T. C., Dolan, N. C., Ferreira, M. R., Tomori, C., Green, K. W., Sipler, A. M., et al. (2001). The role of inadequate health literacy skills in colorectal cancer screening. *Cancer Investigation, 19,* 193–200.

Dewalt, D. A., Berkman, N. D., Sheridan, S., Lohr, K. N., & Pignone, M. P. (2004). Literacy and health outcomes: A systematic review of the literature. *Journal of General Internal Medicine, 19,* 1228–1239.

Diefenbach, M. A., & Butz, B. P. (2004). A multimedia interactive education system for prostate cancer patients: Development and preliminary evaluation. *Journal of Medical Internet Research, 6*(1), e3.

Doak, L., Doak, C., & Root, J. (1996). *Teaching patients with low literacy skills* (2nd ed.). Philadelphia: Lippincott.

Dolan, N. C., Ferreira, M. R., Davis, T. C., Fitzgibbon, M. L., Rademaker, A., Liu, D., et al. (2004). Colorectal cancer screening knowledge, attitudes, and beliefs among veterans: Does literacy make a difference? *Journal of Clinical Oncology, 22,* 2617–2622.

Echeverry, D. M., Dike, M. R., Washington, C., & Davidson, M. B. (2003). The impact of using a low-literacy patient education tool on process measures of diabetes care in a minority population. *Journal of the National Medical Association, 95,* 1074–1081.

Educational Testing Service. (2005). Test content for health activities literacy tests. Retrieved November 29, 2005, from www.ets.org

Elkind, P. D., Pitts, K., & Ybarra, S. L. (2002). Theater as a mechanism for increasing farm health and safety knowledge. *American Journal of Industrial Medicine, 42*(Suppl. 2), 28–35.

Endres, L. K., Sharp, L. K., Haney, E., & Dooley, S. L. (2004). Health literacy and pregnancy preparedness in pregestational diabetes. *Diabetes Care, 27,* 331–334.

Estrada, C. A., Martin-Hryniewicz, M., Peek, B. T., Collins, C., & Byrd, J. C. (2004). Literacy and numeracy skills and anticoagulation control. *American Journal of Medical Science, 328,* 88–93.

Evers, D. B. (2001). Teaching mothers about childhood immunizations. *MCN, American Journal of Maternal Child Nursing, 26,* 253–256.

Flesch, R. (1948). A new readability yardstick. *Journal of Applied Psychology, 32,* 2211–2223.

Fortenberry, J. D., McFarlane, M. M., Hennessy, M., Bull, S. S., Grimley, D. M., St. Lawrence, J., et al. (2001). Relation of health literacy to gonorrhea related care. *Sexually Transmitted Infections, 77,* 206–211.

Friedman, D. B., Hoffman-Goetz, L., & Arocha, J. F. (2004). Readability of cancer information on the Internet. *Journal of Cancer Education, 19,* 117–122.

Fry, R. (1977). Fry's readability graph: Clarifications, validity, and extension to level 17. *Journal of Reading, 21,* 241–252.

Galloway, G., Murphy, P., Chesson, A. L., & Martinez, K. (2003). MDA and AAEM informational brochures: Can patients read them? *Journal of Neuroscience Nursing, 35,* 171–174.

Gaston, M. A. (2002). Low literacy: A problem in health care. *Journal of Dental Hygiene, 76,* 172–173.

Gausman Benson, J., & Forman, W. B. (2002). Comprehension of written health care information in an affluent geriatric retirement community: Use of the Test of Functional Health Literacy. *Gerontology, 48,* 93–97.

Gazmararian, J. D., Baker, D., Parker, R., & Blazer, D. G. (2000). A multivariate analysis of factors associated with depression: Evaluating the role of health literacy as a potential contributor. *Archives of Internal Medicine, 160,* 3307–3314.

Gazmararian, J. A., Williams, M. V., Peel, J., & Baker, D. W. (2003). Health literacy and knowledge of chronic disease. *Patient Education and Counseling, 51,* 267–275.

Glanville, I. K. (2000). Moving towards health oriented patient education (HOPE). *Holistic Nursing Practice, 14,* 57–66.

Golbeck, A. L., Ahlers-Schmidt, C. R., Paschal, A. M., & Dismuke, S. E. (2005). A definition and operational framework for health numeracy. *American Journal of Preventive Medicine, 29,* 375–376.

Goldney, R. D., Fisher, L. J., & Wilson, D. H. (2001). Mental health literacy: An impediment to the optimum treatment of major depression in the community. *Journal of Affective Disorders, 64,* 277–284.

Gordon, M. M., Hampson, R., Capell, H. A., & Madhok, R. (2002). Illiteracy in rheumatoid arthritis patients as determined by the Rapid Estimate of Adult Literacy in Medicine (REALM) score. *Rheumatology, 41,* 750–754.

Hahn, E. A., Cella, D., Dobrez, D., Shiomoto, G., Marcus, E., Taylor, S. G., et al. (2004). The talking touchscreen: A new approach to outcomes assessment in low literacy. *Psychooncology, 13,* 86–95.

Harvey, H. D., & Fleming, P. (2000). A rapid appraisal method for the selection and pre-testing of environmental health leaflets. *Journal of the Royal Society of Health, 120,* 112–116.

Herman, A. D., & Mayer, G. G. (2004). Reducing the use of emergency medical resources among Head Start families: A pilot study. *Journal of Community Health, 29,* 197–208.

Hochhauser, M. (2002). Which prescription for the illegible and unreadable DTC (direct-to-consumer) brief summary—Major surgery or euthanasia? *Managed Care Quarterly, 10*(3), 6–10.

Horner, S. D., Surratt, D., & Juliusson, S. (2000). Improving readability of patient education materials. *Journal of Community Health Nursing, 17,* 15–23.

Houts, P. S., Witmer, J. T., Egeth, H. E., Loscalzo, M. J., & Zabora, J. R. (2001). Using pictographs to enhance recall of spoken medical instructions II. *Patient Education and Counseling, 43,* 231–242.

Howard, D. H., Gazmararian, J., & Parker, R. M. (2005). The impact of low health literacy on the medical costs of Medicare managed care enrollees. *American Journal of Medicine, 118*(4), 371–377.

Hwang, S. W., Tram, C. Q., & Knarr, N. (2005). The effect of illustrations on patient comprehension of medication instruction labels. *BMC Family Practice, 6*(1), 26.

Institute of Medicine. (2004). *Health literacy: A prescription to end confusion.* Washington, DC: National Academies Press.

Jorm, A. F. (2000). Mental health literacy: Public knowledge and beliefs about mental disorders. *British Journal of Psychiatry, 177,* 396–401.

Kalichman, S. C., Benotsch, E., Suarez, T., Catz, S., Miller, J., & Rompa, D. (2000). Health literacy and health-related knowledge among persons living with HIV/AIDS. *American Journal of Preventive Medicine, 18,* 325–331.

Kalichman, S. C., Cain, D., Fuhrel, A., Eaton, L., Di Fonzo, K., & Ertl, T. (2005). Assessing medication adherence self-efficacy among low-literacy patients: Development of a pictographic visual analogue scale. *Health Education Research, 20*(1), 24–35.

Kalichman, S. C., & Rompa, D. (2000). Functional health literacy is associated with health status and health-related knowledge in people living with HIV-AIDS. *Journal of Acquired Immune Deficiency Syndrome Human Retrovirology, 25,* 337–344.

Kaphingst, K. A., Rudd, R. E., DeJong, W., & Daltroy, L. H. (2004). Literacy demands of product information intended to supplement television direct-to-consumer prescription drug advertisements. *Patient Education and Counseling, 55,* 293–300.

Kaphingst, K. A., Rudd, R. E., DeJong, W., & Daltroy, L. H. (2005). Comprehension of information in three direct-to-consumer television prescription drug advertisements among adults with limited literacy. *Journal of Health Communication, 10,* 609–619.

Kaufman, H., Skipper, B., Small, L., Terry, T., & McGrew, M. (2001). Effect of literacy on breast-feeding outcomes. *Southern Medical Journal, 94,* 293–296.

Kim, S., Love, F., Quistberg, D. A., & Shea, J. A. (2004). Association of health literacy with self-management behavior in patients with diabetes. *Diabetes Care, 27,* 2980–2982.

Kirksey, O., Harper, K., Thompson, S., & Pringle, M. (2004). Assessment of selected patient educational materials of various chain pharmacies. *Journal of Health Community, 9,* 91–93.

Kirsch, I., Jungeblut, A., Jenkins, L., & Kolstad, A. (1993). *Adult literacy in America: The first look at the results of the National Adult Literacy Survey (NALS).* Washington, DC: U.S. Department of Education.

Koo, M. M., Krass, I., & Aslani, P. (2003). Factors influencing consumer use of written drug information. *Annals of Pharmacotherapy, 37,* 259–267.

Kubba, H. (2000). Reading skills of otolaryngology outpatients: Implications for information provision. *Journal of Laryngology & Otolology, 114,* 694–696.

Kutner, M., Greenberg, E., & Baer, J. (2005). *A first look at the literacy of America's adults in the 21st century* (NCES 2006-470. U.S. Department of Education. Washington, DC: National Center for Education Statistics.

Kutner, M., Greenberg, E., Jin, Y., & Paulsen, C. (2006). *The helth literacy of America's adults: Results from the 2003 National Assessment of Adult Literacy* (NCES 2006-483). U.S. Department of Education. Washington, DC: National Center for Education Statistics.

Leiner, M., Handal, G., & Williams, D. (2004). Patient communication: A multidisciplinary approach using animated cartoons. *Health Education and Research, 19,* 591–595.
Leyva, M., Sharif, I., & Ozuah, P. O. (2005). Health literacy among Spanish-speaking Latino parents with limited English proficiency. *Ambulatory Pediatrics, 5,* 56–59.
Li, B. D., Brown, W. A., Ampil, F. L., Burton, G. V., Yu, H., & McDonald, J. C. (2000). Patient compliance is critical for equivalent clinical outcomes for breast cancer treated by breast-conservation therapy. *Annals of Surgery, 231,* 883–889.
Lindau, S. T., Tomori, C., Lyons, T., Langseth, L., Bennett, C. L., & Garcia, P. (2002). The association of health literacy with cervical cancer prevention knowledge and health behaviors in a multiethnic cohort of women. *American Journal of Obstetrics and Gynecology, 186,* 938–943.
Lobach, D. F., Arbanas, J. M., Mishra, D. D., Campbell, M., & Wildemuth, B. M. (2004). Adapting the human-computer interface for reading literacy and computer skill to facilitate collection of information directly from patients. *Medinfo,* 1142–1146.
Mansoor, L. E., & Dowse, R. (2003). Effect of pictograms on readability of patient information materials. *Annals of Pharmacotherapy, 37,* 1003–1009.
Mayer, G. G., & Villaire, M. (2004). Low health literacy and its effects on patient care. *Journal of Nursing Administration, 34,* 440–442.
McLaughlin, G. H. (1969). SMOG grading: A new readability formula. *Journal of Reading, 12,* 639–646.
Miller, L. G., Liu, H., Hays, R. D., Golin, C. E., Ye, Z., Beck, C. K., et al. (2003). Knowledge of antiretroviral regimen dosing and adherence: A longitudinal study. *Clinical Infectious Diseases, 36,* 514–518.
Mosenthal, P. B., & Kirsch, I. (1998). A new measure for assessing document complexity: The PMOSE/IKIRSCH Document Readability Formula. *Journal of Adolescent and Adult Literacy, 41,* 638–657.
Murphy, P. W., Chesson, A. L., Walker, L., Arnold, C. L., & Chesson, L. M. (2000). Comparing the effectiveness of video and written material for improving knowledge among sleep disorders clinic patients with limited literacy skills. *Southern Medical Journal, 93,* 297–304.
Nichols-English, G., & Poirier, S. (2000). Optimizing adherence to pharmaceutical care plans. *Journal of the American Pharmaceutical Association, 40,* 475–485.
NIDCR Workgroup Report. (2005). The invisible barrier: Literacy and its relationship with oral health. *Journal of Public Health Dentistry, 65,* 174–182.
Oermann, M. H., & Wilson, F. L. (2000). Quality of care information for consumers on the Internet. *Journal of Nursing Care Quality, 14*(4), 45–54.
Paasche-Orlow, M. K., Taylor, H. A., & Brancati, F. L. (2003). Readability standards for informed-consent forms as compared with actual readability. *The New England Journal of Medicine, 348,* 721–726.
Pirisi, A. (2000). Low health literacy prevents equal access to care. *The Lancet, 356*(9244), 1828.
Praska, J. L., Kripalani, S., Seright, A. L., & Jacobson, T. A. (2005). Identifying and assisting low-literacy patients with medication use: A survey of community pharmacies. *Annals of Pharmacotherapy, 39,* 1441–1445.
Rich, M. (2004). Health literacy via media literacy: Video intervention/prevention assessment. *American Behavioral Scientist, 48,* 165–188.
Rootman, I. (2004). Health promotion and literacy: Implications for nursing. *Canadian Journal of Nursing Research, 36*(1), 13–21.
Ross, B. S., Potter, L. S., & Armstrong, K. A. (2004). Improving patient educational literature: An understandable patient package insert for "the pill." *Journal of Obstetric, Gynecologic, and Neonatal Nursing, 33,* 198–208.
Ross, L. A., Frier, B. M., Kelnar, C. J., & Deary, I. J. (2001). Child and parental mental ability and glycaemic control in children with Type 1 diabetes. *Diabetic Medicine, 18,* 364–369.

Rossi, M., McClellan, R., Chou, L., & Davis, K. (2004). Informed consent for ankle fracture surgery: Patient comprehension of verbal and videotaped information. *Foot & Ankle International, 25,* 1756–1762.

Rothman, R., Malone, R., Bryant, B., Horlen, C., DeWalt, D., & Pignone, M. (2004). The relationship between literacy and glycemic control in a diabetes disease-management program. *Diabetes Education, 30,* 263–273.

Rovner, D. R., Wills, C. E., Bonham, V., Williams, G., Lillie, J., Kelly-Blake, K., et al. (2004). Decision aids for benign prostatic hyperplasia: Applicability across race and education. *Medical Decision Making, 24,* 359–366.

Rudd, R. E. (2004). Navigating hospitals: Literacy barriers. *Literacy Harvest, 11*(1), 19–24.

Rudd, R. E., Colton, T. C., Das, J. K., DeJong, W., & Hyde, J. (2003). Mutual exchanges support academic and community collaboration. *Public Health Reports, 118,* 80–82.

Rudd, R. E., Comings, J. P., & Hyde, J. N. (2003). Leave no one behind: Improving health and risk communication through attention to literacy. *Journal of Health Communication, 8*(Suppl. 1), 104–115.

Rudd, R. E., & Horowitz, A. M. (2005a). Health and literacy: Supporting the oral health research agenda. *Journal of Public Health Dentistry, 65,* 131–132.

Rudd, R. E., & Horowitz, A. M. (2005b). The role of health literacy in achieving oral health for elders. *Journal of Dental Education, 69,* 1018–1021.

Rudd, R. E., Kaphingst, K. A., Colton, T., Gregoire, J., & Hyde, J. (2004). Rewriting public health information in plain language. *Journal of Health Communication, 9,* 195–206.

Rudd, R. E., Kirsch, I., & Yamamoto, K. (2004). *Literacy and health in America.* Princeton, NJ: Educational Testing Service.

Rudd, R. E., Moeykens, B. A., & Colton, T. C. (2000). Health and literacy: A review of medical and public health literature. In J. P. Comings, B. Garner, & C. Smith (Eds.), *The annual review of adult learning and literacy* (pp. 158–199). San Francisco: Jossey-Bass.

Rudd, R. E., Soricone, L., Santos, M., Zobel, E., Smith, J., & Lawrence, W. (2005). *Skills for health care access and navigation: Health literacy study circles.* Boston: World Education.

Rudd, R. E., Zobel, E., Fanta, C. H., Surkan, P., Rodriguez-Louis, J., Valderrama, Y., et al. (2004). Asthma in plain language. *Health Promotion Practice, 8,* 334–340.

Schillinger, D., Grumbach, K., Piette, J., Wang, F., Osmond, D., Daher, C., et al. (2002). Association of health literacy with diabetes outcomes. *Journal of the American Medical Association, 288,* 475–482.

Schillinger, D., Piette, J., Grumbach, K., Wang, F., Wilson, C., Daher, C., et al. (2003). Closing the loop: Physician communication with diabetic patients who have low health literacy. *Archives of Internal Medicine, 163,* 83–90.

Schwartzberg, J. E., Van Geest, J. B., & Wang, C. C. (Eds.). (2005). *Understanding health literacy: Implications for medicine and public health.* Chicago: American Medical Association.

Scott, T. L., Gazmararian, J. A., Williams, M. V., & Baker, D. W. (2002). Health literacy and preventive health care use among Medicare enrollees in a managed care organization. *Medical Care, 40,* 395–404.

Sentell, T. L., & Ratcliff-Baird, B. (2003). Literacy and comprehension of Beck Depression Inventory response alternatives. *Community Mental Health Journal, 39,* 323–331.

Sentell, T. L., & Shumway, M. A. (2003). Low literacy and mental illness in a nationally representative sample. *Journal of Nervous and Mental Disease, 191,* 549–552.

Sharp, L. K., Zurawski, J. M., Roland, P. Y., O'Toole, C., & Hines, J. (2002). Health literacy, cervical cancer risk factors, and distress in low-income African-American women seeking colposcopy. *Ethnicity & Disease, 12,* 541–546.

Tassi, A. (2004). The emergence of health literacy as a public policy priority: From research to consensus to action. *Literacy Harvest, 11*(1), 5–10.

Thomas, D. M., Ray, S. M., Morton, F. J., Drew, J. S., Offutt, G., Whitney, C. G., et al. (2003). Patient education strategies to improve pneumococcal vaccination rates: Randomized trial. *Journal of Investigative Medicine, 51,* 141–148.

U.S. Department of Health and Human Services. (2000). *Healthy people 2010: Understanding and improving health* (2nd ed.). Washington, DC: U.S. Government Printing Office.

U.S. Department of Health and Human Services. (2003a). *Communicating health: Priorities and strategies for progress—Action plans to achieve the health communication objectives in Healthy People 2010.* Washington, DC: U.S. Government Printing Office.

U.S. Department of Health and Human Services. (2003b). *A national call to action to promote oral health* (NIH Publication No. 03-5303). Rockville, MD: U.S. Department of Health and Human Services, Public Health Service, Centers for Disease Control and Prevention, and the National Institutes of Health, National Institute of Dental and Craniofacial Research.

Van Servellen, G. J., Brown, S., Lombardi, E., & Herrera, G. (2003). Health literacy in low-income Latino men and women receiving antiretroviral therapy in community-based treatment centers. *AIDS Patient Care and STDs, 17,* 283–298.

Weiss, B. D. (2003). *Health literacy: A manual for clinicians.* Chicago: American Medical Association Press.

Weiss, B. (2005). *The newest vital sign.* Retrieved November 29, 2005, from http://www.newestvitalsign.org

Weiss, B. D., & Palmer, R. (2004). Relationship between health care costs and very low literacy skills in a medically needy and indigent Medicaid population. *Journal of the American Board of Family Practitioners, 17*(1), 44–47.

Williams, L. N. (2004). More help for patients trying to become tobacco-free. *General Dentistry, 52,* 478–479.

Wilson, F. L., Baker, L. M., Brown-Syed, C., & Gollop, C. (2000). An analysis of the readability and cultural sensitivity of information on the National Cancer Institute's Web site: CancerNet. *Oncology Nursing Forum, 27,* 1403–1409.

Wilson, H. R. (2003). Hepatitis B and you: A patient education resource for pregnant women and new mothers. *Journal of Women's Health, 12,* 437–441.

Winslow, E. H. (2001). Patient education materials. *American Journal of Nursing, 101*(10), 33–38, 39.

Woloshin, S., Schwartz, L. M., Moncur, M., Gabriel, S., & Tosteson, A. N. (2001). Assessing values for health: Numeracy matters. *Medical Decision Making, 21,* 382–390.

Wydra, E. W. (2001). The effectiveness of a self-care management interactive multimedia module. *Oncology Nursing Forum, 28,* 1399–1407.

Youmans, S. L., & Schillinger, D. (2003). Functional health literacy and medication use: The pharmacist's role. *Annals of Pharmacotherapy, 37,* 1726–1729.

Zarcadoolas, C., Pleasant, A., & Greer, D. S. (2005). Understanding health literacy: An expanded model. *Health Promotion International, 20,* 195–203.

7

Research on Professional Development and Teacher Change: Implications for Adult Basic Education

Cristine Smith and Marilyn Gillespie

There is no doubt that the current educational climate is driven by an overriding concern with student achievement and what promotes it. This is true in K–12 education and, increasingly, in adult basic education (ABE) as well. The role of teachers in student achievement is central to this concern. According to the U.S. Department of Education, "research confirms that teachers are the single most important factor in raising student achievement."[39] Higher standards for teachers accompany the push for higher standards for students and greater accountability for student learning, and professional development is a critical link among new policies, school reform, and improved educational practice (Knapp, 2003). In this chapter we draw on the K–12 and adult literacy education research literature

---

[39]See http://www.ed.gov/teachers/how/tools/initiative/factsheet.pdf.

to examine two topics: (a) what is known about what makes teacher professional development effective, and (b) how teachers change as a result of professional development. Before addressing these topics, we briefly summarize a few of the key research studies that have underscored the central role of teachers in student achievement.

THE ROLE OF TEACHERS IN STUDENT ACHIEVEMENT

In recent years, there has been growing recognition that teachers are the most important factor in student achievement (Carey, 2004; Haycock, 1998). Support for this perspective comes from a landmark study on teacher quality in Tennessee. Sanders and Rivers (1996) used student achievement data for all teachers across the state of Tennessee to determine how "effective" teachers were,[40] then tested and followed specific students over several years. They found that students who performed equally well in second grade, but had different teachers over the next 3 years, performed unequally by Year 5. Fifth graders who had "effective" teachers in third, fourth, and fifth grades scored in the 83rd percentile in Grade 5, but those students who studied in the third, fourth, and fifth grades under the "ineffective" teachers scored much lower (the 29th percentile, a 54-point difference) by the end of fifth grade. Similarly, Sanders and Rivers found that in 1 year, the most effective teachers could boost the scores of their low-achieving students an average of 39 percentile points compared to similar low-achieving students who had ineffective teachers.

One body of research in K–12 has investigated just what role preservice preparation of teachers plays in teacher quality and student achievement. By matching indicators of teacher preparation and background—such as certification, level of formal education, level of experience, degree in the subject in which the teacher is teaching (i.e., a degree in math rather than a degree in education), pedagogical knowledge, and cognitive and verbal ability—with student test scores, researchers hope to isolate those characteristics of

---

[40]Rather than defining an "effective" teacher by specific criteria, Sanders and Rivers (1996) used more than 5 million records from Tennessee students who were tested each year, Grades 3 through 8, in five subjects. With these data, they determined whether the students in a given teacher's class had more or less than a normal year's academic growth in a particular subject. Teachers were then classified as below average, average, or above average in quality or "effectiveness."

teachers linked to higher student achievement. Results are, as yet, contradictory. For example, one analysis (Darling-Hammond & Youngs, 2002) found that the formal preparation of the teacher (specifically, certification and subject-matter degree) predicts higher student achievement. Teachers' cognitive and verbal ability[41] and knowledge of subject matter are not as important to student achievement as teacher completion of a formal degree in the subject matter and pedagogical knowledge.[42] However, another analysis proposed that teacher cognitive and verbal ability and content knowledge are more important than certification or a master's degree (U.S. Department of Education, 2002). Yet other analyses propose that it is not individual teachers but the alignment of content standards, curriculum tied to those content standards, teachers trained to use that curriculum, and accountability that leads to student achievement[43] (Whitehurst, 2002). Other research has supported the notion that specific models of instruction (e.g., Success for All, see Borman & Hewes, 2002; Direct Instruction, see Gersten, Keating, & Becker, 1988; Open Court, see American Federation of Teachers, 1998) can improve student achievement. Regardless of whether it is the teacher's background and qualifications, teaching methodologies, or alignment of standards with curriculum and accountability that leads to student success, each of these depends on effective training and preparation of teachers.

In this chapter we begin to frame our review of how teacher professional development can promote student learning by first summarizing the state of professional development in ABE and grounding our discussion in those realities. This includes an overview of the professional development ABE[44] teachers currently receive and the conditions that affect their ability to get and use professional development to improve what they do in the classroom. We then draw on both K–12 and adult education research to discuss teacher professional development from the perspective of two prevalent models of professional development: traditional and

---

[41] As measured by teacher licensing tests and college aptitude tests.

[42] As measured by teacher licensing tests.

[43] "For standards-based reform to work there is reason to think that two additional components are necessary: 1) teachers must be provided with curriculum that is aligned with the standards and assessments; and 2) teachers must have professional development to deliver that curriculum" (Whitehurst, 2002).

[44] ABE includes adult basic literacy instruction, adult secondary education and general educational development (GED) preparation, and instruction for adult English-language learners.

job-embedded. For each of these models, we examine research findings that indicate what makes the model effective or ineffective, followed by a brief discussion of the current emphasis on standards-based teaching and learning and how each of the two models have been used to provide professional development in standards-based education. We then look at key factors at the individual, school or program, and system level that influence how teachers change through professional development and conclude with implications for professional development practice, policy, and further research.

THE STATE OF PROFESSIONAL DEVELOPMENT IN ADULT BASIC EDUCATION

Although teachers who work in ABE programs are similar in many ways to K–12 teachers, there are several basic differences:

Adult basic education teachers work mostly part time. In their study of more than 2,600 local ABE programs, Young, Fleischman, Fitzgerald, and Morgan (1995) found that 36% of programs do not have any full-time staff (teaching or administration), 59% do not have even one full-time instructional staff member, and the ratio of part-time to full-time teachers is 4 to 1. In addition, teachers who want to work full time in ABE where no such jobs are available often piece together part-time ABE jobs at more than one site, or with more than one organization (Smith & Hofer, 2003). Teachers' part-time status presents challenges for teacher professional development, including limitations on the time teachers have available for professional development, opportunities for integrating what has been learned into instruction, and time available for collaboration with colleagues.

Adult basic education teachers may leave the field more often than do K–12 teachers. High teacher turnover is a concern in K–12 education; however, turnover rates within adult education might be even higher. Currently, no national data related to teacher turnover in ABE have yet been collected. According to the 1995 National Evaluation of Adult Education programs (Young et al., 1995), although 80% of full-time teachers had taught in adult education for more than 3 years, a little more than half of all part-time instructors had taught for fewer than 3 years.

A survey by Sabatini and colleagues (2000)[45] of 423 adult education teachers—of whom almost 60% were full-time teachers—indicated that about 40% had taught in the field fewer than 5 years. In their sample, 43% of part-time teachers (which constitute the bulk of the national population of adult education teachers) had been in the field fewer than 5 years. Out of 104 ABE teachers in one study, 21% were no longer teaching in an adult education program 18 months after the study began (Smith, Hofer, Gillespie, Solomon, & Rowe, 2003).

Adult basic education teachers are often required to teach in multiple subject areas. The National Evaluation of Adult Education programs (Young et al., 1995) also found that more than 55% of teachers teach more than one instructional component, including a combination of adult basic education (ABE, pre-GED,[46] GED, or English for students of other languages [ESOL]). These teachers must master multiple content areas. For example, to effectively teach ABE, a teacher may need to know how to teach basic reading, writing, and math at the elementary level. If that same teacher also teaches pre-GED or GED preparation, he or she must also understand subject matter related to high school equivalency-level language arts, math, writing, science, and social studies. Depending on their instructional context, teachers may also be expected to address other topics, such as workplace or family literacy. Teachers in culturally diverse settings must also be able to address specific knowledge and attitudes that are relevant to teaching English-language learners, such as basic issues of bilingualism and second-language development; the nature of language proficiency; the role of the first language and culture in learning; and how their own and learner attitudes and beliefs about language, culture, and race impact teaching and learning (Clair & Adger, 1999). They may also be required to integrate language and content-area instruction, such as teaching math to English-language learners.

---

[45]This was a self-response survey study, which specifically attempted to target "professional" teachers; sampling was done by mailing surveys to state-identified "quality" programs in large states with greater numbers of full-time teachers, making the self-selected sample deliberately skewed toward more full-time teachers. The final sample was 59% full time, 41% part time (Sabatini et al., 2000), a full-time/part-time ratio substantially different from the U.S. Department of Education 1998 data on numbers of part-time and full-time adult education personnel: 13% of state-administered adult education program personnel (including administrators) are full time, so the percentage of full-time teachers is probably considerably less than 13%. Thirty-nine percent of personnel were part time and 48% were volunteers (see www.ed.gov/offices/OVAE/98personnel.html).

[46]Pre-GED adult students read at approximately the 5–8 grade level, although the exact definition varies state by state.

Whereas the majority of adult basic education teachers are qualified to, and have taught in K–12, they have scant formal education related to teaching adults. The 1995 National Evaluation of Adult Education programs found that 40% of full-time and 33% of part-time instructors had master's degrees or higher (Young et al., 1995). The majority of the adult education teachers in their sample were at one time K–12 teachers. However, what is not known is whether these teachers had training in the specific subject areas they were teaching in adult education (e.g., ESOL, reading, or math). The same study also found that only 18% of full-time staff and 8% of part-time staff were specifically certified in adult education. A recent study of more than 100 ABE teachers in New England (Smith et al., 2003[47]) found that more than half of the sample (53%) reported that they had not completed any formal coursework in adult education (undergraduate or graduate courses in adult education, ABE, adult literacy, or ESOL). Of all the teachers (one quarter of whom identified themselves as ESOL teachers) in this study, less than 20% had participated in three or more formal courses in the field of adult education. Teachers of adults need specific competence in areas such as how to help adults become self-directed learners, how to enhance adult learning by relating what is learned to adults' previous life experiences, and how to teach adults immediate applications to life outside the classroom (Sherman, Tibbetts, Woodruff, & Weidler, 1999). Teachers who have content knowledge but lack an understanding of how to apply their knowledge and skills to teaching adult learners require different kinds of training than those who lack both content-related knowledge and an understanding of methods for teaching adults. Moreover, it is not known how many ABE teachers have completed formal coursework to prepare them to work with students with learning disabilities, which is of particular importance given the increasing recognition that as many as 40% to 50% of adults in adult education programs, social services programs, or employment-seeking programs may have learning disabilities (National Institute for Literacy, n.d.).

---

[47]This study, *How Teachers Change: A Study of Professional Development in Adult Education*, sponsored by the National Center for the Study of Adult Learning and Literacy, is the only recent intervention study related to professional development specifically conducted with ABE and literacy teachers. Therefore, it is cited frequently throughout this chapter.

In-service preparation is adult basic education teachers' primary form of professional development. The K–12 system has a well-developed method of preparing and certifying future teachers through higher-education-based teacher education and master's programs; potential K–12 teachers who invest time and money in such programs do so in the belief that their investment will lead to a stable, living-wage career in education. In adult education, in-service professional development is often the only preparation that teachers receive, as there are few master's programs specifically focused on ABE, and most teachers are not required to be certified specifically in teaching adults or formally trained in teaching adults before they begin teaching. One survey of states (Tolbert, 2001) found that only nine states require adult education teachers to get preservice training specifically related to teaching adults. Therefore, the ABE field depends on in-service professional development to expose teachers to specific theories, methodologies, and approaches to helping adults learn.

Adult basic education teachers are not consistently funded to participate in in-service professional development. In their survey of all states' use of federal monies for ABE professional development, RMC Research Corporation (1996) conducted interviews with state administrators, trainers, and more than 1,000 adult educators. They found that 80% of ABE practitioners surveyed attended at least some professional development the year prior to the survey (1994); of these, 57% attended a conference.[48] There was no difference in participation between full-time and part-time practitioners, but those 20% who received no training were more likely to be younger, have fewer academic degrees, and be less experienced. In many cases, the amount of in-service professional development is limited. Smith and colleagues (2003) found that 73% of their sample ($N = 104$) received 3 days or fewer of paid professional development release time annually, and 23% received none.

---

[48]By comparison, 99% of K–12 teachers participated in some staff development over the past year, according to a national survey (Lewis et al., 1999). They were most likely to attend training, workshops, or conferences (95% of public school teachers and 87% of private school teachers; Choy, Chen, & Bugarin, 2006). In another national survey, 85% reported having attended some staff development in the past year (National Education Goals Panel Report, 1999); however, another study reported that 50% of teachers in one national survey attended fewer than 2 days of staff development per year (Wenglinsky, 2000).

Adult basic education teachers have access mostly to short-term training and conferences. Professional development attended by adult education practitioners is typically organized at the state rather than the local level (Wilson & Corbett, 2001). Although it varies by state, much of the professional development attended by adult education practitioners is offered at centrally organized workshops and conferences rather than in local or program settings. The predominant form of professional development in ABE is short-term training and single-session workshops (Crocker, 1987; Kutner, Herman, Stephenson, & Webb, 1991; Tibbetts, Kutner, Hemphill, & Jones, 1991; Tolbert, 2001). Even with the advent of alternative forms of professional development, the reliance on this model persists. In their national study of professional development, RMC Research Corporation (1996) found that single-session workshops accounted for 38% of all professional development activities, followed by institutes or courses (24%), and statewide or regional conferences (11%). Only 27% of activities were alternative kinds of professional development, such as study groups, on-site technical assistance, or independent study. Conferences also accounted for 40% of the money spent, even though they accounted for only 11% of the activities.

Systemic constraints hinder adult basic education teachers' ability to participate in professional development. The difficulty of providing high-quality professional development in adult education is exacerbated by the structure of the system itself. Teachers in adult education are hindered by factors that make it hard for them to know what professional development opportunities are available, and then to participate (Burt & Keenan, 1998). After interviewing 60 adult education "decision makers" and practitioners from 10 states, Wilson and Corbett (2001) found the most important hindering factors included the following:

- *Time constraints.* Working part time makes it hard for teachers to participate regularly or for extended periods of time.
- *Financial constraints.* Often teachers are not paid to participate in professional development.
- *Distance.* Professional development is not offered locally through the program but at state-organized, centrally located venues, which requires practitioners to travel.
- *Information gaps.* Teachers often teach in decentralized locations and have infrequent contact with other practitioners in and out of the program. They may not hear about professional development

unless their program directors or other supervisors who serve as "gatekeepers" pass information along.
- *Lack of face-to-face interaction.* Due to the part-time nature of staff, in many programs staff meetings are rare, so teachers have limited opportunities to meet and talk.
- *Mismatch of goals.* There may be a mismatch between the goals of the professional development and individual practitioners' professional interests. This may result from the diversity of settings and instructional contexts in which teachers work, or can be due to differing perspectives on the overall goals of adult education; for example, between preparing students to pass a test, such as the GED, or preparing them for civic, work, and family life.

Wilson and Corbett (2001) concluded that:

> Currently, the conditions of the ABE occupation are such that those in the field will never be able to participate systematically in the very activities they see as necessary to doing their jobs well. Educators claim the desire for professional development is present; readily accessible opportunities to fulfill that desire are most notably not. (p. 26)

Taken together, the conditions just described create a challenging context for ABE teachers to access the professional development they need to prepare to teach adults. Thus, it is even more important that the professional development teachers are able to attend be as effective as possible.

CONTRASTING MODELS OF PROFESSIONAL DEVELOPMENT

Although the situational and resource constraints in ABE make it difficult to implement the type of professional development often tested in K–12 professional development research, there is so little research on the effectiveness of ABE professional development that we must learn what we can from K–12 research. In this section, we frame our discussion around the two most commonly researched K–12 professional development models—traditional professional development and job-embedded professional development—and provide an overview of the evidence of their effectiveness.

1. *Traditional professional development.* This model consists of workshops, conference sessions, seminars, lectures, and other short-term

training events. We describe this as traditional professional development because it is the standard, most commonly offered type of professional development in both K–12 (Elmore, 2002) and in ABE (RMC, 1996).
2. *Job-embedded professional development.* This approach, which became popular in the 1990s, locates training within the school, program, or local context. Activities such as study circles or inquiry groups allow teachers greater participation in shaping the content of instruction and also provide them with the opportunity to investigate problems of student learning more closely tied to their own contexts. This model emerged in K–12, in part, as a response to the research identifying the ineffective features of traditional professional development, and it is not yet common in the ABE context.

Although there is, of course, overlap between these two models of professional development, they can be distinguished by different goals, formats, and content, as shown in Table 7.1.

Although there is not much argument that professional development can help teachers gain new knowledge and adopt new practices (Whitehurst, 2002), opinions differ concerning the factors—professional development model, school or program context, system or policy directives—that must be in place for teacher learning and change to take place. By comparing and contrasting these two models, we illustrate that professional development, like all other educational efforts, is subject to changes in direction, paradigm, philosophy, and approach, sometimes driven by policy changes and sometimes driven by advances in the knowledge base as a result of research.

The Traditional Professional Development Model

Short-term or one-session workshops, trainings, seminars, lectures, and conference sessions are the mainstay of the traditional professional development model. School districts, professional agencies, and teacher-training colleges (or, in ABE, state professional development systems) offer a menu of topics such as cooperative learning or classroom management, and training on topic areas such as math, science, or language. Teachers, sometimes in conjunction with their school or program leadership, choose to attend specific activities throughout the year, depending on their availability, interest, need for continuing education units as part of recertification efforts, or motivation to learn more about the topic.

TABLE 7.1
Models of Professional Development

Features	Traditional Professional Development	Job-Embedded Professional Development
Primary goal	Increase individual teacher general knowledge, skills, and teaching competency; introduce new instructional models or methodologies	Improve student learning, help teachers with specific teaching problems they face
Location ("site" is school or program)	Mostly off-site	On-site
Intensity	Single session or series	Long-term, ongoing
Common format of this professional development	Workshops, seminars, conferences	Study circles, practitioner research, inquiry projects
Content for this professional development	Range of knowledge and skills teachers should know and be able to do (competencies, special issues, new approaches to teaching)	Student thinking and learning (examining student work), teaching problems
Research related to this model	Joyce & Showers (1995), Loucks-Horsley, Hewson, Love, & Stiles (1998)	Ball & Cohen (1999), Little, Gearheart, Curry, & Kafka (2003)

This model, which has dominated K–12 professional development for decades, is based on the belief that students will benefit when teachers acquire competencies and good teaching behavior over their career (Fenstermacher & Berliner, 1985). By being exposed to new information and approaches emerging from research and developments in the field of education, teachers will change their thinking and adopt behaviors that lead to student achievement.

There is a significant amount of research on this model, partially because it is the most common and enduring. Although this model has some benefits, such as being more easily planned, overall K–12 research in this area indicates that short-term workshops and trainings leave much to be desired. For example, in one study of 31 K–12 teachers attending a 6-day workshop on "effective teaching," teachers implemented only 3 out of 18 concepts and strategies, and were more likely to just "bolt on" new strategies to existing practices ("horizontal" integration of new ideas), rather than to really change their existing beliefs and practices ("vertical" integration; Gardner, 1996). In their study of one school, Joyce, Wolf, and

Calhoun (1993) found that K–12 teachers, even with extensive training, only adopted 10% of practices learned in professional development, unless the training was followed by coaching or action research. Even in cases in which what is learned is implemented at first, research by Stallings and Krasavage (1986) of 11 teachers in two California schools shows that implementation of new practices declined over the long term if teacher excitement and momentum was not maintained by the professional development effort, and that this caused a corresponding downward turn in student achievement. One longitudinal study of K–12 professional development (Porter, Garet, Desimone, Yoon, & Birman, 2000), using self-reports of change from 287 teachers, found "little change in overall teaching practice" after 3 years. The authors found that "teachers changed little in terms of the content they teach, the pedagogy they use to teach it, and their emphasis on performance goals for students," although some individual teachers did sometimes show moderate change. Porter and his colleagues felt that their findings "add support to the concept that both teaching and professional development are typically individual experiences" for teachers (p. ES-10). Elmore (2002), a critic of traditional professional development, claims that it is a "gargantuan task" (p. 25) for teachers to apply what they have learned in an off-site workshop once back in their classrooms and isolated from other teachers.

Given its prevalence in education, however, recent K–12 reviews and studies have outlined the design elements and conditions under which the traditional professional development model can be most successful at promoting change or affecting student achievement (Knapp, 2003). A summary of the K–12 research indicates that professional development within the traditional model can be more effective if it is designed to:

- *Be of longer duration.* Professional development is more effective in changing teachers' practice (at least as self-reported) when it is of longer duration (Porter et al., 2000; Supovitz & Turner, 2000). Longer term professional development permits more time for teachers to learn about their own practice, especially if it includes follow-up (Joyce & Showers, 1995; Stein, Smith, & Silver, 1999). In their study of ABE teacher change, Smith and colleagues (2003) found a direct and positive correlation between the number of hours teachers participated in professional development activity and the amount and type of change related to the topic of the professional development they demonstrated in the following year. Studies of the professional development of K–12 educators teaching English-language learners

have also shown that creating change in teachers is a time-consuming process that requires many meetings and workshops over an extended period of time (Anderson, 1997; Calderón & Marsh, 1988; Ruiz, Rueda, Figueroa, & Boothroyd, 1995).
- *Make a strong connection between what is learned in the professional development and the teacher's own work context.* This is especially relevant if the professional development is organized outside of the school (as most is). Professional development needs to help teachers plan for application and to identify and strategize barriers to application that they will face once back in their programs: "Devoting no time or little time for synthesis, integration, and planning beyond the (professional development) program is inadequate preparation for application. Helping participants anticipate and plan for barriers may facilitate practice changes" (Ottoson, 1997, p. 105).
- *Focus on subject-matter knowledge.* In K–12, a strong correlation exists between student achievement in K–12 science and mathematics and the level of knowledge of K–12 teachers in science and math (Committee on Science and Mathematics Teacher Preparation, 2000). Teachers themselves report that professional development focused on content knowledge contributes to changes in instructional practice (Garet, Porter, Desimone, Birman, & Yoon, 2001).
- *Include a strong emphasis on analysis and reflection, rather than just demonstrating techniques.* Guskey (1997, 1999) and Sparks (1994, 1995) advocated professional development that focuses on learning rather than on teaching, on problem-solving and reflectiveness rather than on acquiring new techniques, and on embedding change within the program rather than on individual change. Carpenter, Fennema, Peterson, Chiang, and Loef (1989), in an experimental study of 40 first-grade teachers, found that when teachers were introduced— through professional development—to the research on how students learn math concepts and how children think about math, but were not given specific teaching techniques, they were able to implement their own strategies for teaching math, and student achievement improved, compared to the students of teachers who did not attend this intensive professional development.
- *Include a variety of activities.* These might include theory, demonstration, practice, feedback, and classroom application (Joyce & Showers, 1995; Mazzarella, 1980). If professional development is short term or single session, it needs to be followed by assistance to

help teachers implement what they learned (Stein & Wang, 1988), because "teachers are more likely to learn from direct observation of practice and trial and error in their own classrooms than they are from abstract descriptions of teaching" (Elmore, 1996, p. 24). Professional development should also follow principles of adult learning: establish a supportive environment, acknowledge teachers' prior experience, help teachers consider how new learning applies to their specific teaching situation, and encourage teachers to make their implicit knowledge about teaching (their "craft knowledge") explicit (Gardner, 1996). In their multiyear study of more than 700 K–12 bilingual teachers who participated in multidistrict training focused on literacy development, Calderón and Marsh (1988) found that to ensure that the training would be used, it is necessary to present theory, model the instructional strategies, and give teachers the opportunity to practice with feedback and extensive support.

- *Encourage teachers from the same workplace to participate together.* "Professional development is more effective when teachers participate with others from their school, grade, or department" (Porter et al., 2000, p. ES-9). In research on adult basic education professional development, Smith and colleagues (2003) also found that teachers from the same adult basic education program participating together in professional development changed their thinking and acting more after the professional development, as compared to teachers who participated without other teachers from their workplace.
- *Focus on quality and features of professional development, rather than on format or type.* Research indicates that the model or type of professional development matters little, as long as it has features of high-quality training. A survey of 1,027 teachers (Garet et al., 2001) found that the most important professional development features for increasing knowledge and self-reported changes in practice were a focus on content knowledge; opportunities for hands-on, active learning; and greater coherence (professional development was aligned with other professional development activities or with state or district standards). The authors concluded: "To improve professional development, it is more important to focus on the duration, collective participation, and the core features (i.e., content, active learning, and coherence) than type" (Garet et al., 2001, p. 936). Smith and colleagues (2003), in their study of 100 ABE teachers participating in up to 18 hours of professional development that

addressed the issue of adult student persistence (how to help adult students continue to work toward their educational goals), concluded that type of professional development (multisession workshop, mentor teacher group, or practitioner research group) was not as important as the amount and quality of professional development teachers attended; high-quality professional development was characterized by strong facilitation, good group dynamics among the teachers participating, and flexible but clear adherence to the professional development design.

The Job-Embedded Professional Development Model

Professional development under the job-embedded model is located within a school, program, or other local context as part of an effort to create ongoing professional communities (Hord, 1997). Schools and programs develop site-based learning communities where professional development is woven into the fabric of the school community, balanced at times with the cross-fertilization of new ideas from outside the school (Taylor, Pearson, Peterson, & Rodriguez, 2005). Professional development activities include study circles, sharing groups, or inquiry groups made up of teachers from the same school or division. The focus is on developing teacher knowledge in the content area, analyzing student thinking, and identifying how that knowledge can be applied to changes in instructional practices tailored to the local educational context. Teachers participating in this type of professional development model often work together over extended periods of time (a year or more), bringing in and examining "artifacts of teaching" (Ball & Cohen, 1999). These include examples of student work that teachers analyze to discover what it tells them about student thinking and learning. The difference between traditional and job-embedded professional development is that "in conventional forms of in-service training and staff development, outside experts do most of the talking and teachers do the listening." In "new" approaches to professional development, "teachers do the talking, thinking and learning" (Feiman-Nemser, 2001, p. 1042).

This model, which gained popularity in the 1990s, is rooted in the belief that students will benefit when teachers are knowledgeable about their subject matter and about the problems students face in their learning. When teachers study students' work together with other teachers and try new tactics to address teaching and learning problems, students achieve more. Proponents of this model claim that professional development cannot be viewed as an event that occurs on certain days in the school year, but rather must be part of the daily work of teachers, administrators, and others in the system. This approach is supported by a growing body of cognitive science research on the conditions that facilitate the building of expertise. This research is built on the findings of studies of adults who had moved from being a novice to being an expert in their fields, such as science, mathematics, and chess. The research stresses the importance of supporting learners to activate their prior knowledge related to a topic they want to learn; to explicitly monitor new learning in light of their past experiences; and to evaluate how the new learning transfers into real-world practices. Studies show that to develop expertise, individuals need to develop not only factual knowledge but also procedural knowledge of when, how, and under what conditions to use their new skills. This kind of knowledge can only be developed by actually practicing the new skills and then reflecting on those practices (Bransford, Brown, & Cocking, 1999; Greeno, Resnick, & Collins, 1997).

Recent K–12 research demonstrates the effectiveness of the job-embedded model when it includes:

- *A focus on helping teachers to study their students' thinking, not just try new techniques.* Carpenter and Franke (1998), studying 22 math and science teachers, found that change was sustained over longer periods of time when math teachers were trained and supported to really understand what their students were thinking, and teachers had a base from which to generalize practices to other situations and continue learning. Ancess (2000), interviewing 66 teachers in three high schools, identified teacher inquiry about student learning and student work as a powerful tool for changing teacher practice and ultimately changing school structure.
- *Collaborative learning activities among teachers.* Langer (2000), in a qualitative study of 25 schools (44 teachers in 14 high-performing schools and 11 average-performing schools) over 5 years concluded that professional development contributes to high performance when it focuses not on individual teachers but on groups of teachers within schools, especially where school culture supports the "professional lives" of the teachers. Professional development schools constitute another collaborative approach to teacher professional development that is becoming popular in many teacher-education programs. In this model, teacher-education students, cooperating teachers, and university supervisors discuss and analyze classroom experiences

with the aim of combining forces to improve instruction (Neubert & Binko, 1998).
- *Activities in which teachers make use of student performance data.* In a longitudinal study of the impact of professional development in 13 schools, 92 teachers, and 733 students in Grades 2 through 5 in high-poverty areas, Taylor and colleagues (2005) investigated the effectiveness of job-embedded professional development on reading scores, where teachers working together were introduced to the research on reading instruction and analyzed their school's reading achievement data as part of a larger reform effort to improve reading scores. Increased comprehension and fluency scores (after 2 years) were found in schools where teachers collaborated in reflective professional development and used data to improve their teaching practice, aided by changes at the school level—effective school leadership, commitment to the reform effort—that supported such change.
- *Help from facilitators to organize job-embedded professional development.* Because job-embedded professional development is a new experience for many teachers, they need assistance to overcome their natural reluctance to sharing their concerns and their own and students' work with other teachers in the sharing or inquiry group. In addition, facilitators need training and support to guide the group's development over time. In their work with a small group of math teachers in one school, Kazemi and Franke (2003) found that teachers needed to learn how to examine student work together, with a facilitator structuring teacher meetings to help them focus specifically on the details of student work. Richardson and Placier (2001), in their study of middle school teachers in six schools participating together in inquiry groups to implement changes in reading instruction, found that such groups go through stages of development (introductory, breakthrough, empowerment), and that a trained facilitator can help to guide such groups through initial stages. McDonald (2001) described a variety of "protocols" or methods for studying student work (some of which he used with Connecticut K–12 teachers in a working group) to help teachers learn how to speak with each other; one such protocol, called a *setaside,* brings teachers together for 45 minutes "set aside" after school to say what interests them in a child's drawing, page of math, or any other work collected from students that day, followed by a general discussion among the teachers about students' work.

The author claims that the "disciplined conversations" that follow from using these structured discussion protocols help teachers learn how to analyze student work without judging, and promote teachers' beliefs about students' potential for learning. Sharing or inquiry groups also can benefit from the help of university experts or even Web sites that can provide an infusion of information about research or relevant instructional strategies when teachers feel the need to look outside the group for solutions to challenging instructional problems (Taylor et al., 2005).

PROFESSIONAL DEVELOPMENT IN A STANDARDS-BASED ENVIRONMENT

Standards-based teaching and learning has gained momentum in K–12 education in the past decade as states have been required to comply with mandated standards-based reform efforts associated with No Child Left Behind legislation. The need to develop content standards (what students should know and be able to do), curriculum matched to the standards, and teaching approaches that will help students prepare for assessments based on the standards has had a significant impact on the nature and delivery of teacher professional development in many K–12 settings.

Understanding what effective standards-based professional development looks like at the K–12 level is important for adult educators. Although they are not yet mandated at the federal level, standards-based reform efforts are increasingly being initiated by state adult education organizations (see www.adultcontentstandards.org). Over the past 2 years, the Office of Adult and Vocational Education at the U.S. Department of Education has sponsored the Adult Education Content Standards Warehouse project to assist states to build capacity in the development, alignment, and implementation of state adult education content standards in reading, mathematics, and English-language acquisition. The U.S. Department of Education also sponsors a Web site containing information about state initiatives and about Equipped for the Future, a national standards-based system reform initiative sponsored by the National Institute for Literacy, to share information among states and help them to either adopt or adapt existing standards, or to develop their own (often with links to their state K–12 standards in given content areas).

Professional development to help K–12 teachers implement standards-based education often has features of both traditional and job-embedded models. Reform, by its nature, takes intensive resources, and researchers

(Knapp, 2003; Stein & D'Amico, 2002) seem to agree that intensive professional development is key to changing not just policy but the "educational core": the way in which teachers and students interact in classrooms around subject matter (Elmore, 1996). Combining features of both traditional and job-embedded professional development is part of what—in comparison to the professional development that ABE teachers typically receive—appears to be much more intensive training efforts to truly change practice. For example, Stein and D'Amico (2002) described a multiyear effort in New York City's District 2 to improve literacy scores through the adoption of a balanced literacy approach: Teachers attend a multitude of professional development activities, including workshops, observing expert teachers, a professional development lab (3 solid weeks observing a mentor teacher), study groups, and grade-level, school-based meetings with other teachers and the principal. Dutro, Fisk, Koch, Roop, and Wixson (2002) described the professional development for implementing English-language-arts curriculum frameworks in four school districts in Michigan: 48 teachers participated in 2 week-long institutes, 4 days of training, 24 monthly meetings, workshops, and a conference. In a San Francisco Unified School District reform project (Bye, 2004) to upgrade services for limited-English-proficient students in Grades 6 through 12, 200 middle school and high school teachers participated in various combinations of in-service workshops, week-long summer institutes, training and support to use new curricula, site-based inquiry seminars, and certification training (although the report does not provide information about the total number of professional development hours in which teachers participated).

Despite serious investment in professional development as part of standards-based reform efforts, there is as yet little data on the effectiveness of different "packages" of professional development supporting standards-based education, and recent research indicates that other contextual features, such as school culture, leadership, and district policies, also have an impact on how and whether such professional development is related to improved student achievement. The existing research, however slim, suggests that standards-based professional development contributes to teacher change when it includes:

- *Professional development linked to curriculum based on the standards.* There is some research that indicates that professional development linked to a standards-based initiative improves the possibility that teachers will implement what they have learned in the classroom.

A study by Cohen and Hill (2000) investigated self-reports of teacher changes in the practice of 1,000 teachers from 250 California schools who attended either "special topics" workshops on topics of their own choosing or attended "curriculum-related" professional development that focused on the California Framework (a math curriculum) and related assessments for fourth-grade math. They found that more teachers who attended the curriculum-related professional development reported the kind of classroom practice in mathematics that the California Framework advocated, and that their students performed better on the assessment.

- *Leadership focused on reform of instruction, not just greater accountability.* Although standards-based professional development programs are making an effort to use the latest research on what makes training effective, these programs face the same challenges as professional development not connected to standards-based reform: the need for a supportive school culture and leadership within the school. A recent study of the impact of high-stakes accountability on teachers' professional development in 24 southern schools (Berry, Turchi, & Johnson, 2003) revealed that although the accountability system did help teachers to focus on the content to be taught, the professional development experiences did not always build on what is known about best practices within the content areas. Teacher collaboration did exist but it was often incomplete and sporadic, rather than sustained with systematic follow-up. School systems often did not have the organizational capacity to help teachers direct their teaching toward better student outcomes. The advances in system reform were tempered with concerns on the part of teachers and administrators about the extent to which instruction under the standards-based system had become too test driven, limiting teachers' opportunities for innovation and individual choice, as well as requiring that teachers spend increasing amounts of time on assessment-related activities. Successful professional development experiences were most frequently driven by strong superintendents and principals who were able to build organizational capacity to respond to integrated system reform, rather than simply focusing professional development on responding to high-stakes accountability assessments. Taylor and colleagues (2005) also found that school leadership was an important factor in improved student achievement among teachers in 13 different schools trying to implement research-based reading instruction strategies.

- *Multiple, district-wide efforts supportive of reform, in addition to professional development for teachers.* Professional development is more likely to be effective when there is recognition that "professional learning is not the only condition supporting the improvement of student learning" (Knapp, 2003). In a review of standards-based efforts in Connecticut, New York City, and Kentucky, Knapp concluded that standards-based professional development can serve as an effective "pathway" to policy-instigated reform, under certain conditions, including when:

  - Administrators, as well as teachers, see themselves as learners.
  - States and districts implement multiple successful strategies for professional learning (strengthening professional community, increasing instructional leadership capacity, bringing in external partners such as researchers and professional associations).
  - There is a recognition that it is not only what teachers learn and do that supports the improvement of student learning, but also when the standards, curriculum assessments, and accountability system are linked and aligned.

It is also important to ensure that the needs of special populations, such as language-minority learners and special education students are taken into account.[49]

FACTORS AFFECTING HOW TEACHERS CHANGE

Teachers do not exist in a void; they are individuals with different backgrounds and ambitions who work in varied school and system contexts. In the same way that student achievement is affected by factors other than the instruction they receive (including socioeconomic status, race, and class size), teacher change is also affected by individual and school factors that influence how they provide instruction. Although the teacher is always the link between professional development and student achievement,

---

[49]The publication *Implementing the ESL Standards for PreK-12 Students Through Teacher Education* (available at http://www.cal.org/eslstandards/), for example, contains guidance for assuring that the needs of language-minority children are taken into account. The Center for Applied Linguistics (www.cal.org) maintains a searchable database of information on how states, districts, and schools are working on standards-based educational reforms that include English-language learners.

teacher practice is only one of many factors affecting student learning. Researchers call this the "dilution" effect of professional development: The actual impact of the professional development is diluted by all of the other factors that support or hinder teachers from making change. The dilution effect is the primary criticism behind arguments against judging professional development according to process–product research (i.e., the process of professional development does not always result in the product of student achievement; Adey, 1995).

Several researchers have categorized factors that mediate the influence of professional development. Guskey and Sparks (1996), for example, discussed three categories of factors:[50]

1. *Content characteristics.* "What" the professional development covers; the credibility and scope of the practice or concept being conveyed.
2. *Process variables.* The "how" of professional development, the models and type of follow-up.
3. *Context characteristics.* The who, when, where, and why of the professional development; the organizational or system culture; and expectations and incentives for using new practices.

Ottoson (1997) named five factors that affect "application" of what is learned in training:

1. *Educational factors.* The characteristics of the professional development, including quality of facilitation, organization, and methods.
2. *Innovation.* The ideas, practices, and strategies taught or suggested to teachers during the professional development.
3. *Predisposing factors.* The characteristics of the teacher, including their motivation for attending, background knowledge, and preexisting attitudes.
4. *Enabling factors.* The teacher's skill in applying the new strategy; factors in the context of the teacher's program, including resources, authority, and opportunity to apply what has been learned.
5. *Reinforcing factors.* The factors in the context of the teacher's program that support the teacher in applying knowledge, such as help from colleagues, the director, and students.

---

[50]Guskey and Sparks (1996) also considered administrator knowledge and practices, plus parent knowledge and practices, to be important factors mediating teacher change and student learning because parents and administrators affect curriculum policies that dictate the types of changes teachers can make.

In this section, we choose a simpler framework for understanding the factors that mediate professional development. We first review the research on individual factors—who teachers are as they come to the professional development—and we then review the research on school factors that support change after professional development. Understanding these factors can help professional developers and policymakers take action to provide the conditions supportive of teacher change and, ultimately, student achievement.

Individual (Teacher) Factors

A significant body of research exists on the social psychology of teachers, some of which is relevant to the question of whether teachers' experience, dispositions, and motivations support or prevent them from learning and changing.

Teacher Motivation for Professional Development. Teachers' motivation to attend professional development appears to be a key factor in change. Stout (1996), for example, proposed four motivations teachers have for participating in professional development: salary enhancement, certificate maintenance, career mobility (building their resume to move up the ladder into administration or pursue other careers), and gaining new skills or knowledge. Livneh and Livneh (1999) surveyed 256 K–12 educators in Oregon to gauge their motivation to learn, background characteristics, and the amount of professional continuing education they had attended in the previous year. Two motivational factors predicted participation: high internal motivation to learn and high external motivation to learn (wanted career advancement or to network with others).

Joyce (1983) studied K–12 teachers' motivation to participate in professional development and categorized teachers as learners and consumers of professional development. Based on teachers' participation in three domains—(a) formal systems (courses, workshops, coaching or supervision), (b) informal systems (exchanges with other teachers and professionals), and (c) personal activities (reading, leisure activities)—Joyce proposed five categories to describe teachers' states as learners:

1. *Omnivores* are teachers who "actively use every available aspect of the formal and informal systems available to them" (p. 163).
2. *Active consumers* are teachers who keep busy in one or more of the domains or systems.

3. *Passive consumers* are teachers who go along with professional development opportunities that arise but do not seek them out.
4. *Entrenched* teachers are suspicious of change and take courses only in areas where they already feel successful; they may actively or surreptitiously oppose new ideas.
5. *Withdrawn* teachers are actively opposed to engaging in one or all three domains.

Joyce (1983) claimed that omnivores generate energy for the system in which they are engaged, whereas entrenched and withdrawn teachers consume energy from the system. An entrenched or withdrawn teacher with influence within the school—even informal power—can act as a "gatekeeper," preventing any type of collective action, change, or improvement from occurring. Even the best professional development will not have an impact if there is a poor culture in the school, one in which there is a poor fit between teachers' states of growth and the culture that could support growth and new ideas from professional development.

In their ABE research, Smith and colleagues (2003) found that stronger motivation to attend the professional development was related to teacher change: Those ABE teachers with a strong need to learn, either on the topic or about good teaching and student success, demonstrated more change in knowledge and action after participating in professional development.

Teacher Concerns. Another thread in the literature relates to what Fuller and Bown (1975) called teachers' "concerns." They proposed that teachers have three types of concerns: (a) *self-survival*—controlling classes, having adequate knowledge, finding one's place in the school, satisfying others' expectations of them; (b) *task*—planning instruction and handling the administrative work, and (c) *impact*—meeting students' individual needs and increasing students' motivation. Ghaith and Shaaban (1999) argued that these kinds of concerns change over time; new teachers are more concerned about classroom tasks and experienced teachers are more concerned about impact. Kagan (1992) supported the idea that beginning teachers are more concerned about self-survival.

Hord, Rutherford, Huling-Austin, and Hall (1987) expanded on this theory to explain that as teachers change by adopting new attitudes and practices, they have different types of concerns: *personal concerns* about how change will affect them, *task concerns* about how to manage new practices, and *impact concerns* about how new practice will affect students.

Differing concerns may dictate what types and subjects of professional development teachers select. A 1999 National Center on Educational Statistics survey on K–12 teacher participation in professional development found that experienced teachers are less likely to participate in professional development on topics of classroom management and new teaching methods; newer teachers are more likely to participate in mentoring than more experienced teachers (Lewis et al., 1999). Other researchers challenge the notion that new teachers are only interested in classroom management and techniques, claiming that new teachers are concerned with content and teaching ethics as well as with classroom management (Grossman, 1992).

Teacher Self-Efficacy. Another individual factor well studied in relation to teacher change is teachers' level of self-efficacy, a concept first outlined by Bandura (1995). Bandura defined self-efficacy as "beliefs in one's capabilities to organize and execute the courses of action required to manage prospective situations" (p. 2). Stronger self-efficacy among teachers has been related to student achievement (Goddard, Hoy, & Hoy, 2000; Tschannen-Moran, Hoy, & Hoy, 1998). Professional development researchers have tested hypotheses about whether teachers' level of self-efficacy was related to how much they changed. Overall, they found that:

- *Self-efficacy is related to individual factors.* Ross (1994) found that new teachers had high levels of general self-efficacy[51] but low levels of personal self-efficacy (i.e., a strong belief in the power of education but a weak belief about whether they personally could be successful as teachers), whereas experienced teachers felt just the opposite (i.e., they held a strong belief in their own competence as teachers but a weak belief in education's power to reach all students; and believed that success is "limited by factors beyond school control," p. 382). Ross felt that this research confirms that teachers' sense of self-efficacy is more stable among more experienced teachers and that "to change it in a material way (would)

---

[51]*General self-efficacy* is the belief that education itself can be successful with all students, regardless of background and abilities. *Personal self-efficacy* is the belief that teachers themselves are "instrumental to the learning of their students" (Smylie, 1988, p. 23). *Collective self-efficacy* is the common belief held by groups of teachers that together they are successful.

likely take something more substantial (e.g., a dramatic shift in teaching assignment that often comes with a change of school or an involuntary alteration of curriculum) than a routine in-service program" (p. 391).

- *Stronger self-efficacy going into professional development affected teacher change.* Smylie (1988) found that teachers were more likely to change as a result of professional development if they had high personal self-efficacy. Guskey (1988) found that teachers with high levels of self-efficacy were more likely to adopt new practices, but that high self-efficacy was also associated with effectiveness (although how "effectiveness" was measured is not defined), and so teachers with high self-efficacy least needed to adopt new practices. Tschannen-Moran and colleagues (1998) concluded that teachers with strong self-efficacy may be less motivated to learn and try new strategies.
- *Professional development in turn affected self-efficacy.* Stein and Wang (1988) found that those who implemented a new practice showed an increase in self-efficacy. Ross (1998) found that teachers who did try new strategies initially showed a drop in self-efficacy but that self-efficacy increased again when they saw that the new strategy worked. Roberts, Henson, Tharp, and Moreno (2000) found that teachers who entered professional development with high levels of self-efficacy did not change their feelings of self-efficacy much, no matter how long the professional development was, but that teachers who entered professional development with low levels of self-efficacy increased their sense of self-efficacy, proportional to the length of the professional development.

Teacher Cognitive Styles or "Ways of Knowing." Other characteristics of teachers as individuals that researchers believe relate to teacher change include cognitive style. Joughin (1992) proposed that some teachers have an analytic ability to understand a strategy and how to use it, whereas other teachers lack this ability and need more structure to grasp and then apply a new strategy. Similarly, developmental theory (Kegan, 1994) holds that all adults have "ways of knowing" that they bring to a learning task; specifically, a learner with an *instrumental* way of knowing would tend to see the trainer as an expert and look for the right answer; a learner with a *socializing* way of knowing would learn from others and see the trainer as a mentor; and a learner with a *self-authoring* way of knowing would want to bring his or her own knowledge to the learning process and understand that there may be no one right answer. Theories of cognitive style or development have implications for the fit between individual teachers' ways of knowing and the style of the professional development in which they participate; for example, teachers with an instrumental way of knowing may feel more comfortable in workshops led by experts, whereas teachers with a self-authoring way of knowing may feel more comfortable in professional development activities (e.g., practitioner research) that allow or ask them to generate knowledge on their own.

Teacher Reflectiveness. In the professional development and teacher education literature, there is a strong concern for teachers' reflectiveness. Schon (1983) began the discussion of how to help teachers develop a "stance" of looking at their own practice by analyzing, adapting, and always challenging their assumptions, in a self-sustaining cycle of reflecting on their own theory and practice, learning from one problem to inform the next problem. In a qualitative study of 18 extension educators, Ferry and Ross-Gordon (1998) found that a reflective stance was not automatically related to years of teaching experience. Some new teachers had already adopted a reflective stance and demonstrated a cyclical approach to problem solving, whereas some very experienced teachers used a sequential (noncyclical) approach to problem solving: When faced with a problem, they summoned their existing knowledge and chose the best fit solution from what they already knew.

Teacher Formal Education and Years of Experience. Research in both K–12 and adult education points to the impact of teachers' level of formal education on participation in professional development and in change. Livneh and Livneh (1999), in their study of 256 K–12 teachers, found that those with lower levels of formal education participated in more professional development. The researchers argued that this finding:

> lends support to the notion that people with comparatively lower educational levels in professional fields often recognize the need to upgrade their educational skills and abilities. They may also be beginning their professional career, a time when they recognize the need for additional information and skill building. (Livneh & Livneh, 1999, p. 100)

Amount of formal education and teaching experience may also be related to teacher change. In their study of 100 ABE teachers and the change they demonstrated after participating in different types of professional development,

Smith and colleagues (2003) identified the following individual characteristics as influencing how much, and in what ways, teachers changed after participating in professional development:

- *Years of experience in adult education.* Those teachers with fewer years of experience changed more.
- *Venue of first teaching experience.* Those teachers who began their teaching career in adult education (not K–12) changed more.
- *Level of education.* Teachers with a bachelor's degree or less changed more.

School, Program, and System Factors

In addition to individual factors, school, program, and system factors also mediate teacher change by either hindering or supporting it. In this section, we provide an overview of a few of the most prominent system factors that research has shown to influence teacher change and their relevance to adult education professional development.

Leadership. Research in K–12 indicates that school leadership plays a role in readying teachers for change by creating a positive culture that lets teachers' attitudes change naturally when they see how and whether a new practice helps students' learning (Sparks, 1995). Principals that were too controlling and principal turnover negatively affected teacher education programs (Bollough, Kauchak, Crow, Hobbs, & Stoke, 1997). Such findings are relevant to adult educators because adult education programs are structured like schools, with program administrators that influence the program's culture. However, in the adult education context, part-time teachers working in diverse and sometimes isolated settings often have less access than K–12 teachers to the leadership in their program. Research in ABE indicates that those teachers with greater access to decision making within the program demonstrated more knowledge and action change after participating in professional development (Smith et al., 2003).

Coherence Between Professional Development Topic and School Reform. *Coherence* is defined as the match between school adoption of particular reforms and individual professional development of teachers in that school; that is, whether the school is trying to improve the same problem or issue addressed by the professional development. The match can either be required (by the district) or voluntary (the school or teachers sought professional development related to the school improvement issue). Recent research by Garet and colleagues (2001) indicates that K–12 teachers gained more knowledge and changed practices more often when there was a match between school or district standards and goals. When change is voluntary (i.e., there is no concurrent reform effort at the school level), then leadership or supportive school factors (e.g., teachers' access to decision making) were not as important in promoting change as the teachers' own beliefs (Smylie, 1988). Such findings will become more relevant to the field of adult education as the effort to institute content standards gains momentum, and professional development systems will respond with training for teachers in how to implement these standards.

Collegiality Within the School. The movement for teacher professional communities within schools grew from the belief that one cannot take individual teachers out of their environment, train and change them, then put them back into the same environment and expect them to change that environment. Rather, teachers need a community of teachers within the school, so they can learn together about their work as they apply that learning (Calderón, 1999; Grossman, Wineburg, & Woolworth, 2000). The issue of collegiality as an organizational support that increases the efficiency of professional development is especially relevant to adult education, because so many part-time teachers work in satellite locations apart from other teachers (Smith & Hofer, 2003). In a review of previous research about the relationship between K–12 school culture and the effectiveness of professional development, Olson, Butler, and Olson (1991) found that collegiality emerged as a key indicator. Interactions with colleagues seemed to help teachers develop a "body of technical knowledge about what teaching practices are likely to be effective" (Olson et al., 1991, p. 23) and a sense of their own competence (Smylie, 1988). Other research suggests that more collaboration within a school increases teachers' commitment to teaching (Rosenholtz, 1986), which may in turn support openness to new knowledge and practices. When teachers, both K–12 and adult education, do not have the opportunity to talk to colleagues about strategies learned during professional development, they are less likely to implement them (Gardner, 1996; Huberman & Miles, 1984; Smith et al., 2003); the greater the communication, the more likely teachers were to adopt the new practice (Adey, 1995). By contrast, Joyce (1983) found that professional development was less effective when there was an entrenched teacher who acted as gatekeeper to spoil or prevent other teachers from adopting new strategies. In short:

Teaching practice is unlikely to change as a result of exposure to training, unless that training also brings with it some kind of external normative structure, a network of social relationships that personalize that structure, and supports interaction around problems of practice. (Elmore, 1996, p. 21)

Teachers' Working Conditions. Although we found no K–12 studies that investigate teachers' working conditions (full time vs. part time, salary and benefit level, etc.) on the effectiveness of professional development, we did find studies indicating that working conditions have an effect on teacher turnover (Ingersoll, 2001). K–12 "dissatisfied" teachers who had low salaries, lack of support from administration, problems with student discipline, or lack of input in decision making were more likely to migrate to other schools, or to leave teaching entirely.

Only one study in ABE (Smith et al., 2003) has investigated the relationship between teacher change and teachers' working conditions, which the researchers defined as access to (a) resources, (b) professional development and information, (c) colleagues and directors, (d) decision making, and (e) well-supported jobs.[52] They found that the following factors influenced the amount and type of change that ABE teachers ($n = 100$) demonstrated after participating in professional development:

- *Access to prep time.* Those who received prep time were more likely to change.[53]
- *Access to benefits.* Those teachers who received one or more benefits from their adult education job (health or dental insurance, vacation, etc.) were more likely to change.[54]
- *Program situation.* Teachers who worked in programs that were not already taking action to address learner persistence and where teachers had a voice in decision making were more likely to change.

These findings indicate that the ABE field has structural constraints that influence how much teachers change after participating in even high-quality professional development.

---

[52]Well-supported jobs are defined as "full-time, relatively well-paid, and stable jobs that include benefits (medical coverage, paid vacation and sick time, pension plans, etc.), paid preparation time, and paid professional development release time" (p. 2, Summary Report).

[53]Only 42 out of 78 teachers in this study (54%) received any amount of paid preparation time.

[54]Less than half (48%, $n = 78$) of the teachers in the study received benefits as part of their ABE jobs.

IMPLICATIONS FOR POLICY, PRACTICE, AND RESEARCH

The obstacles to professional learning and teacher change in ABE are many. Thus, professional developers and policymakers need to make what little professional development teachers do receive as optimally effective as possible. The following sections suggest some ideas for further research and some key implications and recommendations that can promote the implementation of more effective research-based professional development policies and practices.

Implications for Policy

The message for policymakers is that ABE teachers need considerably more access to professional development if they are to contribute to significant improvements in student achievement, especially because they come into the field without much formal education in teaching adults. The research is unequivocal that professional development is more effective in changing teachers' practice when it is of longer duration, allows for the collective participation of teachers, and includes opportunities for follow-up activities that make a strong connection between what is learned and how to apply it in the teacher's own context.

This means that the ABE field needs well-resourced professional development systems in states and programs to provide professional development opportunities with these features, and that teachers should be paid to attend professional development for longer periods of time. The scope of knowledge and skills that adult educators need—from GED teachers needing to know enough about science, history, math, reading, and writing to help students both increase skills and pass the test, to ESOL teachers who need to know about second-language acquisition, strategies for improving oral communication skills, and ways of working with students from different cultures—means that a wide range of professional development offerings must be available in a state and program, and must be accessible to teachers throughout their lives as practitioners.

Increases in funding for professional development would help to put such professional development systems into place in states that do not currently have a comprehensive system; however, other supports also need to be in place. Because the research also indicates that working conditions such as access to benefits and paid preparation time for ABE teachers are not simply perquisites to the job but may actually influence the effectiveness of the professional development in bringing about teacher change, state and federal policymakers should consider whether any increased funding for adult education could be channeled into expenditures such as benefits and paid preparation time that support teachers to better use what they learn in professional development, even if fewer students are served as a result.

Finally, because research in the K–12 system indicates that intensive professional development is desirable to implement standards-based reform efforts, policymakers at the state and federal level should be prepared to fund comprehensive "packages" of professional development for programs and practitioners that are required to adopt standards-based curriculum and assessment. Professional development should play a role, as it often does in K–12 reform efforts, not just in preparing teachers to adopt standards but to adapt them: By working with other teachers in job-embedded professional development, ABE teachers can develop and try out lessons and assessments, aligned to the standards, that are relevant to a wide range of adult students' needs.

Implications for Practice

Obviously, with more funding for teacher preparation and support, the design of professional development could also be more easily changed to offer longer term, more job-embedded models of professional development. However, even without a significant infusion of new funds, professional development systems and ABE programs could change the current configuration of professional development activities to promote more effective professional development in their states and programs. Although we know of no research project that directly tests the efficacy of traditional versus job-embedded models of professional development, the latter, by design, has more of the features of professional development demonstrated to be effective: It is of longer term, focused on student learning, and built around teacher collegiality and reflection.

For example, states should make single-session workshops the exception, rather than the norm, and increase the incidence of mentoring, study circles, inquiry projects, or teacher sharing circles. This may mean that practitioners, especially part-time teachers, go to fewer sessions each year, but the ones they do attend are longer term and more embedded in their actual teaching. States might consider reducing funds for statewide conferences (by, perhaps, holding them every 2 or 3 years rather than annually) and diverting these funds to longer term and more targeted professional development offered at the program or regional level. If reducing the scope or frequency of state conferences is not an option, states might consider alternatives such as summer institutes, adding extended training activities (e.g., full day within the conferences, with follow-up at sites), team teaching activities, and inclusion of planning time for curriculum and assessment task forces inside programs.

States and ABE programs should experiment, even modestly, with job-embedded professional development. Programs that are already providing some time each month for teacher sharing could, without too much difficulty (but with some training and preparation), provide a structure for ongoing professional development sessions focused on challenges in adult student reading, for example. Professional development staff at the state level could help by offering facilitation and technical assistance within programs to initiate job-embedded professional development activities. There are some states (e.g., Rhode Island and Maryland) where professional development monies and activities are managed at the program level; experimenting with job-embedded models using achievement data and focusing on student learning could be done within the current structure. To do so, program administrators would need a model for such professional development and help from professional developers at the state level to implement it. This would require the professional development system to reallocate some of its funding from stand-alone workshops to programs in which facilitators would help start job-embedded professional development. Such changes might also mean using subject-matter experts in new ways; rather than bringing the teachers to the experts, for example, professional developers could explore ways to send the experts into programs to work with staff as a team.

Finally, states should continue to develop distance education technologies as methods to bring teachers from different programs together for professional development, reducing teacher travel and allowing teachers to participate in learning online. Such online learning opportunities may be the only type of professional development activities readily accessible to teachers from small, geographically isolated programs across larger states. However, professional development planners need to ensure that teacher collegiality can still be an essential feature of such distance professional development, so hybrid or "blended" distance professional development models (in which one part is face-to-face or conference call and the rest is online) hold promise for reaching ABE teachers while still giving teachers a network of other practitioners with whom to problem solve and share ideas.[55]

Implications for Research

First, we need research about the effectiveness of professional development in supporting student achievement in an adult education context. Research about the relationship between teacher preparation and teacher quality would be particularly important in standards-based reform situations, as K–12 research indicates that major investments of time and training—both of which are in short supply in ABE—are warranted to bring about real reform. Because teacher preparation requires investment of scarce adult education dollars, state and federal policymakers need information about the minimum per-pupil cost that will support the retention and preparation of adult education teachers.

Second, because research indicates that teachers' working conditions influence the effectiveness of professional development, we need more research on the optimal configuration of teacher working conditions—program structure, paid preparation time, job benefits, working hours, and paid release time for training—and their relation to teacher quality, student achievement, and teacher retention. As there is no research in K–12 on many of these conditions because K–12 teachers typically have full-time jobs with paid preparation time and benefits, this is one area of special importance, particularly in a climate in which overall resources for adult education are limited. Findings would provide states with guidance about how to allocate scarce funds for teacher support and preparation.

We also need research comparing the outcomes of participating in job-embedded, traditional, and standards-based reform professional development "packages" in ABE, so that state policymakers and professional developers have good information on which to base decisions about what types of professional development to offer and under what conditions such models are most effective in promoting teacher change and student achievement.

Finally, we need systems to collect more data at the state and national level about the background, needs, and formal education of practitioners

---

[55]For models of ABE distance professional development, see Project IDEAL (http://projectideal.org), the Student Achievement in Reading (STAR) project (http://www.ed.gov/about/offices/list/ovae/pi/AdultEd/starnewsDec05.doc), or AE PRO Online Professional Development (http://www.aeprofessional.org/).

to plan effective professional development initiatives. After all, adult basic educators include, for example, teachers of adult ESOL students, tutors who work with youth preparing to take the GED test, administrators who supervise programs for low-literate adults with learning disabilities, and counselors who provide transition assistance to adult education students aspiring to attend college. Each of these practitioners will also have different backgrounds, perceived professional development needs, and years of experience in the field, factors that, among others, affect the type and amount of change practitioners demonstrate after participating in professional development.

CONCLUSION

We can help adult education students achieve higher standards only if we also enhance the effectiveness of our adult education teachers. The research in both K–12 and adult education demonstrates that professional development can, under the right conditions, help teachers be more effective. However, questions remain: Over the long term, we need more research that helps us understand the relationship among student achievement, professional development, and such factors as adult education program structure, teachers' backgrounds, and working conditions. Such information can guide decisions about the design and funding of teacher preparation and support. However, there is much we can do in the short term to promote more effective research-based approaches to teacher professional development in ABE.

REFERENCES

Adey, P. (1995). *The effectiveness of a staff development program: The relationship between the level of use of innovative science curriculum activities and student achievement*. Washington, DC: Education Resources Information Center. (ERIC Document Reproduction Service No. ED 383567)

American Federation of Teachers. (1998). *Building on the best, learning from what works: Seven promising reading and language arts programs*. Washington, DC: Author. Retrieved March 31, 2006, from http://www.aft.org/pubs-reports/downloads/teachers/seven.pdf

Ancess, J. (2000). The reciprocal influence of teacher learning, teaching practice, school restructuring and student learning outcomes. *Teachers College Record, 102*, 590–619.

Anderson, P. J. (1997). Professional development schools: A balanced wheel makes it better for everyone. *TESOL Journal, 7*(1), 19–24.

Ball, D. L., & Cohen, D. K. (1999). Developing practice, developing practitioners: Toward a practice-based theory of professional education. In L. Darling-Hammond & G. Sykes (Eds.), *Teaching as the learning profession: Handbook of policy and practice* (pp. 3–32). San Francisco: Jossey-Bass.

Bandura, A. (1995). Exercise of personal and collective efficacy in changing societies. In A. Bandura (Ed.), *Self-efficacy in changing societies* (pp. 1–45). Cambridge, UK: Cambridge University Press.

Berry, B., Turchi, L., & Johnson, D. (2003). *The impact of high-stakes accountability on teachers' professional development: Evidence from the south.* Chapel Hill, NC: Southeast Center for Teaching Quality. Retrieved March 31, 2006, from http://www.teachingquality.org/pdfs/Spencer_FinalReport.pdf

Bollough, R. V., Kauchak, D., Crow, N., Hobbs, S., & Stoke, D. (1997). Professional development schools: Catalysts for teacher and school change. *Teaching and Teacher Education, 13,* 153–169.

Borman, G., & Hewes, G. (2002). The long-term effects and cost-effectiveness of Success for All. *Educational Evaluation and Policy Analysis, 24,* 243–266.

Bransford, J. D., Brown, A. L., & Cocking, R. R. (Eds.). (1999). *How people learn: Brain, mind, experience and school.* Washington, DC: National Academy Press.

Burt, M., & Keenan, F. (1998). *Q & A: Trends in staff development for adult ESL instructors.* National Clearinghouse for ESL Literacy Education (NCLE). Retrieved November 18, 2003, from http://www.cal.org/ncle/DIGESTS/TrendQA.htm

Bye, T. (2004). *Project ALACASA: Academic Literacy Across the Curriculum for Achieving Standards Biennial Evaluation Report 2002–2004.* San Francisco: San Francisco Unified School District.

Calderón, M. (1999). Teachers learning communities for cooperation in diverse settings. *Theory Into Practice, 38,* 94–99.

Calderón, M., & Marsh, D. (1988, Winter). Applying research on effective bilingual instruction in a multi-district inservice teacher training program. *NABE Journal,* pp. 133–152.

Carey, K. (2004). The real value of teachers: Using new information about teacher effectiveness to close the achievement gap. *Thinking K–16, 8*(1), 3–42.

Carpenter, T. P., Fennema, E., Peterson, P. L., Chiang, C., & Loef, M. (1989). Using knowledge of children's mathematics thinking in classroom teaching: An experimental study. *American Educational Research Journal, 26,* 499–531.

Carpenter, T. P., & Franke, M. L. (1998). Teachers as learners. *Principled Practice in Mathematics and Science Education, 2*(2), 1–3.

Choy, S. P., Chen, X., & Bugarin, R. (2006). *Teacher professional development in 1999–2000: What teachers, principals, and district staff report* (NCES Rep. No. 2006-305). Washington, DC: National Center for Education Statistics.

Clair, N., & Adger, C. T. (1999). *Professional development for teachers in culturally diverse schools* (CAL Digest EDO-FL-99-08). Washington, DC: Center for Applied Linguistics. Retrieved March 31, 2006, from http://www.cal.org/resources/digest/profdvpt.html

Cohen, D. K., & Hill, H. C. (2000). Instructional policy and classroom performance: The mathematics reform in California. *Teachers College Record, 102,* 294–343.

Committee on Science and Mathematics Teacher Preparation. (2000). *Educating teachers of science, mathematics and technology: New practices for the new millenium.* Washington, DC: National Academies Press.

Crocker, J. (1987, October). *ABE statewide staff development programs: Analysis of program dimensions, characteristics, and contextual factors.* Paper presented at the American Adult and Continuing Education Conference, Washington, DC.

Darling-Hammond, L., & Youngs, P. (2002). Defining "high-qualified teachers": What does "scientifically-based research" actually tell us? *Educational Researcher, 31*(9), 13–25.

Dutro, E., Fisk, K., Koch, R., Roop, L. J., & Wixson, K. (2002). When state policies meet local district contexts: Standards-based professional development as a means to individual agency and collective ownership. *Teachers College Record, 104,* 787–811.

Elmore, R. F. (1996). Getting to scale with good educational practice. *Harvard Educational Review, 66*(1), 1–28.

Elmore, R. F. (2002). *Bridging the gap between standards and achievement: The imperative for professional development in education.* Retrieved March 31, 2006, from http://www.ashankerinst.org/Downloads/Bridging_Gap.pdf

Feiman-Nemser, S. (2001). From preparation to practice: Designing a continuum to strengthen and sustain teaching. *Teachers College Record, 103,* 1013–1055.

Fenstermacher, G. D., & Berliner, D. C. (1985). Determining the value of staff development. *The Elementary School Journal, 85,* 281–314.

Ferry, N. M., & Ross-Gordon, J. M. (1998). An inquiry into Schon's epistemology of practice: Exploring links between experience and reflective practice. *Adult Education Quarterly, 48,* 98–112.

Fuller, F., & Bown, O. H. (1975). Becoming a teacher. In K. Ryan (Ed.), *Teacher education: The seventy-fourth yearbook of the National Society for the Study of Education, Part 2* (pp. 25–52). Chicago: University of Chicago Press.

Gardner, J. (1996). *Professional development which provides an icing on the pedagogical cake.* Washington, DC: Education Resources Information Center. (ERIC Document Reproduction Service No. ED 400589)

Garet, M. S., Porter, A. C., Desimone, L., Birman, B., & Yoon, K. S. (2001). What makes professional development effective? Results from a national sample of teachers. *American Educational Research Journal, 38,* 915–945.

Gersten, R., Keating, T., & Becker, W. (1988). The continued impact of the direct instruction model: Longitudinal studies of follow through students. *Education and Treatment of Children, 11,* 318–327.

Ghaith, G., & Shaaban, K. (1999). The relationship between perceptions of teaching concerns, teacher efficacy, and selected teacher characteristics. *Teaching and Teacher Education, 15,* 487–496.

Goddard, R. D., Hoy, W. K., & Hoy, A. W. (2000). Collective teacher efficacy: Its meaning, measure, and impact on student achievement. *American Educational Research Journal, 37,* 479–507.

Greeno, J. G., Resnick, L. B., & Collins, A. M. (1997). Cognition and learning. In D. Berlinger & R. Calfee (Eds.), *Handbook of educational psychology* (pp. 15–46). New York: Simon & Schuster/Macmillan.

Grossman, P. L. (1992). Why models matter: An approach view on professional growth in teaching. *Review of Educational Research, 62,* 171–179.

Grossman, P., Wineburg, S., & Woolworth, S. (2000). *What makes teacher community different from a gathering of teachers?* (Occasional paper). Washington, DC: Center for the Study of Teaching and Policy and Center on English Learning & Achievement.

Guskey, T. R. (1988). Teacher efficacy, self-concept, and attitudes toward the implementation of instructional innovation. *Teaching & Teacher Education, 4,* 63–69.

Guskey, T. R. (1997). Research needs to link professional development and student learning. *Journal of Staff Development, 18*(2), 36–40.

Guskey, T. R. (1999). Moving from means to ends. *Journal of Staff Development, 20*(1), 48.

Guskey, T. R., & Sparks, D. (1996). Exploring the relationship between staff development and improvements in student learning. *Journal of Staff Development, 17*(4), 34–38.

Haycock, K. (1998). Good teaching matters ... a lot. *Thinking K-16, 3*(2), 3–14.

Hord, S. (1997). *Professional learning communities: Communities of continuous inquiry and improvement.* Austin, TX: Southwest Educational Development Laboratory. Retrieved March 31, 2006, from http://www.sedl.org/pubs/change34/

Hord, S., Rutherford, W., Huling-Austin, L., & Hall, G. (1987). *Taking charge of change.* Alexandria, VA: Association for Supervision and Curriculum Development.

Huberman, A. M., & Miles, M. B. (1984). *Innovation up close*. New York: Plenum.
Ingersoll, R. M. (2001). *Teacher turnover, teacher shortages, and the organization of schools* (Rep. No. R-01-1). Seattle: University of Washington Center for the Study of Teaching and Policy.
Joughin, G. (1992). Cognitive style and adult learning principles. *International Journal of Lifelong Education, 11*(1), 3–14.
Joyce, B. (1983). *The structure of school improvement*. New York: Longman.
Joyce, B., & Showers, B. (1995). *Student achievement through staff development: Fundamentals of school renewal* (2nd ed.). White Plains, NY: Longman.
Joyce, B., Wolf, J., & Calhoun, E. (1993). *The self-renewing school*. Alexandria, VA: Association for Supervision and Curriculum Development.
Kagan, D. M. (1992). Professional growth among pre-service and beginning teachers. *Review of Educational Research, 62*, 129–169.
Kazemi, E., & Franke, M. (2003). *Using student work to support professional development in elementary mathematics* (Document No. W-03-1). Seattle: University of Washington, Center for the Study of Teaching and Policy.
Kegan, R. (1994). *In over our heads: The mental demands of modern life*. Cambridge, MA: Harvard University Press.
Knapp, M. (2003). Professional development as a policy pathway. *Review of Research in Education, 27*, 109–157.
Kutner, M., Herman, R., Stephenson, E., & Webb, L. (1991). *Study of ABE/ESL instructor training approaches: State profiles report*. Washington, DC: Pelavin Research Institute.
Langer, J. A. (2000). Excellence in English in middle and high school: How teachers' professional lives support student achievement. *American Educational Research Journal, 37*, 397–439.
Lewis, L., Parsad, B., Carey, N., Bartfai, N., Farris, E., & Smerdon, B. (1999). *Teacher quality: A report on the preparation and qualifications of public school teachers* (NCES 1999-080). Washington, DC: National Center for Education Statistics, U.S. Department of Education.
Little, J. W., Gearhart, M., Curry, M., & Kafka, J. (2003). Looking at student work for teacher learning, teacher community, and school reform. *Phi Delta Kappan, 85*, 184–192.
Livneh, C., & Livneh, H. (1999). Continuing professional education among educators: Predictions of participation in learning activities. *Adult Education Quarterly, 49*, 91–106.
Loucks-Horsley, S., Hewson, P. W., Love, N., & Stiles, K. E. (1998). *Designing professional development for teachers of science and mathematics*. Thousand Oaks, CA: Corwin.
Mazzarella, J. A. (1980). Synthesis of research on staff development. *Educational Leadership, 38*, 182–185.
McDonald, J. (2001). Students' work and teachers' learning. In A. Lieberman & L. Miller (Eds.), *Teachers caught in the action: Professional development that matters* (pp. 209–235). New York: Teachers College Press.
National Education Goals Panel Report. (1999). *Teacher education and professional development*. Retrieved November 18, 2003, from http://www.negp.gov/reports/ 99rpt.pdf
National Institute for Literacy. (n.d.). *Bridges to Practice: The project*. Retrieved February 20, 2006, from http://www.nifl.gov/nifl/ld/bridges/about/project.html
Neubert, G. A., & Binko, J. B. (1998). Professional development schools: The proof is in the performance. *Educational Leadership, 55*(5), 44–46.
Olson, T. A., Butler, J. A., & Olson, N. L. (1991). *Designing meaningful professional development: A planning tool* (Field test version). Portland, OR: Northwest Regional Educational Laboratory. (ERIC Document Reproduction Service No. ED 334671)
Ottoson, J. M. (1997). After the applause: Exploring multiple influences on application following an adult education program. *Adult Education Quarterly, 47*, 92–107.

Porter, A. C., Garet, M. S., Desimone, L. D., Yoon, K. S., & Birman, B. F. (2000). *Does professional development change teaching practice? Results from a three-year study: Executive summary*. Washington, DC: U.S. Department of Education, Office of the Undersecretary.

Richardson, V., & Placier, P. (2001). Teacher change. In V. Richardson (Ed.), *Handbook of research on teaching* (4th ed.). Washington, DC: American Educational Research Association.

RMC Research Corporation. (1996). *National evaluation of the Section 353 set-aside for teacher training and innovation in adult education* (Contract No. EA 93064991). Portsmouth, NH: Author.

Roberts, J. K., Henson, R. K., Tharp, B. Z., & Moreno, N. (2000, January). *An examination of change in teacher self-efficacy beliefs in science education based on the duration of in-service activities*. Paper presented at the annual meeting of the American Educational Research Association, Dallas, TX. (ERIC Document Reproduction Service No. ED 438259)

Rosenholtz, S. (1986). Educational reform strategies: Will they increase teacher commitment? *American Journal of Education, 95,* 543–562.

Ross, J. A. (1994). The impact of an in-service to promote cooperative learning on the stability of teacher efficacy. *Teaching & Teacher Education, 10,* 381–394.

Ross, J. A. (1998). Antecedents and consequences of teacher efficacy. In J. Brophy (Ed.), *Advances in research on teaching* (Vol. 7, pp. 49–74). Greenwich, CT: JAI.

Ruiz, N. T., Rueda, R., Figueroa, R. A., & Boothroyd, M. (1995). Bilingual special education teachers' shifting paradigms: Complex responses to educational reform. *Journal of Learning Disabilities, 28,* 622–635.

Sabatini, J. P., Daniels, M., Ginsburg, L., Limeul, K., Russell, M., & Stites, R. (2000). *Teacher perspectives on the adult education profession: National survey findings about an emerging profession* (Tech. Rep. No. 00-02). Philadelphia: National Center on Adult Literacy.

Sanders, W. L., & Rivers, J. C. (1996). *Cumulative and residual effects of teachers on future student academic achievement*. Knoxville: University of Tennessee.

Schon, D. A. (1983). *The reflective practitioner: How professionals think in action*. New York: Basic Books.

Sherman, R., Tibbetts, J., Woodruff, D., & Weidler, D. (1999). *Instructor competencies and performance indicators for the improvement of adult education programs*. Washington, DC: Pelavin Research Institute.

Smith, C., & Hofer, J. (2003). *The characteristics and concerns of adult basic education teachers* (NCSALL Rep. No. 26). Boston: National Center for the Study of Adult Learning and Literacy.

Smith, C., Hofer, J., Gillespie, M., Solomon, M., & Rowe, K. (2003). *How teachers change: A study of professional development in adult education* (NCSALL Rep. No. 25). Boston: National Center for the Study of Adult Learning and Literacy.

Smylie, M. A. (1988). The enhancement function of staff development: Organizational and psychological antecedents to individual teacher change. *American Educational Research Journal, 25,* 1–30.

Sparks, D. (1994). A paradigm shift in staff development. *Journal of Staff Development, 15*(4), 26–29.

Sparks, D. (1995). Focusing staff development on improving student learning. In G. Cawelti (Ed.), *Handbook of research on improving student achievement* (pp. 163–169). Arlington, VA: Educational Research Service.

Stallings, J., & Krasavage, E. (1986). Program implementation and student achievement in a four-year Madeline Hunter follow-through project. *Elementary School Journal, 87,* 117–138.

Stein, M. K., & D'Amico, L. (2002). Inquiry at the crossroads of policy and learning: A study of a district-wide literacy initiative. *Teachers College Record, 104,* 1313–1344.

Stein, M. K., Smith, M. S., & Silver, E. (1999). The development of professional developers: Learning to assist teachers in new settings in new ways. *Harvard Educational Review, 69,* 237–269.

Stein, M. K., & Wang, M. C. (1988). Teacher development and school improvement: The process of teacher change. *Teaching & Teacher Education, 4,* 171–187.

Stout, R. T. (1996). Staff development policy: Fuzzy choices in an imperfect market. *Education Policy Analysis Archives, 4*(2). Retrieved March 31, 2006, from http://epaa.asu.edu/epaa/v4n2.html

Supovitz, J. A., & Turner, H. M. (2000). The effects of professional development on science teaching practices and classroom culture. *Journal of Research in Science Teaching, 37,* 963–980.

Taylor, B. M., Pearson, P. D., Peterson, D. S., & Rodriguez, M. C. (2005). The CIERA School Change Framework: An evidence-based approach to professional development and school reading improvement. *Reading Research Quarterly, 40,* 40–68.

Tibbetts, J., Kutner, M., Hemphill, D., & Jones, E. (1991). *Study of ABE/ESL instructor training approaches: The delivery and content of training for adult education teachers and volunteers.* Washington, DC: Pelavin Research Institute.

Tolbert, M. (2001). *Professional development for adult education instructors: State policy update.* Washington, DC: National Institute for Literacy.

Tschannen-Moran, M., Hoy, A. W., & Hoy, W. K. (1998). Teacher efficacy: Its meaning and measure. *Review of Educational Research, 68,* 202–248.

U.S. Department of Education. (2002). *Meeting the highly qualified teachers challenge: The Secretary's annual report on teacher quality.* Washington, DC: Department of Education, Office of Postsecondary Education, Office of Policy, Planning and Innovation.

Wenglinsky, H. (2000). *How teaching matters: Bringing the classroom back into discussions of teacher quality* (a Policy Information Center Report). Retrieved November 18, 2003, from http://www.ets.org/research/pic

Whitehurst, G. (2002, March 5). *Research on teacher preparation and professional development.* Speech given at the White House Conference on Preparing Quality Teachers. Retrieved December 29, 2006, from http://www.ed.gov/admins/tchrqual/learn/preparingteachersconference/whitehurst.html

Wilson, B., & Corbett, D. (2001). Adult basic education and professional development: Strangers for too long. *Focus on Basics, 4*(D), 25–26.

Young, M. B., Fleischman, H., Fitzgerald, N., & Morgan, M. A. (1995). *National evaluation of adult education programs* (Executive summary, Contract No. LC 90065001). Arlington, VA: Development Associates.

8

Opportunities, Transitions, and Risks: Perspectives on Adult Literacy and Numeracy Development in Australia

Rosie Wickert, Jean Searle, Beth Marr, and Betty Johnston

This chapter provides an account of the development of adult literacy and numeracy in Australia. As with any attempt to capture a history in a few pages, it is selective and partial.[56] We aim to convey a flavor of the major national events and influences that have shaped adult literacy and numeracy, particularly those we believe have contributed to Australia's international reputation as an innovator in this field (Coben & Chanda, 2000; McKenna & Fitzpatrick, 2004a). The trajectory of adult literacy and numeracy's development in Australia is uneven, reflecting changes in government priorities, the varying beliefs and commitments of practitioners, external

---

[56]Indeed, as readers may discern, the personal experiences of the four authors of this chapter result, sometimes, in shared interpretations and, at other times, in different ones.

influences, and the complexity of how this area of work is organized and experienced. As the priorities and influences shifted, so did the nature of adult literacy and numeracy provision.

A recurrent theme through this account is how purposeful actions by literacy and numeracy advocates helped ensure that adult literacy and numeracy survived and grew through a volatile Australian policy environment over the last 15 to 20 years. With specific reference to adult numeracy, we present some of the distinctive characteristics of adult literacy and numeracy's beginnings, and explore the conditions enabling its move into mainstream postcompulsory policy and provision from the late 1980s, when it became an integral part of the broader vocational education system. What brought adult literacy and numeracy from the "billabong to the mainstream" (Kell, 1998)[57] in Australia was a complex array of events and circumstances; among them particular constellations of coalitions and advocacy networks, a reformist Labor (Democrat) government, a radical education and training minister, and the impact of external influences such as the Organization for Economic Cooperation and Development (OECD) and World Bank reform agendas and the United Nations Educational, Scientific and Cultural Organization (UNESCO) International Literacy Year in 1990.

The first national survey of adult literacy and numeracy skills in Australia (Wickert, 1989) also played an important role in this change-ready environment, not only by virtue of the data reported, but also because the report articulated some substantial arguments for change (Brock, 2001). Eight years later, under a newly elected conservative federal government and falling on less fertile ground, the International Adult Literacy Survey (IALS) data (Australian Bureau of Statistics [ABS], 1997) had less impact than might have been expected in furthering adult literacy and numeracy policy and provision (Hagston, 2002; McKenna & Fitzpatrick, 2004b), As a result, influences shaping Australia's adult literacy and numeracy policy and practice differ from those of many other English-speaking OECD nations (e.g., Ireland, England, and New Zealand) where the IALS data have spurred governments into action.

Positive influences on adult literacy and numeracy's development that we explore in this chapter include the following:

---

[57]A billabong is a pool or waterhole formed by a side channel of a river during the wet season.

- The federal Labor government's adoption of the 1991 Australian Language and Literacy Policy (ALLP)[58] (Department of Employment, Education and Training [DEET], 1991b).
- A coordinated ALLP implementation strategy based on extensive consultation on the ground and the presence of key influencers in decision-making roles.
- A strong community of practice linked via various networked coalitions around activities such as research, professional development, and advocacy.
- A "policy literacy"[59] (Lo Bianco, 2001b) among advocates, exemplified in a willingness to adapt to change, try new approaches, and grab opportunities to lock numeracy and literacy into mainstream policy initiatives and priorities.
- A history of activism in relation to equity initiatives and to language and literacy policy (Lo Bianco, 2001a; Wickert, 2001).]

The development of adult literacy and numeracy in Australia is typically regarded as occurring in three 10-year eras—starting roughly in the mid-1970s (Kell, 1998; McKenna & Fitzpatrick, 2004b; Searle, 1999). We follow this tradition here and characterize the three periods as (a) the mid-1970s to mid-1980s, "at the margins: emerging from the ground up"; (b) the mid-1980s to mid-1990s, "into the mainstream: building a national infrastructure for growth"; and (c) mid-1990s to present day, "intensification, integration, and fragmentation: living with tensions and contradictions."

We identify some key defining characteristics of each of these decades and make specific reference, where appropriate, to adult numeracy as a distinctive aspect of Australian adult education. In this way, we aim both to explain this distinctiveness and show how numeracy's development was influenced by broader events. We draw attention, especially, to events in the middle era (mid-1980s to mid-1990s), described by some as Australia's "literacy decade" (McKenna & Fitzpatrick, 2004b, p. 66), and to three transformative documents that have made a strong impact on how Australia understands and manages adult literacy and numeracy practice.

---

[58]A list of acronyms can be found in the Appendix.

[59]Lo Bianco (2001b) described policy literacy as "a critical understanding of the policy process" which, he argued, "brings about a more reflective and full participation in the processes of public policy making" (p. 212).

We conclude with some observations about how adult literacy and numeracy are currently positioned in relation to broader government priorities. To set the scene, we first provide a very brief and selective impression of Australia and its population.

ABOUT AUSTRALIA

Australia is a vast island continent of 7,686,850 square kilometers, similar in size to the mainland United States. Its population of approximately 19.2 million is concentrated on a narrow strip of the east coast, with smaller cities and communities on the south and southwest coasts. Inland Australia is largely dry and arid. It is here that you see the colors of the Aboriginal flag, the red ochre of the earth, the black night sky, and the burning gold of the sun. The colors also symbolize the history of the Indigenous Black population since the White, mainly British, invasion: the blood shed during massacres of whole clans, such that only 2% of the Indigenous population remained at the end of the 19th century, and the loss of traditional lands, rights, and languages.

Colonial rule, which commenced with the transportation of convicts and later encouraged free settlers to take up land, resulted in small settlements across Australia becoming independent colonies. Subsequently, in 1901, these colonies formed a federation that adopted a three-tiered system of government: national (commonwealth), state (six states and two territories), and local. Adult literacy and numeracy policy is generally developed and implemented at both the national and state or territory levels. Although overarching policy directions and associated funding may be set at the commonwealth level, local policies, strategic initiatives, funding, and implementation also occur at the state or territory level. The focus in this chapter is largely on national directions.

At the beginning of the 20th century, Australians believed that the nation would be secure and prosperous, with a substantially increased population. However, there was a net decline in birth rates during World War I and World War II and the Depression of the 1930s. Immigration patterns reflected concerns that Australia was too thinly populated to ensure its security, provide the labor required to build major infrastructure projects, and develop its industrial and economic potential, which was then mainly dependent on extractive industries and agriculture.

However, the "White Australia" policy, in place during the first half of the 1900s, sharply restricted the admission of non-White immigrants and immigrants largely came from southern Europe and the United Kingdom to fill a shortage of manual labor. More recent immigrants have predominantly come from Southeast Asia (Vietnam, Hong Kong, and Taiwan). Australia also accepts a limited number of refugees, mainly from Africa and the Middle East. As of 2000, 23% of Australians were born overseas. Immigrants born in mainly English-speaking countries represent 9.2% of the Australian population; immigrants born elsewhere comprise 14.4%. To provide an indication of the makeup of the immigrant population in 2003, 26% of immigrants were from the United Kingdom (compared with the peak of 67% in 1947), 28% from other European countries, 13% from Southeast Asia, and the remaining 33% from a wide range of other English- and non-English-speaking countries (Department of Immigration and Ethnic Affairs, 2003). Indigenous Australians make up a mere 2.4% of the Australian population (ABS, 2004).

According to the 1996 IALS survey in Australia (ABS, 1997), larger proportions of people whose first language was other than English were at the lowest skill levels on each of the three scales compared with people whose first language was English. Whereas 42% of those with English as their first language scored at Levels 1 and 2, and 58% at Level 3 and above, the figures for those for whom English was not their first language were 72% and 28%, respectively (ABS, 1997).

Data about the English-language literacy levels of Indigenous populations is patchy. The ABS survey excluded certain remote areas of Australia. Almost 50% of Aboriginal and Torres Strait Islanders live in nonurban or remote areas, and up to 50% of these may not speak English as their first language (Kral & Schwab, 2003). Eighty-eight percent of the urban Aboriginal and Torres Strait Islander population people speak English. Of the Indigenous peoples in the 1996 IALS sample, significantly greater proportions were at low literacy levels compared with other people who spoke English as their first language. Forty-one percent were at Level 1 on the prose scale, compared with 14% of the rest of the sample, for whom English was their first language. Different education experiences contribute in large measure to results like this, as the secondary school completion rate for Indigenous students is less than half that of the non-Indigenous student population.

As with other industrialized countries, Australia now requires a more highly skilled workforce, with strong literacy and numeracy skills. Globalization, competition, and environmental concerns have forced much manufacturing to overseas countries where there are cheaper sources of labor. The subsequent rise in service industries, communications, and other technologies in Australia have led to skill shortages in these areas. These workforce changes have influenced the nature of adult literacy and numeracy provision such that early emphases on citizenship, individual rights, inclusion, and remedial education have given way to a stronger focus on work preparation and vocational competence.

PHASES OF ADULT LITERACY AND NUMERACY IN AUSTRALIA

Introduction: Setting the Context

Scholars interested in comparative studies of adult basic education (ABE) often ask for quantitative data. How much provision? How many students? How much government funding? Such questions are almost impossible to answer with any degree of accuracy in relation to Australia for at least four reasons: (a) Australia's federated system, with at least nine education and training bureaucracies, has no consistent national system of categorization and reporting of all participants or programs; (b) the long history of immigration and the many different kinds of support programs that emerged for immigrants during the latter half of the 20th century implicitly incorporate literacy and numeracy skills development, but they do not report on this aspect of their work; (c) deliberate moves to integrate or embed literacy and numeracy learning in vocational education, workplace training, and programs for specific groups (e.g., women returning to work or adults with disabilities) means that there is overlap between basic education and broader educational programs so it is difficult to separate basic education; and (d) the increasing number of private and nongovernment providers in this market, for whom information about basic education is deemed "commercial-in-confidence," which means that accurate data cannot be compiled. Also, despite some commonly held misconceptions, provision does not neatly divide into programs for immigrants and for those with English-speaking backgrounds.

Rather than attempt to engage the reader further in these complexities, the material in this chapter relates predominantly to what is conventionally referred to as adult literacy and numeracy or ABE. Although this may include many adults from non-English-speaking backgrounds, for a number of reasons such as differing funding arrangements or priorities, it does not include provision specifically targeted at newly arrived immigrants or specified groups, such as women or Indigenous communities.

The Mid-1970s to Mid-1980s: At the Margins—Emerging From the Ground Up

As in much of the Western world, in Australia in the 1970s, social movements demanded a better situation for many previously marginalized citizens. Adult literacy and numeracy provision in this early period depended on the initiative and energy of committed individuals—often working in isolation under considerable physical and financial constraints, typically with strong humanist, political, or religious convictions—to assist adults who lacked access to education and other social capital. During this time, programs made extensive use of volunteers along with paid teachers, many of whom identified strongly with the principle of literacy as a fundamental human right.

In the mid-1970s, the newly elected Whitlam Labor government, fired up with a reformist, social justice zeal, charged the Technical and Further Education (TAFE) system with responsibility for adult literacy (Zimmerman & Norton, 1990). This was in line with a highly influential report (Kangan, 1974) that resulted in the reorientation of postcompulsory education toward addressing equity and access concerns alongside its traditional industry training focus. By the end of the 1970s, education and training authorities implemented affirmative-action policies and broadened their focus to embrace previously disadvantaged or equity groups such as women, Indigenous people, people from non-English-speaking backgrounds, and people with disabilities, all of whom were underrepresented in the broad spectrum of training programs.

Along with this widening of their charter, many TAFE colleges established learning centers to provide individual assistance with English and mathematics to students who needed extra support to succeed in their vocational courses. Gradually, teachers in these centers reached out to the wider community and offered specialized sessions in mathematics to the public, some following individualized tuition models, others providing a more social learning atmosphere. The Mathematics Workshops in New South Wales were just one example of this approach, where a small group of adults "came together to learn through understanding and to foster pleasure in mathematical experience" (Thiering, 1981, p. 1).

Many of the early adult literacy and numeracy pioneers considered themselves part of a larger education and social movement (Nelson, 1981; Searle, 1999; Wickert, 2001). They formed statewide professional voluntary organizations, an influential national council active in political advocacy and professional formation, and local networks of practitioners such as the Numeracy Network in Victoria in the early 1980s, an arm of the local state adult literacy council. These state and national voluntary professional associations continue to provide important forums for literacy and numeracy practitioners. Also, during the early 1980s, a number of states established professional support agencies to provide assistance to volunteer tutors and others, and to refer adults seeking help to appropriate literacy programs. These agencies operated as "strong networks for practitioners in the field, hubs of activity and ideas" (Hazell, 2002, p. 49). They conducted professional development, developed literacy and numeracy resources, and maintained unique libraries of material for teachers to use. They were the places where a numeracy or literacy teacher who felt isolated might meet people of like mind and passion.

The strengths of this era of emergence "from the ground up" rested on enthusiasm, conviction, and student-centeredness in an environment in which there were no formal literacy and numeracy curricula, few articulated pathways for student progression, and little system accountability. Indeed, one senior bureaucrat described the field in the late 1980s as "isolated and marginalized" with "largely unqualified practitioners," "limited" infrastructure and a "virtually nonexistent" research base (Elwell-Gavins, 1994). Securing a sustainable future for adult literacy and numeracy was the major challenge for the next decade.

Australian Adult Numeracy's Distinctive Beginnings

In Australia, adult numeracy is so often paired with literacy that it might be assumed that this has been the case since ABE provision began to integrate numeracy into instruction in the 1980s. However, literacy has not been numeracy's only—or even its most crucial—influence. Like literacy, social justice and equity concerns of the 1970s spurred and shaped the provision of numeracy. However, unlike literacy, the strongest impetus for numeracy's initial and ongoing development grew out of the specifically feminist commitment of many of its advocates, a fact that has had important repercussions for its development.

In the mid-1980s, the newly elected Hawke Labor government's commitment to equity supported improving the position of women in relation to education and training. Vocational training, science, and technology-based courses that required mathematical skills were almost entirely male domains. The limited female presence was partly attributed to the fact that girls tended to opt out of mathematics in compulsory education earlier than boys. Mathematics avoidance (Willis, 1989) among women and teenage girls became the subject of much study.

Women with mathematics teaching backgrounds joined and lobbied Equal Opportunity committees, resulting in funding for more women's courses. In 1985, funding for a Women Who Teach Women Maths and Science conference in Victoria allowed many teachers to share their pioneering experiences. Discussion centered on alternative teaching methodologies and curriculum approaches, and identified the need for new instructional materials, because nothing "reflecting the lives, needs, and interests of adults—particularly women—was available" (Marr & Helme, 1990, p. 82). Working in a spirit of collectivity and cooperation engendered through past experiences in the women's movement, interested women backed by affirmative action funding came together to develop a teaching resource. This Teaching Mathematics to Women Project team investigated existing courses for adult women in Australia and established a framework and activities for successful learning, and ideas for related teaching activities (Marr & Helme, 1987).

Enthusiastic teachers also designed courses to meet the needs of other socially disadvantaged groups. These efforts brought a multiplicity of voices—including those from mathematics education, from adult learning theory, and from vocational education—to conversations that shaped the early approaches to adult numeracy education, its definitions, its curriculum and professional development, and its teaching materials. As its proponents worked to carve out numeracy's distinctiveness from remedial mathematics and functional literacy, numeracy evolved into a concept that involved social and cultural practices, as well as skills (Tout, 1990).

The period of networking and creativity prior to numeracy entering the mainstream in accredited courses pushed the issue into the social and public realm, where the needs of the less numerate adults could be translated into demands for government provision and programs. It politicized the numeracy needs of adults. Along with success in getting government funding for numeracy programs, however, came the requirements and regulations of government.

Late 1980s to 1995: Into the Mainstream—Building a National Infrastructure for Growth

The crash of the U.S. stock market in 1987 resulted in worldwide financial instability. In Australia, the Hawke Labor government chose to respond through microeconomic reform aimed at transforming the nation from "the complacent Lucky Country to an [active] Productive Country, the Innovative and Hard-Working Country" (Hawke, cited in Kelly, 1992, p. 386). From a myriad of state- or territory-based arrangements, the Commonwealth government formed a national training system designed to provide greater flexibility and national consistency, including nationally accredited qualifications. The associated restructuring of industrial awards linked wages to national qualifications,[60] a move that strengthened the vocational education and training sector. Over the next few years, each industry determined the specific skills, knowledge, and attitudes required for workers to operate effectively at each level of employment. These became reified as competency standards, made up of units of competency.[61] Some working in adult literacy and numeracy were concerned that the push for training to be driven by competency standards related to employment and training outcomes put at risk previous funding commitments to programs oriented to social justice, access, and equity (Sanguinetti, 1999; Searle, 1999). Others saw the focus on preparation for work through a range of targeted programs as an important equity initiative and a welcome shift from the protective gatekeeping that some considered characterized too much adult literacy and numeracy teaching practice (McKenna, 1997; Wickert, 1988). This kind of well-meaning, but perhaps shortsighted, perspective saw some students reenrolling in the same programs over many years, with little evidence of literacy and numeracy learning outcomes. Such learning environments were perhaps more oriented to instilling a sense of security and belongingness with students than challenging them to more actively move from welfare to work.

This period of major change to industry structuring and training coincided with UNESCO's declaration of an International Literacy Year in 1990. The coming of International Literacy Year prompted a small but significant policy commitment to adult literacy in 1987 through the National Policy on Languages (Lo Bianco, 1987), which, for the first time in

---

[60]An award is a legally enforceable decision, made by industrial tribunals, that sets out the wages and conditions employees are entitled to receive from their employer. At the time of writing, new industrial-relations legislation is passing through the Commonwealth government that will radically change the Australian Industrial Relations system of awards.

[61]*Competency* (also *competence*) means the ability to perform tasks and duties (generic and occupation-specific) to the standard expected at different levels of employment. A competency standard is the description of the tasks and duties at these different levels.

Australia, provided some resources for a small number of strategic projects aimed at better understanding aspects of literacy and numeracy need and raising awareness and appreciation of the issue, including a substantial Adult Literacy Action Campaign in the build-up to 1990. A watershed event during this time was a gathering, organized through the auspices of the Australian Council for Adult Literacy, that galvanized the attention of key opinion leaders in industry, the union movement, social advocacy organizations, and senior bureaucrats about the place of adult literacy and numeracy in economic and workplace reform (Gilding, 1999). In addition, Australia, along with other OECD countries during this period, was aligning itself with the OECD Active Society policy initiative, which strongly endorsed job-seeker participation in welfare-to-work programs in line with an expectation that welfare recipients work, or actively show intent to develop the capacity for work, in exchange for welfare payments (OECD, 1989). In Australia, this policy approach is known as *mutual obligation* (Curtain Consulting, 2000).[62]

Advocacy groups successfully used these hooks to bring adult literacy in from the margins by persuading government and industry leaders of the integral place of literacy and numeracy in these reforms (Gilding, 1999; Lo Bianco, 1997). A Commonwealth government policy discussion paper on literacy policy (DEET, 1991b) provided the vehicle for this persuasion by delivering a policy commitment to adult literacy in the ALLP (DEET, 1991a), which was more comprehensive than the earlier National Policy on Languages. The ALLP consolidated a number of previously fragmented and uncoordinated language and literacy programs across, for example, work-based provision and assistance for the unemployed.

Forcing a closer connection between language and literacy in the ALLP caused concern about a weakening of distinct ESL provision, particularly for specialist ESL providers such as the Adult Migrant English Service (Moore, 2001). Positioning numeracy as part of literacy, although strategically useful as described later, also caused similar concerns. The parallel and strengthening government commitment to deregulation[63] and the

---

[62]In Australia, there is a specified range of mutual obligation options available to welfare recipients. One of these is attendance at literacy and numeracy programs.

[63]*Deregulation* is the removal of regulations that control or restrict the operation of an industry or enterprise. Previously, Commonwealth government-funded adult literacy and numeracy programs were delivered through government agencies. Now, provision is open to a competitive tender process, and private agencies also deliver services.

associated managerial and contractual requirements were further sources of disquiet for adult literacy and numeracy educators concerned about the potential threat of these policy moves to the professionalization, stability, and quality of the field (Lo Bianco & Wickert, 2001). We discuss these concerns later in the chapter. Nonetheless, the achievement of a specific policy commitment from the Commonwealth government was a major milestone and provided a not-to-be-missed opportunity to consolidate the place of adult literacy and numeracy in national mainstream policy priorities for economic, industry, training, and welfare reform.

Positioning Numeracy

The term *numeracy* was first officially acknowledged in the Australian Council for Adult Literacy's 1989 *Policy Statement*, which stated categorically that "literacy . . . incorporates numeracy":

> Literacy involves the integration of listening, speaking, reading, writing and critical thinking. It incorporates numeracy. It includes the cultural and social knowledge which enables a speaker, writer or reader to recognise and use language appropriate to different social situations. (www.acal.edu.au)

This influential definition was adopted for International Literacy Year and was reflected in the companion volume to the ALLP. Clearly, though, the exact definition of numeracy is open to interpretation in such a statement. This move to "incorporate" later created some tensions for adult numeracy educators who were advocating a greater prominence for numeracy education and became concerned about a loss of visibility for numeracy in policy and practice.

However, the Australian Council for Adult Literacy's strategic move of incorporating numeracy in its definition of literacy gave numeracy an acknowledged place in subsequent policy and program development and widened the opportunity for numeracy teachers and researchers to access resources for numeracy programs, teaching materials, research, and professional development. During the 1990s, numeracy progressively appears alongside literacy in the naming of government programs, professional activities, and publications, thus legitimizing it as a distinct but complementary field.

Although the incorporation of numeracy still left numeracy officially undefined, by the mid-1990s, numeracy teachers in Australia had developed a common working language. They had debated the concept of numeracy and how to teach and assess it, and they had questions to ask about its relationship to literacy, mathematics, and vocational education. One definition argued that being numerate means "being able to situate, interpret, critique, use, and perhaps even create mathematics in context, taking into account all the mathematical as well as social and human complexities which come with that process" (Yasukawa, Johnston, & Yates, 1995, p. 2). Although several definitions did appear in relation to various initiatives, in 2004 the literacy definition used in the tender documents for federal government programs for job seekers was the same as the 1989 Australian Council for Adult Literacy definition, although with the important elaboration of numeracy as "the ability to use mathematics effectively to meet the general demands of life at home, in paid work and for participation in community and civic life" (Department of Education, Science and Training [DEST], 2004, p. 4).

Recognizing the place of adult literacy and numeracy in economic reform, providing new funding, and realigning previously unrelated initiatives within the framework of the ALLP had several important consequences. Adult literacy experienced rapid growth across a variety of types of provision, such as literacy and numeracy assistance for the unemployed, and literacy and numeracy support for participants in vocational education and training, on and off the worksite. Although still a small commitment given the extent of need, federal funding for adult literacy and numeracy provision approximately tripled, to over $30 million (Australian).[64] State governments, keen to win tenders for such provision and build their market share, threw themselves into the task of developing competency-based curricula and getting them onto a national register of approved, accredited literacy and numeracy courses to be eligible for Commonwealth funding. As this was an area of education unfamiliar to many bureaucrats, the increased funding available to the states and territories provided a "once-in-a-lifetime" opportunity (Gilding, 1996, p. 1) for a network of insider literacy and numeracy advocates to gain influential and strategic positions within government agencies and advisory bodies.

---

[64]Note comments earlier about the difficulty of capturing exact expenditures given the variety of programs and various ways of categorizing population groups.

A number of these people became members of the National Adult Literacy Taskforce, created by the Ministerial Council of State and Territory Ministers of Education and Training to oversee implementation of the ALLP. In 1993, this Taskforce achieved agreement from Commonwealth, state, and territory governments to a National Collaborative Adult English Language and Literacy Strategy (Australian Education Council and Ministers of Vocational Education, Employment and Training, 1993). The strategy was strong and ambitious, providing a blueprint for the Commonwealth, state, and territory governments to work with the industry, community, and research sectors to develop and deliver an integrated national language and literacy program. The National Strategy (as we refer to it here) proposed several areas for action that defined the basic frame of reference for implementation. These included (a) setting nationally consistent directions for policy and program management, (b) diversifying and expanding provision, (c) ensuring quality outcomes and equitable access, and (d) demonstrating value for money. The national focus on these priority areas resulted in the creation of many of the initiatives that continue to shape adult literacy and numeracy in Australia today, three of which we now describe: the first, a framework of learner competence; the second, a system for reporting; and the third, a framework for professional development.

The National Framework of Adult English Language, Literacy and Numeracy Competence. The National Framework of Adult English Language, Literacy and Numeracy Competence (the National Curriculum Framework; Australian Committee for Training and Curriculum, 1993) aimed to provide an educationally defensible approach to describing adult English language, literacy, and numeracy competence in ways that could guide curriculum development and reporting across a range of learning contexts (Luke, 1995). The National Curriculum Framework makes available a common point of reference for the identification and development of language, literacy, and numeracy competence in differing contexts of use, such as in public life, at work, or in the home. Recognizing that states or territories have different ABE curricula, it also provides a means of describing, with common terminology, student progress in ways that can be applied to these various curricula. The seeds of the approach lay in an ABE accreditation framework under development in Victoria at the time (State Training Board, Victoria, 1992), although the National Curriculum Framework project was also, in part, an attempt to provide theories of language, culture, and learning to inform and deepen the rather technical and monodimensional competency-based approaches embraced in vocational training.

Rather than a skills-based approach, the authors of National Curriculum Framework advanced notions of language, literacy, and numeracy as both constructing and arising from sociocultural contexts of use. So, because language, literacy, and numeracy gain meaning through widely different and ever-changing contexts of use, they argued that it should be possible for curriculum models to build profiles of competence (and curricula and assessment) related to context; that is, "to move educators' and employers' attention to workers' cultural and gender resources, and to prescriptively shift their attention towards broader repertoires of effective social activity [that defied single-digit assessment of individuals], as opposed to narrow definitions of psychological and behavioural skill. . . . By definition this richer model demanded of educators more complex, multicultural and multilingual descriptive assessment rather than 'single-shot' testing" (Luke, 1995, pp. 91–92).

The multidimensional hexagonal framework design of the National Curriculum Framework (shown in Fig. 8.1) thus departs from traditional notions of literacy represented either as a unitary construct or as a linear developmental progression. It conveys the more complex notion of language, literacy, and numeracy as socially and culturally context-dependent practices. The construct denotes, first, a view of competence that connects performance with social goals in particular contexts, described as *aspects* of communication. These six aspects are (a) performing tasks (procedural), (b) using technology (technical), (c) expressing identity (personal), (d) interacting in groups (cooperative), (e) interacting in organizations (systems), and (f) interacting with the wider community (public).

The second dimension reflects the reality that at any one time a person's literacy and numeracy performance may require one or a combination of these aspects in one of three modes. These ways are described as *stages* of learning, but as well as reflecting stages of learning, any one mode could be adopted at any level of literacy and numeracy competence. The stages are performing with assistance, performing independently, or performing collaboratively. These various modes are also likely to be context specific. For example, a person might work for the most part independently when using technology, but might have to refer to a manual or ask for assistance. At other times, a person may work collaboratively to produce a report. The third dimension of the National Curriculum Framework is that, within each aspect, allowance is made for *phases* of learning; that is, through four "moments of pedagogy": (a) reflecting on experience, (b) engaging in activities, (c) broadening applications, and (d) critically reviewing (see Fig. 8.2).

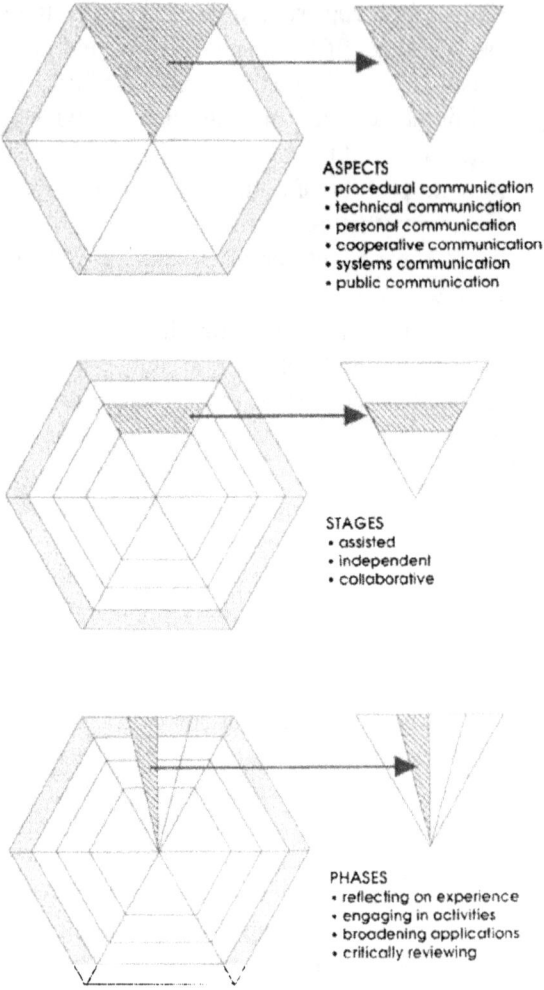

FIG. 8.1. The National Framework of Adult English Language, Literacy and Numeracy Competence. Note: Reproduced with permission from The National Framework of Adult English Language, Literacy and Numeracy Competence (Australian Committee for Training and Curriculum, 1993, p. 16).

This complex "multi-leveled and multifaceted model of competence" (Luke, 1995, p. 92) project was not without its critics. Although well received by many literacy and numeracy experts, others thought it conceptually confusing and some practitioners did not find it easily accessible. Its impact on curriculum development has varied across states and territories. Although not often explicitly referred to these days, its ongoing

8. ADULT LITERACY AND NUMERACY DEVELOPMENT IN AUSTRALIA   261

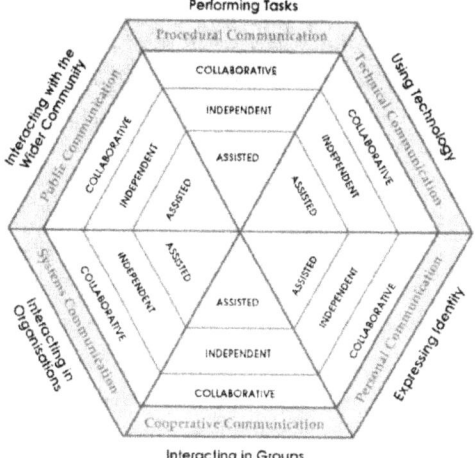

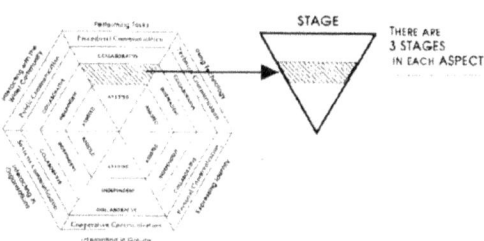

FIG. 8.2. The relationships between the aspects, stages, and phases of the National Framework of Adult English Language, Literacy and Numeracy Competence. Note. Reproduced with permission from The National Framework of Adult English Language, Literacy and Numeracy Competence (Australian Committee for Training and Curriculum, 2003, p. 18).

influence is still evident in some recently designed or reaccredited[65] state-based curriculum documents. Despite this mixed impact, we consider it to be an important legacy of this period. It provided a strong counter resource for adult literacy and numeracy practitioners during a time of

---

[65]*Accreditation* is the formal recognition of a course by the state or territory course accrediting body in accordance with the Standards for State and Territory Registering Course Accrediting Bodies (Australian National Training Authority, 2001). Courses are accredited for a set period of time. Once accredited, they are placed on a national register and available for use throughout Australia.

intense production of narrow, decontextualized lists of competencies as standards for industry training. Most significant, perhaps, is its influence on the National Reporting System (NRS), which currently guides how the Commonwealth government manages the provision of Commonwealth-funded adult literacy programs.

> **Putting the Frameworks Into Action: Numeracy Curriculum and Reporting**
>
> ABE courses in the 1980s began to include mathematics as well as literacy. By the early 1990s, after much debate in the field, programs and practitioners began to use the concept of numeracy, rather than the traditional concept of math. Curricula derived from the National Curriculum Framework, such as the Certificates of General Education for Adults (Adult, Community, and Further Education Board, 1996; Butcher et al., 2002), clearly differentiate numeracy from school mathematics, stressing the application aspects of numeracy, which keep realistic, whole-task situations uppermost in the specified learning outcomes, indicators, and examples of assessment tasks. The approach works to counteract the limited vision of numeracy as number calculations, broadening it to encompass a wide range of practical functions, from measurement and design to data analysis, and from money manipulation to map navigation. Such curriculum documents, therefore, incorporate most strands of formal mathematics—space and shape, measurement, chance and data, and not just number—within a contextualized approach. Evaluative research into the "Mathematics and Numeracy" section of the Certificate of General Education for Adults (Wallace-Clancy, Smith, Halliday, & Goddard, 1998) found that most teachers had expanded the scope of their numeracy teaching because of this inclusion. The research also found that the numeracy component was well received by new and experienced teachers alike, possibly because continuous input and feedback from experienced adult numeracy teachers during the developmental process ensured that it was based on existing good practice.
>
> To promote more holistic and realistic learning opportunities, these curricula offered an integrated approach to teaching adult numeracy and literacy that has proven to be an enormous strength when undertaken by teachers with knowledge and confidence in both areas of teaching, or by teachers from both disciplines working as a team. Note that without these conditions, and without supportive professional development for new teachers, numeracy is in grave danger of being invisible in an integrative approach.

The strength of curriculum documents such as the Certificate of General Education for Adults for supporting numeracy instruction is apparent. They allow sufficient flexibility for teachers to design their own learner-centered programs within the broad parameters of the curriculum frameworks. They also keep assessment in the hands of teachers, acknowledging the importance of ongoing observation and formative assessment in both the learning and assessment process. They support built-in systems of moderation and verification,[66] rather than centrally set tasks or tests. The assessment strategies include such things as teacher observations, performance of practical tasks, oral explanations, portfolios of tasks and investigations, self-assessments, and student journals. These are far removed from the common assessment strategies of short-answer tests and rote-learned processes applied to sets of abstract exercises too often used in more traditional mathematics teaching contexts.

The National Reporting System. In 1994, the Commonwealth government commissioned a project to develop a mechanism for reporting learner outcomes of Commonwealth-funded language, literacy, and numeracy programs. The resulting NRS (Coates, Fitzpatrick, McKenna, & Makin, 1995) is a reporting, rather than a curriculum, framework. It is mainly used for reporting entry and exit standards for learners supported through Commonwealth government funding schemes. Unlike its U.S. counterpart, and despite its name, the NRS is not an overall program reporting system in that it only refers to English language, literacy, and numeracy competence rather than to a wider range of learner outcomes or provider impact, such as getting a job or provider performance. The Australian NRS provides indicators of competence at five levels covering reading, writing, oral communication (listening and speaking), numeracy, and learning strategies.

The theoretical underpinnings for development through the five levels take into account text and task complexity of language and literacy activities; the interplay between identifying and doing mathematical activities and the language and critical reflections associated with numeracy tasks and texts; student familiarity with contexts and variables

---

[66]*Moderation* refers to meetings of teachers in which they compare samples of their locally designed and customized assessment tasks and resulting student performance to ensure consistency of interpretation of the framework descriptors. Verification is similar to moderation except that samples of tasks and student work are sent to an external verifier for judgment and written feedback.

such as the participants involved in the numeracy activity, the mode of communication, and the learner's background knowledge; and information on the maximum types of support an individual might require to perform an activity.

The NRS construct incorporates the six aspects of the National Curriculum Framework in that these provide a set of domains for contextualizing language, literacy, and numeracy performance—a horizontal axis. Other elements of the National Curriculum Framework are evident in the indicative performance conditions, features, and learning strategies described at each level of the NRS, such as the complexity of the text and task with which people engage; the nature of their role in the activity; and the conditions, including degree of support, under which the task is carried out. In summary, a report of a person's competence is meant to derive from the interplay between the chosen activity, the features of the text or task, and the context and level of support under which the activity is carried out.

In most cases the NRS is used alongside the state or territory curriculum frameworks that contain more detail to assist teachers in planning their teaching content, practice, and assessment methods. To assist the teachers, most states have published an equivalence "mapping" between their own frameworks and the NRS.

Using the NRS

At each of the five NRS levels are four indicators: one dealing with locating information, one about selecting strategies and applying strategies, another regarding the evaluation of results in context, and finally, an indicator relating to communication of mathematical processes using appropriate language and symbols. These change in their level of complexity and familiarity as they progress from level 1 to 5.

For example, numeracy indicators at the second of the five levels are:

2.9 Locates relevant mathematical information in a familiar real-life activity or text.
2.10 Selects and uses straightforward mathematical actions in familiar and predictable contexts.
2.11 Uses estimation and prior experience to examine purpose and check reasonableness of the process and outcomes of a mathematical activity.
2.12 Uses oral and written informal and formal language and representation including some symbols and diagrams to communicate mathematically.

The indicators place emphasis on a logical, mathematical approach to real-world tasks involving mathematical skills and reflection on the outcomes in real-world terms. All of these are seen as important features of good numeracy teaching and learning, as opposed to traditional mathematics teaching practices.

The indicators are supported by descriptors of conditions of performance, which specify degrees of support, available models, and familiarity of tasks expected at each level. These are further elaborated by a page of "Numeracy Features and Performance Strategies" subdivided into strategies for meaning making, problem solving, mathematical knowledge, and representation. Some examples include:

- Relies on personal experience and prior knowledge within context to make predictions and check reasonableness (a meaning-making strategy).
- Uses a blend of personal "in-the-head" methods and pen-and-paper calculator procedures (a problem-solving strategy).
- Begins to include symbols and diagrams in producing written records of tasks (mathematical representation).

The mathematical knowledge section indicates the scope of numeracy expected, with items such as:

- Interprets, compares, and calculates with natural numbers and money in personal and some unfamiliar contexts.
- Uses coordinates in a variety of contexts (e.g., street directories, games).

Further assistance is provided by a selection of sample assessment tasks, for instance:

- Uses a street directory to find a route to a familiar place (e.g., locates own street and shows route to local shops).
- Calculates with time (e.g., how long until tea break).
- Uses timetable and fare information to compare different ways of making the same journey (e.g., cost, time taken, convenience in using different forms of transport for a familiar journey; Coates et al., 1995, n.p.).

The Certificates of General Education for Adults (Adult, Community and Further Education Board, 1996; State of Victoria, 2002), which several Australian states and Corrections Education Service use, were developed after the NRS. The writers, having learned from the NRS development process and the strengths and weaknesses of the resulting descriptors, created a document that described the expected numeracy skills and knowledge in sufficient detail for teachers while retaining the flexibility to cater to local and individual needs and interests. Rather than attempting to describe all numeracy at a given level with one compact set of indicators, the document describes seven or eight separate outcomes at each of four levels. For example, one second-level outcome is:

Numeracy for Practical Purposes—Measuring

Can use straightforward measurement and the metric system to estimate and measure for the purpose of interpreting, making or purchasing materials in familiar practical situations.

This is then elaborated by a list of assessment criteria including:

- Interpret and use the concept of length, mass, volume, and temperature.
- Make initial estimates of measurements.
- Choose appropriate measuring instruments and use them correctly to measure.
- Choose and perform arithmetic operation where appropriate.
- Interpret the measurement in terms of the purpose of the practical situation (Butcher et al., 2002, p. 250).

Currently the two major Commonwealth-funded programs use the NRS to report progress: (a) the Workplace English Language and Literacy Program, and (b) the Language, Literacy and Numeracy Program (LLNP) for unemployed job seekers. A recent analysis of the use of the NRS reveals that it is not widely used as a reporting tool other than for these two Commonwealth-funded programs (Perkins, 2005). State and territory providers tend to report on student progress in relation to particular curriculum modules, as this is how they are funded. The Perkins report confirms, however, that when used well, the NRS framework does provide "the scaffolding upon which many things can be built" (Perkins, 2005, p. 9) and that, because the construct can be used for a range of purposes, its impact is wider than might initially be thought. For example, it is used for identifying and naming literacy and numeracy competencies in industry standards and identifying how to integrate literacy and numeracy into the vocational education and training system.[67]

---

[67]For examples, see www.nrs.dest.gov.au.

Perkins (2005) proposed that a simpler version may increase use and thus inform the vocational education and training system and its literacy and numeracy providers more effectively than at present. A major national project is currently underway following Perkins's recommendation, as captured in the title of her report about the NRS: *Reframe, Rename and Revitalize* (Perkins, 2005). Its effect on shaping adult literacy and numeracy provision is likely to grow as governments increase pressure for evidence of the impact of programs.

The National Framework for Professional Development of Adult Literacy and Basic Education Personnel. In February 1992, the TAFE National Staff Development Committee (a body representing all states and territories as well as the Commonwealth government) published the National Framework for Professional Development of Adult Literacy and Basic Education Personnel (National PD Framework; TAFE National Staff Development Committee, 1992), following a funding commitment in the ALLP for professional development activity. This was based on a national agreement, reflected in the National Strategy, to clarify the skills necessary to be a competent adult literacy or numeracy teacher (later published in Scheeres, Gonczi, Hager, & Morley-Warner, 1993) and to develop a more systematic, nationally coordinated, and improved approach to teacher professional development, recruitment, and induction. The National PD Framework targeted particular skill areas, such as working with Indigenous students, numeracy, managing volunteers, competency-based training and assessment approaches, and using information technology. Adult Numeracy Teaching, referred to in the next box, and its sister course, Adult Literacy Teaching, were two of the many influential professional development products associated with this National PD Framework. States and territories used these resources heavily over the ensuing 5 or 6 years. Unfortunately, the current emphasis on cost reduction and the subsequent increase in the employment of staff on short-term or casual contracts, who are considered to be responsible for their own professional development, has significantly reduced the subsidized provision of professional development support (McKenna, 2002; McKenna & Fitzpatrick, 2004a).

The National PD Framework was intended to provide a nationally coordinated mechanism that would embed national policy priorities in the work of adult literacy and numeracy educators. According to the National PD Framework, competency-based training, for example, was to be the major vehicle for enabling a more open market for vocational education and training provision, and for providing more flexible and "transportable" approaches to assessment. If adult literacy and numeracy were to be effectively integrated or embedded in vocational units of competence, as strongly argued in a major report published by the National Board for Employment, Education and Training in 1993, they would need to be constructed in the competency-based language of industry standards.

Constructing these professional development products required the assistance of experts, and although the projects to develop the training products were put to open tender, in reality there were few outside the existing fields of adult literacy and numeracy who had the appropriate expertise to apply for them. Winning these tenders and the substantial funding that accompanied them was one of the great opportunities for influence available during the 1990s, as illustrated later in relation to numeracy.

Building Up to a Professional Development Strategy for Numeracy

The publication resulting from the Teaching Mathematics to Women Project, *Mathematics: A New Beginning—A Resource Book for Teachers of Adults Returning to Study* (Marr & Helme, 1987), reflected numeracy's history of collective processes of development and innovation. The publication encouraged gender-inclusive strategies to reintroduce adults to learning, and it included many ideas drawn from the practical constructivist methodologies espoused by school mathematics reformers of the time, both in Australia and overseas (e.g., http://equals.lhs.berkeley.edu/). Small-group activities and problem solving were adapted to suit adult environments, and mathematical problems were framed in adult contexts. Aware that many teachers of numeracy would not necessarily have strong mathematics backgrounds, the authors included advice about mathematics content, as well as about teaching strategies. Experiential workshops engaged participating teachers in the group work and hands-on activities described in the resources and proved to be highly popular with adult numeracy and literacy teachers eager for new ideas. The Teaching Mathematics to Women team later documented their professional development principles, processes, and activities in a kit, *Breaking the Maths Barrier: A Kit for Building Staff Development Skills in Adult Numeracy*, thus disseminating their approach across Australia's dispersed adult teaching population and enabling others to conduct the professional development themselves (Marr & Helme, 1991).

Johnston and Tout (1995) carried these principles forward into an 80-hour teacher-education program, Adult Numeracy Teaching, that grew from

> consultation with educators and an investigation of existing good practice. As with the earlier professional development resources, the Adult Numeracy Teaching project team designed the course for a range of teachers, from those with mathematics backgrounds but no adult-teaching skills, to those with literacy teaching backgrounds and little mathematics. Adult Numeracy Teaching's goal was to help participating teachers move from an understanding of numeracy as doing basic mathematics, to being comfortable with mathematics, and further, to an understanding of numeracy as a bridge connecting mathematics to the real world. In the words of the program, "Numeracy is not less than maths but more" (Johnston & Tout, 1995, p. 378). The Adult Numeracy Teaching program was piloted in two states in 1994, and its publication, as part of the National PD Framework, ensured its wide dissemination.

Under the National PD Framework, opportunities for professional development for teachers expanded, resulting in a significant professionalization of the field. At the same time, there was an explosion of research and development activity, much of it policy-related research linked to the implementation strategy of the ALLP. Importantly, the Commonwealth DEET established the Adult Literacy Research Network during this period, initially with a strong focus on teacher development through action research[68] (Shore, 2004). By the mid-1990s, the adult literacy and numeracy field had established a "culture of training." Teachers expected access to professional development and teacher-education programs, and they expected to receive recognition for their participation in them (Wickert, Scheeres, & Ward, 1994). By the mid-2000s, for a number of reasons, the opportunities for professional development and, thus, teacher expectations, diminished significantly at all levels of training, from university courses to short workshops (McKenna & Fitzpatrick, 2004a). Explanations for this decline are strongly associated with changes to program funding introduced by the Commonwealth government for their literacy- and numeracy-related programs, which we explore in more detail in the next section. In brief, the changes included:

---

[68]The Adult Literacy Research Network was later renamed the Adult Literacy and Numeracy Australian Research Consortium and its research program gradually became more closely tied to national vocational training agendas. Funding ended in 2002, but its publications are available at www.staff.vu.edu.au/alnarc/.

- Changing patterns of employment for teachers, with more short-term and casual appointments associated with less support from employers for professional development.
- A decline in career opportunities, or at least predictable work, for literacy and numeracy teachers, which has reduced the incentive for teachers to pursue further study.
- A reduction in entry-level qualifications for workers in vocational education and training.
- A profit, rather than a service, motive for some of the new providers entering the training market.

These developments confirm one commentator's prediction in 1997 that a "separate notion of adult literacy and numeracy provision *with infrastructure support* can no longer be assured" (McKenna, 1997, p. 21).

Mixed Reponses to the Developments of the Middle Era. Not everyone in the field supported the developments of this era. Some (as reported by Lo Bianco, 1997; Sanguinetti, 1999) saw the National Strategy and its implementation mechanisms as a betrayal of the origins and core values of adult literacy and numeracy in Australia, but its supporters were strongly committed to a more strategic and managed approach, particularly managers and bureaucrats in the states and territories who struggled daily with the competing pressures of federal and state priorities and directions as they tried to manage change (Gilding, 1995, 1996; Persson, 1995). These people were convinced that the future for adult literacy and numeracy and the ongoing recognition of literacy and numeracy as a strategic priority for the development of the strongly emerging national vocational education and training system required a consistently articulated position across systems, providers, and industry. This was hard work and one of these activist bureaucrats, Gilding (1995) remarked: "Adult literacy has now been in constant national focus since 1989. It has been measured, criticised, strategised and publicised constantly. It has been much more self-conscious and detailed about quality than required. . . . It has posed more intellectual challenges to itself than any other field" (Gilding, 1995, p. 83).

The nature of politics often means the dissolution of the initiatives of previous administrations as other policy priorities take over. Such was the fate, following a change of federal government in 1996, of the National Adult Literacy Taskforce and the ongoing implementation activities of the ALLP. However, through its brief existence, the Taskforce had:

- Achieved a national coordinated policy position.
- Garnered attention to literacy and numeracy in state and Commonwealth funding agreements, in industry training plans, and in industry competencies.
- Established numeracy as an entity in its own right.
- Supported a well-funded, albeit short-lived, national professional development strategy that provided a sound basis for a sustained program of development.
- Instituted measures to tackle issues of quality control and the impact of deregulation.
- Created new providers and new relationships between existing providers (Castleton & McDonald, 2002; Gilding, 1996; McKenna & Fitzpatrick, 2004a).

The mid-1990s was probably the high point to date for adult literacy and numeracy in Australia, with the big boost in funding and greater confidence as a result of the new recognition—in mainstream policy objectives and strong professional networks—of the importance of adult literacy and numeracy (Black, 1990; Gilding, 1995; Kell, 1998). In particular, the National Collaborative Adult English Language and Literacy Strategy set the scene for the development of the frameworks that helped to build mechanisms for consolidating the place of adult literacy and numeracy in training and welfare policies. Our vignettes about numeracy's development reflect not only the significance of these enabling mechanisms as vehicles for sustainable action, but also the confidence and the energy such actions can create for change.

1996 to 2005: Intensification, Integration, and Fragmentation—Living With Tensions and Contradictions

Welfare to Work. After 13 years of a Labor government, the federal election in 1996 delivered a conservative government under the leadership of John Howard. The changes to training and welfare policy and programs initiated under the previous Labor government intensified, with a greater focus on deregulation, competition, and user-pays, such that Australia is now said to be a world model in its restructuring of welfare and employment services, including the creation of a "deep-seated competition culture" (OECD, 2005, p. 2). Successive welfare-to-work strategies have strengthened the links between literacy and numeracy learning and welfare payments, stated baldly in *The Australian* daily national newspaper as "learn to read or lose the dole" (cited in Australian Broadcasting Corporation, 1999). Deregulation of the training market continues to open up the provision of adult literacy and numeracy programs to competitive tendering, with cost an important factor in securing a contract. This has enabled both private and welfare (or not-for-profit) organizations not previously associated with adult literacy and numeracy provision to be successful in tendering for programs.[69] As with all organizations, public and private, the quality of these new providers is mixed; some bring new energy and ideas into the field whereas others offer little support for staff, some of whom have minimal adult literacy and numeracy qualifications and experience (DEST, 2005a). A recent unpublished internal review of the literacy and numeracy program for job seekers has confirmed earlier findings (Rahmani, Crosier, & Pollack, 2002) that the Commonwealth LLNP for job seekers is not delivering expected literacy and numeracy outcomes. Starting in 2006, new quality guidelines for tenderers will substantially strengthen requirements regarding appropriate course content and the use of adequately trained staff (DEST, 2005b), although additional resources to support this are unlikely to be made available.

The present LLNP provides literacy and numeracy training for eligible job seekers whose skills are below the level considered necessary to secure sustainable employment or to pursue further education and training and who are assessed as "having the capacity to benefit" from a literacy and numeracy program (DEST, 2005b, p. 7). The Commonwealth government is using the NRS to tie funding to performance targets, albeit in a simplified form. A DEST evaluation of the LLNP (Rahmani et al., 2002) suggests that the requirement for job seekers to leave the program when they find employment undermines the potential for learning benefit, as the majority exit before completing 200 out of a current maximum eligibility of 400 hours. Reported low success rates may also be due to job seekers being placed on long courses when shorter intensive tuition may be more appropriate. Pressure on providers to deliver better outcomes for LLNP participants is likely to increase following a further (unpublished) DEST evaluation and a comprehensive internal national review in 2004–2005, as are the number of eligible hours (DEST, 2005b).

---

[69]Further changes embodied in both welfare reform and industrial relations legislation going through Parliament at the time of this writing in late 2005 are expected to intensify pressure on providers to reduce costs.

Funding for adult literacy and numeracy programs is increasingly tightly managed and incorporated within other, broader welfare changes. Provision is more mediated through employment brokers who are now major purchasers of adult literacy services. Funding is increasingly performance based, with limited resources apportioned to successful contractors for staff training and development of teaching resources.

Training Reform. Since the Hawke Labor government initiated the National Training Reform Agenda in 1987 (Dawkins & Holding, 1987), three national vocational education and training strategies have set the directions: Towards a Skilled Australia (1994–1998), A Bridge to the Future (1998–2003), and Shaping Our Future (2004–2010). Each one has confirmed the importance of adult literacy and numeracy skill development within mainstream vocational education and training and built this into the vehicles for change.

Industry-specific "training packages" and progressive refinements of quality standards for training organizations are the vehicles for the reform of vocational education and training. Training packages are not a program of work, a course, or a folder of resources, but a package of units of competence that can be tailored to meet the specific needs of the employer or the trainee. Training packages are made up of three components: (a) specific competency standards, (b) industry qualifications (certificates and diplomas pertaining to a specific industry), and (c) assessment guidelines that are formally agreed on at a national level for each industry. Each package thus provides an industry with nationally agreed-on benchmarks for training and assessment. Registered training organizations[70] use these packages for designing their training and assessment strategies.

Industry-related literacy and numeracy competencies are meant to be built into the competency standards at each level of training, referred to as the "built-in, not bolted on," or integrated, approach (Wignall, n.d.), although there are mixed anecdotal reports that question how consistently this is being applied. Registered training organizations must meet a number of specified quality standards to deliver this nationally accredited

---

[70]Registered training organizations are providers of training who are registered by state and territory training authorities to deliver nationally recognized training; that is, training that has been accredited to meet the needs of a particular industry, and training that results in a qualification that is part of the Australian Qualifications Framework. A registered training organization can be a government department or a private enterprise, and training does not have to be its core business.

vocational education and training. Recent revisions to the Australian Quality Training Framework,[71] which was established in 2002, clarify the standard that relates to the capacity of a registered training organization to deliver literacy and numeracy assessment and assistance. Workplace assessors and trainers must complete an accredited Certificate in Assessment and Workplace Training (National Training Information Service, 2005) that, starting in 2005, offers more assistance to them to develop this capacity.

Some decry the influence of industry on literacy and numeracy provision, expressing concern that integration threatens the visibility of adult literacy and numeracy as a distinct field, and that it increases the risk of literacy and numeracy needs not being adequately addressed in vocational education and training (VET; e.g., Sanguinetti & Hartley, 2000). Some numeracy educators have voiced similar concerns about the integration of numeracy with literacy in general education courses (McGuirk & Johnston, 1995). Anecdotal evidence and recent research suggest that there is great variability in expertise and confidence about how to embed literacy and numeracy learning alongside vocational skill development (Fitzpatrick & McKenna, 2005; Marr & Morgan, in press). When literacy, language, and numeracy become integrated in VET competencies and are delivered by poorly trained trainers, the threat of invisibility is very real. Despite the availability of a number of literacy and numeracy teaching resources in the last decade designed to strengthen the capacity of providers to integrate literacy and numeracy skill development with vocational and workplace training, there remains a need for focused, thorough, face-to-face professional development.

Despite these reservations, through strongly advocating the "built-in, not bolted on," or integrated approach since the early 1990s, the adult literacy and numeracy field has taken advantage of the possibilities brought about by industry and training reform in Australia. Several successful examples exist of creative and successful responses to such possibilities (Sanguinetti & Hartley, 2000; Wickert & McGuirk, 2005). For instance, there are examples of literacy workers who specialize in the context and culture of a particular industry and build effective partnerships with that industry, thus enabling the industry trainers to embed appropriate literacy and numeracy skills development throughout the organization and thus into the community.

---

[71]The Australian Quality Training Framework sets out the conditions that an organization must meet to be accepted as a registered training organization. See www.dest.gov.au/sectors/training_skills/policy_issues_reviews/key_issues/nts/aqtf/standards_2005.htm

Inevitably, the intensification of welfare and vocational education and training changes under the Howard government has had a major impact on literacy and numeracy practitioners. In some states, long-standing government providers with certified staff award structures and industrial agreements could not compete financially with small private providers that were often formed in response to funding opportunities. Government providers quickly recognized the financial risks inherent in these developments and moved to manage this risk by reducing the number of programs, offering voluntary early retirement to some teachers, and moving toward short-term teaching contracts for others. In many places, full-time practitioners have been replaced by less experienced contract staff required to conduct short-term courses at low cost with very challenging clients, such as disaffected young people who are required to attend literacy and numeracy classes in return for welfare benefits. Ironically, this period also saw the closure of the professional support agencies referred to earlier.

Many teachers left the field. Some became private providers, paradoxically, to retain some control over their pedagogy, and have now become important leaders in their area of specialization. However, others have taken up the challenges of new ways of working and have become corporate or industry-based educators, often driving innovation in relation to adult literacy and numeracy integration as they do so. Still others are taking their expertise to community and welfare organizations working with specific disadvantaged populations (Wickert & McGuirk, 2005).

In these ways, ABE professionals in Australia have demonstrated their ability and willingness to be flexible. They fill new roles as case managers, industry trainers, consultants, and brokers; they have caseloads and clients. They work at multiple sites and actively continue to develop strategies for positioning adult literacy and numeracy in VET and welfare policy and practice.

CONCLUSION

The adult literacy field in Australia developed principled and informed initiatives and responses to legitimate demands for accountability and quality. These initiatives continue to influence and shape this field and its practices in complex ways, affected in part by how the particular histories and commitments of early literacy and numeracy advocates inflect the work of everyday numeracy teaching practice. Without this intensity of engagement, peppered with the pragmatism of experienced advocacy, it is possible that, following the change of federal government in 1996,

Australia's groundbreaking approaches to adult literacy and numeracy in vocational and workplace training and to provision for job seekers may have seriously faltered.

In relation to numeracy in particular, teachers, professional educators, and researchers in Australia have worked hard to keep numeracy on the agenda. As with literacy professionals, they have worked both to develop practical theoretical conceptualizations of numeracy and to construct new approaches to adult numeracy teaching that draw on a wide range of theories and practices (Kelly, Johnston, & Yasukawa, 2003). These two perspectives to numeracy, one articulating theory and the other supporting practice, have informed each other, resulting in a strong and theoretically based teaching practice. As we have shown in this chapter, in the examples of the development of the field of adult numeracy in Australia, it is these two perspectives—the understanding of what numeracy is, and the careful, imaginative, and grounded development of teaching practice and resources—that are the foundation of Australia's achievements in adult numeracy (Coben & Chanda, 2000; Johnston, 2002).

Positioning of literacy and numeracy programs within the mainstream vocational education sector has brought with it ever-increasing pressures related to time, money, standard quality-assurance systems, and accountability, sometimes with little awareness by regulators of the underpinning philosophies of the field and the nature of its students. Although the previous Labor government set these directions (Pratt, 1994), much stricter control of entitlement to provision and registration of providers has reengineered those aspects of adult literacy and numeracy that are funded directly by the Commonwealth government. There is an ongoing sense of professional fragmentation following the impact of these policy moves. Consequently, not all people who work in the field share the claims of strategic success, despite sustained increases in funding. Some agree with Lo Bianco, author of the 1987 National Policy on Languages who wrote in 1997, 6 years after the adoption of the ALLP, that provision:

> although greater, is fragmented and insecure, the workforce has become increasingly casualised,[72] professional networks have been damaged by competitive tendering processes, infrastructure support has dematerialised, working conditions have worsened, curriculum has been "colonised" by competency-based approaches and in the eyes of many, adult literacy has come to be "sublimated to a centralised, controlling, assessing, monitoring, information-demanding mechanism." (Lo Bianco, 1997, p. 6)

---

[72]*Casualization* refers to a process whereby previously fixed-term or permanent jobs become short-term and dependent on the employer winning government contracts.

There is some legitimacy and accuracy to these concerns, yet despite this, the quantity and variety of provision has grown, Commonwealth funding has been maintained, and literacy and numeracy are built into mainstream welfare and training reform. In relation to quality, however, there are renewed fears that legislation currently going through Parliament will intensify the risks to quality provision, pay, working conditions, adequate support, and defensible notions of literacy and numeracy.

In this chapter, we have demonstrated some of the most important ways in which Australian adult literacy and numeracy have weathered the move from adult literacy as a right to basic skills as an economic imperative to the current stage in which both Commonwealth and state or territory governments are beginning to talk again about adult literacy and numeracy in terms of social capital and community capacity building, albeit within a more closely bureaucratically managed funding environment (Balatti & Falk, 2002; Wickert & McGuirk, 2005). This may be an opportunity for a revitalization of the traditional concerns of many literacy and numeracy educators, as indicated next. The reemergence of a policy interest in notions of community provides some new possibilities for adult literacy and numeracy policy and practice, and Australia's involvement in the international Adult Literacy and Lifeskills survey in 2006 will provide an important opportunity for influence at all levels of government.

Part of an International Community

In July 2005, Australian numeracy practitioners and researchers hosted and organized a conference that they had been looking toward for many years, the first-ever national conference on adult numeracy and adults learning mathematics, called "Connecting Voices: Practitioners, Researchers and Learners in Adult Mathematics and Numeracy." It was, in addition, an international gathering—more than a quarter of the participants came from overseas—with substantial representation from every state and territory in Australia. Sessions focused on, for example, disputing narrow conceptions of "the basics," considering mathematical literacy as a civil right, addressing issues concerning Indigenous adults, exploring maths in current events, social justice issues, and bridging maths. The success of the conference—the number, quality, and variety of the presentations; the national and international strategies that were proposed; and the excitement that was generated in a time of low funding and little professional support—sparked hope for a new generation of creative and energetic practitioners and researchers, building on the strengths of the past.

As in other countries (e.g., Bateson, 2003; Cowan, 2006) there is growing agreement in Australia on the need for a collaborative, multisectoral approach to adult literacy and numeracy as all levels of government face the policy conundrums of health, aging, adequate personal finances, information technology, and the social and economic exclusion of rural and remote communities (Australian Public Service Commission, 2004; Castleton, Sanguinetti, & Falk, 2001; Council of Australian Governments, 2003; DEST, 2005b). There are major challenges ahead if there is to be a real broadening of the scope for collaborative action across sectors. Recent independent advice to the Commonwealth (Innovation and Business Skills Australia, 2005; McDonald & Goodwin, 2005) is suggesting the term *essential skills* offers greater policy potential opportunities than the term *adult literacy and numeracy* and proposes a new national approach to planning for adult literacy and numeracy based on a coordinated strategic planning and implementation framework.

We have tried here to convey the volatility of the policy environment of adult literacy and numeracy in Australia. Maybe, as we have successfully argued for the incorporation of literacy and numeracy into so many aspects of postcompulsory education and training, we have contributed to its fragmentation, both as a field of practice and as a construct. On the other hand, perhaps this apparent fragmentation provides new opportunities for influence. The flexibility of adult literacy professionals and their experience in working across sectors enables them to bring a special kind of expertise to collaboration in provision as government agencies now struggle to find innovative and "joined up" approaches to policy issues as challenging as that of low levels of literacy and numeracy skill in the adult population.

REFERENCES

Adult, Community and Further Education Board. (1996). *The certificate in general education for adults.* Melbourne, Australia: Author.

Australian Broadcasting Corporation. (1999). Learn to read or lose the dole. *Lingua Franca.* Retrieved February 6, 2006, from www.abc.net.au/rn/arts/ling/stories/s692578.htm

Australian Bureau of Statistics. (1997). *Aspects of literacy: Assessed skill levels 1996.* Canberra, Australia: Author.

Australian Bureau of Statistics. (2004). *Population characteristics, Aboriginal and Torres Strait Islander Australians* (Cat 4713.0). Canberra, Australia: Author.

Australian Committee for Training and Curriculum. (1993). *National framework of adult English language, literacy and numeracy competence.* Frankston, Victoria, Australia: ACTRAC Products.

Australian Education Council and Ministers of Vocational Education, Employment and Training. (1993). *National collaborative adult English language and literacy strategy.* Sydney, Australia: Adult Literacy Information Office.

Australian National Training Authority. (2001). *Standards for state and territory registering course accrediting bodies.* Melbourne, Australia: Author.

Australian Public Service Commission. (2004). *Connecting government: Whole of government responses to Australian policy challenges.* Canberra, Australia: Author.

Balatti, J., & Falk, I. (2002). Socio-economic contributions of adult learning to community: A social capital perspective. *Adult Education Quarterly, 52,* 281–298.

Bateson, G. (2003). *Moving the mountain: Halfway there? A whole city approach to basic skills development.* Retrieved January 30, 2004, from http://www.coreskills.co.uk/index.html

Black, S. (1990). Adult literacy: From marginal status to centre stage. *Australian Journal of Reading, 13*(1), 5–6.

Brock, P. (2001). Australia's language. In J. Lo Bianco & R. Wickert (Eds.), *Australian policy activism in language and literacy* (pp. 27–74). Melbourne, Australia: Language Australia.

Butcher, R., Davidson. E., Hagston, J., Ibrido, D., Lucas, J., Ridley, C., et al. (2002). *The certificates in general education for adults, incorporating certificates I, II and III in general education for adults.* Melbourne, Australia: Language Australia.

Castleton, G., & McDonald, M. (2002). *A decade of literacy: Policy, programs and perspectives.* Brisbane, Australia: Adult Literacy and Numeracy Australian Research Consortium.

Castleton, G., Sanguinetti, J., & Falk, I. (2001). Wanted: A new national adult literacy policy for Australia. *Literacy and Numeracy Studies, 11*(3), 3–19.

Coates, S., Fitzpatrick, L., McKenna, A., & Makin, A. (1995). *National reporting system: A mechanism for reporting adult English language, literacy and numeracy indicators of competence.* Melbourne, Australia: Office of Training and Further Education.

Coben, D., & Chanda, N. (2000). Teaching not less than maths, but more: An overview of recent developments in adult numeracy teacher development in England—with a sidelong glance at Australia. In D. Coben, J. O'Donoghue, & G. FitzSimons (Eds.), *Perspectives on adults learning mathematics: Research and practice* (pp. 307–327): London: Kluwer.

Council of Australian Governments. (2003). *The COAG Indigenous initiative: Shared responsibility agreement between Murdi Paaki Regional Council and the Commonwealth and New South Wales Government.* Retrieved May 26, 2004, from www.dest.gov.au/schools/Indiginous/coag_indig_initiative.htm

Cowan, M. (2006). Beyond single interests: Broad-based organizing as a vehicle for promoting adult literacy. In J. Comings, B. Garner, & C. Smith (Eds.), *Review of adult learning and literacy: Vol. 6. Connecting research, policy and practice* (pp. 241–275). Mahwah, NJ: Lawrence Erlbaum Associates, Inc.

Curtain Consulting. (2000). *Mutual obligation: Policy and practice in Australia compared with the UK.* Sydney, Australia: Dusseldorp Skills Forum.

Dawkins, J., & Holding, C. (1987). *Skills for Australia.* Canberra, Australia: Australian Government Publishing Service.

Department of Education, Science and Training. (2004). *Language, literacy and numeracy programme guidelines.* Retrieved July 30, 2005, from http://www.llnp.dest.gov.au

Department of Education, Science and Training. (2005a). *Language literacy and numeracy programme: Proposed programme changes for 2006–2008 tender* (Discussion paper). Retrieved February 14, 2006, from http://www.llnp.dest.gov.au/ASP/Related Links.asp

Department of Education, Science and Training. (2005b). *Language literacy and numeracy programme 2006–2008: Final operating policy position.* Retrieved February 14, 2006, from http://www.llnp.dest.gov.au/ASP/RelatedLinks.asp

Department of Employment, Education and Training. (1991b). *The language of Australia: Discussion paper on an Australian language and literacy policy for the 1990s.* Canberra, Australia: Australian Government Publishing Service.

Department of Employment, Education and Training. (1991a). *Australia's language: The Australian language and literacy policy.* Canberra, Australia: Australian Government Publishing Service.

Department of Immigration and Ethnic Affairs. (2003). *Population flows: Immigration aspects, 2001 edition.* Retrieved March 15, 2005, from http://www.immi.gov.au/statistics/publications/popflows2001/c1_1.pdf

Elwell-Gavins, V. (1994, July). *Adult literacy: Changing horizons. The perspective of a departmental officer.* Paper presented at the 17th Conference of the Australian Council for Adult Literacy, Perth, Australia.

Fitzpatrick, L., & McKenna, R. (2005). *Integrated approaches to teaching adult literacy in Australia: A snapshot of practice in community services.* Retrieved January 16, 2005, from http://www.ncver.edu.au

Gilding, N. (1995). Revision and renewal: Adult literacy and its future challenges. In A. Palfreeman (Ed.), *Critical issues, essential priorities: Proceedings of the 18th national conference of the Australian Council for Adult Literacy* (pp. 78–84). Melbourne, Australia: La Trobe University, Victorian Adult Literacy and Basic Education Council.

Gilding, N. (1996, March). *Strategic responses in ABE to contemporary changes in social, economic and educational policy: Collaborative strategic planning at state and national level. A commentary on the implementation of the Australian Language and Literacy Policy.* Paper presented at the World Congress on Literacy, Improving Literacy, Changing Lives: Innovations and Interconnections for Development, Philadelphia.

Gilding, N. (1999). Seizing the moment: Opportunities and challenges at the intersection of literacy and youth policy. In B. Keating (Ed.), *Living literacies: Papers from the 1999 ACAL/ALBEC Conference* (pp. 24–28). Melbourne, Australia: VALBEC.

Hagston, J. (2002). *Exploring the International Adult Literacy Survey data: Implications for Australia.* Melbourne, Australia: Language Australia.

Hazell, P. (2002). *And then there was one: Investigating the Adult Literacy Information Office (Sydney) and the Victorian Adult Education and Resource Information Service.* Sydney, Australia: Adult Literacy and Numeracy Australian Research Consortium.

Innovation and Business Skills Australia. (2005, August). *Strategies for essential skills—Multiple literacies* (Draft discussion paper). Melbourne, Australia: Author.

Johnston, B. (2002). *Numeracy in the making: Twenty years of Australian adult numeracy.* Sydney, Australia: Adult Literacy and Numeracy Australian Research Consortium.

Johnston, B., & Tout, D. (1995). *Adult numeracy teaching: Making meaning in mathematics.* Canberra, Australia: TAFE National Staff Development Committee.

Kangan, M. (1974). *TAFE in Australia: Report on needs in technical and further education.* Canberra, Australia: Australian Government Publishing Service.

Kell, P. (1998). *From the billabong to the mainstream?* Melbourne, Australia: Language Australia.

Kelly, P. (1992). *The end of certainty: The story of the 1980s.* Sydney, Australia: Allen & Unwin.

Kelly, S., Johnston, B., & Yasukawa, K. (Eds.). (2003). *The adult numeracy handbook: Reframing adult numeracy in Australia.* Melbourne, Australia: Language Australia.

Kral, I., & Schwab, R. G. (2003). *The realities of Indigenous adult literacy acquisition and practice: Implications for capacity development in remote communities* (Rep. No. 257/2003). Canberra, Australia: Centre for Aboriginal Economic Policy and Research.

Lo Bianco, J. (1987). *National policy on languages*. Canberra, Australia: Australian Government Publishing Service.
Lo Bianco, J. (1997). Policy proliferation: Can literacy cope? *Fine Print: A Journal of Adult English Language and Literacy Education, 20*(1), 3–11.
Lo Bianco, J. (2001a). From policy to anti-policy: How fear of language rights took policy out of community hands. In J. Lo Bianco & R. Wickert (Eds.), *Australian policy activism in language and literacy* (pp. 13–44). Melbourne, Australia: Language Australia.
Lo Bianco, J. (2001b). Policy literacy. *Language in Education, 15,* 212–227.
Lo Bianco, J., & Wickert, R. (Eds.). (2001). *Australian policy activism in language and literacy.* Melbourne, Australia: Language Australia.
Luke, A. (1995) Getting our hands dirty: Provisional politics in postmodern conditions. In R. Smith & P. Wexler (Eds.), *After postmodernism: Education, politics and identity* (pp. 83–97). London: Falmer.
Marr, B., & Helme, S. (1987). *Maths: A new beginning.* Melbourne, Australia: State Training Board of Victoria.
Marr, B., & Helme, S. (1990). *Women and maths in Australia: A confidence-building experience for teachers and students.* In L. Burton (Ed.), *Gender and mathematics: An international perspective* (pp. 80–86). London: Cassell Educational.
Marr, B., & Helme, S. (1991). *Breaking the maths barrier: A kit for building staff development skills in adult numeracy.* Canberra, Australia: Department of Employment, Education and Training.
Marr, B., & Morgan, B. (in press). *Enhancing teaching: Integrating language, literacy and numeracy into vocational education and training programs.* Canberra, Australia: Department of Education, Science and Training.
Martin, S. (1999). *New life, new language: The history of the AMEP.* Canberra, Australia: Department of Immigration and Ethnic Affairs.
McDonald, R., & Goodwin, S. (2005, June). *An essential skills action plan* (Discussion paper). Canberra, Australia: Department of Education, Science and Training. Retrieved November 30, 2005, from www.dest.gov.au/literacynet/resources1.htm#Policy
McGuirk, J., & Johnston, B. (1995). *Integrating literacy and numeracy.* Unpublished paper, NSW TAFE, Access Division, Sydney, Australia.
McKenna, R. (1997). Instruments of change: Policy implications for adult literacy. *Fine Print: A Journal of Adult English Language and Literacy Education, 20*(1), 19–21.
McKenna, R. (2002). Quality language, literacy and numeracy provision in the Australian Quality Training Framework, *Literacy Link, 22*(3), 3–6.
McKenna, R., & Fitzpatrick, L. (2004a). *Building sustainable adult literacy provision: A review of international trends in adult literacy policy and practice.* Adelaide, Australia: National Centre for Vocational Education Research.
McKenna, R., & Fitzpatrick, L. (2004b). *Building sustainable adult literacy provision: A review of international trends in adult literacy policy and practice* (Support document). Adelaide, Australia: National Centre for Vocational Education Research.
Moore, H. (2001). Although it wasn't broken, it certainly wasn't fixed: Interventions in the Australian Adult Migrant English Program, 1991–1996. In J. Lo Bianco& R. Wickert (Eds.), *Australian policy activism in language and literacy* (pp. 93–120). Melbourne, Australia: Language Australia.
National Board of Employment, Education and Training. (1993). *Incorporating English language and literacy competencies in industry standards.* Canberra, Australia: Australian Government Publishing Service.
National Training Information Service. (2005). *TAA04 training and assessment training package: Language, literacy and numeracy practice competency standards.* Retrieved October 14, 2005, from http://www.NTIS.gov.au/stdpage1.htm

Nelson, A. (1981). *On the importance of being literate.* Armidale, Australia: Australian Council for Adult Literacy.
Organization for Economic Cooperation and Development. (1989). Editorial: The path to full employment: Structural adjustment for an active society. *1989 Employment Outlook.* Retrieved March 5, 2005, from http://www.oecd.org/documents/37/0,2340,en_2649_34495_31736485_1_1_1_1,00.html
Organization for Economic Cooperation and Development. (2005, January). Economic Survey of Australia 2004 (Policy Brief). *OECD Observer.*
Perkins, K. (2005). *Reframe, rename, revitalise: Future directions of the Language, Literacy and Numeracy Reporting System.* Adelaide, Australia: National Centre for Vocational Education Research.
Persson, M. (1995). Critical planning for individual outcomes. In A. Palfreeman (Ed.), *Proceedings of the 18th national conference of the Australian Council for Adult Literacy, Critical Issues: Essential Priorities*(pp. 43–50). Melbourne, Australia: Australian Council for Adult Literacy.
Pratt, F. (1994). The impact of tendering. *Literacy Update, 9,* 4.
Rahmani, Z., & Crosier, T. (2003). Impact of the Australian Literacy and Numeracy Training Program on job seekers. *Literacy and Numeracy Studies, 12*(2), 31–45.
Rahmani, Z., Crosier, T., & Pollack, S. (2002). *Evaluating the impact of the Literacy and Numeracy Training Program for jobseekers.* Canberra, Australia: Department of Education, Training and Youth Affairs.
Sanguinetti, J. (1999). *Within and against performativity. Discursive engagement in adult literacy and basic education.* Unpublished doctoral dissertation, Deakin University, Melbourne, Australia.
Sanguinetti, J., & Hartley, R. (2000). *Building literacy and numeracy into training: Case studies from selected industries.* Melbourne, Australia: Adult Literacy and Numeracy Australian Research Consortium, Language Australia.
Scheeres, H., Gonczi, A., Hager, P., & Morley-Warner, T. (1993). *The adult basic education profession and competence: Promoting best practice.* Sydney, Australia: University of Technology, Sydney.
Searle, J. (1999). *An unsung band of heroes. A history of adult literacy in Queensland, 1970-1995.* Unpublished doctoral dissertation, Griffith University, Brisbane, Australia.
Shore, S. (2004). Practitioner-research as learning: Exploring situated knowledges of adult literacy educators. *Literacy and Numeracy Studies, 13*(2), 5–22.
State Training Board, Victoria. (1992). *Adult basic education accreditation framework project.* Melbourne, Australia: Ministry of Employment, Post-Secondary Education and Training, Victoria.
TAFE National Staff Development Committee. (1992). *A draft national framework for professional development of adult literacy and basic education personnel.* Melbourne, Australia: Author.
Thiering, J. (1981). Maths workshops. *NSW Adult Literacy Information Office Literacy Broadsheet, 4,* 2.
Tout, D. (1990). Mathematics in adult basic education. In J. V. D'Cruz & P. Langford (Eds.), *Issues in Australian education* (pp. 169–189). Melbourne, Australia: Longman.
Wallace-Clancy, L., Smith, P., Halliday, P., & Goddard, R. (1998). *The evaluation of the effectiveness of the mathematics and numeracy stream of the Certificate of General Education for Adults.* Melbourne, Australia: Victorian Adult, Community and Further Education Board.
Wickert, R. (1988). Gatekeepers or advocates? *Literacy Exchange, 4,* 14–18.
Wickert, R. (1989). *No single measure: A survey of Australian adult literacy.* Sydney, Australia: Institute of Technical and Adult Teacher Education.

Wickert, R. (2001). Politics, activism and processes of policy production: Adult literacy in Australia. In J. Lo Bianco & R. Wickert (Eds.), *Australian policy activism in language and literacy* (pp. 75–91). Melbourne, Australia: Language Australia.

Wickert, R., & McGuirk, J. (2005). *Integrating literacies: Using partnerships to build literacy capabilities in communities.* Adelaide, Australia: National Centre for Vocational Education and Training.

Wickert, R., Scheeres, H., & Ward, P. (1994). *Review of teacher education and professional development in adult literacy and ESL* (Report for the Adult Literacy and Language Council of the National Board of Education, Employment and Training). Sydney, Australia: University of Technology, Sydney.

Wignall, L. (n.d.). *Built in not bolted on: Information kit for language, literacy and numeracy coordinators on incorporating skills into training packages.* Canberra, Australia: Department of Education, Science and Training.

Willis, S. (1989). *Real girls don't do maths: Gender and the construction of privilege.* Geelong, Australia: Deakin University Press.

Yasukawa, K., Johnston, B., & Yates, W. (1995). Numeracy as a critical constructivist awareness of maths—Case studies from engineering and adult basic education. In R. P. Hunting, G. E. Fitzsimons, P. C. Clarkson, and A. J. Bishop (Eds.), *Proceedings of the International Commission on Mathematical Instruction Regional Collaboration in Mathematics Education Conference* (pp. 815–826). Melbourne, Australia: Monash University.

Zimmerman, J., & Norton, M. (1990). The challenge for adult literacy in Australia. In J. V. D'Cruz & P. Langford (Eds.), *Issues in Australian education* (pp. 143–168). Melbourne, Australia: Longman Cheshire.

APPENDIX: ACRONYMS

ABS   Australian Bureau of Statistics
ALLP   Australian Language and Literacy Policy
ANTA   Australian National Training Authority
COAG   Council of Australian Governments. COAG comprises the Prime Minister and premiers of all Australian states and territories.
DEET   Department of Employment, Education and Training
DEST   Department of Education, Science and Training
DIMEA   Department of Immigration and Ethnic Affairs
ESL   English as a second language
IALS   International Adult Literacy Survey
LLNP   Language, Literacy and Numeracy Program. The LLNP is a federally funded program that provides basic skills training for eligible job seekers (up to age 64) whose skills are below the level considered necessary to secure sustainable employment or pursue further education and training.
NRS   National Reporting System. The NRS provides a uniform, national framework for reporting on the language, literacy, and numeracy outcomes of students. It is based on five levels of competence, each

signifying an increase in the complexity of literacy and numeracy involved, the broadening of contexts in which these skills are used, and the increasing independence with which a person tackles a range of tasks. The NRS identifies five distinct skill areas: reading, writing, oral communication, learning strategies, and numeracy.

OECD   Organization for Economic Cooperation and Development

PD   Professional development

TAFE   Technical and further education. This phrase refers mainly to places of learning (TAFE colleges). It used to refer to the system of post-compulsory education and training. This is now known as the Vocational Education and Training System. This includes some, but not all, adult and community education as much of the funding in adult and community education is tied to vocational outcomes.

9

Adult Basic Education and Training in South Africa

Veronica McKay

The Republic of South Africa[73] can be classified as a middle-income country, or a country with one foot in the first world and one foot in the developing world. South Africa has a highly sophisticated production and commercial infrastructure, and high gross domestic product and gross national product, which exist alongside high levels of poverty.

South Africa has a low level of literacy, which cannot be viewed independently of the apartheid policies that were in place prior to democratization in 1994, inseparable from the developed–developing context of the country. The implications of apartheid were far-reaching and served to entrench inequalities and poverty along racial (and gender) lines. These inequalities affected the delivery of services such as water and sanitation, and also affected the system of education. As a result, according to 2001 census figures (Statistics South Africa, 2001), 4.7 million adults (16% of

---

[73]South Africa is situated at the southernmost point of the African continent, bordering Namibia, Botswana, Zimbabwe, and Mozambique and surrounding the kingdoms of Swaziland and Lesotho. Its total land area is 1,219,090 km².

the total population above the age of 15) have had no schooling and may be considered illiterate. A further 9.6 million (32%) have not completed primary school and may be considered in need of compensatory basic education. The majority of these adults are found in rural areas. About 24% of Africans, 10% of "coloreds,"[74] 7% of Indians, and 1% of Whites over the age of 20 years are illiterate (Aitchison, Houghton, & Baatjes, 2000).

After the first democratic elections in South Africa, the new government faced a number of challenges, not the least being the high number of adults who were functionally illiterate. There were many unemployed people whose levels of literacy were such that they were virtually unemployable due to the competition for the small number of available jobs requiring little or no literacy skills. In addition, low literacy was associated with poverty and a low level of entrepreneurship in both the formal and informal sectors.

Based on its vision of providing a better life for all South Africans, the new government's Reconstruction and Development Policy[75] (African National Congress [ANC], 1994) placed great emphasis on community development, in which adult literacy and community development were linked. In addition, the new constitutional and legislative framework (discussed later) states that adult basic education (ABE) is integral to South Africa's economic growth and development. All key educational policy documents now mention ABE.

The goal of this chapter is to describe the integration of education and training in the adult basic education and training (ABET) system in South Africa. I first discuss the relationship of apartheid, poverty, and health to the status of adult literacy. Then, I discuss the policy and legislative frameworks related to adult literacy, followed by a discussion of the role of teachers in ABET. Finally, I show how in light of the aforementioned, an endeavor was made to provide basic literacy as part of a national literacy program in South Africa.

---

[74]In terms of apartheid legislation, South Africans were divided along racial lines into African, Asian, and White. Coloreds referred to children of any racial combination of the aforementioned categories. The categories are still used in certain circumstances to monitor employment equity practices.

[75]Literacy was the only reconstruction and development program project that received no funding at all (Aitchison et al., 2000).

APARTHEID AND ILLITERACY

History of Apartheid

One of the Nationalist government's first acts after coming to power in 1948 was to appoint a commission to formulate the principles and aims of education for Natives[76] as an independent race (Troup, 1976). Pursuant to the recommendations of the commission, the government formulated its legislation in the Bantu Education Act of 1953. The government designed this Act to give Africans[77] an education conforming to their needs and opportunities as a separate community. Schooling was to be Bantu-ized[78]: The commission proposed low-quality, separate schooling for Africans, who would be trained for subordination.

The philosophy that informed this Act may be gleaned from the words of the Minister of Native Affairs, articulated during a debate in September 1953:

> When I have control of native education, I will reform it so that the natives will be taught from childhood to realise that equality with Europeans[79] is not for them . . . People who believe in equality are not desirable teachers for natives. (Troup, 1976, p. 22)

Apartheid education was designed specifically to enforce obedience, communal loyalty, ethnic divisions, acceptance of allocated social roles, and identification with rural culture. In the words of the Minister of Native Affairs:

> There is no place for him [the black child] in the European [white South African] community above the level of certain forms of labour . . . Until now he has been subject to a school system which drew him away from his own community and misled him by showing him the green pastures of European society in which he is not allowed to graze. (Verwoerd, cited in Troup, 1976, p. 22)

---

[76]Here referring to Blacks in general, and Africans in particular.

[77]This racial categorization implies those South Africans classified as Black but not Indian, Asian, or so-called coloreds.

[78]Here meaning Black African.

[79]European in this context referred to Whites.

The specific aim of apartheid—and apartheid education—was to keep Africans in a position of subservience and ignorance. In attempting to prepare the African child for a future as "hewers of wood and drawers of water" (Verwoerd, cited in Troup, 1976), the apartheid master plan controlled—economically, socially, psychologically, and spiritually—the education of Black South Africans. This left African parents with two options: exposing their children to inferior Bantu education, or giving them no education at all. Troup (1976) stated that because:

> only one African child in every two of school-going age was actually attending school, it was understandable that parents were unwilling to give up an opportunity to get even some inferior education for those lucky enough to have the opportunity. (p. 22)

The lack of compulsory education, and the fact that the schools were sites of the liberation struggle, meant that many children did not attend or had disrupted attendance between 1976 and 1994, leaving many without education, thus contributing to the massive need for ABET within the country.

When the government established democracy in South Africa, the literacy situation was still dismal: The statistics on the number of people who need a basic education fluctuate depending on who is counting and what yardstick is used to measure and define literacy. With 11 official languages, the difficulty of defining literacy is compounded. Adults may be defined as being literate in a national language, but surveys seldom consider the communicative practices of adults who do not speak the (dominant) language of the economy.

Government statistics show that in 1996, 27% of adults had no schooling at all and that 41% of the adult population had completed some (but not all) primary school (i.e., the first 7 years of schooling; Statistics South Africa, 1996). The official data show that by 2002, 54% of the population had completed only some (but not all) primary education (Presidency, 2003). This group appears to have increased in spite of policy changes and the introduction of compulsory education. This latter-mentioned group (as well as those who have not attended any schooling) also reflects the number of South Africans who fall within the scope of ABET. Moreover, South Africa still has large numbers of out-of-school youth, which will maintain the long-term need for ABE.

There is gender difference in illiteracy: 41% of men and 58% women are considered illiterate. Illiteracy rates are higher in rural areas than in urban areas.

The Relation Between Levels of Literacy and Levels of Poverty

In South Africa, approximately 25% of people in urban areas and 67% of people in rural areas live in poverty. The number of people living in poverty in 1999 amounted to 33% of the population (Presidency, 2003). In the context of poverty, education needs to be coupled with helping people acquire skills to generate income and for sustainable livelihoods.

Presently, about 6.8 million people—approximately 16.6% of the population—receive social grants. Although the number of grants to those living in poverty is increasing, it is still difficult for the illiterate poor to access information about the entitlements they could receive, and for them to deal with the banking and bureaucracy surrounding accessing these grants.

With 33% of the South African population living below the poverty line, the number of job opportunities is shrinking and unemployment rates are rising. This makes creating jobs a pressing issue. Currently, the official unemployment figure is cited at 40% (Presidency, 2003).[80] However, official figures always mask a multitude of problems in the world of work; one problem is that official figures do not factor in the number of unemployed people who have given up trying to find work and are no longer considered to be part of the unemployed workforce.

The recent introduction of social grants offers an indirect indication of those who are unemployed and regarded as the "poorest of the poor," and who engage in "survivalist" informal economic activities. "The number of people engaged in survivalist economic activities have declined with the introduction of the social welfare grants" (Presidency, 2003, p. 17). Statistics South Africa (2004) referred to a 22% decline in informal sector activities in the period between 2002 and 2003. Over the same period, the number of welfare grant beneficiaries increased by 40%.

Poverty in rural areas is estimated to be as high as 67%, due to poor social and economic conditions in rural areas, the lack of basic infrastructure such as electricity and transportation, and the lack of employment opportunities. Without infrastructure, it is difficult for people to engage in entrepreneurial activities. Most small-scale businesses require, for example,

---

[80]There was an increase of 2,361,834 unemployed adults in the period between 1995 and 2002. In 1995, there were 1,909,468 people officially estimated as being unemployed. This number increased to 4,271,302 by 2002.

electricity for refrigeration and cooking, and transportation for selling. In general, women in rural areas are poorer than men (Presidency, 2003), a fact that can be explained by both their disadvantaged position in the labor market and the patriarchal relations of ownership within the family structure.

The problems of poverty are more acute for new arrivals in the urban informal (or squatter) settlements where residents live in shacks and find themselves without services, employment, or reliable social networks. Previously the numbers of urban and rural dwellers were more or less equal. However, with many people migrating from rural to urban areas in search of jobs and decent services, the urban population has increased. Presently, 55% of the population lives in urban areas. About 20% of all households live in shacks without services such as water and sanitation, road infrastructure, or electricity (Statistics South Africa, 2004).

South African women bear the burden of poverty because they are mainly responsible for managing the households and feeding children and eking out a living under the difficult circumstances of poverty, especially in situations in which women are the heads of households. Forty-five percent of female-headed households live below the poverty line, as opposed to 26% of male-headed households. If women are able to obtain employment,[81] they find it more difficult than men to cope with their jobs (McKay, Mokotong, & Sham, 2003) because they have the double burden of having to work and carry out their traditional functions at home.

The situation of the nation's poor is exacerbated by the HIV/AIDS pandemic, which has decimated jobs and eroded household income. In the long term, the workforce of the future is also weakened as children are taken out of school early to help care for sick family members.

In spite of the current policy of universal primary schooling, the most telling education statistic reported by Statistics South Africa (2004) is that, between 1995 and 2002, the school system recorded an enrollment increase of just 0.1%, despite a school-age population increase of 15%. These data reflect not only the growing and future need for ABE, but also the percentage of children who are not in schools due to the high HIV infection rate. In 2004 it was estimated that there were 2.2 million

---

[81]The highest levels of poverty in South Africa are found in the rural areas where women tend to head households, many as wives left behind by men who form part of the migrant worker network in the cities and towns, or single parents or even grandmothers caring for children (in particular AIDS orphans). Many of these older women have had to reenter activities associated with childrearing and income generation to ensure the survival of the second generation.

orphaned children in South Africa who had lost a parent. It was estimated that nearly half of all orphans were orphaned as a result of AIDS-related illnesses. These children are often compelled to leave school to look after their siblings. They are particularly vulnerable to abuse and, in turn, to contracting HIV. With projections suggesting that about one in five children of school-going age in South Africa will be orphaned by 2010, school dropout rates can be expected to increase (Hooper-Box, 2002). This highlights the ongoing need for literacy and basic education for the increasing numbers of children who do not and who will not complete primary school.

PRESENT POLICIES AND LEGISLATION

ABET is closely linked in South Africa. To fully understand the implications of the integration of ABET in South Africa, it is important to understand the difference: ABE refers to the educational base that individuals require to improve their life chances. Adult basic training refers to the foundational income-generating or occupational skills that individuals require to improve their livelihoods and living conditions. Putting the two together, ABET supplies the foundational knowledge, skills, understanding, and abilities that are required for improved social and economic life. When programs bring education and training together, individuals can acquire the full range of knowledge, skills, understanding, and abilities. These kinds of programs also provide learners with a platform for further learning, should they so choose, and with the capacity to bring this foundation to bear on the improvement and development of their own lives and the lives of those around them. ABET provides the foundation of fundamental skills, knowledge, and understanding that gives people a basis from which they can progress along a chosen career and life path (Department of Education, 1997).

It is important to note that the T in ABET refers to more than technical or employment skills. The T refers to a wide range of skills and expertise including technical skills such as plumbing, dressmaking, beadwork, and other crafts, together with specialized skills such as conflict management and negotiation, and also creative skills such as dance and praise poetry or the ritual chanting and singing verses of praise for esteemed people.[82]

---

[82]Praise poetry and singing for esteemed people form part of the rich tradition of South African society.

Since 1994, the South African government has promulgated a suite of policies and legislative frameworks that support ABE and affirm its role in the process of social change and development. There is acceptance that literacy is essential for human resource development because it contributes to the economic development of people and enables them to expand their life choices. The postapartheid government regards ABET as critical to addressing the basic needs and developmental imperatives of the majority of South Africa's poor. For this reason, literacy underlies (at least at the policy level) the government's proposals[83] for human resource development, focusing on skills acquisition and ABE for those who have been deprived of basic schooling (ANC, 1994).

The definition of ABET as propounded in the government policies discussed later implies more than just literacy: ABET is intended to serve a range of social, economic, and developmental needs. It has been constitutionally enshrined as a basic right of all citizens and a "legal entitlement to which every person has a claim." The South African legislation discussed here also describes ABET as the foundation for justice and equality and as contributing to the core values adopted for South Africa: democracy (active participation), access (redressing historical imbalances), and development (Baatjes, 2004).

The specific government acts or policy documents that promote or relate to adult education have included the following:

- Interim Guidelines for ABET (1995).
- South African Qualifications Act (1995).
- National Education Policy Act (1996).
- South African Constitution (1996).
- National Multi-Year Implementation Plan for adult education and training in the Department of Education (1997).
- Skills Development Act (1998).
- Skills Development Levy Act (1999).

A consideration of the legislative framework for ABET is crucial as a backdrop to understanding the gap between legislation and implementation, a gap that exists because of bureaucratic bottlenecks, lack of capacity, inadequate resources for the sector, and general disagreements within

---

[83]These proposals include the range of social grants for people living in poverty and the public works programs intended to create more than 1 million jobs while upgrading roads and other infrastructure.

the sector. Although South Africa has highly impressive legislation for ABET, the fact that an extremely small amount of the education budget is allocated to ABET makes it inevitable that policy is barely implemented (Aitcheson et al., 2000).

Interim Guidelines for the implementation of ABET (Department of Education, 1995) state that, as a result of the high attrition rates in schools and the high number of adults who never attended school, millions of adult South Africans are functionally illiterate, making clear the need for accelerating the development of an ABET system. The Interim Guidelines emphasize that the provision of ABET is linked to the development of human resources within the broader strategy for national development, and that ABET is aimed at restructuring the economy, addressing past inequalities, and contributing to the creation of a democratic society. ABET has to provide people with the basic foundation for lifelong learning and equip them with the skills and critical capacity to participate fully in society. Although these guidelines refer to all adults who "would like to participate" in ABET programs, women (and, in particular, rural inhabitants), out-of-school youth, the unemployed, prisoners and ex-prisoners, and adults with disabilities are singled out as needing special attention and special motivation.

In 1995, the government established the South African Qualifications Authority (SAQA), which helped develop the South African Qualifications Act (No. 58 of 1995). One of SAQA's key functions was to develop and implement the National Qualifications Framework (NQF), which:

- Created a national framework for learning achievements.
- Facilitated access to—and mobility and progression within—education, training, and career paths.
- Enhanced the quality of education and training.
- Accelerated the redress of past discrimination in education, training, and employment opportunities.
- Contributed to the full personal development of each learner and the social development of the nation at large.

The central function of the NQF was to accredit unit standards, which culminate in qualifications for even basic-level learners. It permits portability, accessibility, and transferability of skills, knowledge, and abilities across qualification levels and across the education and training divide.

The National Education Policy Act (No. 27 of 1996) also protects the right to basic education; in particular, "the right of every person to basic education and equal access to education institutions." The right to a basic education implies, by extension, the right to good-quality learning programs with high-quality learner support materials and teaching practices, and appropriate learning sites. The Policy observes that as a result of the high attrition rate in schools, millions of adult South Africans are functionally illiterate. This chapter thus stresses the need for targeting out-of-school youth for basic education.

The Constitution of the Republic of South Africa (1996) states:

> Everyone has the right to a basic education including adult basic education and to further education which the state through reasonable measures must make available all forms of organised education and training that meet the basic learning needs of adults, including literacy and numeracy, as well as the general knowledge, skills and values and attitudes that they require to survive, develop their capacities, live and work in dignity, improve the quality of their lives, make informed decisions, and continue learning.

Section 29 of the Bill of Rights in the Constitution of the Republic of South Africa, 1996 (Act No. 108 of 1996) establishes the right to: (a) a basic education, including ABE; and (b) further education, which the state, through reasonable measures, must make progressively available and accessible (section 29 [1]). Although the constitution defines ABE as a human right—a sentiment also expressed in all education and training legislation—the decline in learners enrolled in basic educational programs and the decline in resources draw attention to the lack of fit between policy and practice.

The Multi-Year Implementation Plan (Department of Education, 1997) stressed the need to target out-of-school youth (as well as other categories of learners, such as the disabled, women, and prisoners). It outlined the proposed model for delivery of all ABET services and spelled out the criteria and norms for quality ABET delivery. The plan aimed to serve 2.5 million learners by the year 2001. However, the plan was not translated into deliverable outcomes and the state did not reach even one third of this number by that time (Aitchison et al., 2000).

Some studies, such as those done by Aitchison and colleagues (2000), French (2002), and the Human Sciences Research Council (1999), even suggest that there has been a decline in ABET provision and delivery while the sector is becoming increasingly marginalized: Funding allocated to ABET is only 0.83% of the national education budget and delivery of ABET programs has declined. In addition, there is a lack of recognition of adult educators and their status is poor.

The National Skills Development Act (1998) underscored the government's commitment to overall human resource development, which included education reform. The Act stipulated that for South Africans to participate meaningfully in the country's economic and social development, as well as in their own advancement, they must have basic competencies, including the ability to read, write, communicate effectively, and solve problems in their homes, communities, and workplaces.

The National Skills Development Act (1998) and the Skills Development Levy Act (1999), introduced by the Department of Labor, reflected the government's commitment to promoting active labor market policies. These acts provided new institutions, programs, and funding policies for skills development. Under the auspices of the acts, the government established a number of sectoral education and training authorities (SETAs), which would act as education and training custodians in their respective sectors.[84] These bodies were established and charged with the responsibility of transforming the skills base in their respective sectors through the implementation of targeted training at all levels of the workforce.

THE ROLE OF TEACHERS IN ABET

The delivery of quality adult education depends on well-trained adult practitioners who play a pivotal role in addressing critical economic, political, and social problems specific to learners across a variety of contexts (e.g., health and HIV/AIDS, the environment, labor, etc.), as well as across a variety of societal contexts—urban, rural, informal, and so on. Well-trained practitioners can do much to enhance the quality of the learning experience for adults (UNESCO, 1998).

The National Education Policy Investigation (1993) conducted by the ANC found that there was a need for 100,000 adult basic educators. This study suggested that distance education offered the only feasible way of meeting such targets, due to the fact that educators and learners were not always in the same place. In South Africa, a number of modes are used to mediate this, such as audio and visual approaches, including television, video, and radio (depending on the context of the learners and the infrastructure available). Information and computer technologies are also included as a mode for some distance-learning contexts.

---

[84]In line with the skills legislation, SETAs were established for a number of sectors (although several were merged and new ones were introduced). They cut across sectors such as local government and water, mining, the chemical SETA, health, education, building, and so on.

Accordingly, the University of South Africa (UNISA) undertook large-scale training of adult educators in South Africa to develop a more professional cadre. UNISA utilized a blended approach to distance education using some contact (tutor-led) training sessions during which learning is mediated and learners are given support to access their materials. The massive enrollment of training practitioners at UNISA and the pressure they brought to bear on the Department of Education led to the recognition of adult educators in the Educators' Act as a specific category of educator personnel. In the past 4 years, South Africa has begun to establish practitioner qualifications. SAQA established the Standards Generating Body (SGB) in 1999. The SGB produced unit standards for four ABET qualifications in 2000; the unit standards ensure competence and quality of ABET practitioners. The generation of unit standards signaled a breakthrough in establishing a qualification framework and creating a career path for ABET practitioners. The adult educator fraternity (primarily comprised of practitioner training providers such as the universities) regards the development of a qualification framework for adult practitioners by the SGB (Adult Learning National Standards Body 05, which oversaw the development of qualifications and standards for education, training, and development practitioners) as one of the most significant areas of development in the training of practitioners for the ABET field.

Teacher Tasks and Responsibilities

Under the Adult Learning National Standards Body 05, the adult educator is required to assume a variety of complex roles and functions pertaining to education, training, and development. The following tasks and responsibilities, laid out by the SGB, give some indication of the skills educators need:

- Plan a learning event.
- Facilitate an adult learning event.
- Assess learners within a learning situation.
- Fulfill administrative requirements of a learning group.
- Evaluate own facilitation performance.
- Help learners with language and literacy across the curriculum.
- Identify and respond to learners who have special needs.
- Facilitate mother-tongue literacy.
- Facilitate an additional language.
- Facilitate numeracy.
- Design, organize, and facilitate a program of learning.

- Evaluate, select, and adapt published learning materials.
- Develop, use, and evaluate own supplementary learning aids.
- Design, implement, and follow up on internal assessment.
- Conduct research related to the learning situation.
- Mediate language, literacy, and math across the curriculum.
- Identify and respond to learners with special needs and barriers to learning.
- Promote lifelong learning.
- Facilitate communication and math.
- Undertake a leadership role in an ABET division of an organization.
- Supervise the work of other ABET practitioners.
- Apply extended skills around research, evaluation, quality assurance, and community development.
- Have sufficient command of the subjects to be taught.
- Offer specialist input on particular aspects of ABET provision.

In addition to mastering these unit standards, practitioners may specialize in a range of electives, from facilitating craftwork or subsistence agriculture, to workplace and occupational programs and small and microenterprises.

For a practitioner to assume these functions, training has to be well conceptualized and presented. One of the main providers of practitioner training in South Africa is the ABET Institute at UNISA, which was established in 1994 in response to the democratic government's expressed desire to reconstruct and develop communities in South Africa. To fulfill this aim, the ABET Institute trains a cadre of practitioners who work in adult education programs across various sectors and in different social contexts (e.g., health, environment, the workplace, and water management) and in different types of settlements (urban, rural, formal, and informal). The recognition that ABE needs to be set up as an interministerial and cross-sectoral program is intended to promote key socioeconomic benefits, especially for the most marginalized and disadvantaged communities, which are the Institute's primary target group. Training ABET practitioners in basic and generic skills allows them to work in a variety of specialized areas, including literacy, numeracy, primary health care and HIV/AIDS, English as a second language, small business development, and environmental education.

With the development and enhancement of livelihoods as the prime rationale for the courses presented by the ABET Institute, the Institute addresses literacy or numeracy needs by locating them within a broader development paradigm. This point of departure made the ABET Institute immediately different from programs that focused primarily on literacy as a method or as a technique and rarely on literacy as a component of a development strategy. The ABET Institute sees the practitioner as central to the enhancement of communities and trains practitioners—nurses, community workers, literacy volunteers, trade unionists, and so on—who will be able to teach skills like basic literacy, numeracy, or health education but with a developmental bias.

For this reason, the ABET Institute program is useful to a variety of in-service and preservice practitioners, including the following:

- Literacy practitioners.
- Trainers for water and sanitation.
- Trainers in health, nutrition, HIV/AIDS, and family planning.
- Environmental educators.
- Job-skills trainers.
- Trade unionists.
- Worker educators.
- Adult educators who teach in state programs.
- Agricultural extension workers.
- Youth workers.
- Community organizers.
- Materials developers.[85]

The distance education program trains up to 12,000 ABET practitioners per year (more than 50,000 practitioners in total since 1994), who work in a variety of fields in community development and community education. The training uses a "blended" approach (part distance, part face-to-face), in which practitioners read assigned text on their own, supplemented by audiotapes and videotapes, and accompanied by regular contact with a designated tutor in their region. It is only by way of distance education that it has been possible to enable the training to reach such a large number of practitioners.

After successfully completing the ABET practitioner course, teachers should be able to demonstrate that they are competent in a range of activities, from conducting research into the learning needs and difficulties of learners and communities to assessing learners' competencies. Specifically, they should be able to do the following:

---

[85]The program has been evaluated continuously over the past 10 years by the U.K. Department for International Development (DFID) teams, including experts such as Professor Lalage Bown and Dr. Anil Bordia. The materials used for training educators received the Commonwealth of Learning award for the best distance materials in 2003.

- Utilize a range of teaching and facilitation methods.
- Utilize a range of assessment methods.
- Refer learners with complex learning difficulties to other professionals.
- Develop teaching material.
- Relate teaching to social context.
- Identify area of research.
- Design a research approach.
- Compile research reports.
- Utilize a variety of qualitative, quantitative, and participatory research methods.

Practitioners are also expected to achieve the following critical outcomes:

- Engage in problem solving.
- Participate in group or syndicate task groups.
- Organize group activities.
- Collect and evaluate information.
- Communicate ideas.
- Understand the world as a set of interrelated systems.
- Use science and technology appropriately.

These critical outcomes are taught indirectly through methodological processes embedded in the Institute's courses. Regardless of whether they are studying for a doctoral degree or a first-year certificate, they should master the critical outcomes.

EXAMPLES OF ABET PROGRAMS IN SOUTH AFRICA: SANLI, NATIONAL PUBLIC WORKS CAMPAIGN, AND EXTENDED PUBLIC WORKS CAMPAIGN

The South African National Literacy Initiative: A Campaign Endeavor

As has been discussed previously, one of the biggest challenges facing South Africa is poverty, particularly in the rural areas and informal settlements, which are characterized by poor social and economic conditions, lack of basic infrastructure such as electricity and transportation, and lack of employment opportunities. Within this context, reducing the level of illiteracy is but one of the many challenges for the South African government. The South African National Literacy Initiative (SANLI) was conceived as a rapid response initiative with the expressed aim of responding to the then Minister of Education's commitment to "breaking the back of illiteracy among adults and youth."

Accordingly, SANLI stressed the importance of enabling learners to obtain literacy and numeracy competence, which would enable them to relate what they learned to their day-to-day activities. In this way, SANLI proposed to provide basic skills that were relevant and applicable to the lives and contexts of its intended target audience. Its concern for contextual relevance is a theme that emerges throughout its strategy and would be achieved, inter alia, through needs analyses and the development and customization of learning materials for specific provinces and varied target groups.

The aims of SANLI were as follows:

- To reduce illiteracy levels in each province by at least 35% by 2004.
- To enable the majority of newly literate adults to take up referrals to further education and economic opportunities.
- To ensure that 60% of newly literate adults maintained their skills through keeping contact with, and accessing materials in, the local resource centers and community development projects.

SANLI proposed, by 2004, to reach at least 65% of the adults who were currently illiterate or semiliterate, an aim that was heavily reliant on the success of the mobilization campaigns and the availability of resources. If the targets set by the initiative were only partially reached, SANLI would nevertheless have achieved a significant contribution to the country's human resource development strategy; this potential underpins the relevance of the initiative. At a national level, these were SANLI's targets:

- To reach 220,000 learners in the first year of the intervention and recruit 2,400 volunteer educators.
- To reach 440,000 learners in the second year of the intervention and recruit 44,000 educators.
- To maintain a learner:educator ratio of 10:1.

In accomplishing these aims, SANLI proposed to mobilize illiterate and semiliterate adults to access literacy programs. A strategy targeted at potential learners needs to address the added dimensions of getting learners into classrooms and providing a variety of support mechanisms for encouraging them to continue until they have achieved the level of learning they initially hoped to reach. In addition, the literacy initiative needed to look beyond the initial stage of learning to read and write, to the continuity of those newly acquired skills. In this regard, SANLI proposed a continuum from preliteracy to postliteracy initiatives including mainstream ABET programs and other educational, social, and economic opportunities, and to expand the participation of all South Africans in the new democracy. The program, currently in its fourth year, is aimed at all adults who have not had the opportunity to attend school or who only attended for a short period, but it targets, in particular, women and out-of-school youth.

SANLI's delivery strategy is to use other agencies already involved in the provision of adult literacy. In this way, the Ministry proposes to go to scale so that the project can reach its targeted number of enrollments.

The UNISA–SANLI Partnership. In 2002, UNISA's ABET Institute was able to harness its graduates to volunteer to teach in SANLI. Some of the volunteers had previous experience teaching in small grassroots programs or even in the public adult learning centers, but for many SANLI provided a first opportunity to put into practice the skills they acquired during their training. Although volunteers were paid a small stipend for each class they taught, the campaign was marketed by community radio, educators going door-to-door to recruit learners, chiefs, counselors, faith-based groups, and community-based organizations. Educators carried out mapping exercises with the communities to identify households with adults who were to be targeted for the literacy initiative.

The UNISA–SANLI partnership focused on delivering literacy training to the most needy learners across the country in some of South Africa's most isolated and impoverished communities. The ABET Institute mobilized its graduate educators to volunteer to teach basic literacy, numeracy, English, and life-skill education to adults needing basic education. The ABET Institute's goal was to make 75,000 adults literate—a target that was exceeded within the first few months of the partnership. The volunteer educators identified learners and profiled the learners' competencies. Those who were assessed as illiterate were placed in a learning group close to where they lived. Learners were required to attend three classes per week for a period of 9 months. Over this period they completed 25 assessment activities; the completion of these activities meant that they had achieved a level of competence equivalent to the first 3 years of formal schooling.

Since 2002, the ABET Institute has consistently achieved its annual targets, reaching more than 350,000 learners (who were taught by 8,880 volunteer educators and supported and monitored by teams of monitors or coordinators) over its 2-year life span. The widespread introduction of SANLI classes in all nine provinces has provided a critical mass of adults attending literacy classes, so that the process has taken on a momentum of its own (Bordia, 2003).

The UNISA–SANLI partnership has also been instrumental in developing the necessary management support systems to effectively control, review, and evaluate activities across the country. This includes creating a database to facilitate payment of expenses to the volunteer educators, and to monitor the learners' growing competencies by recording their scores on various tasks in their structured-assessment portfolio.

The South African ministry's partnership with the ABET Institute established learning centers in the communities where the learners live, a successful delivery structure for literacy and development opportunities throughout the country. Unlike other initiatives, which rely on volunteers who have received only short periods of training, the UNISA–SANLI campaign volunteer practitioners have received at least 1 year of training. In fact, many have been trained for up to 3 years and a significant number hold postgraduate qualifications.

The mass recruitment of learners by the UNISA–ABET Institute for the SANLI classes in 2002 and 2003 meant that UNISA had to distribute more than 600 tons of learner support materials to learners across South Africa before the classes could begin. Most classes were held in rural locations, which meant that volunteer educators had to pick up materials at one of approximately 600 appointed sites across South Africa, and they often carried boxes of books for their classes on their heads.

Because the SANLI campaign was run across South Africa, it was not possible for the UNISA ABET Institute to obtain venues wherever they were needed. Volunteer educators were required to first recruit their learners, and then obtain an appropriate venue for classes. Although most of the educators were able to access learning sites at schools, government offices, clinics, churches, and so on, a number of educators were not able to obtain venues that were equipped for teaching. Therefore, many classes were held in sites such as the local market, a learner's home, garages, under a bridge or tree, in unused shipping containers, or in any other makeshift "classroom" that they could find. For these situations, portable chalkboards were designed and constructed for educators to hang under a tree or on a hook on the wall.

Assessing the Competencies of the UNISA–SANLI Learners. Within weeks of the initiation of the campaign, the ABET Institute had developed a structured portfolio comprising 24 tasks with which to measure learners' competencies. The sequenced competency-based activities (or common assessment tasks) tested learners against the outcomes for ABET Level 1. The activities were sufficiently generic for learners from almost all social contexts—from rural or urban areas, and for a wide range of age groups, environments, and needs. Learners had to complete activities such as these:

1. Draw a map of the area where you live. Your friend wants to visit you. Write down the directions you would give him/her so that he/she can get to your house. Put a cross on the map to show where he/she is (e.g., taxi rank, church, chief's house). Make sure you have marked such places on the map.
2. Look at the book you are writing in. How big is it? Take a ruler and measure:

    What is the length of the book?
    ....cm
    What is the width of the book?
    ....cm
    How thick is the book?
    ....mm

3. Find something in your environment that you can measure.

    What will you measure?
    ....
    Write down the measurements
    ....

The program distributed assessment criteria and calibration information for the activities to the educators and required them to continuously assess their learners. The educators were then required to engage the services of a peer educator to moderate their assessments, a process that was overseen by their coordinator.[86] When learners completed all the activities, educators submitted each learner's results (accompanied by a common assessment test) to the ABET Institute for moderation. If they completed all activities satisfactorily, they were deemed competent and were then certified and recorded in the National Learners' database.

Results of the UNISA–SANLI Partnership. Evaluations (Bordia, 2003) of the program indicate that the learning centers attracted 30,000 more learners each year than was originally targeted, and dropout rates were less than 5%. Learner attendance was regular and learners continued their own learning groups after the conclusion of the campaign. During monitoring visits made by the Department for International Development evaluation team (Bordia, 2003) to literacy learning sites, adult learners who had been attending adult literacy classes in a variety of sites, including shelters for street children and prisons (UNISA ABET, 2003) expressed what literacy meant to them:

> The world was painful because I used to use a cross when I signed a document and sometimes I would be doubtful of the implications.
>
> —(An elderly learner in UNISA–SANLI class, Soshanguvu)

> My husband, who is blind, enjoys it when I read for him. Learning to read and write has made our lives happy. Even our children who stay far from us always ask me about this project.
>
> —(A UNISA–SANLI learner and pensioner, Makenenge Ridge, Qwa Qwa)

> I was always sad and depressed. Not any more. Now I wake up every day, pick up my books and stop complaining. My life feels good!
>
> —(A UNISA–SANLI learner, Mabopane ABET Centre)

> We now know our rights and I can now start a chicken business.
>
> —(Elderly learner in UNISA–SANLI class, East Rand)

---

[86]Educators were arranged in a cascade comprised of provincial coordinators, each supervising 10 to 15 monitors who each supervised the work of 10 to 15 educators.

Through the learning that I gained in the project, being a shoemaker, I can now count the number of stitches as I combine the sole and the top part of the shoe. This is very helpful because I can now make measurements.

—(A 65-year-old man in UNISA–SANLI class, The Makenenge Rural Centre)

I have opened a spaza [informal] shop—I can now count money and I have bought a fridge with the money I have made.

—(A female UNISA–SANLI learner, Western Cape)

We have class in this primary school [a mud and dung structure]. Sometimes the children will visit us in class. They watch us learn, we hug them, and then they leave. The children are very proud of us.

—(A mother of five, UNISA–SANLI learner, The Makenenge Rural Centre)

I have started to teach my grandchildren numbers and letters of the alphabet and it is very exciting.

—(An elderly woman, UNISA–SANLI learner, Duduza)

I can now read my own letters. I used to hate it when the person reading my letters used to laugh at what the letter said before I knew what was in the letter.

(An adult UNISA–SANLI learner, Gauteng)

I can read a letter for myself without the risk of being lied to.

(A 49-year-old UNISA–SANLI learner, Gauteng)

I can now read and write my own love letters. I can now write about my feelings of love.

(Young wife of a migrant worker, UNISA–SANLI Eastern Cape)

We need to be in a position of being able to write letters to our family and to protect our privacy.

(Male prisoner UNISA–SANLI learner, Johannesburg Prison)

If I knew then what I knew now, I would never have landed up here.

—(30-year-old female prisoner UNISA–SANLI learner)

The Future of the UNISA–SANLI Campaign. All campaigns have a life span. Although the UNISA–SANLI partnership had a very limited life span with minimal political support, the campaign served to heighten the awareness of adults (in particularly of rural adults) of the importance of becoming literate (UNISA ABET, 2003). Without budgetary support, the campaign cannot continue, and it is unlikely that the South African government will commit resources to reviving the campaign. As the Minister of Education explained in his March 2000 reply to a national assembly debate, "Of course I am concerned about the inadequacy of public funding for ABET, including the National literacy campaign. But in my call to action document . . . I made it clear that public funds are at present insufficient for this purpose."

The ABET Institute and its 10,000 campaign operatives trained by UNISA ABET face the daily tragedy of seeing adults clamoring to learn but being unable to access the flexible learning possibilities made available by the UNISA–SANLI.

The number of SANLI learners in 2002 and 2003 exceeded any other government and nongovernmental organization programs for ABET delivery within South Africa. The Ministry of Education had previously stated that it would offer a postcampaign and postliteracy education for new literates but it has not fulfilled this promise due to lack of funding. However, the current Minister for Education, Minister Pandor, is looking at the SANLI design in relation to campaigns of other countries (notably the Cuban-driven campaign in Venezuela) in hopes of establishing a literacy campaign in South Africa starting in 2007.

Clearly, the SANLI campaign and the work undertaken by the UNISA ABET Institute may be seen as a valuable "pilot" for any larger literacy campaign. In the interim, it is necessary for other government agencies to continue to provide basic education. In the section that follows, two of the main ABET providers (both of which are associated with the Ministry of Labour and not Education) appear to be leading the struggle for a literate South Africa.

National Public Works Campaigns

As indicated earlier, the National Skills Development Act defined 25 SETAs,[87] which are established by the Department of Labour. Each SETA

---

[87] This refers to a variety of sectors, such as health, retail, military, and so on.

allocates a budget for ABET, which makes lifelong education a real possibility, as the various programs need to target specific sectoral groups, such as health workers; construction, service industry, or manufacturing workers; workers in local government, water, or environment; and so on. The SETAs have made it possible for the campaign to reach a wide spectrum of stakeholders, such as traditional healers, taxi drivers, and informal sector workers (those workers who are not employed within the mainstream economy and who sell their services and products on the streets). The new health care and HIV/AIDS programs all require training, including literacy training.

Whereas the SETA programs disburse funding for the education and training of workers who are employed in respective sectors, workers who are unemployed and who fall outside of the net are served by a National Skills Fund or via the proposed Extended Public Works Programs (EPWPs). In this way, it is hoped that large numbers of adults may receive training where they are employed. The National Skills Fund makes funding available for those adults who are in need of basic education and training but who are not employed.

The Extended Public Works Programs

President Mbeki announced the creation of the EPWPs in his State of the Nation address in February 2003. The Department of Labour heralded the EPWPs as a central pillar of the South African government's strategy to address poverty and unemployment. The newly launched EPWP was described as being able to do the following:

- Create and maintain essential infrastructure, such as roads and school buildings for communities in high-poverty areas.
- Address poverty and unemployment through the creation of work.
- Transfer skills from skills-development facilitators and trainers to the unskilled workforce.

The EPWP was expected to "contribute to job creation, reinforcement of infrastructure investment and maintenance, provision for higher education transformation and skills development, and further investment in municipal infrastructure and services" (Manuel, cited in McKay, Mokotong, & Morr, 2004, p. 17). The EPWP was designed to give workers training in specific areas on a certain number of workdays per person. In addition, workers will be given on-the-job training to improve their ability to earn an income in the future.

Within the context of increasing unemployment, the EPWP complements and enriches existing[88] skills-development programs aimed at employment generation and poverty alleviation. Through the EPWP, the Department of Labour expects to create 1 million jobs (albeit mostly temporary work) to address conditions of poverty and joblessness.

Collectively, the three goals given—the creation of infrastructure, the creation of work, and the transfer of skills (job skills and basic education)—underlie the rationale for the EPWP. The challenge is now for the program to achieve tangible results for all three goals and this cannot be done without ensuring first that people have a sufficient level of literacy and numeracy for them to learn job-related skills. Moreover, the work environment requires that people acquire a minimal level of life skills to be able to cope with everyday matters like working out a budget, buying on credit, or dealing with conflict. ABET as an essential component of the EPWP makes literacy accessible to many more people who have not as yet been reached through other interventions.

WHAT DOES THE FUTURE OF ADULT LITERACY IN SOUTH AFRICA LOOK LIKE?

Although the EPWP aims to develop skills, the EPWP pilot programs have tended to pay only cursory attention to teaching foundational learning skills, such as reading and writing (McKay et al., 2004). An evaluation of the pilot program recommended that more training days be allocated for teaching literacy-related skills.

McKay and colleagues (2004) also suggested that the Department of Labour make its strategy for ABET more explicit within the context of skills transfer because the targeted 1 million jobless people are to be drawn from among the ranks of the illiterate unemployed. At the time of writing, the Department of Labour is reexamining these suggestions for future implementation and a newly established Ministerial Committee of experts has begun to craft a strategy for implementation in 2007.

The importance of the SETAs in education and training is apparent. Each SETA targets adults with little or no schooling within their respective

---

[88]Different ministries conduct programs aimed at the poor. For example, the Department of Science and Technology has a program on beekeeping to enable the selling of honey and the Department of Trade and Industries provides seed funding for hawkers and vendors in the informal sector.

sectors. Moreover, given the important role of training attributed to the Department of Labour, it is clear that over the next 5 years, adult education could shift from the Ministry of Education to the Department of Labour if the proposed new literacy campaign is not implemented. Presently it seems as if the education sector has failed to deliver adult education (at a notable scale) subsequent to the creation of our democratic government in 1994. In this regard, the Department of Labour offers hope to employed workers who require literacy, and to adult learners who are not employed and who constitute the poorest segment of the South African population.

Although UNISA ABET continues to train adult educators, tracer studies (Lamont, 2003) indicate that educators are being absorbed into the programs being implemented by the various SETAs and not into programs being implemented by the Department of Education. This suggests that the Ministry of Education does not show as much of a commitment to the subsector of ABE as does the Department of Labour.

Although the SETAs make a valuable contribution to the development of human capacity, it is lamentable that the Department of Education—the custodian of education—has played a relatively small role in the implementation of basic education in the past 10 years of South Africa's new democracy. Adult education is and should be interministerial but the poor response by the Ministry of Education means by implication that basic education and adult literacy are still the "stepchildren" of the education sector. This neglect underpins the relatively poor investment into adult education and the reluctant delivery across the country.[89]

REFERENCES

African National Congress. (1994). *The reconstruction and development programme: A policy framework.* Johannesburg, South Africa: Umanayano.

Aitchison, J., Houghton, T., & Baatjes, I., with Douglas, R., Dlamini, M., Seid, S., & Stead, H. (2000). *University of Natal survey of adult basic education and training: South Africa.* Pietermaritzburg, South Africa: University of Natal, Centre for Adult Education.

Baatjes, I. G. (2004). *Norms and standards for funding PALCs: Towards a submission.* Unpublished manuscript.

---

[89] After concluding work on this chapter, the author was appointed to the Minister of Education's Committee on Literacy and basic education, a committee charged with making recommendations to the Cabinet on a proposed new strategy for the mass delivery of ABE that draws on the lessons learned through SANLI.

Bordia, A. (2003). *Evaluation of the UNISA ABET programme—Incorporating SANLI* (DFID Rep. No. PCR 059550088). Pretoria, South Africa: DFIDSA.
Bown, L. (1999, July). *Evaluation of the UNISA ABET programme* (Report compiled for DFID South Africa). Pretoria, South Africa: DFIDSA.
Department of Education. (1995). *White paper on education and training.* Cape Town, South Africa: Author.
Department of Education. (1997). *A national multi-year implementation plan for adult education and training: Provision and accreditation.* Pretoria, South Africa: Author.
French, E. (2002). *The condition of ABET 2002: Qualitative ABET sector review.* Pretoria, South Africa: Human Sciences Research Council.
Hooper-Box, C. (2002). *AIDS orphans time bomb.* Health Systems Trust. Retrieved April 11, 2006, from http://new.hst.org.za
Human Sciences Research Council. (1999). *Annual survey of public adult learning centres.* Pretoria, South Africa: Author.
Lamont, T. (2003). *Evaluation of impact: UNISA ABET practitioner training.* Unpublished report.
McKay, V., Mokotong, E., & Morr, H. (2004). *An evaluation of Gundo Lashu: An extended public works programme.* Unpublished report.
McKay, V., Mokotong, E., & Sham, B. (2003). *Our graves are open: A survey of the informal sector in South Africa.* Unpublished report.
Presidency. (2003). *Towards a ten year review: Policy coordination and advisory services.* Pretoria, South Africa: Government Printers.
Statistics South Africa. (1996). *General population census.* Pretoria, South Africa: Author.
Statistics South Africa. (2001). *General population census.* Pretoria, South Africa: Author.
Statistics South Africa. (2004). *General population census.* Pretoria, South Africa: Author.
Troup, F. (1976). *Forbidden pastures.* London: International Defence Aid Fund.
UNESCO. (1998). *Series of booklets documenting the 5th International Conference on Adult Education.* Hamburg, Germany: UNESCO Institute for Education.
UNISA ABET. (2003). *Literacy matters: A commemorative booklet of the first year of the UNISA SANLI partnership.* Pretoria, South Africa: UNISA.

10

Annotated Bibliography on Workplace Education

Connie Nelson

Throughout the 20th century, businesses, unions, and the military sometimes offered English language classes to new immigrants, or helped workers gain reading and writing skills (Sticht, 1975). The modern version of *workplace education*—basic skills instruction offered to employees at the workplace or union hall—emerged in the 1980s as higher skill requirements and an increase in the number of immigrant workers converged to make upgrading workers' basic skills[90] appear attractive—or necessary—to business, labor, government, and workers themselves. This increase in awareness was accompanied by a surge in state, employer, and union worker education initiatives throughout the 1980s. In 1988, the federal government introduced the National Workplace Literacy Program, which continued for 10 years and funded more than 300 projects around the

---

[90]*Basic skills* as used in this article refers to adult basic education (ABE), English for speakers of other languages (ESOL), and adult secondary education (ASE), which includes preparation for the tests of general educational development (GED) and in some states, the adult or external diploma.

country. Since that time, several states have continued or developed state-level programs to encourage workplace education (Foucar-Szocki, 2004).

Workplace education is interconnected with, yet distinct from, related services. Workplace education is a subset or specialty of adult basic education (ABE), which focuses on the basic skills needed by a broad population, for a wider range of roles (work, family, and community) and services are delivered in a range of venues and to a range of populations. Workplace education offers access to education; a context for creating relevant curriculum for basic skills such as literacy, numeracy, and ESOL; a community of learners sharing common experience; and opportunities and incentives for further education and training related to that context (in this case, a workplace or industry). Workplace education projects are always partnerships, involving, at least, an employer, an educational provider, and learners. Additional partners can be representatives of labor, government, foundations, customers, and various groups of workers, such as those on a particular shift; in a particular job classification or department; or from a particular language, cultural, or ethnic group.

Workforce development is yet a broader endeavor, encompassing a number of services, such as job counseling, job placement, and special services geared toward helping unemployed and underemployed workers overcome obstacles to employment. ABE and job-skills training are sometimes offered in workforce development programs. In a workforce development context, ABE focuses on a broad range of skills required by adults in their role as workers. Those skills include reading, writing, math, and language skills, as well as job-specific basic skills and the skills needed to get a job. Workforce development services are offered to those who have not yet entered the workforce, as well as to employed and dislocated workers, through a diverse group of providers from the workplace and the community.

The Workforce Investment Act (WIA) of 1998 pushed workforce development and ABE agencies to develop new collaborative relationships. WIA provides public funding for workforce development and ABE, and links both to economic development. Through this funding, the federal government addresses both employers' needs for qualified workers, and workers' needs for increased wages and job security. The loss of skilled and semiskilled manufacturing and service jobs to computerization, downsizing, and offshoring has been massive and is likely to continue. The need for basic skills as a foundation for higher level skills training is also likely to grow as the skill requirements of jobs increase.

Models of workplace education programs range from programs offering general reading, writing, math, or language instruction that is physically located at the workplace, to programs in which instruction teaches specific language and math skills needed to do jobs at the particular workplace. Other programs use the community of coworker-learners and the content of workplace knowledge as a foundation for instruction that teaches literacy, numeracy, and English-language skills. These programs use authentic workplace materials, such as forms, routing sheets, safety information, or benefit packages, and they construct scenarios from workplace experiences to build a contextualized curriculum, customized for the workplace.

The full gamut of teaching styles and educational philosophies are found in workplace education. One approach makes a clear philosophical distinction between broad education and narrow job training, whereas another blurs that distinction in theory and practice: Job skills are changing and workers need a broad educational base to adapt to those changes (Levenson, 2004). Various skill standards, such as those developed by the American Society for Training and Development (ASTD) and Equipped for the Future (EFF), take this latter approach. Still other programs focus on workers' rights and help workers gain skills to move ahead in their careers (Rosenbloom, 1996). For example, in the hospitality industry, fluency in English can help workers move "from the back of the house to the front of the house" (i.e., from washing dishes in the kitchen to positions such as wait staff that include customer contact and additional income from tips). Many programs, and some employers, seek to balance the interests and needs of employers, unions, and workers (Jurmo & Folinsbee, 1994).

In this chapter I discuss the changes in the workplace and workforce that precipitated the increased need for workplace education, the interests of workplace education stakeholders, the incidence of workplace education, and lessons learned about implementing workplace education.

Changes in the Workplace and Workforce

Three changes in the U.S. economy and workplace in the last three decades have increased the need for a more skilled and literate workforce: (a) higher skill requirements for many jobs (especially jobs likely to remain in the United States) resulting from computerization of repetitive tasks and combination of higher level tasks (which require additional or cross-training), (b) reorganization that shifts decision-making responsibility to the front-line worker, and (c) technological change that makes computer literacy necessary while shifting traditional craft knowledge to computer data (Zuboff, 1988). As computers are able to do more routine work, human jobs are likely to be those that can analyze computer data and make personal judgments using that data, as well as those involving interpersonal contact and relationships (Murnane & Levy, 2004; Thomas, 1996). More is being asked of the front-line worker in many industries. For example, in the insurance industry, customer-service representatives are expected to give more personalized service, rather than simply referring a customer to another department (Murnane & Levy, 1996).

Government, corporate, and labor awareness of demographic changes in the population have increased attention paid to the need for workplace education. One such demographic change is the increase in the percentage of the workforce whose first language is not English (Hunt, 1996). Immigrant workers need instruction in speaking, reading, and writing in English to communicate with supervisors, coworkers, union representatives, and customers. A second demographic change is the aging of the workforce: In the near future, a larger proportion of workers will not be entering the workforce directly from school. Older workers are likely to remain in the workforce longer as the general population ages and retirement age goes up. Education reform efforts geared to improving the preparation of today's school population for tomorrow's jobs must be augmented by raising the skill level of the present workforce (Munnell, Cahill, Eschtruth, & Sass, 2004).

STAKEHOLDER INTERESTS

Effective workplace education must serve its constituent interests. Partners, known as stakeholders, each have a stake in the success of the program. The program must address each stakeholder's needs. The more completely this happens, the greater the buy-in and support from all parties.

Employers may be interested in workplace education to further business goals such as improved communication, higher productivity, increased safety, and fewer job errors, or they may see it as primarily an employee benefit, thereby resulting in improved recruitment, retention, and morale. Typically, in business, spending decisions must be justified in terms of cost–benefit analysis or return on investment (ROI). However, workplace education programs do not always fit into traditional ROI formulas. It can be very difficult and prohibitively expensive to isolate the effects of education programs on productivity or quality, because so many other factors are involved, such as work organization, equipment, availability of materials, or staffing. Some employers see workplace education as a way to help their businesses become "learning organizations" or to extend that culture from the managerial corps to the front-line workers (Bloom, 2003; Geissler, Knell, McVey, Powell, & Brenner, 1995; Levenson, 2004).

Organized labor (Rosenbloom, 1996) represents the interests of workers in such matters as wages and working conditions. Organized labor has always had a political commitment to the education of working-class children (e.g., public schools) and this commitment extends to education and training for adults. Education programs can help workers get access to promotions, use and understand their negotiated benefits, deal with technological changes at the workplace, and become more active in union leadership (Levine, 2000).

Groups of workers (e.g., from different ethnic or language groups, or different departments, job classifications, or shifts) may have a wide variety of motivations for and concerns about an education program. Some may want to learn basic or more advanced levels of English; get help with reading, math, or computer literacy; or get tutoring to pass a GED test. Workers may want to improve very specific skills required for their current jobs, or they might want to learn skills they can transfer to a new job, get technical training required for a new career, or obtain assistance with tasks they face outside the workplace (e.g., helping their children succeed in school, managing their personal finances). On the other hand, workers may be reluctant to come forward and reveal what may be considered (by themselves or, in their perception, by employer and coworkers) a deficit. This fear of embarrassment or of being pigeonholed as "less able" is one reason why confidentiality is critical in workplace education.

Local, state, and federal governments are interested in a skilled, literate workforce that will retain or attract employers and thus increase employment. An estimated 64 million workers in the United States need additional basic skills or credentials to meet the demands of the 21st-century economy (Comings, Reder, & Sum, 2001). Additionally, immigrant labor plays an increasingly important role in the U.S. economy (Sum, Palma, & Khatiwada, 2001). Government also views workplace education as a promising venue in which to offer its adult education services to working adults because low-skilled and low-wage workers often need to work multiple jobs, which limits their ability to participate in ABE programs outside of work. Because government is also interested in an educated populace that demonstrates responsible parenthood and citizenship, workplace education is an opportunity for government to leverage private investment through employer-match grants.

Education providers constitute another stakeholder in workplace education partnerships. The changes in workforce development present opportunities and challenges for adult educators. One opportunity is for increased funding of education services by employers who see foundation skills as necessary to increase the skills of the workforce. Education providers can also broaden their offerings to learners by tapping into workforce development areas. Local, state, and federal programs and funding streams include workplace education, such as *career ladder programs* (in which education and training are customized to career paths in a workplace or industry) and *sector initiatives* (in which incumbent and newly entering workers are trained as a qualified pool for several employers in a particular industry).

Although workplace education programs have demonstrated their potential for serving the interests of the multiple stakeholders already discussed, workplace education providers find it challenging to maintain high-quality instruction and provide sufficient instructional time for learners to make real progress, whatever the context or funding stream. In many cases, it is up to adult educators to inform employers, funders, and other stakeholders about what is required to create and sustain high-quality workplace education programs. Educators can also help workers make connections to learning opportunities in the community to continue their education.

In short, while needing to balance the interests of all stakeholders, workplace education is a convenient venue for serving adult learners where they spend much of their time, and it offers opportunities to make the instructional curriculum relevant to workers' current job skills, to take advantage of the community atmosphere among coworkers at a work site, and to generate investment by employers in the development of their own workforce.

INCIDENCE OF WORKPLACE EDUCATION

Although employers have an interest in the basic skills of their workforce, only a few consistently provide training of any kind for their lower wage workers (Frazis, Gittleman, Harrigan, & Joyce, 1998). Training does represent a substantial cost for the employer, and it can be difficult to justify the expense in traditional ROI formulas, particularly in the short term (Levenson, 2004) either initially or after the government funding concludes, raising an important question of whether taxpayer funds should go to businesses that would otherwise offer workplace education to their employees at their own expense.

According to human capital theory (Becker, 1964), employers see the benefit of firm-specific training, but not the benefit of building general skills, which is what basic education generally does. Employers fear that employees will leave once they have learned these skills, representing a lost investment.

In reviewing literature regarding employer-provided workplace education (Ahlstrand, Bassi, & McMurrer, 2003; Bassi, 1992; Geissler et al., 1995; Hollenbeck, 1993; Levenson, 2004), employers' use of state grants (Abelmann, 1996) and continuation of programs after state grants (Nelson, 2002), firm size stands out as the most frequent and significant factor: Large firms are more likely to provide it on their own. They are also more likely to use state grants and to continue programs after those grants end.

Other factors may play a role in the decision to offer workplace education, although this evidence is not as strong as the evidence concerning firm size. Workplace education may be more likely to continue in companies that:

- Are closely held (i.e., not publicly traded) corporations or make decisions locally.
- Experience external pressures for increased skill requirements, such as needing certification from the International Standards Organization (ISO) to trade internationally.
- Have a corporate philosophy supporting training or identify themselves as a "learning organization."[91]
- Have a specific reason to invest in the skills of their current workforce (e.g., companies with a cohort of experienced older workers or those that lack a skilled hiring pool).

Although any or all of these factors may be present in particular workplaces, it is still necessary to evaluate potential workplaces on a case-by-case basis to determine whether they are good candidates for workplace education programs.

---

[91]A *learning organization* is one that implements continuous improvement and learning throughout the organization on an ongoing basis.

LESSONS LEARNED ABOUT IMPLEMENTING QUALITY WORKPLACE EDUCATION PROGRAMS

Given the range of stakeholder needs and the complexity of workplace cultures, creating quality programs can be a daunting challenge. Some programs and states have developed guidelines for creating quality workplace education programs drawn from formal evaluations of programs, or based on field experience gained in individual companies, unions, or statewide workplace education initiatives, such as the lessons learned from Northeastern Illinois University's program in the textile industry, or the state guidelines produced by Ohio and Massachusetts. Some states, such as Pennsylvania and Virginia, have developed Web sites that share practitioner wisdom as well as research, resources, and professional development opportunities; the National Institute for Literacy (NIFL) sponsors a workplace education listserv and special collection Web site.[92]

Gowen's (1992) extensive ethnographic study of a workplace education program in a Southern hospital highlights the importance of investigating the needs of all stakeholder groups, including learners, and taking them into account in program design. In the program Gowen studied, the interests of workers and employers conflicted: Housekeeping employees were not only uninterested in contextualized curriculum—their motives for learning to read related more to family and Bible reading—they were also offended at the suggestion that being able to read housekeeping bulletins would make them better cleaners.

A five-site qualitative study of workplace education programs in manufacturing, hospitality, health care, and service industries (Belfiore, Defoe, Folinsbee, Hunter, & Jackson, 2004) demonstrated that all stakeholders need ongoing training and support about how the program and the workplace affect each other; both workplace educators and their colleagues at the workplace, such as supervisors, trainers, union representatives, and human resource professionals, need professional development. This study also showed that, in addition to assessment of literacy skill levels, it is important to evaluate how and to what extent the workplace culture encourages workers' use of these skills.

Bloom (2003) interviewed practitioners, employers, union representatives, and learners in several joint labor–management programs around

---

[92]Please see the Annotated Bibliography for more information and URLs.

the country and identified common elements of successful practice. Those elements shared by a majority of the programs included the following:

- Balanced collaborative consultation between labor and management at each stage of development of the program.
- Analysis of learning needs.
- Career-planning services.
- Voluntary participation of workers.
- Access to continuing education opportunities and financial assistance.
- Employee involvement in program design and evaluation.
- Specific criteria for selecting education providers.
- Multiple learning strategies for worker-students.

In-depth evaluations of two statewide and three local workplace education initiatives (Moore, Myers, & Silva, 1998) emphasized the importance of adequate instructional time, acknowledging the constraints and difficulties of providing it. The study also made suggestions for local and state support to workplace education programs, such as technical assistance with how to start programs, gain employer support, and maintain quality.

Jurmo and Folinsbee (1994) also pointed out the need for an oversight committee and a workplace needs analysis. An *oversight committee* makes decisions about what kinds of classes are offered, which workers will attend, and the logistics of where and when classes will be held. The committee must reflect and represent the major stakeholders that will benefit from and be affected by an education program at their workplace and may be comprised of a human resource manager, union representative, line supervisor, quality-control person, worker-learner representative, and the teacher. The committee plays a useful role in identifying program goals that are meaningful in the workplace, and in making sure evidence of the program's achievements reaches the right decision makers when seeking financial support for the program.

The *workplace needs analysis* (WNA) systematically investigates the needs at a particular workplace, so that the provider, working with the oversight committee, can clarify the role that basic skills can play in the development of both the organization and the workforce and can thereby ensure the relevance and efficiency of the education program. The WNA can provide a detailed understanding of stakeholder needs and interests, which will enable the committee to identify a common ground for program activities. The WNA also uncovers potential pitfalls—especially logistical issues and turf sensitivities—that must be worked out to maximize participation while minimizing disruption. While conducting the WNA, the provider will also uncover a wealth of authentic materials and resource persons that can be incorporated into the program. The WNA also identifies workplace goals that can be used in program evaluation design. Forming and maintaining an oversight committee with effective stakeholder participation and using a WNA to determine needs can keep an education program focused while avoiding preventable problems.

As workforce skill requirements change and place new responsibilities on the front-line worker, and as the reliance on immigrant labor increases, the need for well-designed workplace basic skills programs grows. Program planners and funders should learn from the valuable research and experience already available in this field.

REFERENCES

Abelmann, C. (1996). *Policy off center: Lessons from Mississippi's effort to offer state incentives to promote workplace education.* Unpublished doctoral dissertation, Harvard Graduate School of Education, Cambridge, MA.

Ahlstrand, A. L., Bassi, L. J., & McMurrer, D. P. (2003). *Workplace education for low-wage workers.* Kalamazoo, MI: W. E. Upjohn Institute for Employment Research.

Bassi, L. (1992). Workplace education for hourly workers. *Journal of Public Analysis and Management, 13*(1), 55–74.

Becker, G. S. (1964). *Human capital: A theoretical and empirical analysis.* Chicago: University of Chicago Press.

Belfiore, M. E., Defoe, T., Folinsbee, S., Hunter, J., & Jackson, N. (2004). *Reading work: Literacies in the new workplace.* Mahwah, NJ: Lawrence Erlbaum Associates, Inc.

Bloom, M. (2003). *What works in workforce development.* Arlington, VA: American Society for Training and Development.

Comings, J., Reder, S., & Sum, A. (2001). *Building a level playing field: The need to expand and improve the national and state adult education and literacy systems.* Cambridge, MA: National Center for the Study of Adult Learning and Literacy.

Foucar-Szocki, D. (2004). How states approach workplace education. *Focus on Basics, 7*(B).

Frazis, H., Gittleman, M., Horrigan, R., & Joyce, M. (1998). Results from the 1995 survey of employer-provided training. *Monthly Labor Review, 121*(6), 3–13.

Geissler, B., Knell, S., McVey, J. W., Powell, S., & Brenner, B. (1995). *Learning that works: Basic skills programs in Illinois corporations.* Champaign: Illinois Literacy Resource Center.

Gowen, S. G. (1992). *The politics of workplace literacy.* New York: Teachers College, Columbia University.

Hollenbeck, K. (1993). *Classrooms in the workplace.* Kalamazoo, MI: W. E. Upjohn Institute for Employment Research.

Hunt, E. (1996). *Will we be smart enough? A cognitive analysis of the coming workforce.* New York: Russell Sage Foundation.

Jurmo, P., & Folinsbee, S. (1994). *Collaborative workforce development, collaborative needs assessment, collaborative program evaluation.* Don Mills, ON, Canada: ABC CANADA.

Levenson, A. (2004). Why do companies provide workplace education programs? In J. Comings, B. Garner, & C. Smith (Eds.), *Annual review of adult learning and literacy* (Vol. 5). San Francisco: Jossey-Bass.

Levine, T. (2000). *Learning for our lives: A union guide to worker-centered literacy.* Ottawa, ON, Canada: Canadian Labour Congress.

Moore, M. T., Myers, D., & Silva, T. (1998). *Addressing literacy needs at work: Implementation and impact of workplace literacy programs.* Washington, DC: Mathematica Policy Research.

Munnell, A. H., Cahill, K. E., Eschtruth, A. D., & Sass, S. A. (2004). *The graying of Massachusetts: Aging, the new rules of retirement, and the changing workforce.* Boston: Massachusetts Institute for a New Commonwealth.

Murnane, R., & Levy, F. (1996). *Teaching the new basic skills.* New York: The Free Press.

Murnane, R., & Levy, F. (2004). *The new division of labor: How computers are creating the next job market.* Princeton, NJ: Princeton University Press.

Nelson, C. (2002). *After the grant: Institutionalization of seed-funded workplace education programs in Massachusetts.* Unpublished doctoral dissertation, Harvard Graduate School of Education, Cambridge, MA.

Rosenbloom, S. (1996). *Union-sponsored workplace ESL instruction* (Rep. No. EDO-LE-96-03). Washington, DC: National Clearinghouse for ESL Literacy Education. (ERIC Document Reproduction Service No. ED 392317)

Sticht, T. (1975). *Reading for work.* Englewood Cliffs, NJ: Prentice-Hall.

Sum, A., Palma, S., & Khatiwada, I. (2001). *The story of household incomes in the 1990s.* Boston: Massachusetts Institute for a New Commonwealth.

Thomas, R. (1996). *What machines can't do.* Berkeley: University of California Press.

Zuboff, S. (1988). *In the age of the smart machine.* New York: Basic Books.

RESOURCES

Ahlstrand, A. L., Bassi, L. J., & McMurrer, D. J. (2003). *Workplace education for low-wage workers.* Kalamazoo, MI: W. E. Upjohn Institute for Employment Research.

Focus: Reasons employers offer workplace education
Audience: Researchers
Level of background required: Medium
This book reports on a three-phase study that included analysis of data on training incidence from the American Society for Training and Development, telephone surveys of 40 employers, and several case studies of workplace education programs. The authors found the following main reasons for offering workplace education to low-wage workers: philosophical commitment, improved retention and recruitment, and improved customer service. This adds to the body of research on why employers offer workplace education, and practitioners can use it to understand employer needs. Firms reported using Levels 1 through 3 on the Kirkpatrick Scale. This instrument is widely used by businesses to evaluate training. Level 1 measures employee reactions. Level 2 measures

employee learning (e.g., pre- and posttests). Level 3 measures changes in job performance (using employee and supervisor surveys). Level 4 measures results for the firm based on improved performance and Level 5 refers to return on investment (ROI).

Bloom, M., & LaFleur, B. (1999). *Turning skills into profit: Economic benefits of workplace education programs.* New York: The Conference Board.

Focus: Benefits of workplace education
Audience: Researchers, practitioners, business and labor partners
Level of background required: Basic
In this research report, the authors interviewed 40 employers, 39 employees, and 12 union representatives involved with workplace education and found several economic benefits to the programs. This book is interesting for researchers and practitioners alike, particularly in exploring where the various stakeholder groups agreed and disagreed on benefits of programs.

Geissler, B., Knell, S., McVey, J. W., Powell, S., & Brenner, B. (1995). *Learning that works: Basic skills programs in Illinois corporations.* Champaign: Illinois Literacy Resource Center.

Focus: Reasons employers offer workplace education
Audience: Policymakers, practitioners, researchers, business partners
Level of background required: Medium
This researchers in this study interviewed managers representing 22 Illinois firms. Half (11 firms) provided workplace education. Slightly over half of those who sponsored workplace education did so to achieve quality improvements, and another third were motivated by a commitment to worker education in their corporate culture. The authors also found that companies found technical assistance and seed grants to be the most useful forms of government assistance.

Hollenbeck, K. (1993). *Classrooms in the workplace.* Kalamazoo, MI: W. E. Upjohn Institute for Employment Research.

Focus: Characteristics of firms that offer workplace education
Audience: Researchers
Level of background required: High
This study is useful in its contribution to differentiating firms offering workplace education from those that do not. The study researchers surveyed

1,123 Michigan firms by mail and telephone, and also conducted 28 case studies of firms that offered workplace education programs. Hollenbeck found that the size of the firm was the greatest difference between firms that offered workplace education and those that did not; this held in both manufacturing and service industries. Another difference was that higher paying nonmanufacturing firms offered it; in manufacturing firms, those that were introducing new forms of work organization such as quality circles or increased responsibility for front-line workers were more likely to offer it.

Levenson, A. (2001). *Investing in workers' basic skills: Lessons from company funded workplace based programs.* Washington, DC: National Institute for Literacy.

Focus: Reasons employers offer workplace education
Audience: Researchers, business partners
Level of background required: Medium
Levenson interviewed and visited eight organizations for this in-depth study: four manufacturing companies, two health care organizations, one insurance company, and a consortium of hotels. The study identified factors that affected companies' decisions to fund their programs, such as a protraining company philosophy; having a cohort of older workers with low skills; lacking a skilled pool of workers from which to make new hires; experiencing high worker turnover; and needing to increase worker skills to run new equipment, improve customer service, and improve internal communication.

Levenson, A. (2004). Why do companies provide workplace education programs? In J. Comings, B. Garner, & C. Smith (Eds.), *Annual review of adult learning and literacy* (Vol. 4). San Francisco: Jossey-Bass.

Focus: Reasons employers offer workplace education
Audience: Researchers, practitioners
Level of background required: Medium
This article reviews theory and literature regarding employer motivation to provide workplace education. It provides an in-depth discussion of such issues as employee retention, program implementation, and impact measurement, and draws lessons for practitioners about program design and marketing.

Murnane, R., & Levy, F. (1996). *The new basic skills.* New York: The Free Press; Murnane, R., & Levy, F. (2004). *The new division of labor: How computers are creating the next job market.* Princeton, NJ: Princeton University Press.

Focus: Skills required for changing job market
Audience: Researchers, policymakers, practitioners
Level of background required: Basic
Both books make an argument for an expansion of the definition of basic skills to include literacy and numeracy, but also problem solving and teamwork based on research into employer demands. The second book makes a case that the new division of labor is between humans and computers, and analyzes which jobs can best be done by computers (e.g., those with regular rules) and which will likely continue to require human judgment. Both books can help program planners, as well as business and labor partners, think about skills workers need to retain jobs or skills they will need to get new jobs should theirs be eliminated or outsourced.

Guides to Practice and Design of Workplace Education

AFL-CIO Working for America Institute. (1999). *Worker-centered learning: A union guide to basic skills.* Washington, DC: AFL-CIO.

Focus: Guide to practice
Audience: Practitioners, labor partners
Level of background required: Basic
This guide provides information for union representatives about why and how they should be involved in basic skills programs for their members. It offers practitioners insight into the union's stakeholder interests, as well as practical guides for program development.

Belfiore, M. E., & Burnaby, B. (Eds.). (1995). *Teaching English in the workplace.* Toronto: Pippin.

Focus: Guide to practice
Audience: Practitioners
Level of background required: Basic
This book is useful to program planners and also offers rich stories from experience that can be used in teacher training. It is particularly insightful regarding the necessity of fitting the program into the culture of the workplace, and gives useful advice for how to do so.

Belfiore, M. E., Defoe, T., Folinsbee, S., Hunter, J., & Jackson, N. (2004). *Reading work: Literacies in the new workplace.* Mahwah, NJ: Lawrence Erlbaum Associates, Inc.

Focus: Ethnographic study of literacy use in workplaces
Audience: Researchers, practitioners
Level of background required: Medium
The authors did extensive participant-observation studies in five Canadian workplaces, in manufacturing, hospitality, and health care. The authors show the ways literacy skills are used—or not—in actual job performance, and that literacy and numeracy skill level is only one factor in the overall fabric of workplace culture. They show the need for professional development not only among workplace educators but their colleagues based at the workplace: supervisors, union representatives, and human resource and training professionals. This work is of interest to researchers and to practitioners trying to integrate programs into the workplace culture.

Bloom, M. (2002). *What works in workforce development.* Arlington, VA: American Society for Training and Development.

Focus: Common features of successful programs
Audience: Researchers, policymakers, practitioners, business and labor partners
Level of background required: Medium
In this study, the American Society for Training and Development surveyed 21 programs in several industries and Bloom conducted in-depth interviews with administrators, participants, and business and labor partners in three large programs in the information technology, health care, and hospitality industries. They found a series of practices the education providers and other stakeholders considered necessary to quality programming.

Folinsbee, S., & Jurmo, P. (1994). *Collaborative workforce development, collaborative needs assessment, collaborative program evaluation.* Don Mills, ON, Canada: ABC Canada.

Focus: Guide to practice
Audience: Practitioners
Level of background required: Basic

This series of guides gives detailed, step-by-step advice for practitioners interested in planning and evaluating programs meeting a range of stakeholder needs. It includes sample questionnaires and forms for interviewing various stakeholder groups and a wealth of how-to—and what-not-to-do—guidelines.

Gillespie, M. K. (1996). *Learning to work in a new land.* Washington, DC: Center for Applied Linguistics.

Focus: Guide to practice
Audience: Practitioners
Level of background required: Basic

This sourcebook begins with a section on the growth of immigrant workers and the need for instruction in English for speakers of other languages (ESOL), and a historical view of policy and funding issues. It also describes and compares several useful models both for providing ESOL in preemployment vocational training programs and for workplace education, as well as reviewing several tools and resources.

Gowen, S. G. (1992). *The politics of workplace literacy.* New York: Teachers College, Columbia University.

Focus: Book-length case study of one program
Audience: Researchers
Level of background required: Medium

This in-depth case study follows a workplace education program for housekeepers in a Southern hospital. It is particularly insightful into the stakeholder interests of the learners, showing that the learners' motivations to improve their reading skills were more often tied to personal and family, rather than career, goals.

Hull, G. (Ed.). (1997). *Changing work, changing worker: Critical perspectives on language, literacy and skills.* Albany: State University of New York Press.

Focus: Lessons from practice and critical essays
Audience: Researchers, policymakers, practitioners
Level of background required: Medium

The 14 articles in this book discuss curriculum innovation, philosophical orientation, and policy implications of various approaches to workplace education. Most lessons are drawn from particular workplace education or job training programs and raise issues of balancing worker and employer goals, as well as balancing general education and specific skills.

Levine, T. (2000). *Learning for our lives: A union guide to worker-centered literacy.* Ottawa, ON, Canada: Canadian Labour Congress.

Focus: Guide to practice
Audience: Practitioners, labor partners
Level of background required: Basic
This handbook from the Canadian Labour Congress Literacy Project, written for trade unionists, gives an overview of the interests of the union stakeholders, models of programs with union involvement, and steps to establishing effective programs.

Massachusetts Workplace Literacy Consortium. (1999). *Workplace education guide.* Malden: Massachusetts Department of Education.

Focus: Guide to practice
Audience: Practitioners
Level of background required: Basic
Several program coordinators in the National Workplace Literacy Program wrote this guidebook, which covers WNA, planning teams, labor–management partnerships, curriculum development, assessment, evaluation, institutionalization, and consortia of several businesses working together.

Moore, M. T., Myers, D., & Silva, T. (1998). *Addressing literacy needs at work: Implementation and impact of workplace literacy programs.* Washington, DC: Mathematica Policy Research.

Focus: Evaluation of National Workplace Literacy Program
Audience: Researchers, policymakers
Level of background required: High
This study evaluated the National Workplace Literacy Program (NWLP), which was established by Congress in 1988 and ended in 1996. The authors conducted in-depth studies of three local and two state-level programs, including an experimental design with random assignment in the local sites. Because of the scope of the NWLP, this study is important for policymakers. The study found an association between program effectiveness and instructional time, and stressed the importance of staff experience and state or local infrastructure that can help programs.

Utech, J. L. (2004). *Workplace educators' training.* Boston: Massachusetts Worker Education Roundtable.

Focus: Training for ABE and ESOL teachers going into workplace classrooms
Audience: Practitioners
Level of background required: Basic
This guide contains 60 activities that can be used to train ABE and ESOL teachers to teach in the workplace (especially unionized workplaces). The author developed the activities based on interviews with teachers in the Massachusetts Worker Education Roundtable's statewide network of union and labor–management programs. The guide contains information on WNA, conducting programs that are labor–management partnerships, curriculum development, and assessment and evaluation. There is also an accompanying collection of readings.

World Education. (2004). *Focus on Basics: Connecting Research and Practice* (Workplace Education Issue), 7(B).

Focus: Research, policy, and practice
Audience: Practitioners, researchers
Level of background required: Varies, mostly medium
This issue contains 10 articles and lists additional useful resources on a wide range of workplace education issues: policy, practice, research, philosophy, and historical development of workplace education.

Worker Writing

Baca, J. S. (Ed.) (2003). *The heat.* San Diego, CA: Cedar Hill.

Focus: Anthology of student writing
Audience: Practitioners, participants
Level of background required: Basic
This is a collection from classes at the Institute for Career Development, a joint program of 13 steel mills and the United Steel Workers of America. It contains several moving stories and poems by steelworkers. They can be used as powerful starting points in programs that teach writing.

SEIU Worker Education Program. (1996–2002). *Working writers.* Boston: SEIU Local 2020.

Focus: Anthology of student writing
Audience: Practitioners, participants
Level of background required: Basic
There are seven volumes of these collections of worker writing, mostly by health care workers, including many ESOL learners. These collections can be used as texts for intermediate ESOL and reading levels.

Web Sites

Focus: Resources, reports, and tools
Audience: Practitioners
Level of background required: Basic
- AFL-CIO Working for America Institute: www.workingforamerica.org
  This site features union programs and labor–management partnerships, and is also a reference for broader policy discussions in workforce development and its relationship to economic development. The site has several reports written by Institute staff.
- National Institute for Literacy (NIFL): www.nifl.gov
  Click Workforce to find a wide range of resources and research reports. Resources are organized by stakeholder, as well as by topic. The site includes a Learning Activities Bank (LAB) where practitioners can contribute and find lesson plans on work-related topics. NIFL also sponsors a workplace education listserv that can be accessed through this site.
- National Adult Literacy Database of Canada: www.nald.ca
  This site is a national clearinghouse of valuable resources from workplace education in Canada. Like the NIFL Web site, it contains many research reports and lessons from Canadian programs.
- Pennsylvania Workforce Improvement Network (PAWIN): www.pawin.org
  This site features a monthly newsletter, a reference sheet identifying components of successful programs, and many facts and arguments providers can use to convince employers about the usefulness of education programs. It also provides links to research and to discussions of issues.
- Virginia Workforce Improvement Network (VAWIN): www.jmu.edu
  In addition to access to a range of research reports and discussions of workforce development topics, this site features an online course for workplace education practitioners through James Madison University. It also offers an electronic peer-reviewed journal.

About the Editors

John P. Comings is the director of the National Center for the Study of Adult Learning and Literacy (NCSALL) at the Harvard Graduate School of Education. Before coming to Harvard, he spent 12 years as a vice president of World Education. Comings worked on adult education programs in Nepal for 6 years and in Indonesia for 2 years, and he has helped design and evaluate adult education programs in several countries in Asia, Africa, and the Caribbean. In the United States, he has served as the director of the State Literacy Resource Center in Massachusetts, assisted in the design of instructor training programs, and directed projects that focused on improving the teaching of both math and health in adult education programs. His research and writing have focused on the impact of adult literacy programs on reading ability and life changes such as health and family planning practices, the program factors that lead to that impact, and the issue of persistence in learning in the United States and developing countries.

Barbara Garner is a consultant who specializes in adult literacy. She edits many NCSALL publications, including *Focus on Basics* and a variety of technical reports and training materials. Former director of publications for NCSALL and senior program officer for World Education, she guided that organization's literacy efforts in Africa. She has held many different positions in the field of adult basic education: teacher, staff developer, program administrator, curriculum writer, and even funder.

Cristine Smith is Visiting Associate professor at the University of Massachusetts, Amherst. She previously served as deputy director of NCSALL and directed NCSALL's dissemination efforts, including the Connecting Practice, Policy and Research Initiative run by NCSALL. She also served as principal investigator of NCSALL's 5-year study of staff development in adult basic education and literacy. She has served as a consultant, researcher, and coordinator for World Education's literacy projects and research in South Asia. Smith has worked on staff development issues in the field of adult literacy for 18 years.

About the Contributors

Jennie Epstein Anderson, ScM, focuses her work on health communication, public health program implementation and evaluation, and health literacy. She is the coordinator of health literacy studies at the Harvard School of Public Health and has served as a research associate at the New York State Department of Health AIDS Institute. She is the coauthor of *The Health Literacy Environment Review*, a guide for hospitals and health centers to identify literacy-related barriers within their facilities. She coauthored *Guidelines: The HIV/AIDS Experience—The Roles of State Government in Promoting Implementation of Clinical Practice*, and several patient education booklets including *Making Sense of HIV Treatment: A Patient's Guide to the Federal Antiretroviral Therapy Guidelines*.

Patricia Bennett is the state director of adult education for Maryland. She has provided state leadership to adult education programs for more than 15 years in various roles. Accomplishments under her leadership include the implementation of the Workforce Investment Act, development of the statewide online data and accountability system, development of state content standards, a sevenfold increase in state funding for adult education, and the introduction of distance learning programs. Bennett is a member of the Executive Committee of the National Adult Education Professional Development Consortia (NAEPDC) and cochairs the Policy Committee for the National Council of State Directors of Adult Education (NCSDAE). She also represents the NCSDAE on the Board of the National Coalition for Literacy. Bennett has authored numerous grants for workplace literacy, community technology centers, and grants for services for individuals with learning disabilities and traumatic brain injury. She has also been the president of the Maryland Rehabilitation Association and the American Society for Training and Development (ASTD) Maryland chapter. Bennett has an undergraduate degree in English and a master's degree in education from Western Maryland College (now McDaniel College).

Mary Beth Bingman is an associate director of the Center for Literacy Studies at the University of Tennessee. Her work there includes coordination of the NCSALL work Connecting Practice, Policy and Research, development of training resources for Equipped for the Future, and other professional development work. She has published and presented at state and national conferences on professional development and assessment and accountability in adult literacy education and on women's learning in Appalachian community organizations. She holds a PhD with a concentration on adult education from the University of Tennessee. Before coming to the Center for Literacy Studies, Bingman worked as a county coordinator for a literacy program in Virginia.

Dr. Marilyn Gillespie is a senior educational researcher at the Center for Education Policy at SRI International. Her work focuses on research and evaluation related to literacy and lifelong learning, English language learning, workforce development, and adolescent literacy. She began her career in adult literacy and lifelong learning 25 years ago as an ABE and ESOL teacher and later served as a local program director, staff development specialist, curriculum developer, and director of the National Center for ESL Literacy Education at the Center for Applied Linguistics. Since joining SRI in 2000 she has conducted research related to the development of adult education standards and assessments at the national and state level, served as an advisor for the development of standards-based training for adult educators, and evaluated various technology-based education and teacher training projects. In addition, she has managed a national literacy panel charged with synthesizing research related to the literacy development of language minority children and youth, and has evaluated high school reform efforts such as the Gates Foundation Early College High School Initiative. She is the author of numerous teacher handbooks, training materials, and research articles related to teaching, learning, and professional development in adult education.

Betty Johnston has been involved in mathematics and numeracy education at different levels of the education system, and in a number of countries. Until recently, she was a lecturer in adult numeracy and adult basic education at the University of Technology, Sydney (UTS). Before her time at UTS she had extensive involvement in the field of mathematics teacher education, building on her previous experience teaching math in primary and secondary schools and at the university level. She has taught in New Zealand, Papua-New Guinea, Ghana, the United Kingdom, and Australia. Over the last 20 years she been closely involved in debates about the nature of numeracy, and has worked on a number of professional development projects in relation to adult numeracy, in particular Adult Numeracy Teaching, a course for teachers wanting to teach numeracy to adults. Her doctoral research focused on how mathematics has shaped gendered "mathematical identities" and how women have resisted this shaping. After 5 years as coordinator of the NSW state branch of the national Adult Literacy and Numeracy Australian Research Consortium (ALNARC), Johnston is currently working as a research consultant on projects related to the history of adult numeracy, financial numeracy, and numeracy in the workplace. Her most recent publication, available online, is *Adult Numeracy: Policy and Practice in Global Contexts of Lifelong Learning*.

Noreen Lopez is an adult education trainer and consultant who specializes in the areas of adult education technology and public policy. Her previous experiences include serving as director of LiteracyLink, a Public Broadcasting Service (PBS) project based in Alexandria, Virginia; manager of new product development at Contemporary Books; state director of adult education for the Illinois State Board of Education; faculty member in the graduate studies program at Northern Illinois University; and several years as a teacher and program director at the local level in Illinois. Lopez has served on advisory groups for the National Institute for Literacy, National Center for Adult Literacy, the National Education Goals Panel, and the **PBS CONNECT** project. She has held numerous positions in state and national adult education professional organizations, including currently serving as the co-chair of the Public Policy Committee of the National Coalition for Literacy. She obtained her BA from Mundelein College in Chicago and her MEd in urban education from Loyola University in Chicago, and completed her post-master's work in adult and continuing education at Northern Illinois University.

Beth Marr has more than 20 years of experience in adult mathematics and numeracy education. She has been involved in teaching, curriculum development, professional development, and research across a vast range of adult education sectors. These include vocational education, industry training, adult community education, and university-level teacher training. Marr has played a leading role in the creation of innovative teaching resources for teachers of adults, including *Mathematics: A New Beginning, Strength in Numbers, Breaking the Maths Barrier, Numeracy on the Line: Language Based Numeracy Activities for Adults*, the interactive

CD-ROM *Measuring Up,* and a number of online resources for adult numeracy educators. These publications, written with the needs of inexperienced teachers in mind, promote the use of student-centered teaching strategies suitable for adults. More recently, Marr has been involved in researching adult numeracy teaching, curriculum, and assessment; completing a master's of education research thesis, *Enhancing Mathematical Discourse: A Study of Small Group Interactions in an Adult Numeracy Classroom;* and a number of other related projects. Marr is currently at RMIT University, in Melbourne Australia, where she is a lecturer and researcher in adult teacher education at the Centre for Research in Post Compulsory Education and Training, specializing in instructional design, principles of adult learning and teaching, and adult numeracy.

Veronica McKay is founding director of the Institute for Adult Basic Education (ABET) at the University of South Africa (UNISA), which is renowned for training about 60,000 adult educators since 1994, for implementing a program enabling 342,000 adults to become literate, and for winning the Commonwealth of Learning excellence award for teacher training materials. McKay has published in a number of books and journals and has developed a range of teaching materials for new literate learners and university students. As an educator and sociologist, her research areas are broad and include educational policy, social development and poverty, HIV and AIDS, gender, and ways of enhancing learning, particularly through using the methods of distance education. In addition to her work in training adult educators, McKay is also involved in presenting a presidential lead program, which trains community development workers who facilitate service delivery and enable the poor (across every ward in South Africa) to access services and, where eligible, social grants. Recently, McKay was appointed to the ministerial committee for literacy, which is designing and implementing a strategy for a national literacy campaign in South Africa.

Charlotte Nath, RN, CDE, EdD, has been a faculty member in the Department of Family Medicine at West Virginia University School of Medicine for more than 20 years. She was a finalist for the American Association of Diabetes Educators Educator of the Year award and was the recipient of the Heebink Award for distinguished service to the state of West Virginia. An elective rotation developed by Dr. Nath received the Patient Care Award for Excellence in Patient Education by a Family

Practice Residency Program. She was on the editorial board for the *Core Curriculum for Diabetes Educators, 6th Edition, 2003–2004*.

Connie Nelson is the director of the Massachusetts Worker Education Roundtable, a network of worker education programs dedicated to promoting partnerships of employers, unions, and educators that provide high-quality education and training for Massachusetts union members. She conducts workplace needs analyses, facilitates labor–management oversight committees, develops curriculum, trains teachers, and provides all-around support to programs. The Worker Education Roundtable works with groups such as Working for America, the AFL-CIO, and the Association of Joint Labor–Management Education Programs, as well as education and training groups such as the Massachusetts Coalition for Adult Education and Massachusetts Workforce Alliance. She holds a BA in Adult Training and Development from University of Massachusetts at Boston and EdM and EdD degrees in Community Education and Lifelong Learning from Harvard University, where her research focused on sustainability of workplace learning programs.

Sarah C. Oppenheimer, ScM, focuses her work on social behaviors, institutional forces, and program and resource availability that influence individual health and larger public health trends. She currently works as the housing services program manager for Cambridge Cares About AIDS. Previously, Oppenheimer worked as a research assistant in Health Literacy Studies at the Harvard School of Public Health. There she developed a literacy assessment tool comprised solely of diabetes terms, which was validated and published in 2001. She has sought and received funding in the areas of diabetes and the incorporation of health literacy awareness into medical education at the graduate and postgraduate levels. In 2004 she completed a 6-month sabbatical leave with Dr. Rima Rudd at the Harvard School of Public Health, during which she contributed to the *Health Literacy Skills: Chronic Disease Management Study Circle Guide*. She was coinvestigator for an HRSA Title VII Grant that culminated in the production of a Resident as Teacher OSTE Training Video and supporting materials in 2005.

Perrine Robinson-Geller is a research assistant for NCSALL-Rutgers University. She has also been involved in other Rutgers projects, such as policy work assessing the delivery of adult basic education services in

New Jersey and making recommendations for improvement. She has a master's degree from Kent State University, where her work concentrated on reading and writing instruction for adults. While at Kent State she worked for the Ohio Literacy Resource Center as a research assistant. She helped to develop and deliver statewide professional development workshops on using authentic literature in the ABE classroom. Robinson-Geller has been a teacher and administrator for a community-based ABE program, as well as several workplace-based literacy programs. Prior to entering the adult literacy field she worked for 9 years in the computer industry as a technical writer and computer instructor.

Rima E. Rudd, MSPH, ScD, is senior lecturer on society, human development, and health at the Harvard School of Public Health and a senior fellow of NCSALL. She teaches graduate courses on innovative strategies, program planning and evaluation, and health literacy. She has been focusing her research inquiries on literacy-related disparities and literacy-related barriers to health programs, services, and care. She works closely with the adult education, public health, and medical sectors. Rudd is a member of several national and international committees related to national programs and policy. She served on the National Research Council Committee on Performance Levels in Adult Literacy and on the Institute of Medicine Committee on Health Literacy and wrote sections of both committee reports. The IOM report, *Health Literacy: A Prescription to End Confusion,* is considered a core policy document for health literacy. She wrote several other reports that are helping to shape the agenda in health literacy research and practice. They include the health literacy chapter of the Health and Human Services book *Communicating Health: Priorities and Strategies for Progress* (2003) and the Educational Testing Services report, *Literacy and Health in America* (2004).

Dr. Jean Searle, a senior lecturer within the School of Vocational, Technology and Arts Education, Faculty of Education, Griffith University, teaches subjects focusing on adult literacy in the bachelor of adult and vocational education, bachelor of training program, and the master of adult and vocational education and master of training and development programs. She is also a program leader for research on access, equity, and transitions in the Centre for Learning Research. She was also the director of the Queensland Centre of the Adult Literacy and Numeracy Australian Research Consortium (ALNARC); many of her publications are archived on the ALNARC Web site (www.staff.vu.edu.au/alnarc). Her research interests include adult and workplace literacy, the history of adult literacy, social and e-literacies, flexible delivery, and academic literacies. Searle has been involved in the field of adult literacy for more than 20 years. She began as a volunteer tutor and later became a program organizer and tutor trainer and was later involved in the development of distance literacy programs and resources. She has held several executive positions in state adult literacy and in the Australian Council for Adult Literacy (www.acal.edu.au).

Heidi Silver-Pacuilla has more than 20 years of experience with literacy learning, research, and professional development. She has taught and tutored students in literacy across the life span, collaborated with and coached literacy teachers of all grade levels from preschool to postsecondary, and conducted and participated in research into literacy development and learning disabilities. She has focused on helping students who struggle and their teachers find the diagnostic teaching or assistive technology that would support students' access to the general curriculum and materials that are personally motivating and relevant. She is particularly interested in how established special education best practices can be provided and updated through a digital teaching and learning environment. Currently employed by the American Institutes for Research in Washington, DC, she is conducting research on assistive and accessible mainstream technology innovation.

Dr. Rosie Wickert is a professor of education and literacy at the University of Technology, Sydney (UTS) and is also director of academic policy and projects. She has worked in adult education since 1970, initially as an adult literacy teacher in the United Kingdom. She emigrated to Australia in 1981 and, in the mid-1980s, became state literacy coordinator for the NSW Board of Adult and Community Education before moving to UTS in 1988. At UTS she has held the positions of head of the department of language and literacy, director of the Language and Literacy Research Centre, and director of the NSW center of the Australian Adult Literacy Research Network. Wickert has served as the president and vice-president of the Australian Council for Adult Literacy and is currently a coopted member of the executive. She was president of the NSWAdult Literacy Council for several years. She has provided policy advice to federal and state governments and was a member of the

National Consultative Council for the 1990 International Literacy Year and a member of the federal minister's advisory body (the Australian Language and Literacy Council). She has represented Australia at OECD and UNESCO expert meetings on adult literacy. In addition to authoring several papers and reports, Wickert is a coeditor of the refereed journal *Literacy and Numeracy Studies: An International Journal in the Education and Training of Adults.*

Mary Ziegler has been consulting at the local, state, and national levels in adult literacy for more than 15 years. She currently works at the University of Tennessee where she serves as associate professor in the Educational Psychology and Counseling Department specializing in adult education. She formerly served as the director of the Center for Literacy Studies at the University of Tennessee. Ziegler has directed numerous grant-funded adult literacy projects in professional development, accountability, workforce development, community literacy, curriculum development, and reading. She serves on the editorial boards of *Adult Basic Education and Perspectives: The New York Journal of Adult Learning* and is a member of the Adult Literacy Research Working Group (ALRWG) of the National Institute for Literacy. She holds an EdD from Columbia University in adult education and has numerous publication and conference presentations in the area of adult literacy.

Author Index

A

Abelmann, C., 317, 320
Adey, P., 226, 233, 239
Adger, C. T., 209, 240
Adult, Community and Further Education Board, 262, 265, 278
AFL-CIO Working for America Institute, 324
African National Congress, 286, 292, 309
Agre, P., 192, 198
Ahlers-Schmidt, C. R., 190, 199
Ahlstrand, A. L., 317, 320, 321
Aitchison, J., 286, 293, 294, 309
Alamprese, J., 60, 89
Alexander, R. E., 191, 197
Algazy, J. I., 186, 197
Allinder, R. M., 112, 129
Allington, R. L., 121, 129
Alspach, G., 192, 197
Alt, M. N., 96, 131
Alvermann, D. E., 97, 131
American Council on Education, Business-Higher Education Forum, 51, 89
American Federation of Teachers, 207, 239
Ampil, F. L., 189, 201
Ancess, J., 220, 239
Anders, P. L., 114, 130
Anderson, P. J., 217, 239
Anderson-Inman, L., 115, 130
Arbanas, J. M., 187, 201
Arif, M., 51, 89
Armstrong, K. A., 192, 193, 201
Arnold, C. L., 182, 187, 188, 197, 201
Arocha, J. F., 186, 199
Askov, E. N., 126, 130

Aslani, P., 193, 200
Australian Broadcasting Corporation, 272, 278
Australian Bureau of Statistics, 246, 249, 278
Australian Committee for Training and Curriculum, 258, 260, 261, 278, 284
Australian Education Council and Ministers of Vocational Education, Employment and Training, 258, 279
Australian National Training Authority, 261, 279
Australian Public Service Commission, 278, 279
Axelrod, A., 192, 198

B

Baatjes, I., 286, 292–294, 309
Baca, J. S., 328
Baer, J., 179, 200
Baker, D. W., 182, 188, 189, 192, 197, 199, 202
Baker, L. M., 192, 203
Balatti, J., 277, 279
Ball, D. L., 215, 219, 239
Baldrige National Quality Program, 69, 89
Bandura, A., 35, 45, 229, 240
Barnes, D. E., 189, 197
Bartfai, N., 211, 229, 242
Bassi, L. J., 317, 320, 321
Bateson, G., 278, 279
Beck, C. K., 182, 201
Becker, G. S., 317, 320
Becker, W., 207, 241
Beder, H., 27, 28, 32, 45, 137, 139, 146, 150, 154, 157, 161, 162, 170

Belfiore, M. E., 318, 320, 324, 325
Belzer, A., 39, 45, 169, 170
Bennett, C. L., 182, 189, 201
Benotsch, E., 188, 200
Berkel, H. J., 182, 188, 197
Berkman, N. D., 178, 182, 197, 198
Berland, G. K., 186, 197
Berliner, D. C., 215, 241
Bernstam, E. V., 185, 198
Berry, B., 224, 240
Berryman, S., 162, 171
Bierria, T., 186, 198
Bingman, M. B., 77, 89
Binko, J. B., 221, 242
Birman, B., 216–218, 233, 241, 243
Birru, M. S., 186, 198
Black, M., 116, 131
Black, S., 271, 279
Blazer, D. G., 188, 189, 192, 199
Bloom, M., 315, 318, 320, 322, 325
Bollough, R. V., 232, 240
Bonham, V., 187, 202
Bonstingl, J. J., 51, 89
Boothroyd, M., 217, 243
Bordia, A., 298, 302, 304, 310
Borman, G., 207, 240
Borrayo, E. A., 187, 194, 198
Borsum, L. A., 51, 89
Bos, C. S., 114, 130
Bowden, J. A., 51, 89
Bown, L., 298, 310
Bown, O. H., 228, 241
Boyd, F. B., 97, 131
Boylan, H. R., 125, 130
Boyle, P., 51, 89
Bradley, K. A., 189, 198
Brancati, F. L., 185, 201
Bransford, J. D., 220, 240
Brenner, B., 315, 317, 320, 322
Brock, P., 246, 279
Brockett, R. G., 145, 172
Broder, M. S., 186, 197
Broderick, M., 165, 166, 171
Brooks, C., 160, 161, 164, 173
Brown, A. L., 220, 240
Brown, D. A., 147, 170

Brown, S., 188, 203
Brown, W. A., 189, 201
Brown-Syed, C., 192, 203
Brozo, W. G., 97, 131
Brulle, A., 125, 132
Brunken, C. D., 112, 129
Bryant, B., 114, 130, 193, 202
Bryant, D. P., 114, 130
Bugarin, R., 211, 240
Bulgren, J. A., 127, 130
Bull, S. S., 189, 199
Burnaby, B., 324
Burns, L., 116, 117, 131
Burt, M., 212, 240
Burton, G. V., 189, 201
Butcher, R., 262, 266, 279
Butler, J. A., 233, 242
Butz, B. P., 187, 198
Bye, T., 223, 240
Byrd, J. C., 189, 199

C

Cahill, K. E., 314, 321
Cain, D., 195, 200
Calderón, M., 217, 218, 233, 240
Calhoun, E., 216, 217, 242
Cameron, K. S., 49, 51, 91
Cammack, D. W., 98, 124, 132
Campbell, M., 187, 201
Canadian Public Health Association, 195, 198
Capell, H. A., 189, 199
Carey, K., 206, 240
Carey, N., 211, 229, 242
Carino, C., 160, 161, 164, 173
Carpenter, T. P., 217, 220, 240
Carter, J. B., 144, 145, 163, 173
Casazza, M., 125, 130
Castleton, G., 271, 278, 279
Catts, H., 96, 134
Catz, S., 188, 200
Cavalier, A. R., 117, 120, 124, 132
Caverly, D. C., 125, 130
Cella, D., 186, 199
Cervero, R. M., 86, 89

Author Index

Chanda, N., 245, 276, 279
Chapman, C. D., 96, 131
Chard, D. J., 95, 97, 134
Charles, L., 186, 198
Chelf, J. H., 192, 198
Chen, X., 211, 240
Cheney, L., 192, 198
Chesson, A. L., 187, 192, 199, 201
Chesson, L. M., 187, 201
Chestnutt, I. G., 191, 198
Chew, L. D., 189, 198
Chiang, C., 217, 240
Chou, L., 194, 201
Choy, S. P., 211, 240
Clair, N., 209, 240
Coates, S., 263, 265, 279, 284
Coben, D., 245, 276, 279
Cocking, R. R., 220, 240
Cody, J., 71, 89
Cohen, D. K., 215, 219, 223, 239, 240
Cohen, K., 116, 131
Coiro, J. L., 98, 124, 132
Cole, D. D., 192, 198
Coleman, E. A., 194, 198
Coleman, S., 53, 90
Coles, G. S., 167, 170
College Board, 51, 90
Collins, A. M., 220, 241
Collins, C., 189, 199
Colton, T. C., 176, 179, 184, 185, 188, 191, 202
Comings, J., 23–27, 32, 43, 45, 121, 130, 191, 202, 315, 320
Committee on Science and Mathematics Teacher Preparation, 217, 240
Comptroller General of the United States, 142, 170
Condelli, L., 53, 55, 56, 90
Conlin, K. K., 182, 185, 192, 198
Conners, C., 93, 134
Conrad, K., 192, 198
Conway, M., 94, 134
Coon, S., 194, 198
Corbett, D., 212, 213, 244
Corley, M. A., 94–96, 124, 130
Cornia, P. B., 189, 198

Council of Australian Governments, 278, 279
Cowan, M., 278, 279
Cox, K., 185, 198
Coyne, C. A., 194, 198
Coyne, P., 116, 130
Crandall, D. P., 150, 151, 158, 170
Crocker, J., 212, 240
Crosier, T., 272, 282
Crow, N., 232, 240
Cuban, S., 25, 28, 31, 32, 43, 45
Curry, M., 215, 242
Curtain Consulting, 255, 279

D

Daher, C., 182, 189, 202
D'Alessandro, D. M., 186, 198
Dalton, B., 116, 130
Daltoy, L. H., 193, 194, 200
D'Amico, L., 223, 243
Daniels, M., 209, 243
Darkenwald, G., 24, 45, 142, 153–155, 162, 172
Darling-Hammond, L., 207, 240
Das, J. K., 191, 202
Davidson, E., 262, 266, 279
Davidson, M. B., 194, 198
Davis, K., 194, 201
Davis, T. C., 182, 188, 197, 198
Dawkins, J., 273, 279
Dawson, L., 113, 130
Deary, I. J., 182, 189, 201
Defoe, T., 318, 320, 325
Degener, S., 126, 133, 167, 170, 172
DeJong, W., 191, 193, 194, 200, 202
De La Paz, S., 119, 132
Deng, W., 137, 157, 162, 170
Department of Education, 291, 293, 294, 310
Department of Education, Science and Training, 257, 272, 278–280
Department of Employment, Education and Training, 247, 255, 280
Department of Immigration and Ethnic Affairs, 249, 280

Deshler, D. D., 127, 130
Desimone, L., 216–218, 233, 241, 243
Development Associates, 25, 45, 154, 159, 171
DeWalt, D. A., 178, 182, 193, 197, 198, 202
Diefenbach, M. A., 187, 198
Di Fonzo, K., 195, 200
Dignan, M., 194, 198
Dike, M. R., 194, 198
Dismuke, S. E., 190, 199
Doak, C., 184, 198
Doak, L., 184, 198
Dobbins, D., 56, 91
Dobrez, D., 186, 199
Dolan, N. C., 188, 198
Doña, J., 125, 130
Dooley, S. L., 189, 199
Dorland, J., 142, 149, 173
Dowhower, S., 112, 130
Dowse, R., 187, 193, 201
Drago-Severson, E., 165, 166, 171
Drennon, C., 154, 161, 165, 171
Drew, H., 186, 198
Drew, J. S., 194, 202
Dunse, L., 112, 129
Dutro, E., 223, 240
Dysher, S., 116, 130

E

Eagleton, M., 116, 130
Eaton, L., 195, 200
Echeverry, D. M., 194, 198
Edmister, J. H., 125, 130
Educational Testing Service, 188, 199
Edwards, L., 114, 131
Edyburn, D. L., 99, 111, 114, 130
EFF Assessment Consortium, 75, 90
EFF Center for Training and Technical Assistance, 77, 90
Egeth, H. E., 187, 200
Ehri, L., 114, 120, 130, 131
Elkind, J., 116, 117, 122, 131
Elkind, K., 116, 117, 131
Elkind, P. D., 194, 199
Elliott, M. N., 186, 197

Elmore, R. F., 214, 216, 218, 223, 234, 241
Elwell-Gavins, V., 252, 280
Endres, L. K., 189, 199
Equipped for the Future, 162, 171
Ertl, T., 195, 200
Eschtruth, A. D., 314, 321
Estrada, C. A., 189, 199
Evers, D. B., 193, 194, 199
Eyre, G., 142, 171

F

Falk, I., 277–279
Fanta, C. H., 194, 202
Farris, E., 211, 229, 242
Feiman-Nemser, S., 219, 241
Felton, R. H., 112, 132
Fennema, E., 217, 240
Fenstermacher, G. D., 215, 241
Fernald, G., 112, 131
Ferreira, M. R., 188, 198
Ferretti, R. P., 117, 124, 132
Ferry, N. M., 231, 241
Figueroa, R. A., 217, 243
Fingeret, H. A., 154, 161, 165, 171
Fisher, D., 117, 121, 131
Fisher, L. J., 192, 199
Fisk, K., 223, 240
Fisk, S., 32, 45
Fitzgerald, N., 25, 33, 45, 46, 154, 156, 173, 208–210, 244
Fitzgibbon, M. L., 188, 198
Fitzpatrick, L., 245–247, 263, 265, 267, 269, 271, 274, 279–281, 284
Flannery, D., 31, 45
Fleischman, H., 33, 46, 154, 156, 173, 208–210, 244
Fleming, P., 185, 199
Flesch, R., 184, 199
Flum, D. R., 189, 198
Folinsbee, S., 313, 318–320, 325
Ford, J., 71, 89
Forman, W. B., 185, 199
Fortenberry, J. D., 189, 199
Foucar-Szocki, D., 312, 320

Author Index

Francke, C. A., 51, 89
Franke, M. L., 220, 221, 240, 242
Frazis, H., 316, 320
Freebody, P., 98, 132
Freire, P., 126, 131, 170, 171
French, E., 294, 310
Frey, N., 117, 121, 131
Friedman, D. B., 186, 199
Friedman, T. L., vii
Frier, B. M., 182, 189, 201
Fry, R., 184, 199
Fuhrel, A., 195, 200
Fuller, F., 228, 241
Furey, S., 158, 171

G

Gabriel, S., 186, 190, 203
Gadsden, V., 158, 171
Gaebler, T., 50, 90
Gagnon, J., 124, 132
Galloway, G., 192, 199
Garcia, P., 182, 189, 201
Gardner, J., 215, 218, 233, 241
Garet, M. S., 216–218, 233, 241, 243
Gaston, M. A., 191, 199
Gausman Benson, J., 185, 199
Gazmararian, J. A., 182, 188, 189, 192, 197, 199, 200, 202
Gearhart, M., 215, 242
Geissler, B., 315, 317, 320, 322
General Accounting Office, 142, 171
Gersten, R., 95, 97, 134, 207, 241
Ghaith, G., 228, 241
Gibson, R. S., 194, 198
Gilbert, D., 32, 45
Gilding, N., 255, 257, 270, 271, 280
Gillespie, M., 209–211, 216, 218, 228, 232–234, 243, 326
Ginsburg, L., 126, 131, 209, 243
Gittleman, M., 316, 320
Glanville, I. K., 192, 199
Goddard, R., 229, 241, 262, 282
Golbeck, A. L., 190, 199
Goldney, R. D., 192, 199
Golin, C. E., 182, 201

Gollop, C., 192, 203
Gonczi, A., 267, 282
Goodwin, M., 114, 130
Goodwin, S., 278, 281
Gordon, M. M., 189, 199
Goslin, D., 162, 171
Gowen, S. G., 318, 320, 326
Graham, S., 118, 119, 131, 132
Green, D., 182, 189, 197
Green, K. W., 188, 198
Greenberg, D., 114, 131
Greenberg, E., 179, 200
Greenleigh Associates, 147, 171
Greeno, J. G., 220, 241
Greer, D. S., 190, 191, 203
Gregoire, J., 185, 191, 202
Grimley, D. M., 189, 199
Grossman, P. D., 95, 131
Grossman, P. L., 229, 241
Grossman, P., 233, 241
Grumbach, K., 182, 189, 202
Gunter, P. L., 113, 130
Guskey, T. R., 217, 226, 230, 241

H

Hager, P., 267, 282
Hagston, J., 246, 262, 266, 279, 280
Hahn, E. A., 186, 199
Hall, G., 228, 241
Halliday, P., 262, 282
Hampson, R. R., 189, 199
Handal, G., 187, 201
Haney, E., 189, 199
Hardin, S., 194, 198
Harman, D., 142, 171
Harper, K., 193, 200
Harris, V. L., 51, 91
Hart-Landsberg, S., 27, 28, 32, 45
Hartley, R., 274, 282
Harvey, H. D., 185, 199
Haycock, K., 206, 241
Haynes, J. A., 119, 132
Hays, R. D., 182, 201
Hayward, K., 71, 89
Hazell, P., 252, 280

Heckelman, R. G., 112, 131
Hecker, L., 116, 117, 131
Helme, S., 253, 268, 281
Helsing, D., 165, 166, 171
Hemphill, D., 212, 244
Hennessy, M., 189, 199
Henson, R. K., 230, 243
Herman, A. D., 194, 199
Herman, R., 212, 242
Herrera, G., 188, 203
Hewes, G., 207, 240
Hewson, P. W., 215, 242
Hickok, D. S., 140, 150, 151, 171
Higgins, E. L., 119, 131, 133
Higgins, K., 114, 130
Hill, H. C., 223, 240
Hinchman, K. A., 97, 131
Hines, J., 189, 202
Hobbs, S., 232, 240
Hochhauser, M., 193, 200
Hock, M. F., 127, 130
Hofer, J., 143, 154, 156, 168, 173, 208–211, 216, 218, 228, 232–234, 243
Hoffman-Goetz, L., 186, 199
Holding, C., 273, 279
Hollenbeck, K., 317, 320, 322
Holschuh, J. L., 114, 133
Holsinger, E., 167, 172
Hooper-Box, C., 291, 310
Hord, S., 219, 228, 241
Horlen, C., 193, 202
Horner, S. D., 192, 200
Horney, M. A., 115, 130
Horowitz, A. M., 191, 202
Horrigan, R., 316, 320
Hoskyn, M., 97, 134
Houghton, T., 286, 293, 294, 309
Houts, P. S., 187, 200
Howard, D. H., 189, 200
Hoy, A. W., 229, 230, 241, 244
Hoy, W. K., 229, 230, 241, 244
Huberman, A. M., 233, 242
Hughes, C., 119, 124, 132
Huling-Austin, L., 228, 241
Hull, G., 326
Human Sciences Research Council, 294, 310

Hunt, E., 314, 320
Hunter, C. S. J., 142, 171
Hunter, J., 318, 320, 325
Hwang, S. W., 187, 200
Hyde, J., 185, 191, 202

I

Ibrido, D., 262, 266, 279
Ingersoll, R. M., 234, 242
Innovation and Business Skills Australia, 278, 280
Institute of Medicine, 175, 178, 181, 189, 197, 200

J

Jackson, K., 100, 132
Jackson, N., 318, 320, 325
Jackson, R. H., 182, 188, 197
Jacobson, E., 126, 133, 167, 172
Jacobson, L., 114, 131
Jacobson, T. A., 193, 201
Jenkins, L., 178, 197, 200
Jenzer, J., 150, 151, 158, 170
Jin, Y., 179, 200
Jitendra, A., 114, 131
Johnson, D., 224, 240
Johnson-West, J., 186, 198
Johnston, B., 257, 268, 269, 274, 276, 280, 281, 283
Johnston, J., 126, 130
Jones, E., 212, 244
Jorm, A. F., 192, 200
Joughin, G., 230, 242
Joyce, B., 215–217, 227, 228, 233, 242
Joyce, M., 316, 320
Juliusson, S., 192, 200
Jungeblut, A., 178, 197, 200
Jurmo, P., 313, 319, 320, 325

K

Kacandes, J. G., 144, 152, 153, 171
Kafka, J., 215, 242
Kagan, D. M., 228, 242
Kalichman, S. C., 182, 188, 195, 200

Author Index

Kane, M., 162, 171
Kanellos, M., 102, 131
Kangan, M., 251, 280
Kaphingst, K. A., 185, 191, 193, 194, 200, 202
Karp, S. A., 31, 46
Kasworm, C. E., 129, 131
Katz, L., 116, 117, 131
Kauchak, D., 232, 240
Kaufman, H., 188, 200
Kaufman, P., 96, 131
Kazemek, F. E., 166, 167, 173
Kazemi, E., 221, 242
Keating, T., 207, 241
Keenan, F., 212, 240
Kegan, R., 165, 166, 171, 230, 242
Kell, P., 246, 247, 271, 280
Kelly, J., 102, 131
Kelly, P., 254, 280
Kelly, S., 276, 280
Kelly-Blake, K., 187, 202
Kelnar, C. J., 182, 189, 201
Khatiwada, I., 315, 321
Kim, S., 189, 200
Kingsley, P., 186, 198
Kinzer, C. K., 98, 124, 132
Kirk, H. M., 125, 133
Kirksey, O., 193, 200
Kirsch, I., 178, 179, 182–184, 190, 197, 200–202
Knapp, M., 205, 216, 223, 225, 242
Knarr, N., 187, 200
Knell, S., 315, 317, 320, 322
Knight, J., 127, 130
Knobel, M., 98, 131
Knowles, M. S., 145, 171
Knox, A. B., 142, 153–155, 162, 172
Koch, R., 223, 240
Koepsell, T. D., 189, 198
Kolstad, A., 178, 197, 200
Koo, M. M., 193, 200
Kral, I., 249, 280
Krasavage, E., 216, 243
Krass, I., 193, 200
Kravitz, R. L., 186, 197
Kripalani, S., 193, 201
Kruidenier, J., 97, 131

Kubba, H., 185, 200
Kutner, M., 55, 56, 90, 158, 171, 179, 200, 212, 242, 244

L

LaFleur, B., 322
Lamont, T., 309, 310
Lane, C. W., 144, 145, 171
Langer, J. A., 220, 242
Langseth, L., 182, 189, 201
Lankshear, C., 98, 131
LaPlante, W., 148, 172
Lawrence, W., 195, 202
Leahy, M. A., 142, 143, 172
Leiner, M., 187, 201
Lemke, J. L., 129, 131
Lenz, B. K., 96, 127, 130, 134
Lenz, K., 96, 134
Leong, C. K., 120, 132
Lerche, R. S., 150, 151, 158, 170
Leu, D. J., Jr., 98, 124, 132
Levenson, A., 313, 315–317, 321, 323
Levine, T., 315, 321, 327
Levy, F., 314, 321, 323
Lewandowski, L., 113, 132
Lewin, K., 32, 45
Lewis, L., 211, 229, 242
Lewis, R. B., 119, 132, 144, 145, 171
Leyser, Y., 125, 132
Leyva, M., 193, 201
Li, B. D., 189, 201
Lillie, J., 187, 202
Limeul, K., 209, 243
Lindamood, C. H., 122, 132
Lindamood, P. C., 122, 132
Lindau, S. T., 182, 189, 201
Lindzey, G., 32, 45
Little, J. W., 215, 242
Liu, D., 188, 198
Liu, H., 182, 201
Livneh, C., 227, 231, 242
Livneh, H., 227, 231, 242
Lloyd, P., 162, 172
Lobach, D. F., 187, 201
Lo Bianco, J., 247, 254–256, 270, 276, 281
Loef, M., 217, 240

Lohr, K. N., 178, 182, 197, 198
Lombardi, E., 188, 203
London, S., 182, 188, 197
Londoner, C. A., 129, 131
Loscalzo, M. J., 187, 200
Loucks-Horsley, S., 215, 242
Love, F., 189, 200
Love, N., 215, 242
Lucas, J., 262, 266, 279
Luke, A., 98, 117, 132, 258–260, 281
Lux, L., 178, 182, 197
Lyons, T., 182, 189, 201

M

MacArthur, C., 117–120, 124, 131, 132
Maccini, P., 124, 132
Madhok, R., 189, 199
Makin, A., 263, 265, 279, 284
Malone, R., 193, 202
Mangano, J. A., 142, 172
Mansoor, L. E., 187, 193, 201
Marchilonis, B., 150, 151, 158, 170
Marcus, E., 186, 199
Marr, B., 253, 268, 274, 281
Marsh, D., 217, 218, 240
Marsick, V. J., 83, 91
Martin, S., 281
Martin, W. T. J., 144, 145, 163, 172
Martinez, K., 192, 199
Martin-Hryniewicz, M., 189, 199
Massachusetts Workplace Literacy Consortium, 327
Mayer, G. G., 193, 194, 199, 201
Mazzarella, J. A., 217, 242
McCalley, H., 147, 148, 172
McClellan, R., 194, 201
McDonald, J., 189, 201, 221, 242
McDonald, M., 271, 279
McDonald, R., 278, 281
McFarlane, M. M., 189, 199
McGrew, M., 188, 200
McGuirk, J., 274, 275, 277, 281, 283
McKay, V., 290, 307, 308, 310
McKenna, A., 263, 265, 279, 284
McKenna, M. D., 125, 132
McKenna, R., 245–247, 254, 267, 269–271, 274, 280, 281

McLaughlin, G. H., 184, 201
McMurrer, D. P., 317, 320, 321
McNaughton, D., 119, 132
McVey, J. W., 315, 317, 320, 322
Meder, P., 28, 31, 45
Medina, P., 137, 139, 146, 157, 161, 162, 170
Meltzer, A., 162, 171
Meric-Bernstam, F., 185, 198
Merriam, S. B., 145, 172
Merrifield, J., 84, 90
Messner, P. E., 51, 90
Meyer, A., 116, 133
Meyer, M. S., 112, 132
Mezirow, J., 142, 153–155, 162, 172
Michaels, C. A., 100, 132
Mikulecky, L., 162, 172
Miles, M. B., 233, 242
Miller, J., 188, 200
Miller, L., 129, 132, 182, 201
Mishra, D. D., 187, 201
Mocker, D. W., 144, 163, 172
Moeykens, B. A., 176, 179, 184, 188, 202
Mohrmann, C., 194, 198
Mokotong, E., 290, 307, 308, 310
Monaco, V. M., 186, 198
Moncur, M., 186, 190, 203
Montali, J., 113, 132
Montclair State College, 146, 148, 149, 172
Moore, C. S., 140, 150, 151, 171
Moore, H., 255, 281
Moore, M. T., 319, 321, 327
Morabito, S. M., 100, 132
Morales, L. S., 186, 197
Moreno, N., 230, 243
Morest, V. S., 125, 133
Morgan, B., 274, 281
Morgan, M., 33, 46, 154, 156, 173, 208–210, 244
Morley-Warner, T., 267, 282
Morr, H., 307, 308, 310
Morton, F. J., 194, 202
Mosenthal, P. B., 184, 201
Mull, C. A., 94, 133
Munnell, A. H., 314, 321
Murnane, R., 314, 321, 323
Murphy, G., 144, 145, 152, 172
Murphy, P., 187, 192, 199, 201

Author Index

Murray, C., 116, 131
Myers, D., 319, 321, 327

N

Nandy, I., 182, 188, 197
National Adult Literacy and Learning Disabilities Center, 95, 96, 133
National Board of Employment, Education and Training, 268, 281
National Commission on Excellence in Education, 51, 90
National Education Goals Panel Report, 211, 242
National Institute for Literacy, 210, 242
National Institute of Child Health and Human Development, 97, 133
National Performance Review, 50, 90
National Research Council, 75, 90
National Training Information Service, 274, 281
Nelson, A., 251, 282
Nelson, C., 317, 321
Neubert, G. A., 221, 242
New York State Education Department, 152, 172
Newman, A. P., 147, 170
Nichols-English, G., 193, 201
NIDCR Workgroup Report, 178, 191, 201
Nist, S. L., 114, 133
Njie, V., 186, 198
North Carolina State Department of Community Colleges, 152, 172
Norton, M., 251, 283

O

Obermiller-Krolikowski, H. J., 112, 129
O'Brian, M., 98, 134
Oermann, M. H., 192, 201
Office of Special Education Programs, 96, 133
Office of Vocational and Adult Education, 47, 52, 90
Offutt, G., 194, 202
Ofiesh, N., 119, 132
Okolo, C. M., 117, 124, 132
Olson, J., 129, 132

Olson, N. L., 233, 242
Olson, R. K., 120, 133
Olson, T. A., 233, 242
Oltman, P. K., 31, 46
Organization for Economic Cooperation and Development, 255, 271, 282
Orton, S. T., 112, 133
Osborne, D., 50, 90
Osborne, S., 93, 134
Osmond, D., 189, 202
O'Toole, C., 189, 202
Ottoson, J. M., 217, 226, 242
Ozuah, P. O., 193, 201

P

Paasche-Orlow, M. K., 185, 201
Palma, S., 315, 321
Palmer, R., 189, 203
Parecki, A., 162, 172
Paris, S., 162, 172
Parker, R. M., 182, 188, 189, 192, 197, 199, 200
Parrella, A., 23, 24, 26, 27, 32, 45, 121, 130
Parsad, B., 211, 229, 242
Paschal, A. M., 190, 199
Patterson, M., 189, 192, 197
Paulson, C., 179, 200
Pearson, P. D., 219, 221, 222, 224, 244
Peckenpaugh, J., 50, 91
Peek, B. T., 189, 199
Peel, J., 188, 199
Perin, D., 114, 131
Perkins, K., 266, 267, 282
Persson, M., 270, 282
Peterson, C. L., 125, 130
Peterson, D. S., 219, 221, 222, 224, 244
Peterson, P. L., 217, 240
Petty, L. I., 126, 130
Piette, J., 182, 189, 202
Pignone, M. P., 178, 182, 193, 197, 198, 202
Pirisi, A., 189, 201
Pisha, B., 116, 130
Pitts, K., 194, 199
Placier, P., 221, 243
Pleasant, A., 190, 191, 203
Plomer, K., 194, 198

Poirier, S., 193, 201
Pollack, S., 272, 282
Popp, N., 165, 166, 171
Porter, A. C., 216–218, 233, 241, 243
Porter, K., 25, 32, 43, 45
Portnow, K., 165, 166, 171
Potter, L. S., 192, 193, 201
Powell, S., 315, 317, 320, 322
Praska, J. L., 193, 201
Pratt, F., 276, 282
Presidency, 288–290, 310
Prezant, F. P., 100, 132
Pringle, M., 193, 200
Purcell-Gates, V., 126, 133, 167, 172

Q–R

Quigley, A. B., 121, 133
Quigley, B., 27, 28, 30–32, 45, 139, 154, 167, 172
Quistberg, D. A., 189, 200
Rademaker, A., 188, 198
Radwin, E., 141–143, 149, 150, 173
Rahmani, Z., 272, 282
Raich, P., 194, 198
Randall, S. N., 114, 134
Raskin, E., 31, 46
Raskind, M. H., 119, 131, 133
Ratcliff-Baird, B., 186, 192, 202
Ray, S. M., 194, 202
Reder, S., 23, 26–28, 32, 45, 122, 125, 133, 315, 320
Reitsma, P., 112, 133
Resnick, L. B., 220, 241
Riccioni, R., 137, 157, 162, 170
Rich, M., 194, 201
Richardson, V., 221, 243
Ridley, C., 262, 266, 279
Rigg, P., 166, 167, 173
Rivers, J. C., 206, 243
RMC Research Corporation, 211, 212, 214, 243
Roberts, J. K., 230, 243
Rodriguez, M. C., 219, 221, 222, 224, 244
Rodriguez-Louis, J., 194, 202
Roessler, R. T., 125, 133
Roland, P. Y., 189, 202
Rompa, D., 182, 188, 200
Roop, L. J., 223, 240
Root, J., 184, 198
Rootman, I., 192, 201
Rose, D., 116, 133
Rose, S., 25, 45
Rosenbloom, S., 313, 315, 321
Rosenholtz, S., 233, 243
Ross, B. S., 192, 193, 201
Ross, J. A., 229, 230, 243
Ross, L. A., 182, 189, 201
Ross-Gordon, J. M., 231, 241
Rossi, M., 194, 201
Rothman, R., 193, 202
Rowe, K., 209–211, 216, 218, 228, 232–234, 243
Royner, D. R., 187, 202
Rudd, R. E., 176, 178, 179, 182–185, 188, 190, 191, 193–196, 200, 202
Rueda, R., 217, 243
Ruhl, M. L., 51, 90
Ruiz, N. T., 217, 243
Russell, M., 209, 243
Rutherford, W., 228, 241

S

Sabatini, J. P., 160, 161, 164, 173, 209, 243
Sacks, G., 114, 131
Samuels, S., 112, 133
Sanders, W. L., 206, 243
Sandlin, J. A., 167, 173
Sanguinetti, J., 254, 270, 274, 278, 279, 282
Santos, M., 195, 202
Sass, S. A., 314, 321
Satariano, W. A., 189, 197
Satterlee, B., 51, 91
Scanlon, D., 96, 134
Scheeres, H., 267, 269, 282, 283
Schillinger, D., 182, 189, 193, 202, 203
Schon, D. A., 231, 243
Schulte, A., 93, 134
Schumaker, J. B., 127, 130
Schumann, L., 182, 185, 192, 198
Schwab, R. G., 249, 280
Schwartz, L. M., 186, 190, 203
Schwartzberg, J. E., 178, 202

Author Index

Scott, T., 182, 189, 197, 202
Searle, J., 247, 251, 254, 282
SEIU Worker Education Program, 328
Sentell, T. L., 186, 188, 189, 192, 202
Sepede, J. H., 144, 145, 150, 173
Seright, A. L., 193, 201
Seufert, P., 53, 90
Shaaban, K., 228, 241
Sham, B., 290, 310
Sharif, I., 193, 201
Sharp, L. K., 189, 199, 202
Shea, J. A., 189, 200
Shelton, D. M., 185, 198
Sheridan, S. L., 178, 182, 197, 198
Sherk, J., 144, 163, 172
Sherman, R., 56, 91, 210, 243
Shiomoto, G., 186, 199
Shore, S., 269, 282
Showers, B., 215–217, 242
Shumway, M. A., 188, 189, 192, 202
Silva, T., 319, 321, 327
Silver, E., 216, 244
Silver-Pacuilla, H. V., 122, 127, 134
Simpson, M. L., 114, 134
Sipler, A. M., 188, 198
Sitlington, P. L., 94, 133
Skipper, B., 188, 200
Small, L., 188, 200
Smerdon, B., 211, 229, 242
Smiley, F., 51, 89
Smith, C., 143, 154, 156, 168, 173, 208–211, 216, 218, 228, 232–234, 243
Smith, J., 195, 202
Smith, M. S., 216, 244
Smith, P., 262, 282
Smylie, M. A., 229, 230, 233, 243
Soler, M., 126, 133, 167, 172
Solomon, M., 209–211, 216, 218, 228, 232–234, 243
Solórzano, R. W., 159, 173
Soricone, L., 23, 24, 26, 27, 32, 45, 121, 130, 195, 202
Southern Regional Education Board, 152, 173
Sparks, D., 217, 226, 232, 241, 243
Stallings, J., 216, 243

State of Vermont, Department of Education, 77, 91
State Training Board, Victoria, 258, 265, 282
Statistics South Africa, 285, 288–290, 310
Stein, M. K., 216, 218, 223, 230, 243, 244
Stein, S., 54, 76, 77, 79, 89, 91
Stephenson, E., 212, 242
Stewart, B., 194, 198
Sticht, T., 24, 45, 311, 321
Stiles, K. E., 215, 242
Stites, R., 126, 129, 134, 209, 243
St. Lawrence, J., 189, 199
Stodden, R., 94, 134
Stoke, D., 232, 240
Stout, R. T., 227, 244
Strawn, C., 122, 133
Sturomski, N., 96, 134
Suarez, T., 188, 200
Sudano, J., 189, 192, 197
Sum, A., 24, 45, 315, 320, 321
Supovitz, J. A., 216, 244
Surkan, P., 194, 202
Surratt, D., 192, 200
Swadley, R., 55, 56, 91
Swanson, H. L., 97, 134
Swartz, J. P., 150, 151, 158, 170

T

TAFE National Staff Development Committee, 267, 282
Tager, I. B., 189, 197
Tassi, A., 179, 202
Taylor, B. M., 219, 221, 222, 224, 244
Taylor, H. A., 185, 201
Taylor, S. G., 186, 199
Taymans, J. M., 94–96, 124, 130
Teachey, W. G., 144, 145, 163, 173
Tennessee Center for Performance Excellence, 71
Terry, T., 188, 200
Tharp, B. Z., 230, 243
Thiering, J., 251, 282
Thomas, D. M., 194, 202
Thomas, R., 314, 321
Thompson, S., 193, 200

Tibbetts, J., 56, 91, 210, 212, 243, 244
Tolbert, M., 211, 212, 244
Tomkins, J., 137, 157, 162, 170
Tomori, C., 182, 188, 189, 198, 201
Tosteson, A. N., 186, 190, 203
Tout, D., 253, 268, 269, 280, 282
Tracy-Mumford, F., 27–30, 32, 45
Tram, C. Q., 187, 200
Troup, F., 287, 288, 310
Tschannen-Moran, M., 229, 230, 244
Turchi, L., 224, 240
Turner, H. M., 216, 244
Turner, J. C., 150, 151, 158, 170

U

Ulmer, C., 142, 149, 173
UNESCO, 295, 310
UNISA ABET, 304, 306, 310
U.S. Department of Education, 25, 45, 53, 91, 207, 244
U.S. Department of Health and Human Services, 175, 177, 178, 180, 181, 191, 196, 203
Utech, J. L., 328
Uvin, J., 25, 45

V

Vacca, R. T., 97, 131
Valderrama, Y., 194, 202
Van Geest, J. B., 178, 202
Van Servellen, G. J., 188, 203
Vaughn, S., 95, 97, 134
Venezky, R. L., 160, 161, 164, 173
Venn, M. L., 113, 130
Villaire, M., 193, 201
Vogel, S., 125, 132

W

Walji, M., 185, 198
Walker, L., 187, 201
Wallace-Clancy, L., 262, 282
Walton, M., 49, 91
Wang, C. C., 178, 202
Wang, F., 182, 189, 202

Wang, M. C., 218, 230, 244
Ward, P., 269, 283
Washington, C., 194, 198
Waterman, R. A., 126, 133
Watkins, K. E., 83, 91
Watts, E., 98, 134
Webb, L., 158, 171, 212, 242
Weidler, D., 56, 91, 210, 243
Weiss, B., 188, 189, 195, 203
Wenglinsky, H., 211, 244
Wenzel, L. B., 194, 198
Whitehurst, G., 207, 214, 244
Whitney, C. G., 194, 202
Wickert, R., 246, 247, 251, 254, 256, 269, 274, 275, 277, 281–283
Wiedmer, T. L., 51, 91
Wignall, L., 273, 283
Wikelund, K., 27, 28, 32, 45
Wildemuth, B. M., 187, 201
Wilkinson, G., 122, 134
Williams, D., 187, 201
Williams, G., 187, 202
Williams, L. N., 191, 203
Williams, M. V., 182, 188, 189, 192, 197, 199, 202
Willis, S., 253, 283
Wills, C. E., 187, 202
Wilson, A. L., 86, 89
Wilson, B., 212, 213, 244
Wilson, C., 182, 202
Wilson, D. H., 192, 199
Wilson, F. L., 192, 201, 203
Wilson, H. R., 194, 203
Wineburg, S., 233, 241
Winn, B. A., 49, 51, 91
Winslow, E. H., 192, 203
Wise, B. W., 120, 133
Witkin, H. A., 31, 45, 46
Witmer, J. T., 187, 200
Wixson, K., 223, 240
Wojcik, B., 98, 134
Wolf, J., 215, 217, 242
Woloshin, S., 186, 190, 203
Woodruff, D., 210, 243
Woolworth, S., 233, 241
World Education, 328
Wright, M., 25, 45

Wydra, E. W., 193, 203
Wyland, S., 125, 132

X

Xu, R., 194, 198
Xue, Z., 87, 91

Y

Yaffe, K., 189, 197
Yamamoto, K., 178, 179, 182, 183, 190, 202
Yasukawa, K., 257, 276, 280, 283
Yates, W., 257, 283
Ybarra, S. L., 194, 199
Ye, Z., 182, 201
Yoon, K. S., 216–218, 233, 241, 243
Youmans, S. L., 193, 203
Young, M., 25, 33, 45, 46, 150, 153, 154, 156, 158, 173, 208–210, 244
Young, S. J., 126, 130
Youngs, P., 207, 240
Yu, H., 189, 201

Z

Zabora, J. R., 187, 200
Zarcadoolas, C., 190, 191, 203
Ziegler, M., 84, 91
Zimmerman, J., 251, 283
Ziolkowski, 55, 56, 91
Zobel, E., 194, 195, 202
Zuboff, S., 314, 321
Zurawski, J. M., 189, 202

Subject Index

A

ABET Institute, 297, 298, 301–304, 306
accent, 101
accommodation, 94, 95, 111, 120, 127–129, 147, 155
accountability
  demands, 7, 48, 51, 89, 252, 275, 276
  improvements, 14, 15
  performance, 48, 49, 51–53, 55, 57, 68, 75, 77, 79, 88, 89
  program, xii, 43, 44, 225
  student, 75, 77, 205, 207, 224
accreditation, 253, 254, 257, 258, 261, 273, 274, 293
active consumer, 227
active learning, 144, 218
Adobe Acrobat, 100
adult diploma program, 78
Adult Education Act, 142, 149, 152, 153, 158
Adult Education and Family Literacy Report, 14
Adult Education Program Study, 20
Adult Education to Community College Transitions Project, 21
Adult Literacy Teaching (Australia), 267
Adult Migrant English Service (Australia), 255
Adult Numeracy Teaching (Australia), 267–269
Adult Performance Level (APL), 147, 150, 151

Advocacy Hall of Honor, 13
AE PRO Online Professional Development, 238
affirmative action, 251, 253
age factor, 33, 34, 37, 121, 122, 164, 183, 211, 278, 303, 314
Agency for Healthcare Research and Quality (AHRQ), 178, 180, 182, 188
AIDDE, xii, 58, 60–68, 81, 82, 85
AIDS, 290, 291, 295, 297, 298, 307
alignment, 63–68, 75–79, 81, 8–88, 207, 218, 222, 225, 236
America's Literacy Directory, 17
American Society for Training and Development, 313, 321, 325
Americans with Disabilities Act (ADA), 94, 125
andragogy, 145
annotation, 101, 108, 110, 114, 115
anthrax, 191
anxiety, 110, 194
apartheid, xiii, 285–288
application procedures, 11
artificial intelligence, 103, 104
assistive technology, xii, chapter 4
Association for Community-Based Education (ACBE), 54, 57
attendance, 169, 255, 293
  and distance education or self-study, 21, 24, 29, 44
  increasing, 29, 48, 301
  motivation, 34, 37–40, 43, 44, 121, 150, 154, 239, 275, 288, 304

355

professional development, 211–219,
223–228, 236
reestablishing, 42, 43, 141, 144
attention deficit hyperactivity disorder
(ADHD), 117, 122
attention deficit, 93, 97, 105, 110, 117, 122
attitude, 28, 30, 34, 143, 226, 2P28, 232,
254, 294
Australian Language and Literacy Policy,
247, 255–258, 267, 269, 270, 276
authorizing legislation, 8–11
avatar, 116

B

Baldrige Award, 51, 54
Baldrige Criteria, xii, 57, 58, 69, 71–73,
81–83
Baldrige Framework for Excellence, 49,
70, 73, 85, 91
Bantu Education Act, 287
basic skills program, 23, 39, 52, 53, 151,
158, 160, 163, 168, 297, 300, 311,
312, 319–324
Beck Depression Inventory, 186, 192
benefits package, 234–236, 238, 313, 315
bias, 167, 298
bilingualism, 209, 218
bipolar disorder, 122
breakthrough, 221
Bridges to Practice, 17, 95
BrowseAloud, 100
business, viii, 51, 52, 69, 71, 74, 81, 82,
289, 297, 311, 314, 317, 322–325

C

cancer, 185, 187, 189, 192, 194
capstone assessment, 79
captioning, 100
career advancement, 227, 291, 296, 313,
315, 316
career ladder program, 316
caregiver, 32, 194
cartoon, 187
casualization, 276

Center for Law and Social Policy
(CLASP), 12
Certificate of General Education for
Adults (Australia), 262, 263, 265
certification, 26, 38, 168, 206, 207, 210,
211, 214, 223, 227, 273, 304, 317
chanting, 291
Cherry Hill Conference, 147–149
chess, 220
child care, 30, 33–38, 125, 154, 290
choral reading, 147
citizenship, 34, 39, 55, 82, 250, 315
class size, ix, 31, 225
classroom management, 151, 164, 214, 229
Closing the Gap, 111
Co:Writer, 106, 107
cognitive style, 230, 231
coherence, 232
cohort, 165, 166, 317, 323
collegiality, 233, 236, 237
comic book, 187
community college, 18, 19, 21, 59, 60,
71, 81, 111, 125, 144
competency, 150, 254, 257, 258, 267,
268, 273, 276, 298, 302–304
completion rate, 29, 249
computer lab, 140
conference, 211–215, 223, 236, 237, 253
confidentiality, 315
content knowledge, 207, 210, 217–219
continuous enrollment, 154, 155, 169
continuous improvement, 49, 51, 53–55,
60, 64, 66, 67, 71, 74, 84, 317
continuous quality improvement (CQI), 51
controlled-reader machine, 143
cooperating teacher, 220
cooperative learning, 95, 214, 253
corporate giving, 19
cost-benefit analysis, 27, 28, 32, 186, 314
Council for the Advancement of Adult
Literacy (CAAL), 19
counseling, 30, 31, 36–39, 42, 239, 301, 312
credential, 52, 53, 56
cultural awareness, 181, 184, 186, 209,
235, 253, 256, 259
customer satisfaction, 49, 50, 54, 73, 85

Subject Index

D

dance, 291
decoding, 97, 101, 113, 117, 122, 125, 161, 163
deficit model, 96
depression, 122, 186, 189, 192, 304
deregulation, 255, 271, 272
diabetes, 189, 193, 194
diagnostic test, 140, 145, 148, 150, 151, 156, 160
dialect, 109
dictation, 102–105, 108–110, 119, 120
dictionary, 101, 110, 114–116, 119
dilution effect, 225, 226
disabilities rights movement, 125
disabilities, xii, 17, chapter 4, 250, 251, 293, 294
discharge instructions, 181
discrete skills instruction, 161
dislocated worker, 9, 312
dispositional influence, 30
distance education, 21, 24, 42, 237, 238, 295–298
downsizing, 312
Dragon Dictate, 119
Dragon Naturally Speaking, 102–104, 119
  dropout, 20, 31, 94
  motivation, 27, 30, 33, 35, 36, 39, 154, 166
  reducing, 29, 30, 39, 117
  returning after, 24, 43, 121, 144, 155
  statistics, 25, 26, 32, 96, 291, 304
dual highlighting, 100
dynamic highlighting, 99, 100, 113
dyslexia, 106

E

Early Reading First, 14
educational manager, 140
Effective Practices in Reading, 17, 21
eligibility standards, 11
e-mail, 100, 103, 122, 138, 159
embedded resources, 100, 105, 110, 114–117, 125

employment status, 15, 20, 33, 37, 38, 53, 128, 272
English as a second language (ESL), 5, 7, 11, 14, 16–19, 23, 33, 64, 88, 126, 297
English for students of other languages (ESOL), 137, 138, 154, 158, 193, 209, 210, 235, 239, 311, 312, 326–329
English language learners (ELL), viii, 78, 207, 209, 216, 223, 225
enrollment limits, 43
entrenched teacher, 228, 233
Equipped for the Future (EFF), xii, 17, 57, 58, 74–80, 82, 83, 85, 88, 91, 222, 313
equity issues, 247, 251, 252, 254, 258, 286
essential skills, 278
ethnicity, 33, 122, 164, 209, 225, 285–287, 312, 315
Even Start, 2, 4, 5, 8, 14, 22
expertise, 220, 268, 274, 275, 278
Extended Public Works, 299, 307, 308

F

Family Literacy Alliance (FLA), 4
fast food coupon, 48
feedback, 50, 61, 71, 95, 144, 217, 218, 262, 263
feminism, 252
filmstrips, 143
Flesch Reading Ease Formula, 184
fluency, 25, 77, 97, 112, 113, 118, 122, 125, 160, 221, 313
food stamps, 9
force-field analysis, 32
Ford Foundation, 143
free writing, 118
Freirian model of literacy, 98
FRY Formula, 184
functional literacy, 96, 150, 182, 253, 286, 293, 294

G

gatekeeper, 213, 228, 233, 254
gender, 33, 122, 164, 167, 183, 252, 253, 259, 268, 285, 288, 290, 294, 301

generative sentences, 117, 118
globalization, 249
glossary, 101, 110, 114–116, 194, 196
goal setting, 28–31, 34, 35, 38, 41, 42, 48, 74, 77, 98, 117, 129, 152
GOALS 2000, 51, 55, 75
going to scale, 58, 66, 83, 91, 301
Government Performance and Results Act (GPRA), 50
governors, 9–11, 14, 74
gradual release model, 117, 118, 121
grassroots activism, xi, 13
Greenleigh study, 146–148

H

Head Start, 14
Health Activities Literacy Scale, 183
Health and Literacy Survey, 188
health issues, 34, 96, 154, 286, 295, 298
health literacy, chapter 6
Healthy People 2010, 177, 180, 196, 197
high school diploma, 6, 11, 14, 15, 26
high school equivalence, 23, 25, 27
high school initiative, 5, 6
highlighting text, 99–101, 110–114, 117
HIV, 290, 291, 295, 297, 298, 307
homograph, 102
homonym/homophone, 107
Horizon Project, 57
horizontal integration, 215
hospitalization, 182, 189
housing, 37
human capital theory, 317
hurricanes, 2, 10, 22

I

IBM ViaVoice, 102
icons, 177
identity, 259, 261
immigration, viii, 25, 33, 183, 248–250, 311, 314, 315, 320, 326
immunization, 194, see also vaccination
impact concern, 228
inclusion, 250

individualized group instruction, xii, chapter 5
Individuals with Disabilities Education Improvement Act (IDEA), 94, 99
informed consent, 181, 184, 185, 194, 196
infrastructure, 285, 289, 290, 292, 295, 299, 307, 308, 327
inquiry, 214, 215, 219, 221–223, 236
in-service, 211, 219, 223, 230
institutional influence, 30
instructional management system, 150
instructional support services, ix
instrumental way of knowing, 230, 231
intake, 28–30, 37–39, 41, 60–62, 64, 68, 74, 87, 139
interactive software, 121, 187
intergenerational illiteracy, vii, 14
International Adult Literacy Survey (IALS), 20, 182, 188, 246, 249
International Literacy Year, 254, 256
Internet, 1, 16, 44, 100, 113, 125, 127, 184–186, 192, 196
intervention, 95, 96, 110, 119, 164, 182, 190, 191, 193, 210, 300, 308
Iraq war, 2, 5, 22

J

jargon, 177, 196
Job Corps, 10, 147, 148
job placement, 312
job training, 9, 26, 147
job-embedded professional development, 208, 213–215, 219–223, 236–238

K

keyboarding, 103–105, 108, 118, 125
Kirkpatrick Scale, 321
Kurzweil reader, 100, 101, 106, 110, 116

L

labor, viii, ix, 248, 249, 287, 290, 295, chapter 10
Language, Literacy and Numeracy Program, 266, 272

Subject Index

large print, 95
Last Gamble on Education, 153
law enforcement, 37, 38
laziness, 34
Leadership in Action, 65
leadership
  funding, 5, 8, 128
  organizational, 13, 18, 22, 70
  program, 56, 60–66, 68, 70, 72, 73, 82, 214
  school, 221, 223–225, 232, 233
  student, 77
  teacher, 297
Learn2Type, 118
Learning Activities Bank, 329
learning center, 140, 251, 301, 302, 304
learning disability, 93–97, 105, 110–123, 128, 163, 210, 239
learning lab, 144, 149, 152, 153
learning organization, 317
Learning Unlimited, 160
library, 32, 36, 38, 42, 55, 252
life demands, 24, 34, 121, 139, 169, 257
LINCS, 16, 17
Lindamood Auditory Conceptualization Test (LAC), 122, 124
lip sync, 100
literacy decade, 247
Literacy President, 13

M

macro, 105
management
  classroom, 151, 164, 214, 229
  conflict, 291
  education, 51, 69, 302
  government, 50, 270, 273
  health, 182
  private sector, 49, 315, 318, 327–329
  program, 54–56, 60–64, 66, 68–71, 81, 83, 84, 258, 319
mandatory student, 37, 38
masking, 100, 101
mastery, 144, 145, 148, 151, 160
Mathematics Workshops, 251
maturity, 33, 37
Mavis Beacon Teaches Typing, 118

medicine label, 187, 193
memory, 93, 97, 99, 113, 114, 120
mental health literacy, 192
mental retardation, 96
mentoring, 229, 230, 236
metacognition, 162, 168
Microsoft Reader, 99, 127
migrant worker, 290, 305
military, 148, 151, 158, 306, 311
mixed-level classes, 155, 157, 168, 169
moderation, 263
motivation
  employer, 322, 323
  student, xii, 27, 28, 31–34, 38, 39, 41, 75, 93, 111, 112, 121–124, 141, 150, 162, 228, 293
  teacher, 70, 214, 226–228, 230
  worker, xiv, 315, 318, 326
moving (relocation), 34
multisensory input, 112–114, 120, 124
mutual obligation, 255

N

NAEDDC, 57, 58, 91
National Adult Literacy Survey (NALS), 176, 178, 182, 183, 185, 188, 197
National Assessment of Adult Literacy (NAAL), vii, 18, 20, 22, 179, 188, 197
National Center for Family Literacy, 4
National Center for the Study of Adult Learning and Literacy (NCSALL), 20, 32, 121, 195, 210
National Coalition for Literacy (NCL), 6, 7, 9, 10, 12, 13, 18, 22
National Council of State Directors of Adult Education (NCSDAE), 1, 6, 7, 10–12, 14, 22
National Curriculum Framework (Australia), 258–262, 264
National Education Policy Act (South Africa), 292, 293
National Evaluation of Adult Education Programs, 154, 159
National Institute for Literacy (NIFL), 1, 8, 13, 16–18, 21, 22, 54, 55, 75, 76, 95, 222, 318, 329

National Literacy Act, 47, 52, 53
National Literacy Advocacy (NLA), 13
National Policy on Languages (Australia), 254, 255, 276
National Public Works Campaign (South Africa), 299, 306
National Qualifications Framework (South Africa), 293
National Quality Initiative (NQI), 60, 63–66
National Reporting System (NRS)
  Australian, 262–267, 272
  U.S., 48, 53, 57, 58, 74, 79, 85–88, 91
National Skills Development Act (South Africa), 295, 306
National Technology Laboratory for the Improvement of Adult Education (TECH21), 21
National Workplace Literacy Program, 311, 327
neurologic impress method, 112
New Literacy Studies, 98
No Child Left Behind, 222
nondiscrimination, 94
nonparticipant, 28, 29, 39
nonprofits, 54
Numeracy Network, 252
numeracy, 177, 181, 189, 190, chapter 8, 294–301, 308, 312, 313, 324, 325
nursing, 190, 192, 193, 298

O

Office of Management and Budget (OMB), viii, 2, 3, 5, 6, 14
offshoring, 312
omnivore teacher, 227, 228
Open Court, 207
open enrollment, 153–155, 157, 168
optical character recognition (OCR), 100–102, 111, 116, 122
orientation, 28–30, 37, 38, 41, 62, 64, 68, 74, 156
orphans, 290, 291
orthography, 97, 120

outsourcing, 324
oversight committee, 319, 320

P

packet, 149, 150
parenting, vii, 4, 123, 124, 226, 288, 290, 315
part-time
  staff, x, 18, 84, 156, 157, 169
  teachers, 71, 81, 150, 208–213, 232–234, 236
passive consumer, 228
passive learning, 144
patient package insert, 193
PDF Aloud, 100
peer learning, 42, 108, 114, 125
Pell Grants, 6, 7
Performance Measurement Reporting and Improvement System (PMRIS), 55–57
performance standards, 11, 14
performance target, 14, 50, 53, 272
persistence, xii, 20, chapter 2, 97, 110–112, 114, 117, 121–124, 129, 140, 219, 234
pharmacology, 190, 193
phonics, 97
phonology, 97, 119, 120, 122, 124, 160
pictograph, 187, 195
placement test, 148, 150
plain language, 177, 191, 194, 195
PMOSE/IKIRSCH, 184
poetry, 291
policy literacy, 247
portfolio, 53, 79, 139, 263, 302, 303
postponement, 39, 41
postsecondary education, 7, 14, 15, 26, 53, 55, 94, 97, 100, 143, 151, 158
poverty, xiii, 141, 221, 285, 286, 289, 290, 292, 299, 301, 307, 308
power writing, 118
predictive word processor, 99, see also word prediction
Premier Assistive Suite, 100, 101

Subject Index

preparation time, 234–236, 238
prescription
  learning, 150, 151
  medication, 178, 181, 193
preservice training, 206
President George W. Bush, vii, viii, xi, 1–5, 7–10, 14, 17, 18, 22
President Lyndon B. Johnson, 141
President William J. Clinton, 50, 51
print literacy, 98
prisoners, 293, 294, 304, 305
problem-based learning, 61, 96
process-product research, 226
productivity, 314
Professional Development Network (Pro-Net), 56, 57
program quality indicators (PQI), 47, 52, 53, 60, 73, 88
programmed instruction, 143, 144, 147, 149, 152, 157, 163
Project 100,000, 148
Project EQuAL, 57
Project Gutenberg, 127
Project IDEAL, 21, 238
pronunciation, 101–103, 105, 109, 115
proprioceptive input, 100, 112, 113, 120
protocol, 221, 222
public assistance, 37, 147
public works program, 292, 299, 306

Q

qualified staff, ix, 30
quality circle, 323
Quality Indicators for Assistive Technology, 111

R

race, *see ethnicity*
radio, 295, 301
Rapid Estimate of Adults' Literacy (REALM), 187, 188
Read and Write Gold, 100, 101, 106
reading disability, 94, 112

ReadPlease, 99, 127
recruitment, 27, 29, 41, 47, 52, 60, 61, 196, 267, 301, 302, 314, 321
reengagement, 41, 43
referral, 30, 36, 38, 43, 61, 125, 128, 299, 300
reflection
  on program improvement, 68, 86, 169, 170, 247
  student, 76, 129, 162, 259, 260, 263
  teacher, 217, 220, 221, 231, 236
reform
  education, vii, xiii, 205, 221–225, 232, 233, 238, 268, 273, 274, 277, 295, 314
  government, 246, 251, 254, 255, 257
  program, xiii, 30
  welfare, 2, 8, 11, 22, 256, 272, 277
registered training organization, 273, 274
rehabilitation, 98
reinforcement, 145, 226, 307
relationships, 33, 34, 70, 166, 234, 271, 314
release time, 211, 234, 238
remedial education, 148, 250, 253
repeated reading, 112
reporting requirements, 11, 53, 67
retention, 24, 27, 52, 74, 125, 165, 169, 238, 314, 321, 323
return on investment, 314, 316, 322
rhythm, 103, 113
RMC Research Corporation, 16, 211, 212

S

salary, 227, 234, see also wages
SAM, 184
sanitation, 285, 290, 298
Save NIFL, 13
scanner, 101, 102, 113
scheduling, 32, 35, 42, 95, 126, 139, 140, 155, 190
scientific method, 61
scribe, 108, 110, 120
second language acquisition, 209, 235
sector initiative, 316

sectoral education and training authority (SETA), 295, 306–309
self-authoring, 230, 231
self-confidence, 35
self-determination, 34, 35, 124
self-direction, 145, 165, 210
self-efficacy, 35, 42, 119, 124, 162, 229, 230
self-study
  program, 69, 71–73, 82, 83, 85
  student, 24, 33, 40–42, 44, 93, 108, 111, 121–124, 138, 141, 144, 158, 159, 168
self-survival, 228
self-talk, 109
sensory input, 95, 99, see also *multisensory input*
setaside, 221
sexual orientation, 33
silo effect, 83
singing, 291
situational influence, 30
Skills Development Levy Act (South Africa), 292, 295
small-group instruction, 93, 95, 108, 124, 140, 147, 153, 156, 158, 159, 164, 168, 268
SMOG Readability Formula, 184
social capital, 251, 277
social justice, 98, 251, 252, 254, 277
social services, 30, 36, 38, 50, 210
socializing way of knowing, 230
socioeconomic status, 164, 176, 182, 225
soft skills, 162, 168
South African National Literacy Initiative (SANLI), 299–306, 309
South African Qualifications Authority, 293, 296
SpeakQ, 102, 103
special education, 94, 96, 99, 164, 225
speech impairment, 96
speech-synthesis technology, 99
spell checker, 105, 106, 118, 119
standardized tests, 53, 61, 79, 88, 120, 122, 128
Standards Generating Body, 296

standards-based reform, xiii, 17, 19, 74–82, 85, 87, 88, 207, 208, 222–225, 236, 238
stereotype, 167
stopout, 39, 121, 154, 169
strategic planning, 50, 63, 67, 68, 70, 85, 105, 278
Student Achievement in Reading Program (STAR), 21, 238
student achievement, xiii, 205–207, 215–217, 223–225, 227, 229, 235, 238, 239
student-centered approach, 146, 252
study circle, 214, 215, 219, 236
stutter, 103
subject-matter knowledge, 207, 209, 210, 217, 219
subvocalization, 100, 112, 113
Success for All, 207
superwaiver, 11, 12
support group, 34
supported text, 115, 128, 129
Supreme Court, 10

T

talking touch screen, 186
tape recorder, 100, 120, 143
task concern, 228
tax cuts, 2
teacher change, xiii, 48, 87, chapter 7
teacher quality, xiii, 168, 206, 238, 272, 294, 295
Technology-Related Assistance Act, 98, 99
Test of Functional Health Literacy in Adults (TOFHLA), 187, 188
text enhancement software, xii
text reader, 99, 102, 106
text-to-speech (TTS), 99–110, 113, 116, 122–127
thesaurus, 101
Thinking Reader, 116
time on task, 161, 164
Title 1, 14
touch screen, 184, 186, 187

Subject Index

Touch Typing, 118
transportation, 30, 34, 36, 125, 212, 289, 290, 299
turnover, 69, 208, 232, 234, 323

U

unemployment, vii, 255, 257, 266, 286, 289, 293, 307–309, 312
union, 298, 311, 313–315, 318, 319, 322, 324, 325, 327–329

V

vaccination, 187, 194
verification, 263
vertical integration, 215
video, 187, 194, 195, 295, 298
vocabulary, 97, 103, 105, 110, 113–117
Vocational Rehabilitation Act, 94
vocational training, 10, 64, 128, 246, 250–254, 257, 258, 266–270, 273–276, 326
voice recognition software, 99, 102–105, 108, 109, 118–120, 123, 125
volunteer, 251, 252, 267, 298, 301, 302

W

wages, ix, 211, 254, 312, 315, 316, 321, see also salary
water safety, 191
ways of knowing, 230, 231

Web Talkster, 100
welfare, xi, 1, 2, 8, 9, 11, 12, 22, 34, 254–256, 271–273, 275, 277, 289
welfare-to-work, 12, 254, 255, 271
White Australia Policy, 248
WIA Plus, 9, 10
window card, 100
withdrawn teacher, 228
word prediction, 106–108, 125, see also predictive word processor
word processor, 99–109, 115, 118, 119, 122
WordQ, 106–108
WordSmith, 106
workforce development, 312, 316, 325, 329
Workforce Investment Act (WIA), xi, 2, 8–10, 13, 14, 22, 48, 53, 57, 312
working conditions, 234, 235, 238, 239, 276, 277, 315
workplace education, xiv, 162, 250, 257, 274, 276, 297, chapter 10
Workplace English Language and Literacy Program, 266
workplace needs analysis (WNA), 319, 320, 327, 328
workshops, 80, 84, 135, 195, 211–217, 219, 223, 224, 227, 231, 236, 237, 251, 268, 269
World Bank, 246
wraparound services, 125
Write:Outloud, 107
WYNN reader, 100, 101, 106

For Product Safety Concerns and Information please contact our EU representative GPSR@taylorandfrancis.com
Taylor & Francis Verlag GmbH, Kaufingerstraße 24, 80331 München, Germany

www.ingramcontent.com/pod-product-compliance
Lightning Source LLC
Chambersburg PA
CBHW071226230426
43668CB00011B/1317